ETHICS AND MORALITY
IN SPORT MANAGEMENT

The Sport Management Library offers textbooks for undergraduate students. The subjects in the series reflect the content areas prescribed by NASPE/NASSM curriculum standards for undergraduate sport management programs.

Titles in the Sport Management Library

Case Studies in Sport Marketing
Developing Successful Sport Marketing Plans
Developing Successful Sport Sponsorship Plans
Economics of Sport
Ethics in Sport Management
Financing Sport
Fundamentals of Sport Marketing (2nd Edition)
Legal Aspects of Sport Entrepreneurship
Media Relations in Sport
Sport Facility Planning and Management
Sport Governance in the Global Community
Sport Management Field Experience

Sport Management Library Titles Forthcoming for the Fall of 2003 and Spring of 2004

Financing Sport (2nd Edition)
Sport Facility Management: Organizing Events and Mitigating Risks

NEW! Professor Packets now available at no charge for many of our bestselling textbooks. Visit www.fitinfotech.com for details.

ETHICS AND MORALITY IN SPORT MANAGEMENT

Joy T. DeSensi

The University of Tennessee

Danny Rosenberg

Brock University

Fitness Information Technology, Inc.
•
P.O. Box 4425
•
Morgantown, WV 26504-4425

Library of Congress Card Catalog Number: 2002113559

ISBN: 188569346X

Copyeditor: Sandra Woods
Cover Design: Jamie Pein
Developmental Editor: Jessica McDonald
Managing Editor: Geoff Fuller
Production Editor: Jamie Pein
Proofreader: Maria den Boer
Indexer: Maria den Boer
Printed by Sheridan
Cover Photo: © SportsChrome

10   9   8   7   6   5   4   3   2   1

Fitness Information Technology, Inc.
P.O. Box 4425, University Avenue
Morgantown, WV 26504 USA
800.477.4348
304.599.3483 phone
304.599.3482 fax
Email: fit@fitinfotech.com
Website: www.fitinfotech.com

Contents

Part IV: What Lies Ahead

Foreword

Over the past several years, the sport industry has grown phenomenally, and it now ranks among the largest industries in North America. Concomitant with this growth is an increase in the number of university sport management programs. Despite the encouraging advances in the preparation of professional managers, the value-based ethical and moral aspects of sport management have not been given due consideration. *Ethics and Morality in Sport Management* represents a landmark effort to bring into focus the moral and ethical issues associated with the management of sport and sport organizations.

Within a sport context, Joy DeSensi and Danny Rosenberg have critically examined a view shared by virtually all business managers and scholars—that ethics and morality in management is not only good for all concerned, but a necessity in terms of the bottom line. The literature clearly indicates that ethical decision making can enhance both the employee work environment and the quality of products and services. The initial difficulties and costs associated with developing ethical practices in management and organizations would be more than offset by increased productivity, profitability, and good public relations. Thus, ethics and morality in sport management is indeed a business imperative.

While the foregoing is generally true of all businesses, the sport enterprise poses a unique problem. Because sport is a pervasive force in modern society and is viewed with such awe, whatever happens in sport may be considered legitimate and right, at least by impressionable young people who pursue careers in sport and/or sport management. DeSensi and Rosenberg have done a great service in writing a book that clearly illustrates how easily one can slip into unethical behavior in sport.

In a step by step progression, the authors introduce the reader to the concepts of values, ethics, and morality and the differences among them. They examine ethical theories that focus on the consequences of behavior toward a common good, as well as theories that espouse justice as a moral standard. In describing the existing theories of ethics, they note the maxims offered by each theory to guide personal and managerial behavior. They discuss the plurality of ethical theories and offer methods of applying a particular theory in a given context. The two sides of ethics—personal and professional—are also cast in terms of social responsibility. Finally, the various models and codes of ethics are discussed in juxtaposition with decision making in general, sport marketing, human resource management, organizational governance, and legal issues in sport management.

When specific cases are addressed, readers are informed of alternative courses of action and are encouraged to decide on their own the merits of certain options. The authors do not necessarily endorse a particular theory or theories, but they provide readers with the necessary tools to shape their professional and personal lives in ethically coherent ways. Thus, the implications of a theory to suit one's personal culture and value systems are couched in moral terms. Moreover, in fulfilling the multiple objectives of their book, the authors employ a consistency of style and clarity throughout the chapters.

Overall, *Ethics and Morality in Sport Management* underscores the need to integrate ethical priorities with economic and administrative interests, and to demonstrate that management practices need not be opposed to ethical and moral demands. It reduces the complexity of the field by clearly defining concepts and theories, and by describing related applied areas where ethical concerns are invoked. Sport management students, faculty, and practitioners will find a comprehensive set of references to works by other leading authors in the field. This useful feature facilitates further inquiry should one be inclined to do so.

Finally, the relevance and significance of ethics to various practical aspects of sport management is so artfully discussed that one wonders if the book is about ethics or about management. That is the point. The book and its content emphasize that good management is good ethics.

Packianathan "Chella" Chelladurai
Ohio State University
June, 2002

Preface

The second edition of Ethics in Sport Management was written in response to many constructive suggestions to improve the text, which we welcome and appreciate. While the book has enjoyed an overall good reputation and has proved a valuable resource in university courses and libraries, we recognize there is still room for improvement. Thus, the aim here is to build on the strengths of the first edition and produce a second quality volume.

In order to create a strong second edition, we are in accordance with the Sport Management Library II Editorial Board Mission and Vision Statement, which indicates that authors have been challenged to adopt a critical perspective acknowledging historical and present power imbalances, oppression, and neglect within society. This critical perspective embraces an integration of thought and action inclusive of gender, race, ethnicity, class, sexuality, age, disability, and religion. To develop a library of textbooks and monographs that contribute to an expansion of understanding, knowledge, and practice in the major content areas in the discipline of sport management in its broadest interpretation.

The major concepts, concerns, and questions posed in the first preface and the reasons for writing the book remain essentially the same. We are still convinced that sport managers must seriously consider ethical issues and apply sound moral arguments to resolve ethical dilemmas. The 21st century will be marked with new challenges for sport management, encompassing a broad range of ethical and moral queries. The expansion and complexity of sport-related bureaucracies, global organizations, governmental agencies, and advanced communication networks will inevitably influence basic values such as fairness, goodness, equity, justice, and rights. Sport managers therefore must be guided by ethical principles in the course of their professional practices in the future. This work is part of an effort to ensure they have the requisite knowledge and skill to deal effectively from a moral point of view.

The basic structure of the following work remains more or less as in the first edition. The first part will examine ethical concepts and theories; the second part, personal and professional ethics; the third part will be an applied section; and the fourth part offers a look to the future. Within this existing framework are a number of amendments we hope will advance the substance and quality of the text.

The first notable revision is the new title, Ethics and Morality in Sport Management. Since explanations of morality, moral reasoning, and moral development were included previously and were extensively applied throughout, a decision was made to highlight the term morality in the title. Whereas ethics are precepts of right and wrong in our behavior and judgments, the word morality often refers to a way of life, to beliefs, attitudes, motives, and values individuals learn and exhibit in social contexts. Therefore, when considering ethical and moral issues in sport management, individuals should be guided by sound principles, well-reasoned arguments, and socially constructed norms.

In addition to the title, the body of the text was revised significantly. The introductory chapter was rewritten and restructured to reflect a smoother transition of themes and ideas. In Part I, a new feature of chapter 2 is an extended explanation and critique of moral relativism. Two chapters in Part I are devoted to major ethical theories. One of these is chapter 3, which includes an exposition of virtue ethics and character education, and the other is chapter 4, where the notion of moral pluralism is examined in greater detail. Part II, entitled "Personal and Professional Ethics," adds discussions on sexual harassment policies and on dealing with spectator and community concerns, and an expanded chapter on codes of ethics. In "Sport Ethics Applied," Part III of the text, new ethical analyses of different cases are offered in each chapter. Finally, Part IV, which contains the concluding chapter of the book, reviews recent developments in sport management and their ethical and moral implications.

We wish to extend our appreciation to a number of individuals who have made significant contributions to this text, without whose assistance, encouragement, and support, this edition would have not been possible. Our sincere appreciation is extended to Dr. Andrew C. Ostrow, President of Fitness Information Technology, Inc., (FIT) for his patience and support; to Geoff Fuller and the production staff of FIT in the preparation of the manuscript for publication; those who published reviews of the first edition and provided us with insightful comments and suggestions; colleagues who personally conveyed to us their constructive thoughts on our work; the European Association for Sport Management (EASM) for awarding our first edition the EASM Outstanding Book Award; Dr. Sue Inglis for her invaluable assistance and sage advice regarding this work; Dr. Jeff Gorbski, whose writing style provided the very real narratives and insightful ethical analyses for the Moral Dilemmas in Sport sections; Katie Renee Caputo, whose artistic gift and drawings offer ethical interpretations for the text; Mrs. Denise Howell, whose persistent efforts with the preparation of this manuscript were always accompanied by genuine warmth and patience.

Deep appreciation is expressed to Dr. P. Chelladurai who was willing to write the foreword for this text. A highly respected professor and scholar in sport management, Dr. Chelladurai has been an inspiration, mentor, and dear friend. We are privileged and honored to have him comment on our work.

This book is dedicated to our students who have influenced and motivated us in our teaching and research about moral excellence in the management of sport. This dedication also includes our colleagues who affirm our belief that even though ethical behavior in sport may not always be apparent, it can be achieved through learning and serious reflection.

As in the first book, we would like to each include a personal note of gratitude. The grace and spirit of my parents, Columbia and Vincent DeSensi are always with me and serve as a guiding force. Family who care are ever present, and those friends and colleagues who always offer encouragement, friendship, affirmation, and love are so very appreciated.

Joy T. DeSensi
The University of Tennessee
Knoxville, Tennessee

Once more I'd like to thank my wife Etty for her unswerving love and constant encouragement, and our children, Leah, Rafi, Orah, and Mira, for the challenges they throw our way. I would like to acknowledge my late mother-in-law, Bertha Matalon, who continues to inspire us to do good. Finally, I can't say enough about two people who have taught me well about life and whose presence I cherish, my parents, Sonia and Joseph Rosenberg.

Danny Rosenberg

PART I:
SPORT MANAGEMENT AND ETHICAL THEORY

Chapter One

Introduction

Chapter Objectives

- To become aware of ethical and moral issues in sport

- To consider the place of sport in society

- To characterize social responsibility

- To establish the value of studying ethics and morality

- To become familiar with ethical and moral concerns related to sport management

- To introduce the ideas of personal and professional ethics

Displays of violence and hatred between opponents, as depicted in some highlight videos, are acceptable ways to market sport.

Winning is everything, and you have to do whatever it takes to win. Everyone cheats, so why shouldn't we?

"Blackmailing" local governments to acquire new stadiums and arenas under the threat of bolting a community makes use of good business and negotiation practices.

Team loyalty is an anachronism because athletes are considered commodities to be bought, traded, and sold to the highest bidder. It's all part of the game!

Accepting bribes and favors to win a lucrative sport contract is culturally defined, and no real harm or injustice is done when everyone does it.

Fair play and sportsmanship—aren't they what sport is all about?

Concepts like truth, justice, honesty, right, and fairness are part of the language of ethics and morality and pose numerous problems for lay people and for those formally versed in philosophy, specifically ethical theory. The meanings and implications of these expressions are often misunderstood. Moreover, the application of ethical rules and moral standards in everyday life involves complex considerations. When the context is sport, this application is further complicated because sport is so pervasive and commonplace in our social lives. Only recently has a serious examination of ethics and morality as related to sport been taken up. For the most part, there is a lack of understanding or appreciation for ethical theories and their relevance to sport because such principles are normative—they refer to what one ought to do—and sometimes they are difficult to operationalize. The study of ethics and morality does not always produce conclusive answers, and this can be frustrating for some. On the other hand, with formal training and diligence, these subjects, even from a sport perspective, can clarify many perplexing issues and result in satisfactory solutions.

Ethics refers to principles of right and wrong conduct and decisions, whereas morality considers social values, motives, and attitudes. More often than not, ethics serves a prescriptive function and is part of normative philosophy that is concerned with how individuals ought to act. Morality critiques the quality and standards in particular societies and social groups, as well as the character of individuals. Moral and ethical concerns related to sport need not be limited to such areas as sportsmanship, the use of performance-enhancing drugs, violence, and cheating (Morgan & Meier, 1996). Those involved in sport management are also responsible for addressing ethical and moral questions pertaining to professionalism, equity, legal and financial management, personnel concerns, governance and policies, league and franchise issues, and matters of social justice associated with all aspects of sport. They must also be aware of and approach these queries logically, rationally, and with sensitivity to ensure the integrity of sport, the sport community, and society at large.

The word *ethics* refers to principles and concepts of right and wrong conduct and decisions.

The word morality refers to the expression of values, attitudes, and lifestyles by specific social groups and individuals.

Ethical Considerations in Sport Management

Professionalism • Equity

Legal and financial management • Personnel concerns

Governance and policies • League and franchise issues

Matters of social justice

The main purposes of this text are to present concepts and theories in ethics and morality and to demonstrate their applicability in sport management. The work is specifically addressed to those interested in the organization and administration of sport, but it also refers to athletes, coaches, owners, journalists, spectators, governmental agencies, and others linked to sport. Sport managers, in particular, must be aware of and concerned about their own obligations, rights, and responsibilities, as well as those they influence directly and indirectly. As such, nothing short of sound ethical and moral reasoning must inform many of their managerial decisions and actions. This text then will try to make clear the nature of ethics and morality, it will introduce several major ethical theories, and it will discuss and analyze the practical ramifications of these precepts in several sport management contexts.

Ethics and Sport

Sport not only reflects a society's ethical standards but also contains its own moral qualities that influence societal structures and institutions. Sport management must confront general and unique ethical problems in the administration and organization of sport.

Ethics and morality are generally viewed as critical areas in today's world, and the sport environment is really no different. It is not so much that there may be too many abuses in sport, but that the magnitude, severity, and far-reaching influence of these ills are staggering. At the time of this writing, the International Olympic Committee (IOC) bribery and corruption scandal is being investigated in several countries; it has led to many resignations from the IOC and other sport organizations, has concerned Olympic Games sponsors, and has dramatically shaken the foundation of the Olympic movement. In light of this example, and there are

Ethical and Moral Issues in Sport

Key Concepts

commercialization

commodification

fair play

massification

sportsmanship

countless others, it is imperative that sport managers engage in the study of ethics and morality and not perceive these areas as trivial, irrelevant, or too difficult to work through. Sport managers must acquire this special knowledge to ensure they are well equipped to serve and preserve sport in an ethically and morally sound manner.

Whereas the established literature on ethics and morality is enormous, there are relatively few available works that specifically address these subjects in relation to sport management (Branvold, 1996; DeSensi, 1998; Doig, 1994; Galasso, 1988; Kjeldsen, 1992; Malloy, 1996; Malloy & Zakus, 1995; Zeigler, 1989, 1992). The steady growth of written material, however, not only reveals a need for more resources, but also explains why it was difficult to learn about this specialty area. Until recently, even studies related to ethical and unethical behavior in management proper and administrative decision making were superficially addressed. The relatively small body of knowledge in these areas also created obstacles toward building efficacious ethical models. Most of the research fell into two general categories. The first included descriptive accounts of particular cases where it was determined whether or not certain decisions were ethical. The second group of studies surveyed managers' attitudes toward ethical and moral dilemmas, questioned the circumstances of the cases, and probed the methods used to resolve any identifiable problems. These accounts, however, often failed to indicate either the reasons for making certain judgments or the rationale leading to ethical conduct (Bommer, Gratto, Gravander, & Tuttle, 1987). Consequently, this state of affairs often diminished the importance of ethical knowledge and relegated it to an unimportant or secondary consideration.

In the past few decades, most business and management schools have recognized the significance of ethical and moral training, and they now include business ethics as a required part of their programs. It is crucial, therefore, to offer specific courses that directly address applied ethics in sport management. The ability to make good ethical decisions must be perceived as a critical skill that necessitates learned, rational thought processes. Present breaches in ethical practices in society, as well as in sport and sport management specifically, require that serious attention be directed toward ethical and moral understanding.

Key Concepts

relationships

responsiblities

types of action

Reasons for unethical behavior in sport and its allied support mechanisms are attributed to many factors and have been examined by sport ethics scholars. The overemphasis on winning, seeking prestige or financial rewards, and persistent social discrimination such as racism and sexism are perhaps some main reasons for many instances of misconduct by individuals (Atkin, 1998). Zeigler (1992) suggests a more general reason when he states, "Lack of a systematic approach to ethical understanding can be blamed on the doctrine of separation of church and state" (p. 2). This situation has typically led to shifts away from traditional values in the U.S., for example, and although it may be partly responsible for some un-ethical practices and social injustices, it is one of several explanations. Social theorists indicate that the capitalist nature of the economic systems of Western countries and the accompanying motivation toward profit making have also influenced ethical behavior. The drive to succeed and the achievement principle in Western nations, together with the "winning is everything" and "win at all costs" attitudes, have adversely affected many people's ethical and

Social theorists point out that Western cultures' preoccupation with winning has adversely affected their moral and ethical judgment.

moral judgments and actions. This is especially so in sport where competition and winning are constitutive features of the activity. Moreover, the commercialization of sport and the influences of the media contribute significantly to a growing awareness of corruption in sport. In this sense, ethical and moral issues must be considered in light of the social context of sport.

Sport in Society

Individuals possess many reasons for ascribing special meaning and relevance to their experiences in sport, and they sometimes recognize that sport can play an important role in moral development. Thus, their involvement in sport may teach them how to differentiate between ethical and unethical conduct. The pervasiveness of sport around the globe, for example, and the idea of sport as a vehicle of socialization have been studied extensively by sport scholars (Eitzen, 1993; Eitzen & Sage, 1993; Leonard, 1993; McPherson, Curtis, & Loy, 1989). They demonstrate that sport is a common experience for many people who are either active or passive participants in the production of this social phenomenon. As a result, sport permeates people's lives to varying degrees as a shared cultural experience.

Key Concepts

constitutive rules

proscriptive rules

rules of sportsmanship
(fair play)

A perusal of the literature in sport sociology reveals a vast number of social issues are related to sport. Historical developments, cultural meanings, socialization and organization, social deviance, religion, drugs, racism, sexism, violence, gender, sexual orientation, youth, special populations, ethnicity, economics, business, schools and colleges, the media, and governments reflect concepts, groups, and formal structures associated with sport (Donnelly, 2000; Leonard, 1993; Nixon & Frey, 1996). In each of these areas, critical questions and problems exist. For example, violence in sport is expressed in the behavior of athletes, the conduct of fans and officials, and the practices of sport-governing bodies, corporations, governments, and the media. How is violence differentiated in each of these spheres? Are there acceptable and unacceptable forms of violence? What measures are needed to curtail violence in sport? What responsibilities do those in sport management positions have in relation to violence? None of these questions are easy to answer, but one must attempt to do so with a serious, critical, and reflective effort.

In addition to sport's place in society, the effects of sport on individuals can be dramatic. People's daily routines, family schedules, and important media, economic, and political initiatives are sometimes altered to accommodate participation in special events such as Super Bowl Sunday, the World Series, the National Basketball Association play-offs, the National Hockey League championship series, the World Cup, and the Olympic Games. Even the language of sport has become part of many people's vernacular in sporting nations. Motivational slogans like "higher, faster, stronger," "go for the gold," and the pseudo-Lombardian expression "win at all costs" are part of common parlance. People have been socialized to judge the better, more powerful individual, team, school, city, region and country based solely on who won and who lost. Politicians recognize and exploit these perceptions to advance their own agendas and to score political points both at home and abroad. Attending sporting events, being seen engaged in sports activities, and following Olympic medal counts closely are methods politicians use to gain personal, local, national, and even international prestige and recognition.

Another feature of modern societies that influences sport is the capitalist orientation of their economic structures. The professional model of sport, with its emphasis on winning, exclusivity, elitism, exhaustive personal demands, and lucrative pay-offs, has filtered down to almost every level of sport. The concept of amateurism exists, if at all, in the spheres of school and community sport. Yet even at these levels, there are enormous pressures to look and act as though one were a professional. It has been said that sport is too much of a business to be a game and too much of a game to be a business. Despite this play on words, sport is indeed big business. Studies of the economics of sport reveal that sport is one of the largest industries in the world, and the financial stakes involved are enormous. This is especially evident when one examines the amount of money paid for advertising during televised sport contests; the fees for the rights to televise the Olympic Games; the gate receipts for attendance at professional sporting events; professional athletes' salaries; the costs of professional team franchises; government and organizational subsidies for sport; the investments needed to fund sport infrastructure including new stadiums and arenas; the financial scope of the sports equipment and apparel industries; and the budgets of school, college, university and community sport programs. All these examples attest to the fact that sport is an integral component of, and is driven by, the capitalist system in modern countries and contributes significantly to the economies of many nations.

> Professional sports have become so popular that only school and community sports remain for amateurs. And, even these are increasingly modeled after the pros.

The idea of sport as work situated in a corporate setting is often at odds with the notion of sport as a pleasurable activity played for sheer enjoyment. Eitzen (1993) indicates that money and all its symbols have superceded the experiential content of sport as its ultimate goal. This shift in priorities partly explains the growing illicit tactics used in various sports to attain success. Sage (1990) draws an implied connection between economic achievement and ethical behavior in sport when he discusses professional leagues that operate as cartels. Accordingly, he defines a cartel as

> an organization of independent firms that has as its aim some form of restrictive or monopolistic influences on the production or sale of a commodity as well as the control of wages. Obviously cartels increase the benefits for the powerful few at the expense of many. (p. 142)

Freedman (1987) points out that sport leagues operate as cartels by (a) restricting team competition for players by controlling the rights of players through drafts, contracts, and trades that reduce competitive bidding between teams for player services; (b) acting in concert to admit or deny new teams and to control the location and relocation of teams; and (c) dividing local and regional media markets, as well as negotiating as a single entity national media rights fees. Professional sports leagues therefore possess economic and legal powers to operate and function outside of an open, competitive, capitalist environment. This situation can and has elicited questionable ethical practices, especially in the realm of social responsibility.

Under the cartel structure, franchise sport owners can use and abuse their power and enjoy tremendous advantages relative to other businesses to manipulate circumstances in their favor and accumulate profit (Sage, 1990). Owners continue to insist that such a controlled and restricted economic system is necessary to ensure league equity and high quality. Years ago under the reserve clause system, professional athletes could rightly complain that they were bitterly exploited at the hands of greedy owners and bureaucrats. In premier sports today, however, with the advent of free agency, arbitration, sports agents and lawyers, and substantial endorsement contracts, most elite athletes are willing to be treated as commodities, and they aggressively pursue the financial rewards of sport and thus assert their so-called economic independence. Of late, the strained relationship between owners and athletes in several professional sports has led to numerous strikes and lockouts and demonstrates that a serious struggle exists between the two sides. Unfortunately, consumers not only bear the burden of sports' costs, by supporting the salaries and profit of athletes, owners, and others in the sport industry, but they also feel the social effects of protracted breakdowns during these crises.

Whether one considers sport from a social, personal, political, or economic perspective, it is a relevant human activity that has ethical and moral implications. Individuals who share an interest in sport must ensure that its integrity remain intact and that those in the sport community be treated with respect and dignity. Sport managers, broadly understood, occupy a unique role toward fulfilling this objective because they are important leaders and decision makers, and they set much of the stage for how sport is perceived and actually carried out.

Sport's Social Role

Sport in society is a relevant phenomenon that permeates the lives of millions of people around the world. It is socially constructed and influenced by cultural, political, economic, and institutional structures. Although sport expresses many positive values, it also contains forms of discriminatory practices deemed unjust. Sport managers must recognize the inherent strengths and weaknesses of sport as a social entity to effectively confront ethical problems associated with sport.

Social Responsibility

The role of sport in society establishes an awareness that individual judgments and conduct extend to a vast network of social relations. Although social responsibility is also addressed in a later chapter, it is important at this point to introduce this concept because it informs much of the content throughout the text.

Social responsibility involves moral and legal accountability on the part of individuals for oneself, others, and social institutions. When reliability, trustworthiness, and regard for others become part of one's behavior, then one assumes important characteristics of social responsibility. An elevated level of social consciousness often leads to a commitment to become socially responsible. Because sport managers and administrators work in a dynamic environment, they must be cognizant of the social impact of their decisions when conducting their affairs. The development of social responsibility, however, is not an easy task in the realm of sport. The pressures and demands of winning and being successful can be excessive. When this occurs, some individuals lose sight of achieving these goals in a responsible and ethical manner.

Social awareness, or the act of being socially responsible and responsive, can be built into the objectives of planning in sport management. For example, nonprofit organizations are based on recognition of real societal needs, thus creating the tendency whereby people are so immersed in their positive work-related tasks that the notions of social awareness and social responsibility are taken for granted. Put differently, these ideas are imbedded in the very nature of their work. One can presume that a volunteer girls or boys club supported by a funding agency meets or tries to meet a number of laudable social goals. One would also expect that the club monitors its programs and participants and is accountable to the funding agency. On the other hand, some or most profit-making organizations, in which profit maximization is the ultimate goal, need to have their practices monitored so they conform to acceptable ethical and moral standards. Thus, the manner by which organizations are structured and operate has an important bearing on the level and quality of social responsibility.

The segment of the population with which one is dealing also influences the nature of social responsibility. Because sport managers interact with diverse populations, they must consider issues surrounding gender, race, sexual orientation, special populations, those with different mental and physical capabilities, and the opportunities, incomes, and social strata associated with these groups. Social responsibility must be extended to all those within range of one's sphere of influence by treating others with dignity, respect, and fairness. If a main program objective is to provide sport for all, then limitations on participation cannot be coherently and ethically sustained. Similarly, the types of activities offered, the quality of instruction and supervision, and the ways in which programs are funded fall within the realm of social responsibility. To implement social justice, sport managers must establish clear program aims and guidelines that ensure fair treatment for those who seek to become involved. As enlightened and reflective practitioners, sport manager should also adopt a personal and professional philosophy of equity and inclusion, rather than one of exclusion (DeSensi, 1998).

Sport management leaders must view social responsibility as an integral aspect of decisions they make with regard to organizational concerns, the management of funds, the treatment of those in the sport community, and the basic integrity of sport. Within college and university settings, administrators must question the value and contribution of athletic programs and recognize that such programs exist for multiple purposes. This leads to questions like "Whom do these programs serve?" and "Who are the primary beneficiaries?" Athletic departments typically try to please various social groups such as alumni, university and athletic administrators, the media, university faculty, the families of athletes, corporate sponsors, boosters, national sport-governing bodies, and the community as a whole, while they attempt to act responsibly to each individual athlete. In some cases, they carry out a gross miscarriage of justice by not ensuring athletes are treated equitably or they fail to provide athletes with a quality education during their tenure of eligibility at the college or university. Moreover, athletic departments sometimes lose sight of the fact that by virtue of being situated in institutions of higher learning, they too must contribute to overall academic integrity and a commitment to excellence under an umbrella of ethical and moral standards (Frey, 1994; Steiber, 1992).

In professional sport, the goal of accruing profit usually takes precedence over other social considerations. The economic impact of franchise sport and major international sporting events has reached incredible proportions toward this objective. Hemphill (1983) noted this trend almost two decades ago when he wrote, "The pursuit of profit maximization has taken first place while sport management and labor have forsaken the public interest in favor of monetary self-interest" (p. 2). Sport managers who assume a posture of social responsibility must come to terms with precisely this point. At what cost are franchise owners and high-priced athletes willing to compromise the public's interest, treat spectators as social dupes, and undermine the integrity of sport as an institution? Taking into account community needs and the value a team franchise holds among its urban denizens is part of being socially responsible. Although cities depend on the revenues generated by professional sport franchises, owners must acknowledge that fans identify strongly with home teams and as consumers contribute to these monies. Moreover, the franchise location stability, the quality of team performance, and the unpredictability of performance outcome are other obligations assumed by owners in relation to the community. The mutual responsibilities and duties of owners, team managers, city officials, and team supporters impact on the level of success of professional sports teams. By directing their judgments and actions based on a shared recognition of meeting overall and particular needs, members of the franchise and community can mutually benefit in a socially responsible manner.

Unfortunately, the cartel-like nature of professional sport and its power structures often relegate the idea of being responsible for or to a given community as a secondary consideration. Flint and Eitzen (1987) describe this state of affairs as follows:

> Because sport is still categorized as simple play, the power of wealthy capitalist owners can be overlooked as simple aberration or eccentric pastime. Although the meritocratic recruitment arguments are held high by the owners as well as the participants (players or consumers), little attention is given to the contradictory fact that owning a team is not based on merit but on enormous wealth. (p. 25)

To elaborate, owners of sport franchises enjoy the entrepreneurial freedom to operate as they please, the refined security of monopoly capitalism, the independent pursuit of self-interest, and the control of market exigencies by corporate directorates. Because the economic structures of professional sport favor owners in atypical fashion, commitments to communities are sometimes breached, and morally objectionable behavior can occur.

Socially responsible sport franchises can emerge if owners and sport managers focus on long-term plans to meet the needs and interests of the public. Sacrificing a community's investment in its local team for short-term monetary gain reinforces the idea that owners and athletes care little for their patrons and are engaged in professional sport for reasons of self-aggrandizement. Unfortunately, the latest trend in professional sport is to buy high-priced athletes, win a championship title, and then sell off these athletes or the team itself for lucrative profit. In these cases, loyalty to the community by owners and athletes is superficial and virtually nonexistent.

Sport managers must realize the seriousness of these types of ethical and moral issues if they are to behave responsibly. The breadth of ethical and moral issues they will encounter will continue to expand as new problems and concerns emerge in sport. Enhancing the integrity of sport with regard to individuals, resources, and rewards is a tremendous and formidable undertaking. However, if sport managers function in a socially responsible manner, keeping in mind the basic purposes and values of sport, they can contribute toward the improvement of sport as a worthy social institution and practice.

Social Responsibility

Social responsibility refers to moral and legal accountability on the part of individuals and corporations toward others and social institutions. Those in leadership positions must be aware of social issues and problems to establish laudable goals and ensure practices are fair and just. As decision makers, sport managers must treat others with dignity and respect, must ensure that the integrity of sport is maintained, and must pledge to do what is best from organizational and communal standpoints.

The Value of Studying Ethics and Morality as Applied to Sport

Throughout the discussion, an implicit claim has been presented that the study of ethics and morality is a significant pursuit. This proposition requires further clarification. Just as philosophy plays an important role in the development of personal beliefs and actions, a careful examination of the axiological (the study of values) realm of philosophy, specifically ethics and morality, will reveal the quality of one's beliefs, judgments, and conduct in a social context. Philosophy is typically considered profound thinking—or, as some prefer, profound living. One's life, according to the latter view, should consist of a unified combination of logically sound, ethical thought and action. If sport matters to an individual, then ethical and moral issues will be part of that person's reflective experiences in sport. In this sense, the study of ethical theories as related to sport is not reserved for theoreticians and philosophers. All members of the sport community must regard themselves as moral agents, and especially sport managers, who are responsible for individuals, programs, organizations, budgets, and revenues.

> By combining a philosophical understanding with a knowledge of sport issues, sport managers can understand and combat the ethical problems that surround sport.

Familiarity with major sport issues in North America and in the world at large from a philosophic perspective gives sport managers an advantage to apply their knowledge, understanding, decision making, and problem-solving skills in a creative manner. A philosophic viewpoint imbued with social awareness can reveal the structural and institutional sources of unethical behavior in sport and provide a deeper understanding of the causes of exploitation, violence, cheating, and other immoral acts. According to Eitzen (1993), "the ethical problems of American sport have their roots in the political economy of society" (p. 118). Critical theorists cite massification and commodification as the dominant structural conditions within capitalist society that explain why some engage in unethical practices. *Massification* refers to the consequences of society's increased level of bureaucratization, rationalization, and routinization. Hughes and Coakley (1984) claim that sport's massification is exemplified by its specialized, technocratic, elitist-controlled, and impersonal nature. Sport is said to mirror the massification in society at large by being displayed as work, spectacle, power politics, and big business (Eitzen, 1993). Factors that lead to an increased level of massification in sport can potentially lead to unethical behavior by participants who sometimes feel alienated from their peers. Young and Massey (1980) explain that

> as the tasks in sport become more complex and specialized, the anonymity of the participants increases. This occurs even on a single team, as in football, for example, when the offensive and defensive units practice separately and meet independently with their specialized coaches. Social contact is minimized and the norms of reciprocity that are essential to community are evaded even among teammates. (p. 88)

The idea that anonymity can possibly lead to unethical conduct is not so far-fetched. Because of short-term and episodic interactions, social relations between participants are segmented, and players may rarely encounter each other in their different roles. Impersonal relationships can result from this lack of social interaction, and because sport is internally and externally competitive, such an environment could lead to the promotion of an "ends justify the means" or a "me-first" attitude or type of behavior. Unethical conduct, exploitation, excessive violence, manipulation, cheating, and fraud have a tendency to occur more frequently when others are perceived to be anonymous adversaries.

Young (1984) indicates that *commodification* "refers to the social, psychological, and cultural uses of social structures for the commercial needs of monopolies" (p. 7). Under this notion, the individual is viewed and treated as an object to be manipulated, bought, and sold. Team owners, managers of sport, and athletes who are fixated on profit maximization can become oblivious to the human qualities of other members of the sport community. Every aspect of sport is seen as an opportunity to produce a valuable entity that can be sold. The sport spectacle, with its pomp and ceremony, is nothing more than a popular hyped-up bazaar for the public's consumption, whether it wants it or not. Because violence is "in," it too sells well on the field and in marketing campaigns. Female and male athletes are often paraded as sex objects for the sake of advertising revenue. Under this guise, sport is featured as "display" for commercial reasons, whereas the experiential and moral values of sport are held in contempt. Sport as entertainment and spectacle either distorts or plays upon personal values and meanings. The packaging, selling, buying, and trading of athletes, more often with their consent, diminishes the human element in sport with which many devotees identify. Instead, the mercenary motives of athletes perpetuate the commodification of sport for the sake of increasing their "market" value, rather than strengthening their value and allegiance to the integrity of sport. What can people expect when athletes have become alienated from each other and the public and have either fallen prey to or have colluded with the economic system of sport? Is it any wonder that members of the sport community are treated as means rather than ends? Finally, does commodification in sport contribute to and perpetuate the "win at all costs" attitude?

In addition to these serious questions from a social philosophic perspective, the concept of relativism is another contemporary idea that has complicated our moral lives. In brief, moral relativism refers to the idea that there are no ethical absolutes and that right and wrong are culturally defined. Consequently, this view asserts that the standards and expectations in a given society can never be deemed correct relative to those of another society. Moral relativism leaves open the door for a society to rationalize its formal policies and social mores. Individuals, too, are in a position to rationalize their decisions and behavior. For example, one may contemplate breaking the law by evaluating the risks of getting caught and the extent of any incurred penalties. Another rationalization strategy is to claim "everyone else is doing it" or "no one will get hurt," and this grants one's judgment or action a modicum of legitimacy. Thus, social rules are regarded as hurdles to be overcome, rather than as guidelines for living equitably and peacefully with one's neighbors. Further still, moral relativism falls prey to its own tenets and collapses as a sound ethical approach, for it cannot recommend itself as superior to other ethical principles. As will be argued later, moral relativism is a skeptical and pessimistic notion that has more often contributed to moral bankruptcy in contemporary life. In contrast, the approach taken in this text, and considered an important value, relies on the conviction that judgments and actions should be based on reasonable, cogent ethical and moral principles.

Ethics and Sport

Philosophical reflection can be a lifelong attempt to understand oneself, others, and the world at large. Since ethical judgments are an unavoidable part of daily life, it makes sense that the same moral questions would arise in sport and sport management. The value in studying ethical and moral issues associated with sport lies in trying to comprehend and answer such ethical queries in the most coherent, reasonable, and logical way possible.

Ethical and Moral Concerns in Sport Management

Sport managers are in a unique position to internalize and act on the value that ethical and moral understanding is relevant, because so many of their daily professional tasks involve these concerns. Moreover, those associated with sport at all levels (i.e., informal sport, organized sport, corporate sport, and pseudo or trash sport) face a continuous ethical tug-of-war in relation to the philosophy, values, and purposes of their programs; the behavior of coaches, athletes, spectators, sponsors, media personnel, and sport-governing body officials; the role of government agencies; and the political and economic infrastructure of sport. The role of sport and the behaviors it elicits on and off the field need to be reevaluated by members of the sport community, especially by its decision-making brokers, to determine the current moral status of sport and how it can be improved.

The spectrum of ethical and moral concerns in sport management is broadly defined and deals with a diversity of issues. The question arises, however, as to whether or not fair and just practices are more easily pursued and exercised in today's competitive sport business climate. For example, a recently held undisputed world heavyweight championship boxing match ended in a draw based on the decisions of three judges. Many in the boxing community criticized and viewed this result as a ploy to hold a rematch so additional millions of dollars could be added to the coffers of companies and the personal bank accounts of individuals. In the United States, college and university athletic program personnel, coaches, alumni, and boosters often engage in illegal recruitment and retention practices. Violence and cheating on the field and the unruly behavior of spectators often distort and mar the competitive atmosphere of contests. Drug abuse, game fixing, gambling, sexual exploitation, and bribery are other instances of corruption in sport that make news headlines. Individual coaches, team managers, and trainers have also been implicated in the violation of laws of human rights, civil rights, and equality.

Sport managers, in particular, must be aware of these ethical and moral shortcomings in sport and know how to confront them. They can set an example by taking bold decisions to ensure the values of sport are upheld and enhanced by offering the public quality programs and performances. In an interview with Ted Lee (1992) on the ethical tug-of-war in sports, sport philosopher Scott Kretchmar notes that certain action in sport that are morally questionable are referred to as technical competence in the execution of skills or as part of the strategy of the game. The intentional foul and excessive rough contact in basketball are two such examples. More often than not, coaches, athletes, spectators, sport managers, and officials accept these forms of play without questioning their moral and ethical implications. Not only is the status quo often accepted, but deliberate attempts also are sometimes undertaken to encourage a more hostile environment to secure victory.

> As organizers and administrators, sport managers are in a position to educate their staff and the public regarding issues of fair treatment and social responsible.

Unfortunately today, many see winning and performing within acceptable moral standards in sport as antithetical pursuits. However, nothing could be farther from the truth. These ideals should *not* be construed as an inverse relationship whereby one's chances of winning are increased by lowering one's ethical conduct. Both objectives, winning and good ethical behavior, can be and should be pursued seriously to ensure that victory is well deserved and noble. Because sport managers do influence the structures and competitive ethos of sport, they must recognize the factors that diminish the stature and practice of sport and seek concrete means to place sport on a moral high ground.

In addition to proactive efforts to correct the ills of sport, sport managers must be cautious, for now more than ever, their judgments and actions will be closely scrutinized. As recent events in public life have demonstrated, a lack of responsibility and accountability for one's behavior can be exposed easily. As long as the value of winning and achievement in sport are overemphasized, then those who are successful and act in an ethical manner will be looked upon with suspicion. Individuals who follow the rules and whose behavior is without reproach are rarely praised and noted for their ethical conduct. On the other hand, organizations and individuals who violate norms and rules like the former East German Olympic movement, some American colleges and universities, the IOC, Ben Johnson, Pete Rose, and Tonya Harding receive far more media attention and greater notoriety. Although it may be understandable that some fall short of moral compliance when the stakes of sport are so high, pushing, ignoring, or violating rules blatantly and illegally cannot be accepted. When individuals or organizations do cross the line, sport managers, administrators, and officials must determine the type of misconduct involved, the intent of the action, the effects of the behavior toward others, the nature of policies and guidelines, and the penalties that may ensue. Efforts to avoid unethical conduct and a fair review process after the fact are two measures sport managers can implement to ensure responsible and accountable behavior on their part and on the part of those in the sport community.

Some of the principles to guide sport and to monitor the administrative practices of sport managers are discussed by Eitzen (1993). He addresses obligations in relation to sport and the ideals sport managers need to pursue as follows: (a) Athletes [and all sport community members] must be considered ends and not means; (b) all forms of competition must be fair; (c) participation, leadership, resources, and rewards must be based on achievement rather than on ascribed characteristics; and (d) the activity must provide for the relative safety of participants (pp. 109-110). A foundational precept underlying these principles is expressed by Weiss (1969) when he states that "sport should begin and be carried out with a concern for the rights of others" (p. 180). Although the preceding ideas and tenets will be taken up in more detail in a later chapter, they provide some indication here how sport managers should orient themselves to their profession on an ethical and moral basis.

Evaluating Values

Ethical and moral concerns in sport management are increasingly significant because of modern sport's complexity and alarming rate of expansion. For those reasons, there are numerous competing values within sport. Sport managers must learn to identify and evaluate values related to the bureaucratic and business aspects of sport. They must then seek to evoke positive change so ethical behavior and practices are championed in sport.

Personal and Professional Ethics

More attention must be given to the need to be ethical that significantly affects individuals generally and professionally. Without influencing personal ethics in people's daily lives, the overall social effect of being truthful, fair, and right is difficult to achieve. Individuals have to believe that good moral behavior starts with them in order to develop sound professional ethics or at least draw the conclusion that few people can separate their personal and professional selves. They also have to recognize their personal beliefs and professional standards of right and wrong do not exist in a social vacuum, nor are they mutually exclusive (Beauchamp, 1988). Ethical theories must provide a reasonable and consistent guide to deal with practical experiences from both these perspectives.

> The study of ethics and morality in sport management must include personal beliefs and professional ethics at the individual level.

Inevitably, individuals bring to the sport management setting different personal beliefs and experiences. However, professional behavior is characterized to a certain extent by the strength of commitment to one's personal values. Honesty, fairness, courage, and integrity are but four important values that influence professional conduct. When such values inform decisions and job-related tasks, they not only express an individual's character, but they also contribute to the working environment and may influence positively the practices of others. Because collective responsibility for ethical and unethical conduct rests upon the convictions of individuals within an organization, personal moral and ethical development is pertinent to responsible action. There are those who believe that business endeavors should focus exclusively on economic and financial criteria irrespective of moral considerations. However this approach to business can lead to the dehumanization of personnel and consumers, unethical practices, and ultimately to poor business decisions. If individuals in business and in sport management recognize that their own human interests, values, and needs often overlap with those of others, they could transform vulgar bottom-line thinking and behavior to ethical and responsible bottom-line decisions and conduct. Professional actions and judgments must be infused with a coherent foundation of personal ethics. To view these realms as a strict dichotomy is morally suspect at best and morally dangerous at worst.

The complementary relationship between personal and professional ethics is not only part of the ethos of organizations, reflecting a certain philosophy and tradition, but it also affects the quality of leadership. By virtue of their roles and duties, sport managers are in positions of leadership to set an example for others and influence the organizational climate. Leaders are capable of expressing explicit and implicit expectations about ethical and moral conduct in the workplace and can impress upon employees and colleagues what is considered acceptable and unacceptable behavior. Once individual leaders clarify the parameters of professional conduct, then others in the organization must assume responsibility and be accountable for their actions (Branvold, 1996).

Together with the preceding ethical constructs and tenets, and particularly in reference to sport management, an analysis of personal values and beliefs toward sport and its place in North American society and throughout the world is necessary. This introspective audit could include the following questions:

- What does sport mean to individuals as athletes and spectators?

- What expectations do individuals have of the institution of organized sport and its athletes and coaches?

- Do individuals in distinct segments of the population, for example, children, high school students, college and university students, and those involved in professional sport, value sport differently, and if so, why?

These sorts of questions and their answers should be part of any general ethical analyses. As individuals become increasingly conscious of many social issues, they must critically reflect on their personal ethical viewpoints toward these concerns. Those engaged in sport management should do likewise. Violence; inequity toward women and racial and ethnic minorities; and discrimination against the elderly and the physically challenged are some of the problems prevalent within the institution of sport. If such concerns are part of people's personal belief systems, then the chances of rectifying problem areas will improve considerably. There must be a recognition, therefore, that the decisions and actions of individual sport managers affect other persons involved in sport such as athletes, coaches, officials, volunteers, and spectators.

> Because social injustices are often inadequately addressed in the sport community, sport managers in particular should consciously develop a moral sensitivity.

Professions like business, medicine, and law have established formal mechanisms like codes of ethics and ethics boards to deal with pressing moral dilemmas in their respective fields so that individuals can better gauge their ethical and moral duties explicitly. Sport management must develop similar operative structures if it is to create a climate that influences its members' personal belief systems (cf., Zeigler, 1989, 1992). This type of effort, together with educational training, should lead to a greater understanding about the complementary relationship between personal and professional ethics, how the two should be reasonably consistent, and how each influences the other when making ethical judgments. Those preparing sport managers must emphasis both these aspects and impress upon their students that personal belief and professional ethics are serious matters.

Summary

This chapter presented an introduction to several areas related to ethics and morality in sport management. A general discussion of ethical and moral issues in sport demonstrated that such concerns are within the purview of sport management. Sport managers should also know some of the causes of moral decay in sport. They should recognize the role of sport in society and understand its economic, political, and social structures. In each of these spheres, there are important moral and ethical implications—one particularly relevant for sport managers is social responsibility. Awareness of societal problems and needs and the vast network of social relations associated with sport can lead to responsive ethical conduct by sport community members. The value of studying ethics and morality in the context of sport lies in the fact that people are moral agents with real human qualities and desires and that forces contrary to this perception undermine sport managerial practices from a moral point of view. Sport managers must be acutely aware of ethical and moral concerns specifically in their profession. As the organizational, bureaucratic, and institutional structures of sport expand and become more complex, the need for clear ethical thinking and sound moral behavior becomes a pressing concern. Finally, sport managers must realize that professional ethics cannot be so easily divorced from personal ethics and that each must develop coherently to complement the other.

The Interplay of Personal and Professional Ethics

In everyday life, ethical decisions, conduct, and moral character combine to influence personal and professional ethics. Although one's personal beliefs can be distinguished from one's professional standards, there is usually some overlap between these dimensions. Strong personal convictions often influence leadership and administrative practices. Sport managers must develop a coherent and consistent personal philosophy, as well as sound, responsible professional guidelines.

This introductory chapter set the stage for numerous questions and analyses in ethics and morality in sport management that are to follow in the remainder of the text. Readers will encounter detailed explications of moral concepts and ethical theories, personal and professional ethics, models and codes of ethics, and the application of ethical and moral principles. They will also read about the future of sport management ethics and morality to better understand the responsibilities and obligations sport managers must assume toward sport and sport community members in the years ahead.

Questions for Consideration

1. How are ethics and morality generally defined and specifically defined in relation to sport management?

2. What value, if any, is there in studying ethics and morality in sport and in sport management?

3. Provide three concrete examples of social responsibility in sport management.

4. What are the sources of unethical behavior in sport?

5. How are personal and professional ethics related to one another?

Chapter Two

Basic Concepts and Problems in Ethical and Moral Discourse

Chapter Objectives

- To become familiar with the concepts of values (axiology) and to understand the nature of definitions and clarity in language

- To comprehend the nature of ethics

- To differentiate between ethics and morality

- To consider various ideas on moral development and moral reasoning and critique philosophical relativism

- To know the meaning of ethical conduct and what constitutes misconduct

This text will discuss the ethical and moral dimensions of sport management practices from an applied perspective. That is, in the course of everyday experiences within various sport management settings, there inevitably arise moments when ethical and moral concerns have to be addressed. Questions of honesty, cheating, responsibility, fairness, justice, and personal rights cannot be avoided in most working environments, and sport management is no exception. However, the mere identification of ethical considerations in the workplace is not enough.

Sport managers must make concrete moral decisions, often under circumstances that are unclear. For example, one might ask, are individuals morally responsible when events and the behavior of others are beyond their control? Where does this responsibility begin, and where does it end? When is common sense a factor in demonstrating responsibility, and when is one obligated to assume responsibility? How responsible should one be? These, and certainly numerous other ethical questions, indicate that sport managers must be concerned with issues of a substantially different nature than the technical problems they face on a daily basis.

This chapter will lay a foundation of some of the basic concepts, terminology, and problems in ethics and morality toward understanding the nature of ethical judgments and moral reasoning in sport management. Becoming familiar with the language and concerns of ethics and morality at this point will assist readers in their comprehension of ethical and moral dilemmas. Readers will also acquire enough basic knowledge in these areas to adequately arrive at sound moral decisions when confronted with ethical difficulties. The latter will be taken up specifically in sport management in the applied chapters of the text.

The subsection topics below do not exhaust the terms and issues found in ethics and morality, and they are not treated extensively, but they do provide a sufficient starting point for consideration. In addition to the introduction of ethical and moral terms and problems, specific sport and sport management examples and illustrations will be provided to underscore the meaning of concepts.

According to *Webster's New Collegiate Dictionary* (1977), the word *axiology* refers to "the study of the nature, types, and criteria of values and of value judgments esp. in ethics" (p. 79). Already then there is a clue as to the content of ethics, namely, that it will involve an examination of some aspect of values. However, before the concept of ethics and other important terms are considered, an introduction to axiological concerns and definitional efforts in general seems in order.

Axiology and the Meanings of Value

Axiology is a branch of philosophy that investigates a broad range of areas where value issues arise. For example, one might value a certain belief or opinion, a way of life, a type of individual character, a particular action, a certain physical object, and the like. In general, the things people value and what counts as a value are numerous. Values can be expressed overtly in what one says and does, as well as covertly in individual thinking and feeling patterns. So one may say that one prefers competitive games and sports rather than fitness and jogging sessions because one finds the latter less challenging, or one may behave differently toward female athletes because one holds the belief that it is unbecoming for females to engage in athletic contests and sees their social role as mainly a domestic one. Despite these variations in expression, a *value* is typically anything we assess to be worthwhile, interesting, excellent, desirable, and important.

A value is something that is considered worthwhile.

One serious difficulty that arises when discussing values is determining which values to adopt and express. On what evidence does one accept certain values and reject others? Is there a way to rationally justify some values and not others, or should values and what people value be left to personal preference? These are samples of long-standing and vexing questions that we can address only in a cursory manner in this section. They do, however, indicate to some degree the complexity of axiological concerns.

Although the study of values has been part of Western intellectual history for over 2,000 years, beginning with the Greeks, the term axiology was introduced at the start of the 20th century (Findlay, 1970). In its modern usage it can refer to a strand of ethics or a general notion that deals with *value theory* or *theories of value*. These expressions can include theories about what is good, what is an obligation, what is a virtue, what is truth, what is beautiful, what is right, and the like. These theories would consider such topics in terms of the worthiness of various specific subject matters. In this sense, axiology is a field of study with the aim of leading to concrete resolutions of issues that involve value concerns. For example, in a health club setting, the question of serving alcohol can be considered from a value-theory perspective. Would the sale of alcoholic beverages comply with the purpose and mission of a health club? Should the provision of such an amenity be guided by principles of profit or by the welfare of health club patrons, or perhaps by both?

The preceding questions point to the general value of the health club itself, to economic value and to social and health values held by members and potential members. By raising such questions, the health club manager or owner might consider whether it would be worthwhile to provide alcoholic drinks on the premises. These are only some of the value elements for consideration here, and there certainly could be more. Further, this application of value theory to a specific case may or may not contain any moral imperative, in the sense of prescribing what one ought to do. In general, though, many current value issues include some prescriptive element.

Because the latter is usually the case, let us briefly examine the variety or kinds of values there are in order to distinguish between moral and amoral values. For many people, statements of facts and values are difficult to discern because many of us fail to be objective and honest about our opinions and beliefs. One's own prejudices and biases often color the way one assesses certain objects, human actions, and situations.

> Biases and prejudices can interfere with an individuals' concept of his or her values.

Sometimes it is the social context and historical period in which a person lives that shape the attitudes he or she possesses and hence the claims an individual makes. Often, vague language and unclear usage of words confuse meanings so that fact and value claims are not distinct. Nevertheless, it is imperative that factual propositions be distinguished from value statements. Usually the former can be independently verified, whereas the latter are open matters for discussion (Billington, 1988). For example, to say there has been a steady rate of growth in attendance at the SkyDome in Toronto for baseball games is an empirical or a factual matter. On the other hand, to claim that it is fun going to live baseball games is a value judgment. Some people simply despise or ignore sports and place little or no value on them. Debatable statements then often point out areas where judgments are based on one's values rather than on what can be conclusively verified.

Once value statements are identified, another classification can be proposed to distinguish between values with a moral (prescriptive) content and those that do not have any moral implications. Making this distinction is often difficult because it usually relies on what an individual means by *good*. There are numerous definitions and usages of the word good, and this adds to the problem of sorting out various moral and amoral values. However, the term good as a value-laden expression may not only refer to something that is good but it may be also used to describe the goodness of something or something that has the property of being good (Frankena, 1973). These are two different senses of good. Moreover, a general use of the term good often implies a desire to see such a good come into existence or implies the suggestion that one ought to pursue a particular good, but this need not be so. We sometimes use good without moral intent or a moral foundation. Therefore, saying something is good need not imply a prescription to bring about a particular good or any moral grounds for making such a claim. Some examples will help clarify this point.

To say that this is a good bat and this is a good mitt can refer primarily to the *usefulness* of these objects. Here, the purpose of each object may be the most important consideration, without suggesting to someone that she should go and purchase the same bat and mitt. This sense of good is based on whether the purpose is good or not. The claim that it is a good idea to buy sports equipment when it is on sale points to an *extrinsic* or *instrumental* sense of good, or when good is considered as a means. Here, one would be a careful and prudent equipment manager to make purchases when costs are lower. To exclaim that that was a good hit may indicate that one had a rewarding experience while watching a batter make a solid connection on a pitch. A fine hit, catch, or save may have *inherent* goodness because each evokes a worthwhile experience. Unrelated to the last two amoral senses of good, some things may be given the attribute good to indicate they are good when one experiences them. To say skiing or sailing is good may mean that they are good for their *intrinsic* properties. That is, they are good because they are enjoyable in and of themselves. Finally, one might say, "A world without sports would not be a good one." The meaning here might be that sport *contributes* to what some might call the good or happy life. The latter may be understood in an amoral sense where again no prescriptive or "ought" claims are being advanced. It is not that one wishes everyone to help create a world with sports in it, but that sports, for some, are part of what makes life worthwhile (Frankena, 1973).

The preceding discussion identifies a number of amoral values to contrast to moral values (ought statements) and explains how the notion of good can be used in a variety of senses. These amoral values can be summarized as utility values, extrinsic values, inherent values, intrinsic values, and contributory values. Some can be further divided into those that serve as a means and those that serve as an end, although in some circumstances even this distinction is difficult to ascertain. Because there are a number of differing types of values, it is also sometimes difficult to sort out what particular value one is addressing. Is one speaking about an inherent or an intrinsic amoral value or perhaps even a moral value? Despite the confusing nature of the terms introduced here, it is still essential to identify and distinguish between these various expressions and their meanings.

Amoral Values Include
Utility Values
Extrinsic Values
Inherent Values
Intrinsic Values
Contributory Values

In Brief . . .

Axiology refers to the nature, types, and criteria of values and value judgments.

A value is something we judge to be worthwhile, interesting, desirable, excellent, and important.

Value theory refers to theories about the meaning of good, obligation, virtue, truth, beauty, right, etc.

Utility values refer to the usefulness or purpose of something that makes it good.

Extrinsic or instrumental values consider the term good as a means toward something.

> Inherent values are related to the goodness of an object or person.
>
> Intrinsic values refer to the good one experiences in and of itself when doing something.
>
> Contributory values add to the good one experiences or wishes to experience in life.

There are other characterizations of values that can be considered. First, any discussion of values implies their contrary, or *disvalues*. So if one uses the terms *good, right, just*, and *responsible*, these will all have their opposite corresponding expressions such as bad, wrong, unjust, and irresponsible. In this sense, values may be characterized by being either positive or negative. Second, values can usually be ranked in some type of hierarchy where there are lower and higher values. Finally, values are connected to a particular and distinct content, even if that content is an abstraction. The values of holiness and beauty still refer to separate things that people respond to in concrete ways (Marias, 1941/1967). These points are made in order not to lose sight of the many ways in which values (or disvalues) can indicate what one considers desirable, worthwhile, significant, and the like. It further reveals the degree to which axiological matters involve complicated issues and distinctions, especially when they are implicated in ethical and moral discourse.

Definitions and Language Clarification

Part of the preceding discussion touched on the difficulties associated with defining the term *good*. A number of different meanings were presented, and it was pointed out that confusion could arise if one did not clearly define the word *good*. Everyone has likely experienced breakdowns in conversation because certain terms used were vague or ambiguous. In many cases, expressions that are not clearly defined lead to a lack of understanding, and sometimes misunderstanding. Clarity in language then often hinges on the appropriate definition of words. Analyses and decisions in ethics and morality also involve the clear comprehension of terms, and so it would be useful to briefly examine the area of definitions.

The topic of definitions can be found in many logic textbooks, because the construction and meaning of arguments often rest on the use and comprehension of language. In this chapter, we will consider only five main purposes and five types of definitions as discussed by Copi (1982).

Why does one bother defining words? A simple and immediate answer might be to make oneself better understood in the use of language. Yet the learning of language is a complicated process. It usually begins through observation and imitation. It is also an accumulative process. That is, one builds a store of words, the meanings of which are readily available, and one learns how to use such words in appropriate contexts, but the observation or imitation approach (and perhaps the use of examples and descriptions) reaches a limit until a more formal method for understanding words and increasing one's store of words is required. At some point, when one hears or reads a new word, only a formal, explicit explanation or definition will suffice—like turning to the dictionary. One particular purpose of definitions then is to increase one's vocabulary.

Words that have two or more distinct meanings have the potential to be used in ambiguous ways. The word *good*, discussed earlier, is a classic example of an ambiguous term. How often does one know precisely how good something is or when something or someone is good? Words are often ambiguous when their meaning in a particular context or sentence is unclear. For example, "would you like a punch?," "my sister is mad," and "Marx's *Capital* is a very heavy book" are three statements that include ambiguous words. Without further information, the meanings of these statements are unclear.

When ambiguous terms and phrases and their various senses are used more than once in discussions, arguments, or essays, shifts in meaning can lead to *equivocations*. For instance, the syllogism "Only man is rational. No woman is a man. Therefore, no woman is rational." commits what is known as the *fallacy of equivocation* (Freeman, 1988, p. 119). This argument makes use of two different definitions of *man*, and the reasoning and conclusion here are obviously incorrect. Sometimes entire sentences are ambiguous because their structure leads to confusion. "He has two grown sons and a daughter in a nunnery" could leave the impression that his sons are also in a nunnery. A comma after sons would correct what is known as an *amphiboly*, a structurally flawed ambiguous sentence (Salmon, 1989, p. 325).

Relative terms, such as *small, large, heavy*, and *light*, are sometimes used in speech and in writing in unclear ways. A light elephant is not a light animal. A small mountain is not a small landmass. A change of emphasis or *accent* can also alter the way terms are used and the meaning of expressions. In spoken language, the statement "all men are not liars" can mean that some men are not liars or that indeed each and every man is not a liar. The first meaning is suggested if the emphasis is placed on *all*, whereas the second meaning is implied when the accent is placed on *not*. In these and in most cases of ambiguity, the context of the words and statements can sometimes provide a clue as to their intended meaning. Although many instances of ambiguity should be avoided in language, ambiguity has an important place in literature, poetry, and humor. In general, however, language discrepancies related to multiple meanings identify a second purpose of definitions, which is to eliminate ambiguity.

Definitions of terms are often required when words are vague. Vagueness refers to expressions that require further clarification as to their meaning. Vague terms generally arise when "borderline cases" are discussed. In such instances, it becomes difficult to understand a vague word without specifying more precisely its meaning. Terms like *happy, bald, democracy, old, obscene, maturity*, and *death* are considered vague. Most color words are vague. How red does something have to be to be called red? How bald does someone have to be to be called bald? When is a person mature or old or happy?

In many circumstances, definitions can clarify the meaning of these vague expressions. Sometimes authoritative bodies, the judiciary or government, legally define vague words like *obscene, person*, and *living*. In other contexts, vague expressions, such as *see you later* or *take care*, have a place in our use of language. Some words are both vague and ambiguous. *Heavy* is vague in the sense of how heavy is heavy? It can be ambiguous by referring either to weight or seriousness.

A vague expression, however, lacks meaning not because there are two or more distinct meanings attached to it, but because it does not contain enough information in the meaning one intends to convey. The preceding discussion then suggests a third purpose for definitions, and that is to eliminate vagueness.

Two other purposes for definitions are offered by Copi (1982). In the sciences, many words are given precise definitions to make various theoretical claims. Although vagueness and ambiguity may be avoided by providing such technical definitions, these are not the primary reasons for making use of such definitions. A chemist may define an acid in principle to distinguish it from other substances, and this may have little to do with others who make use of acids such as cooks and sheet-metal workers (Copi, 1982) So, definitions can serve a theoretical purpose. Finally, definitions are sometimes used to influence the attitude of others. Words are sometimes defined to elicit an emotional response or to serve as a rhetorical device. Emotive value is usually attached to words like *abortion, euthanasia, racist, rapist,* and *molester*. Sometimes one defines such words not to provide an explanation of their meaning, but to arouse certain feelings in others or to alter the views or beliefs of others.

Types of Definitions

Ostensive definitions name an object, action, or situation after one points it out.

Stipulative definitions introduce a new word into a language.

Lexical definitions refer to an acceptable meaning(s) of a term as found in a dictionary.

Precising definitions go beyond ordinary meanings to clarify words and are usually set by an authoritative body.

Theoretical definitions are usually accepted in principle and are sometimes needed when proposing new theories.

Persuasive definitions rely on emotive or expressive words to influence people's attitudes.

The various purposes of definitions imply there are several types of definitions, and in the following, we will consider only six different kinds. *Ostensive* definitions are the most rudimentary type of definition. Here, one merely points to an object, action, or situation and assigns it a name. Parents use such definitions with infants and young children by pointing to things and repeating the names of those objects. There are at least two limitations of ostensive definitions. Sometimes children associate the name of an object with something other than the object being pointed out. For example, one's finger, rather than the protrusion on the side of the head, is identified as the ear. Second, if no object is available, then this type of definition cannot be employed. Abstract entities cannot be defined ostensively, nor can waterfalls or caves if photos or videos are unavailable (Salmon, 1989).

Definitions can stipulate new meanings and introduce new terms into language. As products and technologies are created, new names and new meanings attached to existing words are associated with such advances. Computer language today has its own vocabulary with newly invented words like *byte* and *download*, and redefined words like *disk* and *boot*. There are usually two requirements for definitions of this sort. A new term should not already have a widely accepted meaning, and it should provide a useful addition to language (Salmon, 1989). A definition that stipulates is not necessarily true or false; instead, it is offered as a new expression or as a proposed new meaning of an existing term that will be accepted within a specific context.

A *lexical* definition, in contrast, refers to an accepted meaning of a word that is either true or false and that is usually offered as a way to reduce ambiguity. Lexical definitions must conform to standard or conventional meanings and usages of words, and based on this, it can be determined whether or not someone uses a term correctly or incorrectly (Copi, 1982). Dictionary definitions are considered lexical definitions.

The latter two types of definitions do not reduce vagueness, but *precising* definitions do (Salmon, 1989). Because vagueness involves real borderline cases, new meanings cannot clarify vague expressions. Precising definitions utilize meanings already established, but they go beyond an appeal to ordinary meanings to clear up confusion in particular circumstances. Such definitions are often employed in the legal system when new and difficult cases arise. For example, some women today act as paid surrogates for those unable to carry a pregnancy to term. The question of who is the actual mother of the newborn might require a precising definition.

A fifth type of definition is a *theoretical* definition. Such definitions are connected to the proposal of new theories, and because most theories can be questioned, so too are the definitions they introduce. Theoretical definitions seek to provide meanings that can be accepted in principle. They do not necessarily appeal to common usages of terms, though they can be considered correct or incorrect, and they do not propose completely new meanings. Instead, a theoretical definition serves to clarify an expression used when proposing a new theory. Its acceptance is intimately bound to the acceptance of the theory itself.

Finally, there are *persuasive* definitions. These make use of emotive and expressive language to influence attitudes. Many words can be defined in rhetorical language and thereby act as devices of persuasion. Terms like *abortion*, *homosexual*, *communism*, and the like can be defined negatively or positively. In intercollegiate sports, many women's team names carry the prefix lady (e.g., Lady Vols or Lady Badgers), and for some, this conveys a meaning that women's sport is inferior to men's sport. Although persuasive definitions are not always derogatory—they may even be humorous—one must be sensitive to the expressive ways in which words are defined.

> Before you can analyze the ethical issues surrounding a situation, you must clearly establish an even playing field by clearly defining all related terms.

Far more could be said about definitions and the general area of language clarification. By recognizing some of the main purposes and types of definitions, one gains an added sense and appreciation for the nuances of language and the varied usage of words. Most analyses of ethical dilemmas require that one's terms of reference be clearly defined to ensure there is a common base of understanding. As an ethical argument develops, it will rely on shared meanings of words and expressions to advance one's moral claims and prescriptive dictums. This sensitivity to definitions and language will become invaluable as we proceed to examine other ideas in this chapter and other topics in this text.

Many people rarely consider the area of ethics, at least from a formal and rigorous perspective, and yet all people frequently engage in making ethical decisions. How often does a person declare someone's behavior to be right or wrong, good or bad, worthy or unworthy, and the like? How frequently does one say someone ought to do this or should not do that? How many times does one assert that this is worth pursuing and that is worth avoiding? On what rational or reasoned grounds do individuals make such claims? If, broadly speaking, ethics involves principles used to assess human actions and concerns in terms of right or wrong, good or bad, then many ethical judgments are arrived at through conventional wisdom, intuition, or reliance on some authority or by some other readily available means. Few people then engage in serious inquiry into the theories and axioms underlying ethical judgments, yet it would be useful to have a basic understanding of some of these notions. In this section, we will examine the nature of ethics by introducing some of its main themes and ideas.

As mentioned in the previous section, ethics or *moral philosophy* is concerned with value issues and decisions. Matters of value can be referred to as *normative* or *nonnormative*. In the latter case, ethics does not address a particular moral position (e.g., opposing boxing because it is predicated on violence), but is concerned instead with descriptive features of ethics or the meanings of ethical terms and expressions. Normative ethics, on the other hand, involves defending certain ethical principles and standards or virtues in a systematic way or demonstrating the applicability of such systems in an area like sport management (Beauchamp, 1991). This text will be primarily concerned with normative ethics in the latter applied sense.

> Normative ethics defends ethical principles, standards, and virtues while nonnormative ethics concerns the meanings of ethical terms and expressions.

In most instances, the main task of ethics is to evaluate the standards of right or wrong that people assign to behavior, motives, intentions, and persons (Cornman & Lehrer, 1974). Without the moral quality of good or bad attached to such an assessment, then, it is unlikely that ethical decisions are involved. For example, one could say to a tennis player, "After your opponent hits down the line and approaches the net, you should return with a cross-court." Although the term *should* is used, the preceding has no moral relevance here but is strategic or tactical advice. In contrast, to say a player should not call a fault when he or she knows the ball touched the line indicates that it would be wrong to do so. Ethics is primarily concerned with the latter type of instances.

There are generally two types of ethical judgments. As indicated in some of the questions raised in the opening paragraph of this section, ethical decisions may relate to a person's conduct in terms of what an individual should or should not do or to something that is either valued or not valued. Frankena (1973) calls ethical judgments related to human actions *judgments of moral obligation*. Words like ought and should, right and wrong to describe particular and general behavior are included in this category. He calls ethical decisions concerned with intentions, motives, and the character of individuals, *judgments of moral value*. Expressions like *good, bad, praiseworthy, reprehensible,* and *virtuous* can describe the state or condition of one's character, motives, or intentions in particular and general ways. Again, there are also judgments of amoral value, discussed in the previous section, which are not strictly speaking part of ethical considerations, though they are part of axiology.

Ethics vs. Morals

Ethics is the set of theories or principles that determines right and wrong.

Morals involve the practice of these ethical theories or principles.

Ethical judgments contain a moral component as related to conduct or values, yet morals and ethics can differ. Ethics is considered on the level of theory or principles in the determination of right and wrong, whereas morals are observed on the level of practice (Billington, 1988). In ethics, one appeals to rules or maxims as a way to justify certain moral decisions, irrespective of whether those decisions are right or wrong (there are good and bad ethics). On the other hand, morals usually describe a personal set of values expressed in individual actions in concrete situations. So the morals of a sport director would matter to that person's family and friends, and this might differ from the ethical principles she applies to refrain from padding the budget. In most cases, the adjective *ethical* is synonymous with *moral*. That is, the ethical or moral thing to do is considered the right or good thing to do.

Billington (1988) identifies six features of ethical or moral questions to differentiate them from questions raised in other disciplines and areas of study:

1. *No one can avoid dealing with moral questions.* People can live without being concerned or having knowledge about many things, but as long as one lives with and alongside others, or is remotely influenced by others, one encounters moral issues and makes ethical decisions.

2. *Moral decisions involve other people.* There is no such thing as a private ethics. Individuals sometimes feel that certain personal decisions do not affect others, but on closer examination they do. The decision to solo mountain climb on a dangerous cliff seems quite personal and would harm no one else. Yet, should one die from such a venture, others would be deprived from such a loss.

3. *Moral decisions are reserved for things that matter most.* Many disciplines serve to enable others to reach a level of happiness and self-fulfillment in their lives. This is certainly true of education. However, it is probably not that important which pedagogical method one employs to enjoy success as a teacher. On the other hand, deep divisions might exist between teachers over issues like honesty, cheating, bigotry, racism, sexism, and the like. Technical or strategic judgments are usually less pressing than and are qualitatively different from moral ones.

4. *Ethical decisions offer no final answers.* Although many groups of people in society like doctors, lawyers, legislators, and religious leaders es-

pouse clear solutions to moral questions, philosophers usually provide no definitive right or wrong answers. Some ethical theories and behavior may be shown to be more reasonable and correct than others, but to offer a completely satisfactory answer to a moral problem is too ambitious a goal. Although this might frustrate many people, thinking clearly and rigorously about moral issues is in itself challenging without arriving at a final answer.

5. *Choice is a central element of morality.* If someone were forced to act in a way that is morally despicable, one would not generally hold that person blameworthy. The difficulty of course is determining how much and what kind of force the individual experienced to deny him a choice. Are there life situations where choice is impossible? Perhaps issues like blameworthiness can be dealt with only in degrees? If so, then moral decisions might always include choice. One thing is certain, however. Trying to avoid a moral problem is also a choice. In this sense, no one can remain neutral about ethical concerns.

6. *The aim of moral reasoning is to discover right or correct forms of behavior.* Seeking some kind of truth is the aim of most disciplines, as in the sciences where there are accepted methods to verify truths, but this must be precluded when making ethical decisions. Because there are numerous competing ethical theories, all containing some weaknesses, and no singular method for arriving at ethical solutions, no action can be declared absolutely correct or incorrect. This does not mean that no right or correct behavior can be recommended through moral analysis. Certain conduct might be more justified (and hence right or correct) than others, and an appeal to ethical principles might reveal these differences. Ethical discourse can at least try to ensure and encourage honest, open debates about controversial moral issues.

These distinguishing features provide an adequate overview of the nature of ethics, but there is another approach toward identifying other characteristics about ethics, and that is to describe what ethics is not. This is a method employed by White (1988) and one we shall now consider by following his lead.

Ethical decisions have little to do with the way one feels, but rather with the way one thinks or reasons. Statements of feeling are usually personal expressions of one's emotive state, and they often cannot be seriously challenged. If someone feels happy or grief or is in pain, it is almost absurd to question such feelings or to recommend that one ought not to have such feelings. One mainly accepts other people's feelings at face value.

The same is not true of ethical judgments of the normative variety with which we are concerned. Questioning these decisions is most appropriate for it usually means one is asking for some sort of justification for a stance on a moral issue. Why does one oppose the good foul in sport, or why is one in favor of transferring greater funds to men's intercollegiate sport rather than to comparable women's sports? To answer these questions requires an appeal to sound reasons, principles, rational arguments, and the like. One will rely mostly on thinking carefully about these issues.

In fact, emotions would likely hinder or possibly create a bias toward a clear, well-reasoned response to these concerns. If one were to simply answer, "I get upset when I watch a good foul," and "I just feel women's sport is less worthy than men's" and leave it at that, then there is no attempt here to defend one's moral decision, nor would there be any point to challenge these positions. At least two of the features of ethics mentioned earlier indicate why these reactions are unsatisfactory from a moral point of view. Recall there is no such thing as a private ethics, and others are affected by one's moral decisions. Ethics is situated in the public domain.

Because of these characteristics, when making ethical judgments, one is obligated to recommend one's moral decisions to others. Consider if an individual decided that cheating on exams was fine for him, but not for others. If reciprocity cannot be granted for one's ethical judgments, it places suspicion on the strength of one's moral convictions. Further, people generally want others to respect their ethical decisions, and at times people want to convince others of the correctness of their judgments. These goals can be accomplished only through critical thinking and accepting the challenges of others, not merely by expressing one's feelings.

Moreover, feelings can and often do change for no apparent reason. One can feel sincere or guilty over certain issues one day and feel just the opposite the next day. People sometimes then arbitrarily have and express their feelings. Further, it would hardly be appropriate to rely on the strength of emotions as a guide for moral conduct. Feeling sincere about racist causes does not make an assault on a member of a minority group right. Although an examination of one's feelings may reveal certain reasons for making ethical decisions, relying foremost on one's feelings is not part of most ethical considerations.

> In order to command respect for their ethical decisions, people must be willing to think critically and accept the challenges of others, rather than let their feelings dictate their judgment.

Ethics is also not about relying on authoritative voices or bodies to tell us what is right or wrong, good or bad, and the like. This is a posture one assumes for any type of philosophical inquiry. Each of us must ultimately arrive at ethical decisions independently of what others have to say (although we may ultimately agree with others). This does not mean that others do not influence a person's moral judgments, but what counts most in the end is what that person thinks.

Parents, teachers, and government and religious leaders may insist that individuals accept their word as final, not because they have put forth good reasons for accepting their views, but because they are in a position of authority. They may even tempt individuals with various rewards, but manipulation, threats, and coercion have no place in moral discourse. Dialogue on ethical matters must be built on a foundation where people's reasons and rational arguments can be freely offered and rejected and where one can decide for oneself whether to accept or oppose moral positions.

Placing importance on individual thinking, however, should not lead to the idea that ethics is, therefore, dependent on absolute personal authority. Individuality referred to above stresses the point that moral decisions cannot be made for a person and that to a large extent each person is responsible for the moral position she or he assumes. If morality were based strictly on the authority of individuals, whose ethics would people claim is superior and would they want to follow? In fact, such questions could not even be raised on such a view. Nevertheless, people do pose such queries when it comes to moral issues, and this reveals something important.

The ability to distinguish between right and wrong, good and bad compels one to raise questions about the relative worth of moral judgments and the actions guided by such decisions. Because these are comparative matters, they necessarily involve considerations beyond one's private domain. Moral disagreements are between people. One cannot claim a moral decision is correct unless it is held up against someone else's alternative view that might oppose it. This is partly how the scientific method works to verify truths, and this feature has a place in ethics. It ensures that no single person has a monopoly on what is morally right (otherwise, slavery and torture could be justified) and that moral views can change (one can convince someone else that capital punishment is right or wrong). Although individuals must make up their own minds about moral dilemmas—that is, they have to live with and be largely responsible for their ethical decisions—no person can claim to be an absolute authority on moral issues.

Even though no one individual is a moral authority, some people equate what is ethical with what is legal. In other words, nothing is deemed morally wrong if it conforms with the law. Are ethics and the law the same?

At first glance, many laws do seem to prohibit and punish actions considered morally unacceptable like murder, theft, molestation, fraud, and embezzlement, but as a bearer of high moral standards and as a moral authority, the law is questionable. As White (1988) points out:

> But there are problems with making the law an ultimate standard of right and wrong. The law allows many actions that are morally offensive (manipulating people or lying to your friends). It prohibits things that might be morally neutral or even good (certain sexual practices). And it is changeable and contradictory. (p. 15)

Laws in the United States once permitted slavery, laws in Nazi Germany gave sanction to anti-Semitism, and laws in the former USSR denied basic human freedoms. In each case, the laws were abandoned, but only after much bloodshed and civil strife. Other practices like capital punishment, abortion, euthanasia, pornography, and prostitution are illegal in some countries and legal in others. Even within one's own country, laws change or are different with regard to some of these moral issues. Prostitution is legal in Nevada but not in other states in the United States. Does this make prostitution right or wrong?

In any nation, the law may serve to please the majority of its people, a particular political party, or some dictator, and this would have very little to do with the establishment of what is ethical. Even a majority view can condone immoral practices. Moreover, the authority of law can be coercive in many practical instances, whereas ethical principles are held open to be scrutinized and accepted or rejected freely. Ethics, therefore, is unlike the law in many respects when it comes to moral concerns.

> Unlike ethics, laws are by nature coercive and reflect the body that creates them, which may or may not be ethical.

Finally, there is one area many people subscribe to as a moral authority and for moral guidance: religion. In fact, some people claim that without religion there can be no morality at all. Because religion is mostly concerned with how we lead our lives, it has much to say about living a moral life. Many people turn to religious teachings and authorities in times of moral crises and do find acceptable, sound answers. There are, however, differences between religious ethics and philosophical ethics.

White (1988) identifies three main distinctions. Religious ethics focuses on one's spiritual sensitivities and needs, whereas philosophical ethics appeals primarily to one's intellect and reasoning abilities. Second, religious ethics is often expressed in authoritative and emotive terms, and this takes it beyond public and philosophical debate. Finally, those who deny religion altogether (atheists) can still engage in moral discourse as rational human beings and also live decent lives.

Religion is not being denied here as an area where there are answers to moral questions. However, one must recognize that its tasks and objectives are different from those of philosophical ethics. What is sometimes more surprising is to learn about the common moral grounds and solutions they share. Despite the occasional overlap, religious ethics and philosophical ethics are not equivalent.

This section has provided an overview of the nature of ethics by indicating the kinds of value issues taken up by moral judgments and by discussing what ethics is and is not. In the following, we will discuss the characteristics of morality, which is related to the concept taken up here.

Key Concepts

differentiation of ethical questions

ethics and authority

ethics and religion

ethics and the law

judgments of moral obligations

judgments of moral value

nonnormative

normative

morality

Morality

There are important connections and differences between ethics and morality; the latter can be considered the subject area of the former. That is, the principles and theories of ethics derive from or explain the way of life, beliefs, attitudes, intentions, and motives that are judged to possess moral qualities. The term *morality* usually encompasses all facets of life where moral questions can arise. For this reason, religion and morality are closely linked as indicated above.

Beauchamp (1991) describes a morality as "a social institution with a code of learnable rules" (p. 6). The social nature of morality, its application of certain rules, and its expansive concerns separate it from ethics, which has a primary theoretical interest. Morality then is grounded in practical affairs of social life, and this will be the focus of our examination here.

Most social rules are already established and given, and so morality exists prior to any one person. People inherit and appropriate morality at a young age when we are told what to do and what not to do. Brush your teeth after every meal, don't run too fast or you might fall, and don't go into the pool alone are all familiar do and don't expressions. Such rules involve self-interest and teach young people to act in a prudent manner.

On the other hand, leave your sister's toys alone, don't cheat when you play soccer, always tell the truth, honor your mother and father, and the like are considered moral rules. These rules take into account the interests of others, their rights, and the respect they are due as human beings. Such rules teach one how to behave with others and what is expected in one's conduct in relation to others. In most instances, morality is other regarding and is the foundation of every society (though some challenge this view). Morality, more properly speaking then, is concerned with behavior and rules in this social and morally relevant sense (Velasquez, 1992).

According to Frankena (1973), morality is both similar to and different from some aspects of law and certain features of social customs and etiquette. We are introduced and taught about morality and society's conventions through similar patterns of development. However, morality, like law and unlike customs, is not overly concerned with matters of taste and appearance. On the other hand, morality, like conventions and unlike law, does not rely on an authoritative body that might be manipulative and coercive. Some go beyond the realms of law and convention to say that morality is whatever is guided by pure intentions, like benevolence or doing what is right for its own sake. The latter can be important in the exercise of morality, something one would not entirely rule out, but more important, morality differs from prudent behavior, personal or social taste, and threatening actions.

That morality as a social institution serves to guide individual conduct does not necessarily mean that people merely act according to social norms and standards. Society's moral system does indicate what is forbidden and what is permitted in many areas. However, we also learn to take an individual moral perspective on many distinct issues where society's rules may not be very helpful. That is, morality teaches people to understand and apply standards from a personal moral point of view, as well as adopt norms from society at large (Frankena, 1973).

> Though societal norms and values may influence an individual's moral decisions, there is a personal moral component that may also have some effect.

As well as examining the social institution thesis, Beauchamp (1991) identifies four distinguishing marks of morality. Reference has been made to some of these features already, but a short review of each will better establish the nature of morality.

1. Morality is concerned with moral ideals that are accepted as "supremely authoritative or overriding" guides for behavior (Beauchamp, p. 16). This means that issues of self-interest, personal politics, religious influences, and the like cannot supercede a moral principle, but granting such high significance to ideals simply because they are moral may be inadequate. Such principles would require moral justification to be granted an overriding status. Then the entire question of moral weight, competing demands, and moral justification could also lead to a circular argument (a chicken-egg-type dilemma). Moreover, people often behave without placing moral

ideals at the top of their list of concerns, especially when involved in activities with adversarial demands (e.g., when playing sports). The supremacy of moral principles may be a sufficient, but not always a necessary, condition of morality.

2. Morality contains a prescriptive character. Morality guides human action by recommending that one act or refrain from acting in certain ways. Sometimes this is explicitly understood by using words like *ought* and *should not*, but at other times, expressions that appear to be moral may contain a vague or no prescriptive sense. To say, "That was a noble gesture" or "She displays virtue" can tell us relatively little or nothing at all in terms of how we should act. While recognizing this weakness, morality usually prescribes actions for us, and in many instances this is considered the hallmark of morality.

3. Universalizability is a distinguishing feature of morality. This component was briefly mentioned in earlier discussions, but it refers to the notion that moral judgments must be held the same for all people in relevantly similar situations. In principle, this element of morality is quite rational and credible. In practice, however, universalizability has at least three problems. First, there could be serious disagreements as to what counts as relevantly similar situations. Second, this characteristic suggests that moral ideals and principles can be theoretically deduced for all people without any consideration of cultural differences and the real choices people have when making moral decisions. Universalizability is also not applicable to supererogatory acts, behavior beyond acceptable standards, such as giving to charitable causes or acting in heroic ways. This criterion is a foundational element of morality for many people, and in many circumstances it is an exceedingly important criterion, but it has its weaknesses as well.

4. Morality has to have a central concern for the well being of others. It must consider both harms and benefits to others and guide people toward the general enhancement of human beings. Certain virtues like generosity, empathy, justice, and compassion might be expressed to show one's interest in the welfare of others. Unfortunately, these virtues are sometimes manifested in prejudicial ways in terms of favoring one class or group of people. For example, scholarship athletes and athletic perks might indicate inequitable treatment between college athletes and the average college student. Maintaining consistency when expressing such virtues can be a problem. Simply applying action-guiding codes based on this criterion might also display a bias, for instance, in the area of affirmative action and charges of reverse discrimination. Although concern for others is a central element of morality, how morality and the welfare of others are linked must be clear and unequivocal.

> ### *Morality . . .*
>
> Is a set of authoritative ideals that guide behavior.
>
> Is prescriptive in nature—it tells people what they should or should not do.
>
> Necessitates similar judgments for similar situations.
>
> Is concerned with others' well-being.

One can see that each of these four distinguishing marks of morality is deficient to some extent and that it would be difficult to arrive at a satisfactory set of sufficient and necessary conditions for morality. Beauchamp (1991), therefore, considers a pluralistic approach to determine what counts as morality. Perhaps no single unitary definition or set of features can characterize the moral. On the other hand, there may be some characteristics of morality that, if present, adequately tell people that they are dealing with a moral principle or ideal.

After presenting several combinations of the above marks, Beauchamp concludes by saying that different combinations may apply to various behaviors or events, and in each case one could sufficiently determine what counts as morality. This approach is perhaps the most reasonable way to view morality because it accounts for the dominant marks of morality, and it is also linked to specific situations and actions.

Besides addressing the question of what morality is, three other features of morality deserve our attention: the idea of a moral position, the object of morality, and the motives for moral behavior (Beauchamp, 1991). It has already been stated that sport management ethics is an applied area of moral philosophy. Ethical theories and principles would be applied to try to understand, examine, and resolve particular moral dilemmas in sport management. As we shall see immediately below, sport management practices can be, and are, defended by appealing to moral positions.

The Terms of Morality

Morality refers to societal rules that govern most forms of everyday interactive behavior.

A moral position is a stance that dictates moral behavior.

The object(s) of morality refers to the final goal(s) or purpose(s) of morality.

Motives for moral behavior include enlightened self-interest, respect for rules, and other-regarding interests.

Moral development refers to the idea that processes of moral thinking and judgments are acquired and refined in various sequential stages of life.

These positions are usually some important, unquestioned underlying moral stances, free of prejudice, emotional reactions, and personal preference, which are taken up to defend certain behavior. A genuine moral position is difficult to identify. A sports section editor might defend the lack of female sports coverage in the newspaper by saying, "But everyone knows female sports are boring." A sports promoter might defend a certain questionable marketing campaign by claiming, "What they don't know can't hurt them." An athletic director might ignore the fact that athletic department student interns are providing college tours for potential scholarship athletes during prohibited times of the year by claiming, "Any student can show a prospective student the campus." In each case, actions are defended by appealing to a moral position, but in these instances each view may be biased or prejudicial.

People express moral positions about many issues and over many types of behavior, but they rarely state their moral positions so clearly that these positions are free from some sort of rationalization. It may also be unsatisfactory to state one's moral position in such general terms that the connection to morality cannot be clearly acknowledged (Beauchamp, 1991). These difficulties can surface because moral positions usually require the articulation of sound, reasoned ethical principles and ideals, which are hardly ever considered on a day-to-day basis. One should, therefore, remain suspect when moral positions are supplied as reasons to explain various actions and situations.

Like the question of moral positions, the object of morality can also be unclear, yet important toward understanding the parameters of morality. What is one attempting to achieve by morality? What purpose does morality serve? We have already discussed social and personal themes related to morality, but these were just general observations. This should not cause us much despair because many philosophers have left the question of morality's purpose or function vague.

Some have suggested that morality can lead us toward a happy life; others have stressed a good will that might guide one's moral decisions. Still others claim that morality serves to combat deteriorating social relationships. In this view, human relations degenerate because there are limits to resources, sympathy, and information (Beauchamp, 1991). Examples of this deterioration include all kinds of physical and psychological violence, various forms of intolerance and injustice, business and government scandals, and a host of other problems of an interpersonal nature. Morality tends to diminish one's limits of sympathy, for example, so one recognizes and is sensitive to these impaired social relations, and ultimately to better this state of affairs, but who can really say what *the* object of morality is?

Morality can point toward a number of goals and purposes like the ones just mentioned. Morality is concerned with human rights, freedoms, and needs. It also censures selfish and harmful acts toward others so we get along in society. By leading a moral life, it is likely that many people can attain a modicum of happiness and perhaps possess the character to make sound moral decisions and do the right thing. It might be more reasonable then to look for several purposes and functions of morality rather than one all-encompassing object.

Finally, what motives do we have for acting in moral ways? What compels us to follow societal rules that constitute morality? Nowell-Smith (1967) suggests there are three basic motives. *Enlightened self-interest* might make us fearful to act in ways that go against our moral duties and obligations. Few people would want to feel socially isolated because they failed to follow certain moral rules. In some cases, some type of punishment is meted out for violating the tenets of moral codes. Still, most people realize that in the long run adhering to societal rules has social and personal advantages.

Respect for rules is another motive. We are taught at an early age how to follow rules and what rules to follow. Consider going to a foreign country and learning its customs and laws. One might encounter different mannerisms, etiquette, procedures, and regulations that guide all facets of life in a relatively new way. One would also likely be made aware how many of one's own cultural rules are different and go unquestioned. Sometimes one is unable to account for why one does certain things, and one claims that's just the way it's done. Social rules can be deeply ingrained in this sense. At other times, people fail to question not only the rule but also the source or author of a rule. An extreme case of this might be following the rules of cult leaders, who seem to have an incredible hold on their followers. In a milder form, most bureaucratic rules are rarely disputed and are uncritically accepted by most of us. Being accustomed to obey rules then is another motive for morality.

Finally, *other-regarding* motives create in people a commitment to morality. Care, trust, compassion, benevolence, and respect for persons are some of these motives. People often act in moral ways simply because they possess a deep concern for others. This motive is sometimes difficult to identify because the same act might also be compelled by a rule. Nevertheless, people should recognize that genuine instances of selflessness do occur and can serve as a motive for morality.

The discussion of ethics and morality to this point has covered a fair number of themes and ideas. Both areas are closely related, but they can be distinguished. In general, ethics refers to the theoretical aspects of moral philosophy, its standards and principles, whereas morality inquires into the social implications and expressions of ethical judgments. To better understand the nature of morality we briefly considered the way societal rules are taught and apprehended. We will examine this process further in the next two sections, which deal with the interrelated topics of moral reasoning and moral development.

Key Concepts

enlightened self-interest

moral objects

moral positions

morality as overriding concern

other regarding

prescriptive

prudent behavior

respect for rules

universalizability

well-being of others

Moral Development

People begin to learn about morality at a young age, as mentioned above, but questions like, how does one come to know right from wrong, how does one recognize a moral problem, and how are moral decisions arrived at as one matures require more detailed answers. Moral reasoning and development consider these and other similar questions, and we'll discuss the latter first in the next two sections.

For most people, the identification and application of moral standards start in the home. Parents and guardians are usually the first teachers of morality, and the lessons and values they try to instill are extremely varied. They not only provide moral instruction in terms of resolving any number of important and sometimes trivial problems, but they are also instrumental in shaping the moral character of children.

Some of one's early moral education occurs explicitly. At about the time a child can begin to understand language, parents bombard children with all kinds of rules to follow: People admonish children for not doing this or doing that, praise them for appropriate behavior, and tell them to trust and cooperate with others and, occasionally, to be suspicious of some people. In other instances, moral lessons are learned implicitly. Adults use facial expressions, a look, gestures, or body language to convey approval or disapproval with a child's moral behavior.

Through one's immediate family, and especially from one's parents, a wealth of moral values, rules, and standards is appropriated.

Parental figures are certainly not the only moral teachers of children, and the home is not the only place where moral education occurs. Children learn about morality from day-care personnel, schoolteachers, coaches, relatives, other parents, and other children. They also find themselves in different environments like in front of the television, at a friend's home, in public places, or at the day-care center, school, and the playground where ethical problems arise. Despite the many situations they find themselves in and the numerous people they come in contact with, children learn to develop the capacity to deal with moral issues.

> Morality is not inherent, but inherited.

The important word in the last sentence is *learn*. No one is born with the ability to reason about moral concerns. Morality, moral standards, and rules are inherited. We are first exposed to morality, and only later do we acquire the capacity to think critically about moral issues. Most children then cannot use moral reasoning until they possess some language skills, become socialized to some extent, and have sufficient life experiences. This indicates that moral reasoning is acquired in a developmental way, a view that has been recognized throughout Western history. Just as our physical development can be traced, so too can our moral development. Contemporary research on moral development has been most prominently advanced by Kohlberg, and it is to his work that we will now turn to discuss this process.

Building on Piaget's ideas of moral development, Kohlberg (1987) believes, unlike Piaget, that children and adolescents move through distinct moral stages where different levels of moral judgments can be identified. Kohlberg's model consists of three levels: the preconventional, the conventional, and the postconventional. Those generally under the age of nine, and perhaps adolescent and adult criminals, are at the preconventional level. The conventional level refers to the acceptance and conformity to society's laws, rules, conventions, and norms by most adolescents and adults. Finally, postconventional level includes those above the age of 20 who can apply moral principles to social rules and who accept the latter based on such principles and not on conventions.

Kohlberg (1987) sees these levels of moral development in terms of the relationship between the individual and society's rules and expectations. Consequently, Level I is characterized by a separation between conventions and the individual. The person here sees social rules as external to the self. A Level II individual closely identifies with society's rules and expectations, whereas a Level III person has identified his or her values independently of social norms, and in some cases the two may conflict, based on ethical principles.

In each of these levels, there are two moral stages, one being more advanced than the other. Kohlberg (1987) elaborates on each of these stages by considering three areas: (a) what is right, (b) the reasons for doing right, and (c) the social perspective behind each stage. Let us turn to examine his model in greater detail (Kohlberg, 1987, pp. 284-286).

Level I: Preconventional

Stage 1—Heteronomous morality. What is right is to not break rules that have punishments attached to them, to be obedient for the sake of obedience, and to not cause physical harm to others and property. Avoiding punishment and recognizing the power of the authority that sets the rules are the reasons for doing right. From a social perspective, morality is viewed as egocentric. Individuals do not account for the interests of others; they recognize only the physicality of actions, not their psychological aspects, and they cannot differentiate between their point of view and that of an authority.

Stage 2—Individualism, instrumental purpose, and exchange. What is right is to follow rules to achieve one's own interests, to let others do the same, and to deem as fair what is an equal exchange, deal, or arrangement. Reasons for doing right are to serve one's interests while realizing others are fulfilling their interests. Socially speaking, this stage expresses a concrete individualistic point of view. Each person has his or her own interests to pursue, making each right in a relativistic sense.

Level II: Conventional

Stage 3—Mutual interpersonal expectations, relationships, and interpersonal conformity. What is right is to live up to the expectations of those who are in one's immediate sphere of influence, to be good by displaying proper motives and concern for others, to keep mutual relations with others through loyalty, trust, confidence, respect, and gratitude. Reasons for doing right include the desire to be good, to have others recognize this goodness, to show concern for others, to follow the Golden Rule, and to adhere to rules and authority that support general good behavior. Awareness of relationships between individuals is the main social perspective here. One becomes aware of the feelings and expectations of others beyond self-interest, can apply the Golden Rule, and assume another point of view, but does not yet fully recognize the larger social context and system.

Stage 4—Social system and conscience. Doing right involves fulfilling agreed-upon duties, adhering to laws except in extreme cases, and contributing to groups, institutions, and society. The reasons for doing right include ensuring the maintenance of institutions and society, preventing their erosion, and letting one's conscience guide the fulfillment of obligations. One is aware one is a member of society, yet is able to differentiate society's perspective from interpersonal agreements and motives by recognizing roles and rules in the social system and identifying the place of the individual in the social system.

Level III: Postconventional, or Principled

Stage 5—Social contract or utility and individual rights. What is right is being aware that others and individual groups hold different and relative values and rules, accepting these differences by reason of a social contract (to ensure the impartial interest of all), and upholding basic fundamental values, like life and liberty, above any relative values. The reasons for doing right include the recognition that abiding by laws preserves and protects the rights and interests of others, security in the knowledge that others enter into the social contract freely and with commitment, and rational acknowledgment of the utility of a contractual social arrangement. This stage is called the prior-to-society perspective because the individual is aware that values and rights are independent of social agreements. The person tries to integrate various perspectives through formal procedures to arrive at contracts and agreements that maintain impartiality and follow due process. He or she also considers moral and legal matters noting that they are sometimes in conflict and difficult to integrate.

Moral Development Models

Kohlberg's model includes Level I Preconventional—heteronomous morality, and individualism, instrumental purpose, and exchange; Level II Conventional—mutual interpersonal expectations, relationships and interpersonal conformity, and social system and conscience; Level III Postconventional, or Principled—social contract or utility and individual rights, and universal ethical principles.

Gilligan's ethic of care identifies a female-specific moral development scheme that differs from Kohlberg's pattern. Level I Preconventional—caring and responsibility to oneself; Level II Conventional—caring for others and neglecting oneself; Level III Postconventional—a balance between caring for others and oneself.

Stage 6—Universal ethical principles. What are right are self-chosen ethical principles that are the foundation for justifying laws and particular social agreements. When laws and these principles are in discord, one follows the principles. Such universal principles include justice, equality of human rights, and respect for the dignity of individuals. The reasons for doing right are the beliefs that these principles are valid for the rational person and that one has a personal commitment to uphold them. One takes a moral point of view at this stage, and all social attachments derive from this perspective. Persons are recognized as ends in themselves and must be treated as such, and it is acknowledged that rational people understand the nature of morality.

Kohlberg's (1987) model and analysis certainly offer or provide a useful way to understand the stages of moral growth and differences in moral reasoning. As a cognitive-developmental approach, the stages are ranked in a hierarchy, and so there are higher and lower stages. Kohlberg is careful to point out, however, that higher stages are not morally better than lower ones and that individuals at higher stages are not morally superior to those at lower stages. The ranking of moral stages is primarily to indicate that people have a better capacity to solve moral problems at higher stages, especially when issues of justice are considered.

Kohlberg (1987) has tried to demonstrate that his developmental model is universal by developing testing instruments to measure the moral stages, by conducting cross-cultural and gender-difference studies, and by finding relevant connections to personality, cognitive, and socialization theories. In many of these efforts, Kohlberg maintains that justice claims most clearly reveal different levels and patterns of moral reasoning and that the principle of justice has a central place in moral and social philosophy. This view is not shared by everyone.

Velasquez (1992) discusses the work of Gilligan (1982), who agrees with Kohlberg's (1987) moral levels and stages, but she claims that Kohlberg neglects to account for the moral development of girls and women because his studies investigate mostly male subjects. In her own research, Gilligan has tried to show that males employ impersonal, impartial, and abstract moral rules and rely on principles of justice and rights to deal with moral problems as expressed at the postconventional stage. By contrast, women view moral issues in terms of caring for others and feeling responsible for the maintenance of relationships. In the early stages, the preconventional ones, this care and responsibility is primarily to oneself. At the conventional level, women internalize the social conventions of caring for others to the point of neglecting themselves. At the mature or postconventional level, women take a critical stance and strike a balance between caring for others and for themselves.

Although there are studies to indicate there are no gender differences in moral development, Gilligan's (1982) work provides an alternative approach toward understanding moral growth and reasoning. Kohlberg (1987) has responded to Gilligan's criticisms and acknowledges that males may focus more on justice and females on care and that there might be a two-track approach to moral development, even though significant differences between the sexes may not be evident. He, therefore, concedes there may be a stage-type development based on care. He notes that particular moral situations may elicit a justice or a care response, and so the type of moral dilemmas one presents to research subjects can result in different findings. He also believes that caring and sympathy toward others are presupposed by any theory of justice, so there are linkages between caring and justice.

The important points of the preceding discussion are to recognize the areas of agreement between Kohlberg (1987) and Gilligan (1982). Each considers moral development to occur in stages, moving from preconventional to conventional to postconventional levels. These stages are sequential; that is, one moves from a lower stage to a higher one. This does not necessarily mean that everyone reaches Stages 5 and 6. In fact, Kohlberg believes most adults remain at the conventional level. Finally, Gilligan and Kohlberg both assert that moral development and reasoning lead to greater critical awareness about issues of right and wrong, and this motivates some to aspire to the postconventional level where rational, open dialogue can lead to resolutions of moral conflicts (Velasquez, 1992).

Key Concepts

consistency

evidence

Gilligan's ethic of care

Kohlberg's three levels of moral development

parental/guardian influences

social influences

Moral Reasoning

Because most of the preceding discussion focused on moral development, let us now turn to examine the nature of moral reasoning. Some of the following points have been mentioned previously, but they are worth noting again in the present context.

Moral reasoning involves the cognitive procedures people employ to arrive at moral decisions and judgments. There, of course, is no one infallible process to follow, but in general, two important considerations are part of moral reasoning: (a) an understanding of what moral standards require or prohibit and (b) evidence to indicate that a policy, organization, or particular conduct contains features that apply to (a) (Velasquez, 1992). For example, the killing of innocent people is wrong might be a moral standard. If during a war it was known that there were stranded civilians in a village, then it would be morally wrong to order the village destroyed. In sport management, the exploitation of others is wrong might be a moral standard. An athletic director who compelled scholarship athletes to run errands for him and maintain the upkeep of his home would be committing a moral offense.

As one can readily tell, three elements are involved in moral reasoning: moral standards, evidence, and moral judgments. Each component is essential in order to justify moral decisions taken by an institution or individual or the moral directives of a policy.

Although each feature is significant, one or the other may not be explicitly stated or given. In the wartime example above, the moral standard could have been omitted, and the reasoning would have remained intact. In the case of the athletic director, the moral decision about his behavior could have been unstated, and the example would have made reasonable sense. Similarly, there may be evidence that is widely known and accepted that would not require mention (e.g., there is about the same number of men and women in North American society). Still, in reasoning coherently and clearly about ethical matters it is recommended one be explicit about each component to avoid making weak moral arguments and poorly reasoned decisions.

This approach is suggested because too often people fail to make use of sufficient and appropriate evidence to support moral claims; or their decisions, evidence, and moral standards are not relevant to one another. It is also the case that there may be general agreement about moral principles, but some would attach certain qualifications or modifications to them. By doing this, people find exceptions to alter some judgments that follow from a standard (Cornman & Lehrer, 1974). For instance, some who oppose abortion might find this option acceptable in cases of incest and rape. It is also difficult sometimes to distinguish between evidence and a moral standard, especially in practice when one occasionally thinks facts speak for themselves. So finding that fewer women are in positions of authority may not, in and of itself, support the standard that any society that treats men and women as unequal is unjust. Clearly the components of moral issues are much more complex than this, yet in the main, the three elements discussed here are critical parts of moral reasoning.

Elements of Moral Reasoning

Moral reasoning involves the cognitive processes people employ to make decisions about ethical problems. This type of thinking requires a consideration of moral standards, evidence, and judgments. Good moral reasoning requires impartiality, consistency, and reflective judgment.

Now that the constituent features of moral reasoning have been considered, it would be useful to examine next how we evaluate moral reasoning. Terms like *standards*, *justification*, *reasons*, and *decisions*, introduced in the above discussion, sound very much like expressions used in constructing logical arguments. In fact, moral arguments do rely to a large extent on the criteria of logic. Although logic seems to provide an almost foolproof way toward assessing the strength and weaknesses of arguments, its precision as a method of evaluation is not always ideal when considering moral issues.

Now that we have stated these qualifications, let us consider three general criteria of good moral reasoning as suggested by Simon (1991). First, moral reasoning must remain impartial. One must not take a self-interested perspective when making moral judgments. That is, it would be morally incorrect if one were to formulate ethical principles tailored to meet personal desires, interests, and needs. This is not acceptable in moral discourse because it arbitrarily excludes others from such deliberations and places oneself in a morally superior position. No one can justifiably claim the latter. One quickly learns, however, that taking an impartial position is not always easy because it requires one to consider the perspectives of others and to ignore any individual privileges and advantages.

A second criterion of moral reasoning is to take a position that is systematically consistent. For example, if one's moral viewpoint is to generally refrain from harming others, then it would be inconsistent to claim that harming others is acceptable in certain situations, unless the circumstances in each instance could be shown to be relevantly dissimilar. So, the principle of not harming others should equally apply in various public situations and places, but likely not on the front line during a war. The issue of violence in sport hinges on this criterion because some contend a sport environment is relevantly dissimilar to other circumstances, and therefore, certain practices are permitted in sport whereas they would not be in other situations (e.g., one might go to jail for slashing one's neighbor with a stick, yet in ice hockey, a slashing infraction results in a two-minute penalty, if one is caught!). If no relevantly dissimilar features can be found between two situations, then holding the same moral position in each case would lead to a contradiction. That is, if community living and ice hockey are similar, one cannot say that not harming others applies to the first situation and not the second. To do so would be inconsistent.

Finally, in addition to impartiality and consistency, moral reasoning must account for reflective judgments about clear moral examples (Simon, 1991, p. 11). This means that moral standards must be analyzed together with particular cases to reveal the extent of their moral worth. Critically, reflectively challenging and refining moral principles, free from cultural biases and other prejudices, can ensure that dialogue about moral issues continues in an open and uncoercive manner. Moral standards should be tested in the real world, and even on a hypothetical plane (e.g., through counter examples), if such principles are to be considered more than mere abstractions. In this way, principles are linked to actions and possible actions, a kind of test for coherence in practice.

It is rather plain to see that to refute a moral argument or position, one would have to demonstrate in it a lack of impartiality, consistency, or practical moral worth, or all three. Yet even by adhering to these criteria, there is still no guarantee that a single line of moral reasoning is flawless. It may also turn out that several moral viewpoints are reasonable. What the aforementioned criteria provide are guidelines to judge whether some moral standards, arguments, and judgments are better justified than others when rationally evaluated. In many instances, this is the best we can do when we reason about moral issues. Although it has been and will be assumed in this text that ethical concerns can be rationally scrutinized and that moral positions and decisions can be assessed and justified through reason, there is a philosophical position that tries to refute these claims.

Key Concepts

coherence in practice

consistency

evidence

impartiality

moral judgments

moral standards

The Challenge of Philosophical Relativism

Philosophical relativism is a view that rejects the idea there are universal ethical ideals and values and objective rational patterns of moral reasoning. There are several versions of this view, but we will focus on just two well-known approaches.

The first account, known as *descriptive relativism*, refers to the idea that the values, or ethical principles, of individuals conflict in a fundamental way (Brandt, 1967, p. 75). When groups of people disagree in a basic way, then descriptive relativism is sometimes called *cultural relativism* because the disagreement often results from cultural or social differences. In part, cultural relativists claim that moral right and wrong vary from place to place. They add that right is contingent on cultural beliefs, and the concepts of right and wrong are therefore meaningless apart from the specific contexts in which they arise (Beauchamp, 1991, p. 40). Thus, no one social moral code is superior to any other, including the moral code of one's own society. By extension, the values and practices of people or societies may not be criticized, denounced, or interfered with (Williams, 1972). Descriptive relativism can only assert that moral principles, values, and behaviors are diverse among people and cultures, and it makes no claim about the truth of being morally right or wrong (Brennan, 1973).

The second account of philosophical relativism, known as *normative* or *ethical relativism*, refers to the idea that what one thinks or believes is right (wrong) for an individual or group is *indeed* right (wrong) for that individual or group. Here there is a claim for the truth of a particular moral principle, value or practice, but it is framed in relative terms (Billington, 1988). For example, should a person declare it is right to physically harm others when competing in sport, then such behavior is right for that person, although it may not be for others who are also right holding a contrary view. If slavery was an accepted practice in ancient Roman society, then it was right for the Romans, even though slavery is wrong by the moral standards of contemporary Western societies. Thus, ethical relativism claims that as long as people uphold either a personal moral belief or conform to social norms, they assert what is right (wrong) for them and the particular society they live in (Wellman, 1975). By implication, no person or social group can morally judge individuals and other societies because what is right is right for that person or society (Rachels, 1986). What ethical relativism, and philosophical relativism generally, can recommend is that we should be tolerant of diverse personal or culturally defined beliefs and practices.

Relativism in Brief

Philosophical Relativism—There are no universal values or morals.

Descriptive Relativism—Individuals' values conflict on a fundamental level.

Cultural Relativism—The concepts of right and wrong are culturally determined.

Normative/Ethical Relativism—What a person or a group considers right is right for them.

There are several common criticisms that can be leveled against both descriptive and ethical relativism. The first points out a logical inconsistency in the argument proposed by relativism generally. Merely because individuals or cultures disagree about fundamental beliefs and behaviors does not necessarily mean there are no universal moral truths or that truth claims like right and wrong cannot be determined. The conclusion does not follow logically from the premise because one's beliefs or society's norms may be mistaken or misapplied or even exaggerated. Rachels (1986) makes the point in the following amoral example. Suppose some believe the earth is flat whereas most people believe it is more or less spherical. Few people would then claim that because there is disagreement here, the discipline of geography contains no objective truths. At issue is not the truth or falsehood of the conclusion, but rather, the reason supporting the conclusion is not logically connected to the conclusion. Williams (1972) and Porter (1980) raise another logical criticism against relativism. If relativism is to be taken seriously, then it too is a relative idea. No nonrelative notion can slip into its argument. Relativism itself and what it recommends are a theory that has no objective moral truth. Thus, there are no reasons to accept the relativist argument because this would require external, objective criteria that the theory does not permit. It is a theory by definition that asks one to accept it as relative and not to be believed in a firmly objective way. To oblige the theory in fact undermines the theory.

Another shortcoming of relativism relates to a conflict that could arise between personal beliefs and practices and those found in society. Suppose an individual is against capital punishment in a society where lethal punishment is legal. On a relativist account, no judgment could be made about the rightness or wrongness of capital punishment or whether or not society or the individual is right (Porter, 1980). No moral debates can be discussed on these matters because relativism offers no means of self-criticism. Not only would this type of conflict be impossible to resolve, but other untenable implications also flow from a relativist position that are contrary to our moral experiences and intuitions.

According to relativism, cross-cultural criticisms may not be raised because values between one society and another are relative, and each culture's values are right. Thus, ethnic cleansing, racism, anti-Semitism, sexism, homophobia, misogyny, slavery, and torture could not be deemed wrong in particular societies, and people would have no right to condemn these social norms and practices. There would be no grounds to denounce certain values in given cultures because all values are context bound. For most of us, however, being critical of other people's values and attitudes is based on serious moral considerations of what is right and wrong. Such criticism should be raised between people of different cultures if only to search for common agreement on basic humane ideas and attitudes (Brennan, 1973, p. 53).

Another way to criticize relativism is to demonstrate that what appear to be fundamental cultural disagreements are not so. For example, no society could sustain the practice of infanticide completely; otherwise, the society could not perpetuate itself. In societies where infanticide is practiced selectively, there are very specific social and economic reasons for doing so, even though the fundamental value of caring for infants and children is present. Thus, cultural differences between societies may not disclose easily areas of common agreement, yet relativists want to emphasize that such differences are fundamental and no cultural agreements can be achieved (Rachels, 1986).

Finally, relativism questions the very idea of moral progress (Brennan, 1973). If we understand progress as change for the better, then this meaning is prohibited from a relativist posture. There are no standards to judge whether or not one way of life is "better" than another. Each society has its own norms, and any comparative analyses and decisions about moral improvement are prejudiced and ethnocentric. Any value reforms carried out in a given culture are merely to strengthen the status quo. However, from an historical perspective, many would like to think there is sufficient evidence to demonstrate that people and nations have advanced from a moral point of view. For example, in the 20th century, women and minority groups have made important strides toward the attainment of greater equality in many countries. Important leaders like Mahatma Gandhi and Martin Luther King, Jr., inspired significant social changes that are recognized as advances from a moral standpoint. Whereas relativism dismisses the very notion of moral progress, it would be hard to ignore historical trends that show people are more humane than they once were, or they are trying to be so due to a climate of increased moral sensitivity (Porter, 1980).

Even though there are several good reasons for rejecting relativism, the theory does offer at least two positive recommendations (Rachels, 1986). First, cultures express certain customs that are founded on nonbasic values and demonstrate particular preferences or tastes. Differences in dress or etiquette between societies are based on social conventions rather than on disagreements about fundamental values. As relativists would argue, and as most people would agree, most social customs cannot be judged objectively right or wrong. Relativists, however, go too far when they claim that differences of taste or preference demonstrate that *all* values are fundamentally culture bound. Second, relativists do make a point when they ask us to question our feelings of moral superiority and the social prejudices we hold. Many of our attitudes develop through social conditioning, and we sometimes view the cultural practices of others as unnatural or even repugnant. When we learn about the customs in another society, we become familiar with another way of life, and we may, or perhaps should, realize that our way of doing things may not always be the best and only way. These two positive assessments of relativism are important because they help us differentiate between fundamental and nonbasic values, and they point out the diversity and shortcomings of our own cultural traditions and biases.

On the whole though, philosophical relativism is an untenable theory because it possesses logical weaknesses and is contrary to many of our moral experiences. Most of us believe that we can establish right from wrong in an objective way in our everyday lives and that there are universal truths to live by. As stated earlier, this text will presume as much. If moral reasoning based on rational principles is possible, then such reasoning will inevitably lead to actions or possible ones taken up as a consequence of ethical deliberations. The next section will examine the character of ethical conduct.

Ethical Conduct

Key Concepts

criticisms of relativism

descriptive relativism

ethical relativism

Without ethical behavior, all the moral reasoning in the world would seem pointless. Ethical principles and moral standards must at some stage take expression in the form of human conduct. Just as these axioms may be questioned, their corresponding and recommended actions are often judged to be good or bad, right or wrong, justified or unjustified. In fact, many consider the main enterprise of ethics is to define and serve as a guide for moral behavior. As Pepper (1960) states, "the term *conduct* in ethical tradition has generally meant voluntary acts of choice which necessarily involve criteria for deciding whether the choices are good or bad" (p. 4). A serious difficulty, however, is identifying the parameters by which conduct can be determined as ethical or not.

To begin, one needs to establish the domain of moral behavior. What counts as action that complies with or can be linked to moral stan-

> In order to be considered ethical, an action must be voluntary.

dards? As suggested above, ethical conduct has to be voluntary. An action that results from compulsion, coercion, or even force usually cannot be characterized as moral behavior. There would be no grounds for holding people responsible for or commending their actions if they did not act with some measure of freedom. A reasonable question is, how much freedom is required to claim behavior is indeed voluntary? Is the soldier who kills innocent civilians in cold blood merely following orders and therefore not acting freely? Is the behavior of habitual criminals a consequence of their unstable personal backgrounds and the impoverished environment in which they were reared? Is the athlete who is told by the coach to harm opposing players simply following directions and doing what is best for the team? These questions are part of a philosophical debate between two concepts, *determinism* and *free will*, and these ideas have an important bearing on ethical conduct.

Briefly, determinism maintains that there is a cause for everything in the universe. Because all occurrences necessarily have causes, if one can specify a set of conditions, one can predict future events, or the effects of such conditions, each and every time. To a large degree, modern science subscribes to this view.

Determinism goes one step further by claiming that cause-and-effect relationships also apply to human beings. Everything about humanity is caused. Because this is the case, human beings possess neither free will nor the capacity to act in a voluntary manner. Their choices and behavior are determined. They are determined by personality, upbringing, past experiences, and training. Humans do not have the ability to do otherwise than what they do, and everything they do has a causal explanation. This, of course, means that people cannot be held morally responsible or culpable (Minton & Shipka, 1990).

However, in many instances, humans do feel a sense of freedom in their choices and in their conduct. Proponents of free will, or what is also known as *libertarianism* or *indeterminism*, point out that creative and expressive behavior in the arts, for example, is rooted in freedom. Interpretation and selection are central means by which painters, sculptors, writers, musicians, composers, dancers, and even some athletes engage in the creation of art. Some claim that art provides the most radical context for the expression of free will and freedom.

Aside from the arts, it would be hard to imagine having no alternatives or control in human lives, but this would be the case if people lived in a deterministic world. It would also mean that people could neither feel proud of their accomplishments nor feel regret about any possible achievements, because who one is, what one becomes, and what one does are caused. That is, individuals are not responsible for any of their successes or for their failures, even those associated with their moral behavior.

One's experiences, however, tell one otherwise. One does hold people responsible when their conduct breaches moral standards, and one even goes so far as to punish them when they violate morally binding laws. In these instances, one accepts the notion that in general people's actions are voluntary, and they are accountable for what they do and sometimes do not do.

Are determinism and indeterminism the only options available? In fact, there is a third view. *Soft-determinism* takes a moderate approach between the latter positions and claims they are compatible. Rather than denying causality altogether, as radical libertarians would suggest, soft-determinists say that for moral responsibility to exist, some causal determinants are required (Minton & Shipka, 1990). Human decisions and behavior cannot be completely devoid of some causes. Aspects of personality and past experiences do influence one's identity, one's interests, and one's conduct. Freedom cannot be totally separated from causes, but is connected to certain types of causes, like one's personality. By appealing to specific select causes, explanations can be given about one's behavior, reforms can be made in one's conduct, and genuine instances of freedom, those not caused, can be identified. Soft-determinism points out that freedom really means being free from external restrictions when deciding to act and when acting, rather than acting without any antecedent causes.

Determinism—Human action is predetermined, not chosen.

Libertarianism/Indeterminism—Humans have complete free will.

Soft Determinism—Actions are influenced by certain causes, but humans do have some free will.

So is ethical conduct really voluntary? Yes and no. Perhaps the best way to approach the matter is to speak about variability (Shirk, 1965). The voluntary aspects of moral behavior come in different degrees. Good and bad habits, for example, may be construed as having less of a voluntary quality than that found in other practices, but the acquisition and perhaps alteration of habits stem from voluntary acts that are under human control. This is to say that even habits are not entirely determined. On the other hand, acts of kindness, charity, or love seem to possess a greater voluntary character. Despite the voluntary nature and particular forms of benevolent actions, to some degree these are influenced by external constraints.

Moreover, we have not touched on situational factors that would certainly influence the nature of ethical conduct. In some circumstances, certain actions are morally neutral whereas the same conduct in a different situation would lend itself to moral evaluation. Tying one's shoelace is usually a morally indifferent act, yet to do so deliberately in a tennis match as a delaying tactic to irritate one's opponent may be ethically questionable. The extent to which actions are considered voluntary may be also traced over time. We generally hold that children have less capacity to act in voluntary ways than do adolescents and adults. So the scope of voluntary actions expands through growth and maturation. An important point being made here is that one has to have the ability and opportunity to act in an ethical manner. In addition to the question of determinism and free will, possessing the personal capacity and being in appropriate circumstances for moral behavior are also important elements in the notion of variability in ethical conduct (Shirk, 1965).

Part of the above discussion mentioned another feature of moral behavior—responsibility. Ethical conduct would likely be vacuous if it carried no sense of responsibility with it. This characteristic is significant not only from the perspective of identification but also from the standpoint of accountability. What is it that one is responsible for? For a mature, rational adult, one might say, in a cavalier way, everything that is part of and constitutes one's life. This means the sum total of one's adult experiences. Because almost every aspect of people's lives can be couched in normative (valuative) terms, their ethical conduct and responsibility can extend to vast personal spheres. Feibleman (1967) put it this way: "An adult who is in a state of health is responsible for all of his actions" (p. 81).

This is something that goes unrecognized by many people. They often fail to acknowledge the moral implications of their conduct and too easily dismiss accepting responsibility for the things they do and say. Even if people's behavior is involuntary, carried out under compulsion, or beyond their awareness, moral consequences and effects may still arise from such conduct. People are responsible even for the unforeseen results of their behavior. Therefore, responsibility runs deep in almost everything people do.

The voluntary nature of ethical conduct leads naturally then to the notion of being responsible for one's moral action. Just as there is variability of freedom and constraints as related to behavior, so too are there differing degrees of responsibility. Adults are held to be more responsible for their actions than are children. People who are senile or insane or who have some type of personality disorder are generally absolved of some or all responsibility for their behavior. This is why a more complete sense of moral responsibility is usually reserved for adults who are healthy, rational, and mature.

However, the last statement poses a difficulty because it is not always clear what one means by or what counts as being healthy, rational, and mature. Should these considerations include attitudes, emotions, instincts, level of intelligence, etc.?

Are feelings reliable yardsticks by which to make ethical judgments, or should only reason prevail? No single pat answer can satisfy these questions. It would likely be more useful to consider such issues on a case-to-case basis. Defining these terms categorically would probably discount relevant areas that must be considered when making ethical decisions. Although each person can characterize a typical healthy, rational, and mature individual, in some particular cases, mostly the difficult ones, a clearer comprehension of these expressions might be necessary. Once this is done in a satisfactory manner, the type and level of moral responsibility attached to specific behavior can be reasonably determined.

Another significant feature of ethical conduct briefly mentioned above refers to its unintended consequences. People often think, or would like to think, that their moral behavior is a result of carefully thought-out and reasoned deliberations. That is, one is conscious of one's ethical judgments; one acts from reflection and has considered the implications of one's actions (Shirk, 1965). However, as stated earlier in this chapter, many moral rules are accepted and followed through habit. People sometimes know what is customary and expected, and little or no thought is given to their actions. Ethical conduct can therefore include behavior that is unconsciously carried out.

If this is so, then in some instances, people are unaware of the effects of their behavior. They might be unconscious about their decision to act and also the ramifications of their actions. Yet these unintended results may be evaluated and assessed in terms of right or wrong, good or bad. They may have an influence on the environment or on others that is morally relevant. So whether one acts wittingly or not, one's actions can carry moral weight, and one may not even realize the extent of that weight.

Related to the idea of consequences is the notion of inaction or refraining from action, which is also an element of ethical conduct (Shirk, 1965, p. 26). Acts of omission are

Doing nothing can be a type of ethical conduct.

sometimes more difficult to detect because the premise here is that one decides not to act or to act alternatively, but the effects of doing nothing, or of consciously removing oneself from a situation, can be powerful. Gandhi and Martin Luther King, Jr., for example, advocated what is known as passive resistance. Their movements not only created enormous social and political changes but they were also built on a moral foundation. A workers' strike is another example in which choosing not to fulfill one's role as a laborer carries ethical implications. The consequences of some strikes, especially by groups like physicians and teachers, can have far-reaching moral effects. To some avid spectators, a players' strike in professional sports is a moral issue. Boycotting a product or refusing to travel to a country that violates human rights is a moral expression. In each of these cases, doing other than expected, being passive, or doing nothing at all is an instance of moral behavior.

Finally, ethical conduct is characterized by involving others. This goes back to the idea that there is no such thing as private ethics, but the sense of involvement here is extensive. It considers not only direct, interactive moral behavior between people, such as telling the truth or treating others with fairness, but also those private moments when one sometimes catches oneself acting in an ethically suspect manner. When questioning one's behavior in these seemingly solitary instances, one is likely reacting to or reflecting on some moral standard that indirectly involves others. No such thought would ever arise otherwise.

The meaning of *others* is necessarily broad here and might include one's parents, teachers, coaches, clergy, or society at large. Moral rules and sensitivities are learned and acquired from such others. So at times, one's own ethical judgments might reflect their influence even when alone. Ethical conduct implicates others in two directions then. In one instance, one's moral behavior has a direct impact on others as far as moving out toward them and penetrating their sphere of influence. This may be performed in a clear, unambiguous fashion or in a subtle, unassuming manner. In the second instance, others have some bearing on one's moral sense that can be expressed explicitly, or occasionally, in moments of privacy. Because the ethical conduct we are speaking about is expansive, the social implications of such behavior are similarly sweeping.

Implicit in the discussion in this section is the way in which ethical conduct is understood. It usually means and includes behavior that is good, right, correct, just, commendable, and the like. To say that someone displays ethical conduct in her work is to mean that she carries out her tasks in exemplary fashion, morally speaking. So the expression *ethical conduct* generally distinguishes actions that are already virtuous. If this is so, we need to examine the nature of behavior excluded from the domain of ethical conduct.

Key Concepts

acts of omission

determinism or free will

involvement of others

libertarianism or indeterminism

responsibility

soft-determinism

unintended consequences

voluntariness

Misconduct

Three definitions of misconduct are provided by *Webster's New Collegiate Dictionary* (1977). One refers to mismanagement, another to intentional wrongdoing, and a third to improper behavior (p. 734). All three meanings are relevant to the discussion of ethics in this text, and each will be taken up separately in this section.

The most general of the three senses is to claim that misconduct is a form of *improper behavior.* This is a broad category that can involve any behavior from transgressions of etiquette and customs to violations of morally binding laws. So, talking with one's mouth full of food, spitting at someone, and pushing oneself to the front of a queue at the grocery store are usually examples of poor, not to mention boorish, manners. Rape, incest, and molestation are criminal acts that are morally reprehensible, but take the case of adultery. In many societies, it is morally unacceptable, or at least seriously frowned upon, whereas in other cultures having lovers and being married to someone else is socially permissible, or at least tolerated with no stigma attached to it. The same can be said about polygamy.

These examples indicate that improper behavior can be manifested in both serious and mild forms and can be closely linked to one's social conditions. Impolite conduct may be easily identified and corrected. We do this constantly with children, with a fair measure of success. In going to a foreign country, one can be taught the proper way to do certain things to avoid embarrassment. Even in sports, there are specific actions that are traditionally unacceptable. For instance, when an offside is called in ice hockey, it would be improper for the player with the puck to shoot at the goal.

More serious improprieties are either construed as criminal or as being so repugnant they are morally censured by society. Criminal activities are the more obvious and readily identifiable cases, but in instances of adultery, note the following. How many political figures have had or almost had their careers destroyed or tainted by scandals involving adultery? North American society clearly considers adultery to be improper behavior, even though some politicians are able to circumvent the issue and survive. Improper behavior then includes a wide range of various kinds of conduct, and most are easily recognized.

The second meaning of misconduct refers to *intentional wrongdoing*. In one sense, one could claim that forms of conduct here are similar to those categorized as improper behavior, and in numerous instances this would be true. Many criminal activities as well as actions deemed morally repugnant are deliberate acts. In some situations, however, improper behavior can be differentiated from acts of intentional wrongdoing.

The insanity plea is still accepted in criminal cases, and although the actual crime is considered improper, a willful posture was not present when the crime was being committed. In fact, in such cases, the defense tries to establish that the defendant did not have the mental capacity to distinguish between right and wrong and, therefore, could not have deliberately set out to do wrong. Similarly, breaches of etiquette may not involve conscious, voluntary actions. Traditional social customs and mores can develop into habits, and certain behavioral patterns are performed with little or no thought to them. The same can be said for poor habits some might judge to be examples of misconduct. These instances then indicate that we must search for a more precise understanding of intentional wrongdoing.

Let us approach this expression by examining each of its components.

The idea of intention and its connection to action is and has been a difficult problem in philosophy, and so we can provide only a cursory treatment of this issue. To carry out an action with intent at least means that one is free and has the ability to act, one adequately knows what one is about to do, and one is sufficiently aware of the possible consequences and implications of one's actions. To perform an action with intent has traditionally meant that a person acts from some inner desire and with volition, as a sort of antecedent cause of some bodily movement. That is, intent has to do with the power each person possesses to knowingly initiate action (D'Arcy, 1963).

Of course, serious problems can arise from such a view. For example, one can intend one thing but for some reason—a situational factor, perhaps—perform an action that was unintended. One hears pleas such as "I only meant to hurt him, not to kill him," and so the intent may have been different from the outcome. In sports, one might attempt a pass, yet the ball ends up in the net or the basket for a goal. For our purposes here, *intentional* will refer to sufficiently anticipating and planning in advance what actions one is about to take, being reasonably sure one can execute said actions, and realizing the corresponding implications of such actions.

> ## Variations of Wrong
>
> Misconduct refers to questionable, sometimes illegal, behavior that is contrary to ethical conduct.
>
> Improper behavior can include transgressions of etiquette or criminal activity that carries a morally repugnant element.
>
> Intentional wrongdoing is the deliberate planning and execution of some behavior one knows or should know to be wrong.
>
> Mitigating factors refer to conditions that alter the level of responsible for intentional wrongdoing and include a) situational uncertainty, b) difficult to avoid actions, c) degree of involvement, and d) seriousness of injury.
>
> Mismanagement refers to bureaucratic or political wrongdoing such as fraud, embezzlement, bribery, questionable accounting practices, and job discrimination.

This definition suggests that one must be free and have the ability to act (Velasquez, 1992). If this freedom and ability did not exist or were seriously curtailed due to a lack of power, control, access to resources, or to pressure, coercion, mental disability, and the like, then one might be excused from responsibility for wrongful acts. To intend something that is wrongful requires that one knows the difference between right and wrong. In this case, ignorance of some vital information or knowledge that can assist in making this distinction usually excuses one from blame for a wrongful act. If one did not know about certain moral standards in a foreign country, let us say, and acted in a wrongful manner, one could be accused of misconduct, but not be held morally responsible. A similar lack of knowledge might arise because one is unfamiliar with certain situational factors. Ignorance resulting from the circumstances described in these cases would excuse wrongful behavior.

Deliberate ignorance is no excuse for immoral behavior.

On the other hand, deliberately keeping oneself ignorant by not reading a crucial report or memo that might provide some important information provides no excuse for moral culpability. This sometimes occurs in large corporations to "protect" executives and shelter them from moral responsibility. In circumstances where one can control one's ignorance, one can still be accused of intentional wrongdoing. Intentional wrongdoing then characterizes the deliberate and willful (planning, knowing in advance) aspects of carrying out actions that might also be known to be wrong.

Clear cases of cheating, stealing, lying, bribery, conflicts of interest, denying the rights of others, and so forth would fall under this category of misconduct, that is, intentional wrongdoing. As mentioned, there are conditions that can excuse one from responsibility from this type of misconduct. There are also mitigating factors that can reduce the level of responsibility for these kinds of action. Velasquez (1992) identifies four such *mitigating factors*.

First, many moral dilemmas are surrounded by some uncertainty. If one was not quite sure how serious a certain action might be, or was unclear about a moral standard, then although one acted in a wrongful way, one's responsibility might lessen. Second, some actions are difficult to avoid. For example, in the workplace, some people feel enormous pressure either from their superiors or from the demands of their job. Under such conditions, they sometimes act in ways they sense are wrong but feel powerless to avoid, and so they are not held completely responsible for their wrongful actions. Third, if one is not actively involved in the commission or omission of a wrongful act, this lack of involvement is generally accepted as a mitigating factor. The less one actively contributes to the outcome of an event, the less responsibility is attributed to that person for some occurrence. Finally, one also considers the seriousness of the injury that resulted from the wrongful action. If the misconduct is extremely serious, likely few or no mitigating factors will reduce responsibility for such action. On the other hand, less serious misconduct might itself act as a reason to lessen responsibility for such behavior. Despite the presence of conditions that can excuse or mitigate intentional wrongdoing, this form of misconduct may be summarized as the deliberate performance of actions known to be wrong.

The third sense of misconduct concerns a more particular set of actions described as mismanagement. This type of misconduct usually involves wrongdoing in bureaucratic or political organizations. Here, corporate standards of conduct; company policies; social, environmental, and fiscal rules and regulations are violated. Mismanagement might include such issues as fraud, embezzlement, lack of truth in advertising, questionable marketing practices, job discrimination, unjust collective bargaining, and breaches of employee rights.

Several of these examples are clearly criminal, but others could be related to ethically questionable internal procedures of an organization. Some criminal misconduct of this sort may result in huge fines and penalties (especially in consumer, product, and environmental cases) and occasionally prison terms for some executives. On the other hand, less serious forms of mismanagement are easily dealt with and corrected on a day-to-day basis. In most instances, mismanagement involves the power and control mechanisms in place in large firms and bureaucracies, but it can also involve small businesses, the social influence of which is relatively minimal. Misconduct in larger corporations is usually carried out by more than one individual, because the network of staff and flow of information make it almost impossible for one to act alone. The scope then of mismanagement is quite broad, and it refers to misconduct at the corporate or political level. Many of the issues taken up in the applied portion of this text will refer to misconduct as mismanagement.

<aside>

Key Concepts

actions difficult to avoid

active involvement

improper behavior

intentional wrongdoing

mismanagement

seriousness of injury

</aside>

Summary

This chapter covered a substantial amount of terrain, but it sought to focus on and examine some of the central ideas, difficulties, and concerns surrounding ethical and moral discourse. It began by discussing the general area of value inquiry known as axiology, because ethics is basically interested in value issues. In that section, several important distinctions were made between moral and amoral values, and various kinds of values were delineated. The next section included a brief excursus into purposes and types of definitions and the complexities and intricacies of our use of language.

The third section treated the topic of ethics proper. Ethics involves the study of criteria used to judge events, actions, and people in terms of right or wrong. Several features of ethical questions were addressed to indicate the distinctiveness of ethics. This section concluded by considering what ethics is not, and it was compared to feelings, authority, the law, and religion.

Morality, the subject of the fourth section, emphasized the practical aspects of rules and standards as they are situated within a social context. Four distinguishing features of morality were examined, as well as the concepts of a moral position, the object of morality, and the motives for moral behavior. This discussion conveniently led to an examination of moral development in the fifth section. The focus here was on the cognitive-developmental theories of Kohlberg (1987), but we also considered an alternative view as proposed by Gilligan (1982). When we turned to address moral reasoning in the following section, three central elements were identified, namely, moral standards, evidence, and moral judgments. Borrowing from Simon (1991), we suggested that impartiality, consistency, and coherence in practice were general guides toward sound moral reasoning. In the seventh section, we critiqued two versions of philosophical relativism to demonstrate that objective moral truths, rational moral reasoning, and judgments of right and wrong were reasonable concepts to uphold.

In the eighth section, the nature of ethical conduct was considered. The discussion here included such issues as voluntariness, determinism, free will, responsibility, unintended consequences, acts of omission, and the involvement of others. Because the notion of ethical conduct marked off what is generally considered commendable behavior, the final section briefly investigated the character of misconduct. Three senses of misconduct were examined, namely, improper behavior, intentional wrongdoing, and mismanagement.

At several points throughout this chapter, reference was made to ethical principles and moral standards. Yet it was never made clear just what these axioms were, who proposed them, and what justifications might exist for them. The next two chapters will explore, in considerable detail, the main theories of ethics we have inherited from some of the greatest philosophers and thinkers in Western history.

Questions for Consideration

1. Define axiology and the different meanings of value, and describe the various senses of the word *good*.

2. Why are definitions important? What types of definitions are there? Finally, what sorts of problems can be avoided by defining terms appropriately?

3. How do normative and nonnormative ethics differ?

4. Compare the positive features related to ethics Billington presents with the negative characteristics White (1988) introduces.

5. Describe the four distinguishing characteristics of morality proposed by Beauchamp.

6. Explain the relationships between a moral position, the object of morality, and motives for moral behavior.

7. Delineate the salient features of Kohlberg's six-stage moral development scheme. What are Gilligan's main objections to this model?

8. What are the main elements of sound moral reasoning?

9. Explain the two versions of philosophical relativism. What are the main criticisms against relativism? Why would you either support or reject relativism?

10. How are the following terms and expressions related to ethical conduct: voluntariness, free will, determinism, soft determinism, responsibility, unintended consequences, acts of omission, and involvement of others?

11. Describe the various senses and meanings of misconduct.

Chapter Three

Major Ethical Theories I

Chapter Objectives

• To consider ethical theories such that the consequences of behavior are directed toward some stated good, purpose, or end

• To examine ethical theories whereby moral obligations and maxims guide and influence one's conduct

• To understand the tenets of virtue ethics

• To become familiar with the ethical concerns associated with sport management

In this chapter and the next, we will turn to theoretical considerations and examine a variety of classical and modern ethical principles that can be employed when making moral decisions. This diversity is evident because there has never been a consensus among moral philosophers throughout history as to the underlying reasons for ethical judgments. Consequently, numerous questions can be raised that refer to the grounds of ethical conduct, and there are generally no single right or wrong answers to these questions.

For example, do people act primarily out of self-interest? Can they be genuinely concerned for the welfare of others? Do people behave morally out of a sense of duty or moral obligation? Are moral standards universal, or are they culturally bound and relative? Are ethical decisions simply based on individual subjectivity? What are the moral grounds for justice and fairness? What constitutes individual, human, civil, moral, and legal rights?

Once again, these basic questions, and there are a wealth of others, have never been answered in a complete and satisfactory manner. Yet by posing them and trying to arrive at some reasonable answers to them, one should be able to understand and appreciate further the complexity of ethical decision making. The point then is not to become discouraged by plurality. Perhaps the best one can do is to analyze the distinctive character of different ethical principles and, from there, to recognize some of the assumptions of ethical judgments.

This chapter then will proceed by examining three main categories of ethical theories and concepts: teleological, deontological, and virtue ethics. The next chapter will discuss theories of justice and rights. In each category, several specific strands of thought will be introduced and investigated. This taxonomy is neither complete nor exhaustive, nor does it follow any prescribed chronology. Its content, however, provides an adequate theoretical background for the applied purposes of this text. So the reader does not feel utter despair over the prospect of considering a number of alternative theoretical viewpoints, a final section in the next chapter will be devoted to the idea of pluralism in ethics and the issue of choosing a theory.

Teleological Theories

Because we are now trying to assess the rationale for and foundation of moral standards, let us begin with a general description of one of the main categories of ethical principles. Teleological theories in ethics rely on some "concept of the good or the humanly desirable" (Olson, 1967, p. 88). As we noted in the previous chapter, candidates for what is good or desirable are numerous. Frankena (1973) lists pleasure, power, knowledge, self-realization, and perfection as possibilities for what counts as good. He further notes that these are amoral values in the sense outlined in the section on axiology in the last chapter. That is, these sorts of good need not carry a prescriptive meaning, and the means to attain them must conform to ethical principles. To judge an action right, correct, or good, the identification of the amoral sense of good must be made or implied to avoid circularity. For example, if one were to claim that people should pursue healthy activities to reduce health-care costs, the idea that being healthy is good in itself might be established in an amoral sense.

A teleologist then would claim that one has a moral obligation to promote whatever amoral good is deemed worthwhile or that on balance one should seek the greatest measure of this good over its oppo-

> Teleological theories promote what is good or desirable. The best course of action is the one that will result in the most good.

site. So, if one's amoral good is pleasure and one is faced with a moral problem, the moral decision or action taken must reflect pleasure to the greatest extent when compared to pain. In this sense, teleological ethics emphasizes the real and possible consequences of ethical conduct, rather than, let us say, the character or intentions of a moral agent. White (1988) calls this a "results-oriented approach" (p. 41).

Many moral decisions are made using a teleological method. Whenever one weighs the benefits and costs of some action (or inaction) when confronted with a moral problem, one focuses on the consequences of one's behavior. Donating money for charity rather than spending it on some luxury might be based on a teleological calculus. The sports expression *no harm, no foul* is results-oriented (White, 1988). The point is that if the end (a particular action, some slight contact in basketball, for instance) produces less or no harm, then perhaps the greater or greatest good (continued play in the game toward the pursuit of excellence) can be sought. Of course, this sort of view is contentious. What should count as harm? Can one foresee all possible forms of harm that might result from one's actions? These are just two general criticisms of teleological ethics, and more will arise as we examine specific brands of this principle.

Egoism

As mentioned above, teleologists make ethical decisions and act from some accepted amoral good. Disputes about what this good should be are legion. For

> Egoism, the belief that all actions are motivated by selfish interests, negates the concept of altruism—the idea that some acts are selfless or even self-sacrificial.

some, the only good thing worth pursuing is that which fulfills one's personal interests, needs, and desires. The name given to ethical views that subscribe to the idea of self-interest is *egoism*.

This teleological stance has some appeal, for in many instances, it would be highly unusual to act against one's own interests. However, some forms of egoism go further and maintain that all our moral actions are guided by self-interest. Telling the truth, keeping one's promises, not cheating, and the like are adhered to because there are personal advantages or benefits to be gained from doing so (Harman, 1977). Even acts of benevolence such as charity, volunteerism and heroism are, or at least can be shown to be, prompted by self-interest. For example, one might save a drowning child because he wants to be recognized as a hero or he enjoys the challenges of high-risk situations. Therefore, egoism insists that our ethical conduct be invariably motivated by the dictum "what's in it for me?" Is the doctrine of egoism feasible? Do people always act from self-interest?

What is immediately clear is that egoism rules out unselfish or altruistic behavior. *Altruism* claims there are situations where we do act in the interest of others, sometimes to the extent of sacrificing our own interests. Most traditional and religious moral philosophies hold some type of altruistic position (e.g., the Golden Rule, "love thy neighbor"), and other-regarding acts are often considered the hallmark of morality (Palmer, 1991). Basic moral considerations such as respect for persons, justice, and fairness tend to acknowledge the interests of others, yet egoism rejects this sort of concern for other people. If egoism is right, or is at least plausible, then it seriously challenges many commonly held views about morality, and it needs to be examined in greater detail.

There are two main versions of egoism in ethics. The first is known as *psychological egoism*. This view states that it is part of our nature as human beings to act according to our own interests. Human beings simply cannot behave otherwise. They are always motivated to act by placing their own interests above those of others as a matter of course. Even when it looks as though one is acting unselfishly, by helping others for example, upon closer examination, a self-centered motive can be found (Porter, 1980). One wants to feel good, one wants to alleviate the feeling of pity, one wants public recognition, and one wants to elevate one's stature in the community could each be a possible motive for assisting others. To the psychological egoist, there is no escaping some self-interested motive for one's behavior. To think that one can genuinely act from a concern for others is a facade.

In the history of philosophy, Thomas Hobbes (1588-1679) was the first important figure to elucidate the tenets of psychological egoism. He exerted great effort to demonstrate that all actions are guided by self-interested motives. In many ways this followed from his declaration that "the condition of man. . . is a condition of war of every one against every one. . ." (Hobbes, 1651/1962, p. 103). What he meant is that the natural disposition of human beings is to be self-seeking and in conflict with others. If there are actions that seem like personal sacrifices on behalf of others, they can occasionally be performed because such sacrifices can also be interpreted to be in one's own interest. Perhaps by making some sacrifices now, greater personal advantages will accrue later, but as one might suspect, under this scheme, every action can be understood from a self-interested perspective.

This kind of interpretive reasoning about the motives of behavior demonstrates one of the weaknesses of psychological egoism. Merely because the motives of actions can be interpreted or reinterpreted as self-seeking does not necessarily prove the soundness of psychological egoism. This view only demonstrates that it is possible to ascribe self-interested motives to actions, but this possibility does not provide substantive proof for the theory (Rachels, 1986).

Another criticism of psychological egoism as an ethical theory concerns its insistence that by nature we act from self-interest. If it is part of human nature to be self-seeking, then the theory has nothing to recommend to people. They cannot help acting other than in a self-interested way. If this is so, then it excludes the possibility of praising or blaming people for their ethical conduct. They had no choice in the matter to begin with (Porter, 1980). Although there are more persuasive arguments in favor of psychological egoism, and each of them contains flaws, there is one other related major criticism against this ethical standpoint.

What are we to make of a theory that can explain, without exception, the true motives of all human conduct? In the sciences, no such all-inclusive theory is possible. A scientific hypothesis by definition must leave open the possibility of being refuted by counter evidence or a superior competing hypothesis. In fact, it must clearly indicate countervailing conditions in order to demonstrate its strength as a hypothesis (certainly so if the hypothesis is to have predictive value). For example, to show the cogency of the theory of gravity, one would have to know the conditions that prove the theory wrong, namely, seeing things heavier than air float (Palmer, 1991). The same empirical demands can be made of psychological egoism.

If the genuine motive of every action can be identified (in this case, a self-interested one) and no action can be picked out as evidence against psychological egoism (i.e., all expressions of altruism are emphatically denied), then the content of the theory is vacuous. An irrefutable theory is logically impossible. There would be nothing to hold up contrary to the theory to support its validity. As Rachels (1986) eloquently states, "Paradoxically, if we do not allow some way in which we might be mistaken, we lose all chance of being right" (p. 64).

Although the proponents of psychological egoism (especially Hobbes) explain away altruistic or unselfish motives, they also claim that our experiences of concern for others are sincerely wrong, and they discount such experiences. People, of course, know better. This refusal to accept and take seriously a set of real human experiences also weakens their case. Thus, the rejection of altruistic experiences as counterevidence, the restricted sense of our nature as human beings, plus the reinterpretation of motives, are serious criticisms against psychological egoism. Perhaps another version of egoism is more palatable.

Rather than say people are naturally motivated to act out of self-interest—that is, people in fact do act out of self-interest—*ethical egoism* asserts that people should act from a self-seeking posture. The first view, psychological egoism, is therefore an explanation of human nature and the motivation of conduct, whereas the second theory is a justification for how people ought to act, regardless of how they do behave (Beauchamp, 1991). Ethical egoism then tries to supply a basic reason for our actions, and that reason is self-promotion.

So when one is confronted with an ethical dilemma, one's only duty as a moral agent ought to be to advance one's own interests. According to Rachels (1986), three types of arguments are usually offered to support this theory. The first generally claims that by looking after one's own interests, everyone is better off. No one would be meddling in other people's affairs because each individual would be seeking what is best for him- or herself. Conservative economic and political policies often subscribe to this view. From a philosophical perspective, however, this argument is fallacious, and in fact, it supports a nonegoistic position. To assert that "everyone is better off" demonstrates a concern for the interests of others, and this notion, by definition, is foreign to an ethical egoist.

A second argument for ethical egoism states that altruism is a pernicious doctrine because it encourages people to become dependent and reliant on others, and it diminishes the value of the individual. In this view, altruism is criticized for it asks one to make sacrifices on behalf of others and denies the interests of the individual.

Personal ambitions are stifled by altruism, and so the only moral principle devoted to individual achievement and personal worth is ethical egoism.

The difficulty here concerns the extreme presentation of altruism, which practically no one accepts. A more charitable and realistic account of altruism would at least say that both the interests of the individual and the interests of others ought to be considered when making moral decisions. Moreover, describing altruism as an extreme position, rejecting it, and then serving up ethical egoism (another extreme) as an alternative are hardly convincing; one view certainly does not follow from the rejection of the other.

This brings us to the third argument in favor of ethical egoism. This position is less radical and accepts some common moral rules, such as telling the truth, keeping one's promises, and not cheating. This is surprising because these rules typically convey a concern for others. Rather than view these rules as separate, other-regarding guides for behavior, this account tries to demonstrate that common-sense morality can be unified and explained by a single principle, namely, ethical egoism. So in the long run, one ought to tell the truth, keep promises, and not cheat because these actions provide personal advantages. If one consistently violated these moral rules, one would likely be considered untrustworthy, unreliable, and subversive. Having this sort of reputation would not help toward advancing one's own interests. Ethical egoism, therefore, can explain everyday moral standards and preserve the idea of promoting self-interest.

The most moderate argument for ethical egoism promotes some moral behavior on the grounds that it is beneficial to the individual.

Rachels (1986) levels two criticisms against ethical egoism. The theory states that there are personal advantages to be gained in the long run from following common moral rules, say, telling the truth, but the theory does not say that this is always the case. So, in some particular instance, substantial gains could be achieved from not telling the truth. This argument then does not stress seriously enough that moral rules ought to be upheld even in the face of some personal gain. Second, although one might reason that it is in one's best interest not to cheat on exams, for example, there still could be a more basic reason for not cheating on tests. Cheating would lose the complete range of challenges of an exam, and one could prefer to be tested to the fullest extent. Thus, for some activities, there could be fundamental reasons for complying with moral rules. The reason of self-interest might be secondary, and it is definitely not the only reason. Therefore, this enlightened form of ethical egoism is unsatisfactory.

Each of the three arguments for ethical egoism falls short of the mark, but there is a more serious charge against ethical egoism. As discussed in the previous chapter, among the distinguishing features of morality are universalizability and a related notion that one should be able to recommend one's moral standards to others. It is reasonable then to ask how these criteria of sound ethical principles relate to ethical egoism. If each person were a committed ethical egoist, there would likely be constant struggle and conflict to fulfill our own interests (much as Hobbes [1651/1962] described). The ethical egoist could say that some individual interests and advantages would overlap, but this admits to a world that could potentially contain shared rather self-interests and defeats the egoist doctrine (Frankena, 1973). The universalizability of ethical egoism is logically implausible.

A related point is that it would be to the ethical egoist's advantage that not everyone adopts this posture. That is, the greatest gains could be made if some people were not ethical egoists, for there would be less conflict with others. This alternative would seem to follow if universalizability is unobtainable, but this creates a scenario where people are divided between "them" and "us," egoists and nonegoists, and the interests of the first group outweigh those of the second group. This, however, raises the question of the justification that egoists offer to prefer their interests to those of nonegoists. Unless there are relevant differences in the characteristics between each group, no difference in value and treatment between them is warranted. In fact, ethical egoism arbitrarily grants itself this privileged status, just as most racist and sexist theories do. Any ethical principle that arbitrarily places itself on a higher moral plane in relation to others can be confidently rejected (Rachels, 1986).

Utilitarianism

Egoism proved unsatisfactory as a teleological ethical theory because striving for self-interested amoral goods fails to meet some of the central demands of sound moral reasoning. Although none of these goods were specifically examined, like pleasure, knowledge, power, and perfection, the point was that none of these could be pursued from an exclusive self-seeking perspective. There is, however, a popular modern ethical principle that does account for the social well-being of others while seeking to attain certain amoral goods.

Utilitarianism posits that the only good worth pursuing is pleasure or happiness. For this reason, it is sometimes labeled a form of hedonism, from the Greek word *hedone*, meaning pleasure (Raphael, 1981). The only moral duty one has is to promote the greatest amount of happiness. Happiness is usually considered the

Key Concepts
altruism
egoism
ethical egoism
psychological egoism
teleological

totality of different pleasures. Pain is the opposite of pleasure and is bad, and by its reduction or removal, one enhances pleasure. So in general, utilitarians wish to create conditions to maximize pleasure and minimize pain, but the obligation toward achieving this sense of happiness is extended to include and account for the pleasures of everyone.

> Utilitarianism holds that one person's happiness is just as important as the next person's.

The social imperative here is critical. As Mothershead (1955) explains, "Human happiness is the good. This being true, the standpoint of utilitarianism is inevitably democratic. . . . Happiness is primary; whose happiness it is, is secondary" (p. 223). Utilitarianism, therefore, is not grounded foremost in self-interested motives (though some utilitarians do make egoistic claims). Because altruism is not entirely ruled out, the general formula of utilitarianism can be stated as "the goodness of an act depends on its giving the greatest happiness to the greatest number" (Pepper, 1960, p. 112). The determination of whether an action is right or wrong then depends on this principle.

As one can easily see, it is the consequences or possible consequences of behavior that serve as a gauge for conduct to be judged good or bad. This view is known as *consequentialism*. Actions that produce the greatest benefits are correct, whereas those that create harmful effects are to be avoided. So an athletic director who has sufficient funds in his budget to renovate both men's and women's locker rooms should select this option, rather than upgrade one or the other facility. All athletes would be served and benefit from the first choice, whereas the second option accommodates fewer athletes.

From a utilitarian perspective then, conduct is seen primarily as a means toward happiness. More specifically, such behavior must be practical and useful, hence the derivative term *utility* in the name utilitarianism. Not only can particular actions in given circumstances be evaluated from a utilitarian standpoint, but also many bureaucratic and governmental policies are decided by employing this approach. Tax, health, and licensing policies, for example, are often determined according to the utilitarian formula, that is, by or as providing the greatest benefits to the greatest number of people. In many ways, utilitarianism is a convenient and efficient way to make judgments of a practical and ethical nature. What makes a particular behavior or policy right then is that its consequences lead toward pleasurable ends (happiness); the behavior or policy has utility because usefulness generally creates greater benefits for more people, and the pleasure(s) of each person affected by such action is (are) equally valued. The difficulty, of course, is deciding what and how to measure the results of conduct or a policy to determine whether a particular course of action or policy should be followed.

Jeremy Bentham (1748-1832), perhaps the first individual to formally articulate the tenets of traditional utilitarianism (though he did not coin the term), tried to quantify pleasures and pains under the following seven categories: intensity, duration, certainty, propinquity (how soon experiences are felt), fecundity (the likelihood of future pleasurable experiences), purity (how free from pain are the experiences), and extent (the number of others who are affected) (White, 1988). Bentham believed one could calculate the goodness of an action by listing the pleasures associated with the action, applying a numerical value (say +1 to +10) for each of these in terms of the above categories, and then finding the total. After one does the same for any pains (say -1 to -10) associated with the action, then the resultant sum, either in favor of pleasures or of pains, would tell an individual what course of action to follow. A positive total would be good, and the behavior ought to be carried out. A negative total would be bad, and the action ought to be avoided (Wheelwright, 1959).

Bentham's hedonistic calculus is a strictly objective procedure for determining the value of an action. How effective is this method? What does one do if the resultant sum is zero? Can all pleasures and pains be quantified? What should count as a pleasure and a pain? Can the latter be objectively determined? These are all-important questions. However, for Bentham, morality was concerned only with quantity and the final tally, what we presently refer to as "the bottom line." In fact, to avoid some of the above questions, he held that any and all pleasures were equivalent. So whether one enjoys digging ditches, washing cars, playing tiddly-winks, watching sports, performing classical ballet, doing math, or just about anything else, each activity is given the same status as a pleasure (White, 1988). There are no intrinsically better or worse pleasures according to Bentham, although some activities may provide greater pleasure than others may for different people. From a sociopolitical perspective, Bentham also insisted that his form of utilitarianism is strictly democratic ("one person, one vote"). No one can tell another person what to enjoy and what is enjoyable, and if hopscotch provides one with more pleasure than poetry, then hopscotch is a more valuable activity (Palmer, 1991). Is there anything wrong with saying all pleasures are equal? One person who thought so was Bentham's disciple and godson, John Stuart Mill (1806-1873).

Mill, who did introduce the term *utilitarianism*, was dissatisfied with the claims that only the quantity and the equal status of pleasures were the most relevant considerations when estimating the consequences of behavior. If this were the case, many mundane and ignoble pleasures could be legitimately pursued. Mill believed that certain pleasures were superior to others, and these provided greater utility (Billington, 1988). In his view, pursuing knowledge and appreciating cultivated activities like art, music, drama, dance, literature, and science are superior to activities like doing the dishes, sunbathing, attending professional wrestling matches, and watching soap operas on television. Mill feared that if the latter pleasures were equally justified pursuits when compared to the former, and they were also widely accepted, then culture would be reduced to a lowest common denominator. He, therefore, set out to refine Bentham's ideas.

Mill (1861/1969) argued that Bentham's exclusive quantitative approach worked only when dealing with "lower," more basic pleasures. When considering "higher desires," the quality of pleasures, not merely the quantity, was needed to better assess the value of certain actions. If some behavior produces pleasure that is qualitatively more superior, but its duration is shorter, then its cumulative value might be greater than an alternative action that provides longer enjoyment but is relatively mundane.

In some ways, Mill's concern here is intuitively correct. If society decided that to achieve "the greatest good for the greatest number" it had to do away with arts and sciences, many creative, original, and ennobling activities would never be re-

Bentham's Quantification of Pleasure and Pain

1. Intensity
2. Duration
3. Certainty
4. Propinquity
5. Fecundity
6. Purity
7. Extent

alized. Human dignity and imagination might erode to base levels, and general happiness might not be attained. To emphasize this point, Mill (1861/1969) went so far as to say, "It is better to be a human being dissatisfied than a pig satisfied; better to be Socrates dissatisfied than a fool satisfied" (p. 237). Therefore, to preserve intellectual and creative integrity, the quality of pleasures has to be acknowledged. However, Mill's improved version of utilitarianism has several shortcomings.

First, by delineating "higher and lower" pleasures, who is to say which provides the greatest happiness? For many people, the simple pleasures of life (like bowling once a week) offer enormous happiness, whereas some intellectuals and artists have led and continue to lead unhappy, agonizing, and sometimes destructive personal lives (think of the number of "cultivated" individuals in history who have had nervous breakdowns, gone insane, or committed suicide). The mere separation of different levels of pleasures does not guarantee more or less happiness (Porter, 1980). Moreover, who is in a position to judge the quality of a pleasure?

Mill, in fact, believed one has to be competent or cultivated before passing judgment on this issue. That is, if one is unrefined in cultural matters, one is unqualified to decide which pleasures are superior. Along similar lines, Mill also thought plural voting in "democratic" elections should occur, with the vote of the educated counting for more than those of the uneducated (Schneewind, 1967). What these views strongly suggest is a form of elitism. In order to preserve a "high" cultural and sociopolitical standard, Mill designated some people and their judgments to be more valuable than those of others (Palmer, 1991). So by attacking one aspect of utilitarianism, its "lowest common denominator" flaw, Mill abandoned the deeply rooted democratic feature of utilitarianism.

Mill's revision of utilitarianism is also weakened because by asserting the duality of pleasures and the legitimacy of elitism, he ceased to support the hedonistic aspects of the doctrine. The pursuit of pleasure is no longer the supreme amoral good in his account. By introducing the notion of quality of pleasures, only certain pleasures acquired and appreciated by a select segment of the population afford and promote happiness. Other pleasures, the "lower" ones, are deemed less worthy, and some likely unworthy altogether, even though some people may enjoy them. If pleasures and people can be divided as such, and Mill does say it would be better to maintain human dignity and be dissatisfied, then this is a serious departure from hedonism. He seems to be describing a particular way of life as being more valuable than a pleasurable one (Porter, 1980). Although the pursuit of pleasure need not be at the core of utilitarianism, Mill attempted to refine this idea but came up short when he departed from this central utilitarian theme.

However, perhaps the most serious charge against Mill's version of utilitarianism, and traditional utilitarianism in general, is some of the intuitively wrong conclusions one can arrive at when following this principle. Consider the following example. In the most important game of the year, the coach of a Division I football team had a decision to make about whether or not to return a player to the game after he suffered an injury. On an earlier play, the athlete was knocked unconscious but regained his composure after a short while. Both the trainer and the team doctor strongly advised against the player's returning to the game, but on a crucial series of downs, the coach ignored their advice and ordered the player onto the field. On the very next play, the player was involved in a vicious tackle, which led to a game-winning score, and he was rendered unconscious again. This time, however, he lapsed into a coma, and several hours later he died.

When questioned afterwards, the coach reasoned that the athlete looked fine, he often returned players to the game after similar injuries and injury reports, the athlete was recently orphaned and had no known relatives (and therefore was not going to be dearly missed), he was a sophomore and not well known on the team, he was needed in the game to secure a win for his team, and his contribution to the team, the college, and the community achieved a greater level of general happiness.

As far-fetched as this example may appear, the coach's reasoning is sound based on utilitarian grounds. The beneficial consequences of playing the athlete perhaps outweighed any suspected harmful effects. Most people, however, intuitively sense the coach was unjustified and wrong in his action, especially based on the strong advice he was given. The example points out that, in some circumstances, utilitarians can lead to conclusions many people would find hard to accept. The athlete certainly did not deserve to be sent out to play, and to reason that the promotion of happiness ("the greatest good") was attained by the sacrifice of this one life is hardly the kind of justice with which many people would agree (Ewing, 1953). Therefore, to focus principally on the consequences of behavior can sometimes lead to a breach of some deeply rooted moral standards, like justice and granting people their due.

Similarly on utilitarian grounds, one could conceivably lie, cheat, or steal, if these actions lead to greater happiness. It is for this reason that later utilitarians introduced the distinction between *act utilitarianism* and *rule utilitarianism*. The former follows closely with traditional utilitarianism by considering the actual or possible consequences of actions in given situations that produce the greatest utility. There are, however, problems with act utilitarianism. In addition to the difficulty of knowing the full range and extent of all the consequences of an action, two different actions in a specific instance might produce identical outcomes. If the first involved lying or cheating and the second did not, then either action could be followed according to act utilitarianism, because both actions produce the same results (Frankena, 1973). Human intuition would say that one should carry out the second action, but this cannot be recommended from an act-utilitarian perspective.

When faced with this sort of dilemma, rule utilitarians argue that one should formulate a general rule that, when followed, would more consistently lead to a greater amount of happiness. So the second course of action, referring once again to the preceding example, should be exercised because one should adhere to the rule that lying and cheating are generally more harmful and do not lead to greater happiness. Rule utilitarianism has an advantage here by taking into account instances where rules of justice, fairness, equality, and the like are part of ethical problem solving. However, a difficulty with this approach might be that one could make certain exceptions to rules (Palmer, 1991). So one might establish the rule that cheating in sport is acceptable as long as officials do not catch one. However, adding exceptions to rules would likely lead to undermining rule utilitarianism altogether. The more exceptions created, the less clear and consistent the application of rules become (much like what is implied in expressions like "a bureaucratic nightmare" and "a catch-22").

The emphasis on the consequences of actions challenges some basic ideas about behavior many of us deem just plain wrong, like lying, stealing, cheating, breaking promises, abandoning a friend, and failing to repay one's debts. It has been shown that utilitarianism can, in many instances, provide us with a method to resolve ethical dilemmas by pointing to the outcomes of behavior, but in some circumstances, our moral intuitions tend to prevail, and we feel compelled to be guided by them. One question then, which we will address more fully in the next section, is, are there actions that must be followed out of a sense of duty, no matter what their consequences? Before proceeding to examine this question, we will briefly address two additional teleological ethical theories. The first of these tries to combine elements of duty and a concern for consequences.

Situation Ethics

As the name implies, this type of ethical approach is similar to act utilitarianism in that it takes into account particular actions and circumstances when one is faced with a moral problem. That is, ethical decisions and actions will arise exclusive to a set of given social conditions. No two contexts can be treated as similar, but each must be viewed as a separate, distinct episode. As such and in one sense, only the consequences of ethical judgments and behavior directly linked to discrete situations are the most significant. This feature of situation ethics provides a connection to utilitarianism, but where is the character of duty located?

Because each situation is unique, some advocates of situation ethics assert that no predetermined general rules can be applied when one is faced with a moral dilemma (Frankena, 1973). Each case must be viewed from its own perspective. For this reason, Billington (1988) calls situation ethics a type of ethical relativism. Distinct circumstances generate and govern different sets of rules, so what is right is a product of a given situation.

However, rules cannot always inform what one should do because in some contexts, either there are no rules to appeal to, or the rules do not readily apply to a certain situation. This development might demand the creation of particular rules by which to act, but they would be relevant only to a specific situation. Thus, in a given context, telling a lie or turning one's back on a friend might be justified, and this enjoins us to be extremely sensitive to the uniqueness of moral situations. One is, therefore, duty bound under this ethical principle to always search for distinct rules or maxims to follow and to reject the application of general moral standards in a hard and fast manner (Hudson, 1970).

So far, the description of situation ethics has not revealed its teleological dimension. Fletcher (1967), an important proponent of situation ethics from a Christian perspective, did supply one supreme value that should guide all ethical considerations. He maintained that "only one thing is intrinsically good, namely, love: nothing else" (p. 15). From a religious perspective, this has become known

<aside>

Key Concepts

act utilitarianism

Bentham's calculus

consequentialism

critique of Mill's version
of utilitarianism

hedonism

higher and lower desires

Mill's critique of Bentham

rule utilitarianism

utilitarianism

</aside>

as "the ethics of love" or *agapism*. This brand of theological situation ethics contains utilitarian elements as well as a duty-bound feature. In this case, one is obliged to derive all decisions and actions from the value of love. Whether this takes the form of considering only one's actions in a given situation or developing and relying on rules, both must be based on the principle of love. There could, of course, be nonreligious supreme values that could serve as various foundations for situation ethics, like justice, self-realization, and perfection. The point is to demonstrate that specific amoral goods in a teleological sense can guide situation ethics.

Despite such noble overriding values, situation ethics has its drawbacks. In practice, one has general rules, maxims, or principles that one follows, and one implicates these in different situations. How can one simply erase the influence of previously learned ethical guidelines and look at each moral episode in an entirely new and fresh way? Certain moral standards are bound to be part of one's ethical deliberations, and the uniqueness of any situation would not likely convince one to completely give up these principles, if only temporarily. Many people already know that torture, slavery, rape, incest, and a host of other abhorrent activities are morally wrong, no matter what. One hardly, if ever, approaches these issues with a blank slate, and so their moral status is quite plain regardless of the situation. Yet the relativistic strain in situation ethics leaves open the question of the wrongfulness of such acts.

Moreover, at least one important weakness emerges if we consider Fletcher's (1967) situation ethics specifically. Because love is the one unconditional principle here, it becomes difficult to discern and specify how other important principles might apply in a given situation, if they do at all. For example, how does love tell us what to do in the case of distributing justice? Fletcher makes a point to say that love and justice are equivalent and justice is love distributed; but he also imports, to some degree, a utilitarian calculus when making ethical decisions. Borrowing the utilitarian approach at least tells us that love on its own may not be sufficient to handle the demands of some ethical dilemmas, and other nonagapeic principles are also significant. Frankena (1973), for one, argues against a pure morality of love and says it needs to be supplemented by a principle of justice.

Although situation ethics possesses some certain flaws, it offers an interesting combination of ethical principles. It may be viewed from a teleological perspective by reflecting a supreme value; it may contain a utilitarian strain by considering the consequences of behavior in particular situations; and it may possess the quality of insisting one be duty bound to certain rules and maxims once they are established in a given context. In the next section, we will turn to an examination of ethical theories that state that actions and rules are right or correct regardless of the consequences that may follow from them or whether or not they promote some amoral good.

Key Concepts

agapism

combining elements of ethical principles

context and duty

critique of situation ethics

specific rule development

Deontological Theories

Many of us feel an obligation to act in a certain way because we just know it is the correct thing to do. Keeping promises, telling the truth, respecting others, and honoring one's parents are viewed as right in themselves. These maxims, and the behavior generated from them, are rarely questioned, and many would claim they apply in all circumstances. Yet if there are some action-guiding principles or rules we accept as intrinsically valuable, what sort of rules are they, and in what ways are we obligated to them? These are at least two central questions we will investigate in this section.

The term generally used to describe theories where moral obligation does not involve a consideration of the outcomes of action is known as *deontological*. As Garner and Rosen (1967) explain, "Deontological theories of obligation hold that things other than (but, perhaps, in addition to) consequences determine which actions are morally right" (p. 25). The word *deontology* is derived from the Greek, *deon*, meaning "duty" or "obligation" (Beauchamp, 1991). Some have even called this ethical approach the ethics of duty. What this theory emphasizes is the moral nature of specific standards and one's behavior irrespective of the results they produce. Once justification is given for the soundness of these, then one's moral duty can be firmly established in any context.

Deontological theories can be easily contrasted with utilitarianism, because the latter is distinguished as a results-oriented approach. Whereas some reasoning along utilitarian lines can lead to injustice or treating people undeservingly (as demonstrated in the previous section), deontologists are usually not confronted with these sorts of problems. In fact, it will turn out that respect for persons, personal autonomy, motives, commitment, and other similar ideas impose moral obligations that can outweigh whatever benefits might result from our actions. For strict deontologists, it does not matter whether the consequences of behavior are good or bad. One's only duty is to adhere to accepted and well-established moral standards.

> Unlike results-oriented utilitarianism, deontology maintains that moral standards should determine action.

Deontological theories can also be contrasted with certain elements of situation ethics. Whereas the latter can be guided by a commitment to a supreme value (e.g., love) whereby one accepts a principal duty, in most versions of situation ethics, the consequences of actions in a given context are usually assessed, and no previously established rules are brought into consideration. In the main, deontological theories reject these utilitarian and rigid context-bound features, but the question remains: Where do intrinsic principles originate?

Some deontologists appeal to the divine commands of God or a Supreme Being; others claim the moral superiority of certain rules and actions is known through intuition; some hold that reason can tell us what is right; and still others claim there are principles and actions that are correct by their very nature (Beauchamp, 1991). Usually in each case, some rationale is given to establish moral standards to which one owes one's allegiance. Once the soundness of these maxims is in place, one must carry out one's obligation to live up to such standards.

As in the earlier section of this chapter, we will again examine a number of approaches. None of these deontological theories is presented completely, but the variations between them will disclose how the notion of duty is alternately expressed. We will begin with a relatively simple type of deontological viewpoint and move toward more complex versions of this ethical principle.

The Golden Rule

Perhaps the most well-known moral maxim in Western history is the Golden Rule. It is mostly associated with the Torah or Pentateuch and Christian bibles and has been suggested as the foundation for morality both in ancient and modern times (Raphael, 1981). Because the Golden Rule was, and is still, a highly revered moral standard, it deserves our attention from a deontological perspective.

Many people believe the Golden Rule was first enunciated by Jesus in the expressions, "love thy neighbor as thyself" and "do unto others as you would have them do unto you." In fact, however, the Golden Rule has an older tradition that predates the time of Jesus and the emergence of Christianity.

In the Pentateuch, the final portion of Leviticus, XIX, 18 reads, "thou shalt love thy neighbour as thyself," and in verse 34 in the same chapter it is written, "The stranger that sojourneth with you shall be unto you as the homeborn among you, and thou shalt love him as thyself" (Hertz, 1980, pp. 502 and 504). Generations of Jewish prophets and scholars quoted or paraphrased this verse as a supreme teaching to guide human conduct. If we now only consider these religious versions of the Golden Rule, without worrying too much about any differences in their formulation, how should we come to understand this basic principle?

In the first instance, the Golden Rule clearly places an emphasis on altruism. One's primary motive for ethical behavior should be to act unselfishly with regard to others. This seems to be the hallmark of religion in Western history. The ideas of charity, helping those less fortunate, and comforting the sick and weak have a central place in Western traditional religions. Trying to put oneself in the place of others is also an attempt to express a deep concern for the condition and welfare of other people. We have already seen how extreme forms of egoism reject altruism as a motive for ethics. The Golden Rule, however, stresses that we should be kind and thoughtful toward others and should assist those in need. The question is to what extent can we act selflessly?

For one thing, total self-sacrifice would lead to social absurdity. Imagine if everyone worked completely for the good of other people. That is, one would tend exclusively to the needs of others, whereas others would tend to one's own needs. This sort of arrangement would be highly unlikely because differences in individual wants and desires would be so varied that no reasonable level of satisfaction would ever be gained (Mackie, 1977). There could also arise the situation whereby if one worked only for the good of others in the most unselfish manner, no one would accept the benefits of such work, and overall general happiness would decline (Ewing, 1953). So in the extreme, living entirely for others, is an untenable form of altruism, but the Golden Rule does not advocate this. It does not say that one should love another "more than" oneself, but "as thyself." One of its assumptions then is the notion of self-love.

Both Judaism and Christianity espouse the idea that regard for the self is a fundamental feature of human existence, hence the expression "as thyself." Taking into account one's own interests along with those of others is a legitimate enterprise in ethical deliberations. In fact, the self-interested dimension is sometimes understood to be a more basic quality of human beings, whereas our concern for others must be learned (Shirk, 1965). Christianity, more so than Judaism, has often seen self-love as a debilitating, sometimes evil and sinful, human trait. It has proposed doctrines of self-denial or asceticism, the renunciation of material, bodily, and personal pleasures, as a way to curb the desires of the self.

As before, such extreme positions are generally implausible interpretations of the Golden Rule. On the one hand, it is unlikely that if one led a life of self-denial, all others would want to be treated in this same way. As Billington (1988) writes, "I am unlikely to make much of a contribution to my neighbor's wellbeing if I am indifferent to my own" (p. 25). In the opposite extreme, some people exude so much love, concern, and care for others, it is sometimes embarrassing to the recipients, or such sentiments are viewed as disingenuous and can put people off. So the idea of "doing unto others" has its limits in both these negative and positive senses. By bringing together a regard for others as well as consideration for oneself, the Golden Rule tries to temper radicalism in either direction. It also serves as a universal maxim.

Anyone who adopts the Golden Rule is committed to placing everyone on an equal moral plane. The emphasis on impartiality is guaranteed here because one is willing to accept the same actions for oneself as those one recommends to others. No one is therefore considered arbitrarily superior in terms of moral worth. Even though this moral equality exists between individuals, as we saw above, the treatment of individuals as one would like to be treated cannot be taken literally (Ewing, 1953). Again, one person might accept living as a hermit, but many other people would not want to adopt this lifestyle. Moreover, the way one would prefer to be treated may not be the right way a person ought to be treated. So, one would prefer to not receive a parking ticket, but if one clearly breaks the law, getting a parking ticket is rightly what one deserves. Despite not making a moral exception in individual cases, and therefore holding to the idea of universalizability, the Golden Rule can still lead to unappealing and unwarranted practices.

The religious formulations of the Golden Rule have much to recommend them. They teach one to be benevolent toward others, to place some importance on self-interested pursuits, and to regard everyone as moral equals. The desire to adhere to the Golden Rule as one's duty is perhaps a good general guide to behavior. But one drawback alluded to in the problems addressed above is the difficulty of applying this principle in specific cases (Brandt, 1959). Consider the example of capital punishment.

Those who advocate this sort of punishment could invoke the Golden Rule by claiming that some death row inmates agree they should be killed for their crimes. Occasionally, convicted murderers come to realize they do not deserve to live for what they have done, and so they are willing to accept capital punishment as a form of justice. In this case, there is no breach of the Golden Rule for those who face execution for their crimes. Moreover, even though the Bible teaches the

Golden Rule, capital punishment is a justifiable form of retribution, and examples are replete in scripture. By contrast, those who oppose this supreme penalty also point to the Golden Rule and argue that loving one's neighbor means expressing reverence for human life and that other, less severe forms of punishment are more just. Consequently, there are no clear answers in some particular cases if one is to rely exclusively on the Golden Rule.

As we noticed above and in the latter specific case, interpretations of the Golden Rule can vary. If this is so, then how it is understood and applied in different situations can also be diverse. The Golden Rule, therefore, does not prescribe precisely what one ought to do in many specific instances. This is one of the major weaknesses of this maxim. In what follows, a nonreligious deontological theory will be examined that, in one of its pronouncements, has an affinity with the Golden Rule.

Kantian Ethics

One of the greatest philosophers in Western history was Emmanuel Kant (1724-1804), a quiet academician, who lived as a bachelor and never ventured very far from his birthplace, Koenigsberg in northeastern Germany (then known as Prussia). Perhaps his greatest contribution to philosophy was in the area of ethics, and his works continue to have tremendous influence on those who agree and disagree with his thought.

Kant reacted against any hint that moral behavior should and can lead to good or beneficial consequences like happiness, perfection, and self-realization. According to Kant, ethics has nothing to do with satisfying some identifiable end. For this reason, he is definitely not a teleologist. In fact, if one could demonstrate that an act was carried out to arrive at some desirable outcome, this would disqualify the act as an instance of ethical behavior (Palmer, 1991). This raises the question of how moral behavior can be recognized as having no association with some consequence.

> The basic premise of Kantian ethics is that moral decisions arise out of a sense of duty rather than to produce a desired result.

In the early portion of *Foundations of the Metaphysics of Morals*, in a famous quote, Kant (1785/1959) wrote, "Nothing in the world. . . can possibly be conceived which could be called good without qualification except a good *will*" (p. 9). Based on this statement, Kant developed the view that ethical conduct can emanate only from someone who possesses a good character. Someone with such a character behaves morally from a pure sense of duty, rather than from a consideration of the results of actions (Brandt, 1959). From a Kantian perspective, if keeping one's promises, not lying, respecting one's parents, paying one's debts, not turning one's back on one's friends, and the like are performed because they provide some kind of advantage or gratification, they are no longer ethical actions. This is so because there would always be alternative motives attached to these actions. For Kant, the only motive for ethical conduct is what human beings will in a strict, unadulterated sense of duty. He, therefore, was one of the first

asceticism

benevolence

deontological

ethics of duty

golden rules

moral equality

selflessness

self-love

ethicists to seriously examine the notion of duty for duty's sake (Ewing, 1953). He also tried to demonstrate the soundness of this basic tenet by relying on one's ability to reason clearly, and he began by making an important distinction in the way we use the term *ought*.

On the one hand, one could tell someone, "If you want to improve your health, then you ought to start exercising" or "If you desire to be a better racquetball player, then you ought to practice more." These everyday typical examples make use of the term *ought* in a practical way. Although a course of action is being recommended ("start exercising" or "practice more"), it is suggested only as a means to fulfill some wish ("improve one's health" or "be a better racquetball player"). Kant called such "if-then" statements where ought is found, *hypothetical imperatives*. That is, the *ought* refers to a practical plan or requirement one should follow if one wants to satisfy some particular desire. However, this sort of imperative (or obligation) is relatively weak, because if one were to renounce the desire, then one would no longer be bound by the recommended action (Rachels, 1986). The binding force of hypothetical imperatives then depends on what one wants, and there is no moral relevance related to one's desires.

A genuine moral ought, however, is unconditional according to Kant. It does not rely on any desire or on any further qualification. So to say, "You ought to treat your sister in a fair manner, if you love her or if you want her to be fair in return" is not an example of a moral statement because various conditions are attached to the ought clause. Kant would say, "You ought to treat your sister in a fair manner" and stop right there. The imperative (or obligation) here is absolute, and no qualification can be linked to it for it to be a moral claim. For just think, if one did not want one's sister to be fair in return or did not love her (and these are possibilities), then the binding force of the imperative is not very strong; it really involves a practical matter, and hence it no longer falls within the domain of morality.

As mentioned earlier, Kant (1785/1959) relied on human ability to reason carefully about ethical issues because he firmly believed the foundation of human existence is based on the fact that humans are rational beings. His ethics is firmly grounded not in intuition, divine authority, desires, consequences and the like, but in reason. Therefore, his moral arguments, if sound, must be accepted by any rational individual; not doing so would be tantamount to renouncing one's very nature.

It is clear from the above discussion there are different degrees of duty. Hypothetical imperatives involve a weak level of duty only insofar as one wishes to fulfill some desire, whereas genuine moral imperatives demand an ultimate sense of duty based on reason. Yet the question remains: What gives the latter their absolute quality when it comes to duty, for this is the only motive acceptable for moral behavior? Kant (1785/1959) provided three formulations to what he called the principle of the *categorical* (absolute) *imperative*. All moral obligations will necessarily conform to this principle.

The first version of the categorical imperative is as follows: "Act only according to the maxim by which you can at the same time will that it should become a universal law" (Kant, 1785/1959, p. 39). One can easily see that Kant appealed to the idea of universalizability as the supreme test to decide if a particular rule or action is right and, therefore, to be followed or carried out with a pure sense of duty. Before one can employ the categorical imperative as a test, however, two preliminary steps must occur.

The first step requires that an individual have in mind some rule of action, known as a maxim (Garner & Rosen, 1967). This will be the personal guide by which individuals conduct themselves, and so numerous maxims can exist. For example, the beliefs that it is good to marry and have children, to do volunteer work, to give part of one's income to charity, and to help one's neighbor are all maxims of various sorts. There need not be any agreement between people about any particular maxim. So not everyone is required to give to charity, to marry and have children, to be a volunteer, or to help one's neighbor, but Kant (1785/1959) did insist that each person must arrive at or will these maxims autonomously. His idea of autonomy is a difficult one and is often misunderstood.

In brief, what Kant was saying is that each person's action-guiding maxims must be willed from a rational posture, independent of any desire or influence (Beauchamp, 1991). Thus, it is fairly clear when a child is told by her father to help her grandmother up the steps, thereby following a rule like "always help the elderly," the child is not acting autonomously. The child is likely acting from obedience and is being influenced by her father, whom she wishes to please or from whom she wishes to avoid some unpleasant consequence. When the child matures and perhaps later accepts the maxim and autonomously wills it as a rational agent, only then would a resulting action contain moral worth. At this stage, too, the maxim possesses authority because it is derived from a rational stance.

Autonomy of will does not simply involve an individual's capacity to make personal decisions and to create and be responsible for a certain kind of lifestyle. Merely establishing rules by which to govern one's own life is not what Kant meant by autonomy. As Beauchamp, (1991) explains, "Kant's theory of autonomy is to be explicated in terms of moral *self-legislation*: If a person freely determines the principles under whose direction he or she will act, the person is a law-giver unto himself or herself, and thus is autonomous" (p. 181). There is a difference then between rule creator and rule legislator. The former produces action-guiding rules primarily as an expression of his or her liberty, whereas the latter an individual autonomously wills maxims that emerge from one's nature as a being who possesses reason and whose maxims, therefore, are valid for all rational beings. The idea of autonomy is a central feature of Kantian ethics to which we will later return.

The second preliminary step required before using the categorical imperative test concerns the relationship between some moral act and a maxim. In this case, the moral agent must choose to have his or her behavior conform to a maxim, so that the person is indeed acting from the maxim (Garner & Rosner, 1967). If an individual did not choose to have a particular action described under a maxim, the person would only be acting according to some rule, rather than *from* the rule.

The categorical imperative test determines whether a given maxim can be followed consistently by everyone at all times.

Once these conditions are met, the categorical imperative then asks a person to consider whether a given maxim can be followed consistently by everyone at all times. This procedure will determine whether an action-guiding rule can be made an objective and absolute (universal) standard, whose binding force at this point is contained within a law. The maxim as a universal law should possess no contradictions or inconsistencies. As Shirk (1965) explains, "We should act in such a way that everyone else could so act, with consistent and harmonious consequences for all" (p. 187). If the maxim passes the test of the categorical imperative, any rational individual then can accept it. Because people possess reason, they cannot deny their obligation to moral laws (Wheelwright, 1959). For Kant (1785/1959), ultimate respect for moral laws is a derivative of human ability to reason, and this compels people to apply the strictest sense of duty toward such laws. What are some of these universal laws?

Kant (1785/1959) provided several examples. He considered whether suicide could be accepted as a universal law. If a person contemplated self-destruction based on the maxim "end your life when a longer life would lead to more pain than pleasure," then this rule would be self-contradictory when held up against the test of the categorical imperative. In this instance, the maxim assumes a certain love for oneself, the very notion that drives one toward sustaining life, and so the maxim contradicts a principle on which it is founded. Suicide, therefore, cannot be universally willed.

Can the neglect of natural talents be universally accepted? Suppose one was gifted in some area, but instead of developing this gift, one decided to live an idle, indulgent, and pleasurable life on the beaches of the Caribbean. Kant (1785/1959) believed that choosing idleness and pleasure as universal laws over the improvement of natural abilities contradicts the nature of humans as rational beings. He reasoned that even a person devoted to seeking pleasure is still acting as a rational person who wills that his talents be developed. In this case, the individual's abilities have provided him or her with a life of pleasure seeking. It would be contradictory, therefore, to will that natural talents be neglected because we cannot foresee how our gifts might be utilized.

Next consider the person who would decide that she no longer wishes to assist others when they are in need. Can the maxim "do not help others in distress" be willed in a universal manner? No, said Kant (1785/1959), because one would eliminate any future possibility for help for oneself, and again, this would be self-contradictory.

Kant's (1785/1959) main example to demonstrate the existence of universal laws and how they are derived from reason concerns the case of making false promises. Suppose one needed to borrow money from someone else and promised to pay back the money, but knew that one would not repay the debt. Promises of this sort could not be universally willed for that would lead to a contradiction. Ultimately no one would believe such promises, and so the very thing promises do would be nullified, thereby making promises logically impossible. Some have applied the self-contradictory nature of false promises to other examples.

Lying presupposes the general condition of truth telling, whereas cheating in sports assumes the overall condition that most players adhere to the rules of the game. In other words, if everyone lied or cheated, these activities would be self-defeating. People generally have to be telling the truth in order for lying to work, for this is what the person lying counts on in order for the lie to bear fruit. Similarly, the cheater in sports does not want everyone to violate the rules; otherwise, cheating would offer no rewards. So Kant (1785/1959) would declare that maxims involved with lying and cheating could not become universal laws and these actions are immoral in all social contexts.

The first version of the categorical imperative reveals whether one's action-guiding principles are consistent or contradictory. For Kant, this moral test not only appeals to one's sense of reason, but it also ensures that no individual can be considered an exception when acting from a maxim. That is, "when we make an exception for ourselves, declaring that the action is wrong in general but we can do it nonetheless, that is a certain indication that our action is immoral" (Porter, 1980, p. 183). The idea of impartiality then is an essential feature of Kantian ethics, and in this respect it is similar to the Golden Rule. It is also clear that the categorical imperative is a procedure that takes into account the rational nature of others. This other-regarding dimension is so central to Kant's ethics it is the basis of the second formulation of the categorical imperative.

In this version, Kant (1785/1959) asserted, "Act so that you treat humanity, whether in your own person or in that of another, always as an end and never as a means only" (p. 47). Here Kant was stressing the intrinsic worth of human beings as rational selves. The primacy of selfhood, autonomy, and self-determination for all rational beings simply because they are rational ensures that no amount of exploitation of people can be morally justified. Moreover, this formulation of the categorical imperative, whose substance is apparently identical with the first version, cannot place conditions upon people in order that they be treated as ends (Korner, 1955). So one cannot force others to adopt a certain way of life and then treat them with human dignity. Once again, people are ends in themselves by virtue of their existence as rational selves. Slavery, torture, political oppression, sexual harassment, and all forms of exploitation are immoral and cannot be justified and condoned.

Kant was not suggesting that we exclusively, in all our affairs with others, view them as ends. Part of one's relationship with others is on an instrumental level, as it is with employers, clerks, coworkers, and even one's parents. The point is that we should not treat others "as a means *only*" (emphasis added). On a fundamental level and as much as possible, others ought to be accorded genuine respect and be treated with dignity even when they are considered as a means to some end (Beauchamp, 1991). So athletes should not treat a trainer or equipment manager *just* as a specialized servant who performs specific auxiliary tasks on demand, but as an autonomous, independent human being, with her own interests, desires, and needs, who performs essential supportive services.

> As a sport manager, you must be sensitive to the kinds of relationships you have with other people and respect the intrinsic worth of human beings.

The idea of treating others "always as an end" carries other implications like not harming others, respecting their rights, enhancing their well-being, and trying to further their ends (Rachels, 1986). It also means holding in high esteem rationality itself. Respect for persons means that one regards others as having the capacity to make choices, and to deny others the ability to choose is to treat them as a means.

In the above false-promise example, if the borrower told the lender he did not know if he could repay the loan, then the lender would be given the opportunity to decide whether or not to extend the loan on some other basis. Consider how a person might feel if he discovered someone had lied to him. Aside from any practical consequences of the lie, the individual would likely feel insulted, as though it were an affront to his integrity as a person. Some moral experiences, therefore, can tell people whether they treat others primarily as ends or as means. Such experiences can also be utilized as a kind of test to determine whether one's maxims are morally sound or inconsistent. So for Kant, a fundamental aspect of human dignity is to respect others as autonomous, rational beings. When one does treat others as ends as such, this provides a further indication that one's maxims can become universal laws.

By combining elements of the first and second versions of the categorical imperative, Kant provided a third formulation. He basically stated that one should act as ". . . a legislative member in the realm of ends" (Kant, 1785/1959, p. 53). Now the term *realm* extends the idea of willing self-imposed laws to all members of a community (Raphael, 1980). If a society, in principle, could account for and unify each person's capacity to will universal laws and always treat others as ends, then at one and the same time, one would be both a legislator of laws and a subject of them.

What Kant was saying is that, in theory, if every person in society used reason to create self-imposed laws, this would lead all persons to will the same universal laws. One's duty toward the law would then be absolute from a social perspective. No longer would coercion or force be needed to uphold the law because in the realm of ends, all individuals are legislators and subjects. Because in such ideal circumstances, members of society would be collectively willing identical self-imposed laws, not to comply with such laws would be contradictory. In essence, what Kant was describing is a pure form of democracy. Each member of society would be given the freedom to make independent decisions (liberty), all choices would carry the same value (equality), and each person would make decisions as a member of a community (fraternity) (Raphael, 1981).

In the three versions of the categorical imperative, several salient features of Kantian ethics emerge, and it would be helpful to review these at this juncture. In the first instance, the notion of an absolute duty as the only motive for moral action (resulting from a good will) required a coherent foundation based on reason alone. Kant introduced the distinction between hypothetical and categorical imperatives to demonstrate how the term ought is employed. In the former case, which is based on desire, ought claims could not be considered morally relevant, nor could the sense of duty here be deemed very strong. A genuine moral ought creates an absolute (categorical) obligation that must be accepted by all rational beings. To establish this duty as ultimately binding, two conditions need to be met.

First, an individual must autonomously will a maxim, or an action-guiding rule. The notion of autonomy here is linked to people's fundamental nature as rational beings. Second, a person must choose to act *from* the maxim rather than act according to the maxim. Once these steps are taken, one can employ the principle of the categorical imperative, as a sort of test to determine whether a maxim is morally correct. Three versions of the categorical imperative were examined.

The first formulation emphasized the idea of universalizability. One asks, "Can the maxim be followed consistently by all people at all times?" In this way the maxim acquires the character of a universal law that can be accepted by all rational persons and adhered to with a strict sense of duty. Any maxim that turns out to be self-contradictory is immoral. This particular moral test ensures impartiality so that no one can be made an exception to a certain rule. The second version of the categorical imperative stressed the importance of human dignity. People are always to treat others as ends and not merely as means. Here there is an ultimate concern to respect the autonomous and rational capacity of others. Individuals must, therefore, enhance the well-being of others, advance their ends, respect their rights, and not harm them. Finally, the third variation consisted of an ideal political situation in which the collective will of all members of a community creates self-imposed laws and opposition to such laws would be contradictory.

Although many features of Kantian ethics conform to moral experiences and they do seem to be rationally grounded, how cogent are these views? One difficulty surrounds the idea that maxims can be universalized. Frankena (1973) points out that conflicts can arise between two duties. Suppose one upholds the universal laws to never tell lie and, always to help someone in trouble. Then one day one is confronted by a known killer (a hit person) who asks the whereabouts of someone one knows. If one tells the truth one would likely endanger the potential victim's life; if one lies, however, one would be assisting the person one knows. In either case, one could not simultaneously uphold both laws. Where then should one's absolute duty reside? Kant (1785/1959) had no satisfactory way to resolve this dilemma, but consider the following.

> ### Testing a Maxim
>
> 1. Is it universalizable?
> 2. Does it treat people with dignity?
> 3. Does it reflect the collective will of the community?

If one were to modify the maxim by saying, "Never tell a lie unless by doing so you preserve someone's life," the maxim would no longer apply in a universal way, but it would be connected to specific instances. Perhaps if there are two conflicting laws, one could be selected as having greater value over another (Porter, 1980). So in the above example, saving a person's life takes precedence over never telling a lie. In this way, a hierarchy of laws could be established, but again, this would not agree with the principle of universalizability, and the application of laws would be context specific. There would also be the problems of deciding what one law would dominate all others, and whether or not the application of this law is guaranteed in every moral situation. In any event, Kant believed that universal laws did apply in all circumstances without exception, so such modifications to the principle of universalizability are unhelpful.

Difficulties raised in the preceding discussion indicate that, in some instances, certain practices people generally think are wrong could be morally justified. So stealing food to feed one's children during wartime or a famine could be approved by most of us. Doctors sometimes make decisions to withhold medical treatment in extremely severe cases (especially if death is imminent), thereby not acting to preserve life and curtail human suffering, and this behavior may be morally justified. So the idea that a universal law is applicable in all situations without exception may be unrealistic in practical terms. In fact, for some critics, there can be no such laws because no maxims can be identified that apply strictly in all situations (Porter, 1980).

Conflict also arises with regard to the second formulation of the categorical imperative. Suppose one is in a position to help only one of two individuals who equally need one's assistance, how does one decide which person should be helped? If both individuals are to be treated as ends so that one is to further their interests, advance their well-being, and the like, it becomes virtually impossible to resolve this dilemma. Kant's (1785/1959) principle identifies what maxims are moral because they demonstrate respect for human dignity, but in reference to the preceding example "it does not give me a criterion for deciding which of them I should help" (Raphael, 1980, p. 60). If there is no standard to decide which person's ends one should respect, then Kant's principle is of limited value in some contexts.

Also at issue are certain practices we sometimes commend, but either they cannot be carried out universally or it would be too much to require strict obligation to them. For example, on one hand, self-sacrificing conduct can occasionally be recommended and be considered virtuous (we certainly would not want to say it is not virtuous) (Porter, 1980). On the other hand, everyone could not perform such conduct; otherwise, no one would be the recipient of such behavior. Consider another example: heroic conduct. Although acts of heroism are often viewed as morally correct, people cannot be required to act in heroic ways if the opportunity might call for it. No one can morally demand that someone enter a burning apartment building to save some of its tenants. This does not mean that heroic behavior has no moral worth, but that one's moral obligations cannot extend to include certain practices.

It is here that Kant's general notion of duty is sometimes unclear. Many maxims can be universalized and, therefore, be candidates for our undivided duty, but this does not necessarily mean the maxims are moral. So, always put on one's left shoe first or comb one's hair before brushing one's teeth could each be a universal law, (i.e., followed by all people at all times), but what sort of absolute moral obligation do we have to these laws?

Frankena (1973) indicates that Kant did not adequately provide a way to tell whether or not one is dealing with a moral issue and where one's duty lies. Palmer (1991), however, defends Kant on this point and claims, "What gives an act moral worth is not simply the fact it *can* be universalized, but the fact it was chosen as a moral act" (p. 328). That is, when one acts from a posture of duty for duty's sake, the action is said to be a moral one. The difficulty here, of course, is, how do we know what people's motives are? These motives may not be evident from their actions, and it may not be helpful to ask them what their motives are (they might not know, or they might be confused about the matter). For these reasons, the idea of absolute duty remains questionable, and some critics contend no such pure stance is possible. Although one's intentions or motives are surely part of moral reasoning and conduct, they are likely not the *only* factors underlying the notion of duty, and they provide limited help when trying to determine what counts as a moral act.

> The motive for one's actions ultimately decides the moral content of behavior (what issues from a good will).

Despite the shortcomings discussed above, and there are several others we will not address, the appeal of Kantian ethics rests on a number of important points. For one thing, it stresses that people must remain strictly impartial. All rational beings are equally considered from a moral point of view. Moreover, although it may be impossible to will universal laws with no exceptions or to act from a pure sense of duty, these can still be useful guidelines for human behavior in some contexts. That is, as ideals these notions cannot be totally discounted. Perhaps the most significant claims within Kantian ethics concern the stature of the moral agent. Kant elevated the individual as a moral authority based on the ideas of autonomy and rationality. This insight removed morality from the realm of external authorities including religion. Kant altered the focus of ethics by turning toward each person as the ultimate source of morality, and this was a major shift in the history of ethics, felt even today.

Ross's Prima Facie *Duties*

Before leaving the area of deontological theories, one other relatively recent viewpoint in the Kantian tradition will be briefly examined. As mentioned in the previous section, Kant's system could not resolve a conflict between one's duty toward two universal laws without breaking one of them. There was just no way to decide which law was to take precedence unless one was willing to make certain exceptions (e.g., never lie except when it helps someone in danger), and Kant would have none of that. For this reason, some deontologists have introduced the notion of plurality whereby several principles operate to account for certain overriding concerns. The most noted philosopher to develop this line of thought was W. D. Ross (1877-1970), and it is to his work that we now turn.

Like Kant, Ross (1930) was committed to a nonconsequentialist approach toward ethics (e.g., he strongly opposed utilitarianism), and he too placed considerable importance on the notion of duty. But unlike Kant, he did not view duty as an absolute obligation. As we noted above, there was no way to resolve the dilemma when two universal laws came into conflict in a given situation, thereby making it impossible to decide where one's duty resided. Ross, therefore, proposed an alternative to the absoluteness of Kant's sense of duty.

To set out this new position, he presented a distinction between actual or "proper" duty and conditional or *prima facie* duty (Ross, 1930). What we actually ought to do or what is actually right can be derived from rules that permit

Key Concepts

act from a rule

acts of heroism

acts of self-sacrifice

autonomy of will

conflicting duties

consistency and contradiction

duty for duty's sake

good will or character

hypothetical imperative

impartiality

maxim

persons as ends

rationality

self-legislation act according to a rule

strict application

three formulations of the categorical imperative

certain exceptions. So, if one made an appointment to meet a friend for a racquetball match, but learned one's mother had to be rushed to the hospital (she had a known heart condition), breaking the date to play tennis (even leaving the friend unknowingly stranded) would be morally justified in order to be at the mother's side (especially if one promised to do so in such a situation). Here, the rule "never break a promise except in personal emergencies" would be followed so that one's actual duty took into account an exception.

A *prima facie* (which means at first glance, apparently so, or self-evident) or conditional duty follows from exceptionless rules. However, such a duty is not yet an actual duty because other overriding obligations can supercede it. In this instance, there will always be more reason to adhere to a *prima facie* duty unless it is outweighed by another duty. For example, one has a *prima facie* duty to keep one's promises as much as possible. If one is a doctor who makes a date to play tennis with a friend and no emergency arises, one has a moral obligation to show up for the game. However, if one faced a conflict where another *prima facie* duty was pressing, for instance, saving a person's life, then this second duty would likely outweigh the first. It would be at this point that one could then declare one's actual duty, which would follow from a rule containing an exception, although promise keeping and saving lives are each separate *prima facie* duties (Frankena, 1973).

Note that Ross is not committed to the idea of absolute duty, but to the consideration of different competing duties. *Prima facie* duties follow from rules that can be said to be internally without exception. By considering other *prima facie* duties, one is not introducing exceptions to certain rules, but one is instead weighing one "exceptionless" rule against another and trying to formulate what one's actual duty is which can contain an exception clause. Some readers often miss this point.

Now one might ask, "What are some of these *prima facie* duties?" Ross (1930) provided a list that he claimed was not exhaustive, and the correctness of these duties he accepted as self-evident (hence, *prima facie*). Many have been critical of him on these two counts (cf., Garner & Rosen, 1967), but it is still useful to know his list of *prima facie* duties.

Ross's Prima Facie *Duties*

1. To keep promises
2. To make restitution when we harm others
3. To return services when we have benefited from others' services
4. To distribute rewards and punishment based on merit
5. To do good on behalf of others
6. To improve ourselves in terms of virtue and intelligence
7. To not injure others

(Brandt, 1959; Ewing, 1953; Ross, 1930)

On the surface, this pluralistic approach toward duty appears sound and something like *prima facie* duties are more reasonable than Kant's unconditional duty, but here also Ross is not totally out of the clear in relation to conflicting duties. Ewing (1953), Brandt (1959), Garner and Rosen (1967), and Frankena (1973) all point out that Ross has not provided sufficient criteria to decide which *prima facie* duties ought to take precedence over others in conflict situations. Ross (1930) conceded as much when he stated, "For the estimation of the comparative stringency of these *prima facie* obligations no general rules can, so far as I can see, be laid down" (p. 41). Other criticisms include counterexamples that demonstrate how some of Ross's *prima facie* duties are occasionally inconsistent and sometimes can be applied in morally questionable circumstances. Critics have also showed that some of his duties brush up against utilitarian themes and calculations that he strongly opposed.

Notwithstanding these criticisms, Ross's ethical theory can at least be said in some instances to do no worse than other ethical theories (Ewing, 1953). Even utilitarians must often admit to having no criteria for deciding between competing pleasures and pains. Although Ross rejected utilitarian grounds to establish moral obligation, and he preferred a self-evident view for the moral value of *prima facie* duties, his approach is generally in accord with ethical concerns on a common-sense level. That is, many everyday moral evaluations and decisions are based on the notion of duty and are often consistent with our moral intuitions. So on Ross's account, an emphasis on duty might not lead so readily to situations in which better overall consequences might result from some personal injustice (as could happen when following a utilitarian approach). Yet on the other hand, the pursuit of virtuous ends cannot be entirely neglected to make way for moral obligations, for the latter often presuppose such ends (Ewing, 1953). Ross's *prima facie* duties, therefore, provide us with an important ethical concept, yet one we must accept with some reservations.

This ends our discussion of deontological theories, and it was made clear that morality here was based on a number of central themes, such as ultimate moral principles, duty, and motives. The final major theory under consideration in this chapter insists that ethical behavior issues from the character of individuals who should learn to exemplify certain moral virtues.

Key Concepts

actual or "proper" duty

conditional or *prima facie* duty

critique of Ross's ethical theory

nonconsequentialist

weighing *prima facie* duties

Virtue Ethics

In the past few decades, a critical view of ethics has been revived and refined as an alternative to both teleological and deontological ethical theories. The main complaint against the preceding two theories is their reliance on obligations to fulfill certain principles. On the one hand, people must act to achieve some supreme good or end, and on the other hand, others have a duty to adhere to universal, rational imperatives (Statman, 1997). Rather than focus on questions like what rules or guides one ought to follow or what principles are needed to discern between right and wrong, virtue ethics, the theory under discussion here, emphasizes the idea that a virtuous character is all that is needed to arrive at sound, ethical judgments. In the following brief exposition, we will describe the basic tenets of virtue ethics, critique this theory, and show how an ethics of virtue applies in two relevant contexts.

Virtue ethics as a brand of moral philosophy has its roots in ancient Greek philosophy, primarily in the works of Plato and Aristotle. Although modern philosophers like Kant and Mill acknowledge that virtues and character play a role in ethical decision making, these elements are not central features in their respective moral theories. Contemporary advocates of virtue ethics, by contrast, stress the supreme importance of character traits that exemplify moral worth. If individuals aspire and develop into virtuous moral agents, they would engage in the world expressing moral virtues and have no need to devise and follow ethical rules or fulfill specific moral obligations (D. Solomon, 1997). A virtuous character would be sufficient to ground and justify ethical judgments. However, what rationale or underpinning is given for making virtue and character fundamental to ethics? Statman (1997) answers that "the virtues are justified in terms of their essential role in the wellbeing of the agent. Virtues are viewed as necessary conditions for, or as constitutive elements of, human flourishing and wellbeing" (p. 8). On this basis, human beings and their harmonious relations with others and the environment, rather than ethical rules and duties, take precedence when considering moral issues. Before proceeding further, the very notion of a virtue requires explanation.

Beauchamp (1991) claims that "a virtue is, at minimum, a character trait that is socially valued" (p. 213). A moral virtue, he continues, is a feature of character that has moral worth. This implies that there are amoral and immoral virtues as well. Being punctual is an amoral virtue, and being a virtuous terrorist may involve immoral values. Blum (1994) makes an additional distinction between "ordinary" and "noteworthy" virtues. A moral virtue like truthfulness is not merely related to tendencies whereby one tells the truth. The disposition of truth telling could be predicated on a rule or principle, or what is right, or fulfilling one's duty. It could also be that we are typically expected to tell the truth, whereas the virtue of courage says something about going beyond normal expectations in everyday life.

What is important in virtue ethics is that virtues are fundamentally linked to people's motives and intentions for doing the right thing and not only to actions that may be deemed praiseworthy. A compliment to someone for his honesty might be withdrawn if one learned that the person was honest because he feared losing his job. How would one feel if it was discovered that someone was a friend for some ulterior reason? How could one call such a person a genuine friend, and what does that say about the virtue of friendliness? Intentions, feelings, emotions and other aspects of one's inner self, together with outward manifestations, describe the quality of one's character. Thus, virtuous behavior is linked to virtuous motives, and both features are constitutive of moral character.

How strongly one insists on this last point is a contentious issue among proponents of virtue ethics. Some wish to claim that traditional concepts of right, wrong, and obligation can be employed to judge conduct as long as they are derived from virtues and qualities of character. Others take a more extreme standpoint and argue that any moral judgments related to duties or the application of ethical principles are untenable and should be replaced completely (Slote, 1992). In any case, motives play a central role in understanding what we mean by a virtuous character.

The all-encompassing manner by which virtues and character are related reveals an interesting feature of virtue ethics. Some advocates claim that if no duty or applied principles are involved in making practical moral decisions, then one must envision an ideal type of virtuous agent who would respond in a given ethical dilemma. Beauchamp (1991) discusses saints and heroes as virtuous characters in this respect. Therefore, to answer a moral problem that one might face as someone's friend, one would require a sense of a paradigmatic moral agent who exemplifies the virtues of friendship. This ideal friend would have exemplary virtues like love, care, sensitivity, compassion, trust, and respect. One would consider how this imaginary friend might react in a particular situation and what measure of the virtues one possesses to respond as a friend helping another. The concept of an ideal type of virtuous character not only sheds light on how one deliberates on ethical issues from a virtue ethics standpoint, but also reinforces the centrality of the virtues and character when faced with ethical dilemmas.

Virtue ethics not only suggests new ways to consider moral problems, but it has other far-reaching implications as described by Statman (1997). Unlike a utilitarian perspective, an emphasis on virtues creates new priorities in terms of

> Virtue ethics considers a decision's effects on individuals and personal relationships.

moral worth. Whereas social utility is based merely on public goods and advantages, virtue ethics will take into account benefits related to individuals and personal social relationships. Traditionally, learning to do what is right has been achieved by adhering to moral rules, like following the Golden Rule. By contrast, under virtue ethics, moral education consists of identifying moral exemplars, understanding their lives and the virtues they possess, and trying to mimic how they are and what they do. Unlike theories of duty that insist on a clear determination between right and wrong, virtue ethics presumes that most often no absolute answer can be given when faced with moral problems. Many ethical dilemmas suggest reasonable alternative solutions without specifying exactly which option is the correct one. Ethical theories based on obligations require that moral agents act voluntarily; otherwise, responsibility for one's actions could not be considered. This distinction between voluntary and nonvoluntary is not essential in virtue ethics because the quality of a person's character can be judged even when areas of life are beyond one's control. Finally, unlike some ethical theories that rely on transcendent, universal concepts and principles, virtue ethics is usually associated with particular cultures where social norms and values are implicated in the formation of character. Thus virtues are not other worldly but are rooted in specific communities and traditions (Blum, 1994).

Despite the appeal of virtue ethics and its broad ramifications, it is not immune from criticism. D. Solomon (1997) raises three internal criticisms against virtue ethics and these will be the extent of the following critique. The first objection claims that virtue ethics is overly self-centered because it focuses on the character of the agent. We have already seen this with the notion of the paradigmatic or ideal type character that one should aspire to imitate. Thus the acquisition, refinement, and expression of virtues are part of an individual enterprise to improve one's character. For some, this emphasis is contrary to many ethical concepts that point to other-regarding acts like charity and helping one's neighbors. A second objection argues that virtue ethics is unable to provide adequate guidelines toward making practical ethical decisions. At times, moral conflicts require precise judgments when trying to figure out the best thing to do. Because virtue ethics does not presuppose or rely on firm standards of right and wrong or universal ethical principles, it is incapable of formulating exact action guides to resolve moral quandaries. Finally, the third objection is related to personal feelings and how individuals respond to their feelings. For some, like Kant (1785/1959), the moral goodness of a person must be invoked at the point of expressing outward behavior. Certain feelings, like care and compassion, are considered natural reactions that may be beyond one's control, yet they may lead to good conduct. Ethical behavior, however, cannot be based on moral luck. Thus emotive aspects of a moral agent are neither praiseworthy nor blameworthy from a moral point of view. Virtue ethics, however, stresses the inner self, including one's emotions, as essential to one's character, even though these feelings may be beyond one's control.

Proponents of virtue ethics have a reply to each of the preceding criticisms. Against the first objection, virtue ethics can point to the development and display of many other-regarding virtues that can serve as counterweights to a self-centered posture. It also argues that theories of duty and utilitarianism confer emphases that highlight the individual and the public good respectively, and therefore, virtue ethics fares no worse when it stresses the primacy of individual character. Against the second objection, virtue ethics can claim that the objection is overstated. Acquiring virtues and living by them is a lifelong pursuit, where encounters with moral problems are facets of one's overall experiences in leading a flourishing life. Within this kind of life project, there need not be hard and immutable rules and action guides to deal with ethical dilemmas. Against the third objection, it can be shown that moral goodness is not so firmly rooted in both utilitarian and Kantian theories. In the case of utilitarianism, consequences may have all sorts of natural contingencies attached to them that distort goodness, and in the case of Kant (1785/1959), his idea of possessing a good will and invoking one's will to do what is right, unlike feelings, is rather selective and understates the capacities of human consciousness.

Having provided an overview and a critique of virtue ethics, let us now discuss in brief two contexts where the practical application of virtue ethics is considered. For the past decade or so, a number of researchers in business ethics have found virtue ethics to be a departure from a rules-based ethical system in business generally, and a useful way to understand the nature and role of managers. This shift in business ethics is explained and advanced concisely by R. C. Solomon (1997) in the following,

> What is missing from much of business ethics is an adequate account of the *personal* dimension in ethics. Accordingly, I want to defend business ethics as a more personally oriented ethics, not just as public policy, 'applied' abstract philosophy or a byproduct of the social sciences. But business ethics so conceived is not 'personal' in the sense of 'private' or 'subjective'; it is rather self-awareness writ large, a sense of oneself as an intimate (but not inseparable) part of the business world with a keen sense of the virtues and values of that world. (p.209)

Proponents of virtue ethics in business insist that a fundamental change is needed so managers and employees do not appeal merely to rules and are not motivated solely to getting out of a jam when faced with moral problems. Instead, those in business should resolve ethical dilemmas based on the virtues and values that encompass their lives (McCracken, Martin, & Shaw, 1998). Not only would this new orientation require individuals to reassess their roles and responsibilities, but it also would necessitate a re-thinking of the business enterprise itself. For example, Brewer (1997) argues that managerial practice contains all the constitutive features whereby virtues and good character can flourish. Collins (1987) demonstrates how Aristotle's sociopolitical philosophy is not contrary to modern corporations that view their role in society as meeting individual needs and providing social stability. Business therefore should be understood as a practice involved in personal and collective well-being where the exercise of virtue fulfills shared social goals (Mintz, 1996).

Moreover, in business, the virtues are implicated in many practical settings, and managers need to be conscious of circumstances that warrant their expression. R. C. Solomon (1997) argues that business and social harmony can be achieved by exemplifying both moral and amoral virtues. Thus, classical virtues like courage, self-control, generosity, magnificence, gentleness, friendliness, truthfulness, and modesty, as well as intelligence, practical wisdom, understanding, and good sense, are all relevant and sound virtues in a business environment (Mintz, 1996). The main point is that business does not have such separate principles and objectives beyond the norms and ideals of individuals and communities. The integrity of people and shared social values are intimately bound up with making products, providing public services, and accruing profits. Virtue ethics is precisely the kind of approach in moral philosophy that serves personal aspirations and the social good—objectives that are not necessarily antithetical to business practices.

> According to Gough, most ethical problems in sport could be resolved if individuals were to take seriously the idea of developing excellence in character.

Another context in which virtue ethics has been applied is in the area of sport and its related fields. Gough (1997) in fact makes virtue ethics the primary ethical theory of his monograph, *Character Is Everything*. In this work, he argues that most ethical problems in sport could be resolved if individuals were to take seriously the idea of developing excellence in character. For example, if ethics involves being good and doing the right thing in general, then sportsmanship means the same thing in a sport setting. A good character will ensure one's actions in sport are good, honest, trustworthy, fair, respectful, and compliant with the rules. Achieving a good character is like developing good sport skills. It requires personal moral training and practice and knowing what virtues work best in diverse sets of circumstances. Strengthening one's abilities and improving on one's weaknesses are essential toward the attainment of excellence in character. Moreover, one's character is always being tested in the face of new ethical challenges. Most often, people live up to the challenge; however, at times they fall short. When the latter occurs, we should not be so quick to judge others as inherently bad. Instead, we should be empathetic because we all experience shortcomings of character and should help others improve who they are and what they do. Along these lines, Gough discusses high-profile athletes as role models and suggests that in most instances they should not be moral exemplars because so few people have an intimate knowledge of who they really are. Role models, therefore, should be found among virtuous people we admire and respect in our everyday lives. In the next study, character is not the main emphasis, but the source and appropriation of sport-related virtues are.

Arnold (1999) examines the nature of virtues, moral development, and the ways in which sport as a practice cultivates particular virtues. In short, sport can be compared to medicine, farming, education, and the like wherein each of these practices defines particular skills and internal values that exemplify excellence and virtue. One can understand and appreciate completely these elements only through participation and experience in specific sports because each sport has its own peculiar skills and ethos. Arnold identifies two functions of sport-related virtues. Those that preserve the way sport is conducted might refer to virtues like fairness, honesty, and cooperation, whereas those that refer to excellence in skills, strategy, and tactics correspond to courage, persistence, thoughtfulness, and self-control. By calling sport a practice, the virtues are derived from and are situated in a specific social environment. Individuals learn and appropriate virtues in specific contexts, they understand the primacy of virtues in a shared way, and they realize that preserving the internal goods of sport requires upholding skills and virtues that make sport a valued human practice. In the last work to be considered here, the sport manager as a social character is investigated.

Corlett (1997) examines the role of the sport manager and managerial practices against the critical views of three leading contemporary sociopolitical philosophers. There is not enough space here to review and elucidate the thought of each of these philosophers, but the conclusions all three draw and the implications their views have for sport management are challenging. Taken together, these scholars charge that managers portray themselves as ethically neutral so they can be absolved of social responsibility. Managers inaccurately make use of social science knowledge to manipulate others and maintain control. They actively subvert practices by treating tasks and people as commodities for self-serving ends, and they create redundant and useless technocratic layers of management to fulfill corporatist goals. Finally, managers are complicit in the decline of democratic principles, which has detrimental implications for individuals. Social fragmentation, hypercompetition, lack of common social goals, pitting individuals against one another, and legalistic resolutions to conflict have been encouraged by managers who subvert the tenets of classical democracy.

In light of these critical observations, Corlett (1997) poses three questions of those in sport management: Are there honest and open lines of communication in one's sport management environment? Have resources shifted away from conducting the sport activity to the preservation of the sport's bureaucratic edifice? Are athletes and coaches central to the management process? Satisfactory answers to these questions would not only require collective considerations, but would also place individuals at the center of such debates. Corlett suggests that sport managers must demonstrate a concern for ethically sound practices. The means of sport management and not only its ends must be fair and just and be determined within a democratic process. Sport managers must listen to and support athletes and coaches who strive to exemplify excellence and the internal values of sport. Perhaps with these objectives in mind, sport managers can make a difference toward the cultivation of virtues and good character in others, preserve the integrity of sport, and change their own role from the sinister portrayal above to a virtuous one.

Key Concepts

character

critique of virtue ethics

implications of virtue ethics

motives

ordinary and noteworthy virtues

paradigmatic moral agent

virtue

virtue ethics and business

virtue ethics and sport

Summary

This chapter set out to introduce and explain three major ethical theories and concepts. It grouped these around the categories called teleological, deontological, and virtue ethics. In the first category, egoism and its several versions were built on the idea of self-interest. Utilitarianism developed the principle of the greatest good for the greatest number of people, and situation ethics adhered to the idea that every circumstance must be treated independently and on its own terms while fulfilling some supreme value.

Deontological theories, by contrast, emphasized the notion of duty and motive. The first of these duty-oriented theories was the Golden Rule, generally described as "do unto others as you would have them do unto you" or "love thy neighbor as thyself." Stressing the categorical imperative, impartiality, universality, and utmost respect for persons featured Kantian ethics next. Finally, Ross's *prima facie* duties tempered some Kantian principles by dealing with the issue of competing and conflicting duties.

In the third grouping, virtue ethics was discussed as an alternative to the above two theories. It stressed the notion that individual moral character was the foundation of ethical discourse and behavior. For example, a person who is genuinely honest and trustworthy can be counted on to do the right thing in any given situation. A virtuous individual is an exemplar to others, is empathetic to the plight of others, and is sensitive to cultural norms and practices. Thus, virtue ethics was not based on seeking a particular supreme good or feeling duty bound to a universal imperative. The development of one's character, and the appropriation and display of moral virtues can meet the challenges of ethical questions and problems.

Throughout the chapter, and to varying degrees, both sport management and nonmanagement examples were raised to help the reader understand better the above content. The next chapter will examine two additional categories of ethical theories that rely on the notion of social justice and the legal concept of rights. It will also discuss the idea of pluralism and how to select an appropriate ethical theory in a practical setting. These topics will assist the reader to frame ethics and morality in a broader perspective.

Questions for Consideration

1. What are the main differences between teleological and deontological ethical theories?

2. Identify the main types of egoistic theories, and critique each of them.

3. How do Bentham's and Mill's versions of utilitarianism differ?

4. Describe examples that demonstrate weaknesses with utilitarianism.

5. What are some supreme values people might adhere to when following a situation ethics approach? How are these values implicated in this approach?

6. Why is the Golden Rule considered a deontological theory?

7. How do Kant's hypothetical and categorical imperatives differ?

8. Identify the three versions of the categorical imperative and critique each of them.

9. How are Ross's *prima facie* duties an advance over Kantian ethics?

10. What is a virtue? How does the individual expression of virtues fulfill a social and moral function?

11. Identify the basic features of virtue ethics, and compare and contrast this theory with teleological and deontological ethical theories.

Chapter Four

Major Ethical Theories II

Theories of Justice

The notion of justice usually falls under the domain of social philosophy. Here, moral problems are framed by such concepts as fairness, desert (what one deserves), entitlement (what one is entitled to), and distribution of goods and services that people claim as citizens of particular societies (Beauchamp, 1991; Palmer, 1991). Issues of justice more generally involve matters where what is due or owed is considered. For example, company policies, rules, and regulations might be in place to ensure fairness in hiring, nondiscriminatory practices in promotions, fair grievance and negotiation procedures, just benefits packages, and the like. Specific rules are usually governed by more general principles such as equality between people, fair treatment by others, protection from harm, ownership rights and obligations, and distributive and retributive justice (Beauchamp; Frankena, 1973). In most instances, social justice is conceived in both these general and specific senses.

Chapter Objectives

- To investigate ethical theories in which justice is viewed as a supreme moral standard

- To understand the concept of rights, rights and obligations, and types of rights

- To become familiar with ethical concerns associated with sport management

- To comprehend pluralism and methods for choosing a particular ethical theory

> Distributive justice refers to the benefits (e.g., workers comp) and burdens (e.g., taxes) assumed by members of a society.

Because this section is really not concerned with criminal activities and the fairness of penalties attached to such behavior (retributive justice), the focus here will be on *distributive justice*. The latter refers to the distribution of benefits and burdens assumed by members of a society. Paying taxes, for example, is a distributed burden, whereas food stamps and welfare, unemployment and workers' compensation checks are distributed benefits. Distributive justice is usually based on the premise that certain qualities people possess should be linked with the way societal benefits and burdens are correctly distributed. For instance, company promotions ought to be given to those who are in line for a promotion, those who possess excellent skills, those who have improved their performance significantly, and those who have achieved recognized standards of accomplishment.

Many examples of distributive justice involve at least two general features. First, there is usually a comparative component. If two similar individuals in similar situations are treated differently for better or worse, there may be grounds to say an injustice has been committed (Frankena, 1973). So what one person or group deserves is often compared to the desert of another person or group. Not all justice issues are comparative, but many of the distributive variety are. Second, distributive justice involves some element of scarcity over which there are conflicting or competing claims. This usually applies to benefits (Bowie & Simon, 1977). If a promotion is seen as a benefit, the available positions to which people can be promoted are typically limited. A just selection process, therefore, must be established when several people apply for promotion.

The comparative and scarce dimensions of distributive justice are still insufficient bases by which to make decisions of fairness, desert, entitlement, and the like. What are also needed are specific criteria by which to establish just rules, procedures, and regulations. Frankena (1973) lists three major categories that can serve as criteria in these instances. First, justice may be founded on what people deserve or what they merit. This criterion is known as *meritarian*, which refers to the distribution of some good (e.g., happiness) based on the expression of some virtue (e.g., honesty). Second, justice may involve treating others as equals so that the distribution of benefits and burdens is equal as well. An *equalitarian* criterion is typical of democratic societies. Finally, justice may be based on people's needs or their abilities or both. This criterion is the foundation of a Marxist view of justice.

In the following subsections, a further explication and critique of these criteria and their relationship to various theories of justice will be presented. The theories to be covered include egalitarian, libertarian, utilitarian, and Marxist perspectives. This cursory examination should provide a sound overview of a difficult topic.

Criteria for Justice

Meritarian—distribution is based on what people deserve or merit

Equalitarian—distribution is the same for all

Marxist—distribution is based on people's needs and/or abilities

---

Egalitarian

In most ethical theories, the meaning of equality plays a major role. Whether one speaks about the equal status of individuals or the equal value given to people's preferences or the treatment of others as equal, some basic sense of equality is needed. A reasonable understanding of equality is also required to determine relevant differences and inequalities in given situations. Unlike other ethical positions, the meaning of equality and inequality is a central tenet of an egalitarian theory of justice (Beauchamp, 1991).

One form of egalitarianism holds strictly to the dictum that justice means treating equals as equals and unequals as unequal. Based on this formula, one is able to render consistent justice decisions (Bowie & Simon, 1977). This extreme egalitarian view considers people to be sufficiently alike so that all people should be treated equally. That is, all benefits and burdens ought to be equally distributed because, morally speaking, all people are equal. A major flaw here is that people are not identical or equal to one another, and so the premise of the argument is false (Wheelwright, 1959). People do not have the same backgrounds, skills, opportunities, needs, interests, physical appearance, and the like. Consequently, there can be no possible way to distribute benefits and burdens so that identical results are achieved.

Some have suggested that equal treatment rather than equal outcomes is the proper way to understand the egalitarian position. So those who have special needs, like the poor, the sick, and those with disabilities, should be provided with greater benefits so inequalities can be corrected (Raphael, 1981). This revision of egalitarianism tries to create advantages proportional to the needs of others in special cases. What this view does not suggest is that those who have superior talents and skills be given additional incentives and rewards so that the advantages they already possess are enhanced further. If this enhancement were carried out, disparity between the distribution of benefits and burdens would continue to exist, and an egalitarian society would not be established. This modified version is still not free of problems.

Is there a fair financial distribution if parents outfit one child in an ice hockey program and a second child in a soccer program? If the first child is interested only in expensive sports, should the second child be "penalized" as a result? In this case, it may be contentious whether or not a just distribution of benefits and burdens should be based solely on special interests or needs (Bowie & Simon, 1977). Because of such criticisms, a further revision to egalitarianism maintains that an equality of opportunity to fulfill fundamental needs is required. Affirmative action, proactive steps by government and business to correct for past discriminatory practices, is one concrete way to implement this last form of egalitarianism, but here too, there are strong objections to affirmative action programs (Beauchamp, 1991). Rather than continue to explore and critique different versions of egalitarianism, let us turn to discuss one of the most compelling contemporary statements related to this theory of justice.

Over three decades ago, Rawls (1971) produced an egalitarian view of justice in his important book, *A Theory of Justice*. According to Rachels (1989), this work is revolutionary because it returned moral philosophy in the 20th century from a mostly theoretical area of study to one in which working principles could be implemented to create a just society. Second, Rawls's book revived aspects of contract theory in social philosophy and joined it with deontological elements, thus creating the first significant alternative and challenge to utilitarianism, which had dominated social and political philosophy for about a century. Unfortunately, given the relevance of this work, only an outline of Rawls's egalitarian theory can be offered here.

We have already discussed how utilitarianism can lead to situations in which injustices are committed, especially in breach of individual rights or what people deserve, to attain the greatest good for society. The potential to arrive at such a circumstance has no place in a system of social justice. Rawls (1971), therefore, set out to construct a theory to avoid violations of justice, including those that exist only in principle.

The procedure or method he follows to locate and establish sound social principles is rooted in the expression "justice as fairness" (Rawls, 1971). Any social structure or institution that fails to ensure individuals are treated justly needs to be abandoned or reformed, but who determines what counts as "justice as fairness?" Rather than present some utopian vision that people work toward, Rawls proposed a hypothetical situation in which free, equal, and rational people will have to make their own basic decisions about creating the just society. In this way, their decisions are produced by and turned back on themselves. Because of the individual and collective nature of this process, people will be constrained by the judgments of others. People will realize that not everyone can receive the largest share of any particular good. There will be recognition that both cooperative and competitive elements will operate to guide people's decisions. Yet despite potential rivalries, free, equal, and rational people will likely choose to create a society that promotes advantages for all (Falikowski, 1990). This will entail that some form of mutual understanding will exist between people where justice and equality are fundamental considerations. Rawls then understood society as consisting of some type of social contract in which tacit agreements are made between members of a society. How exactly does a Rawlsian society emerge?

Rawls (1971) suggests that, theoretically speaking, people create principles of social justice from an original position where impartiality is maintained. From this standpoint, people are placed behind a "veil of ignorance." That is, individuals have no knowledge of their race, class, physical appearance, mental capabilities, social status, natural talents, monetary worth, society's socioeconomic and political structure, and the like. The veil-of-ignorance construct ensures individuals cannot devise principles of justice that favor only themselves. Members of society must take into account the interests and decisions of others because there is no guarantee that a particular judgment will result in personal advantages. Again, one does not know in advance how one will fare in the end. As Raphael (1981) explains,

> The hypothesis of making the calculation under a veil of ignorance about one's personal situation is a method of adding impartiality. If I have to provide for my own interests in any and every possible contingency, I am providing for the interests of anyone and everyone, not just for my own. (p. 72)

> Rawls suggests that people in society develop their own social contracts to maximize their liberties. This, in turn, distributes wealth, power, self-respect, and opportunities to the benefit of all.

By making free, equal, and rational choices under this thought experiment, Rawls (1971) contended people could devise mutually agreeable principles of justice that are fair. Two main principles arise from his proposed scheme. First, people would maximize the amount of liberty (political, religious, speech) they can exercise, and second, once this liberty is in place, primary social goods like wealth, power, self-respect, and opportunities would be distributed to the advantage of all (Beauchamp, 1991). The latter principle implies that inequalities can exist in a just society, as long as the whole of society benefits from such inequalities and everyone has a fair opportunity to acquire unequally distributed goods. Because these principles are generated from behind the veil, they produce the effect of moving toward greater equality for disadvantaged members of society. The conditions created by Rawls's method, therefore, are consistent with his "justice as fairness" credo. It is also clear from this discussion that Rawls objected to desert and merit as founding principles of a just society, as well as traditional forms of utilitarianism. His preferred society stresses the maximization of equal liberty, greater equality for the disadvantaged, and fair distribution of social goods where inequalities can exist for the benefit of all.

Now that an outline of Rawls's (1971) egalitarian theory of justice has briefly been presented, a sport-related application of his procedure and a short critique are in order. Simon (1991) analyzes the problem of unequal distribution of scarce benefits in elite sports by employing the Rawlsian method of social justice. This problem centers on the issue of whether or not a handful of athletes deserve or merit the enormous fame and fortune they receive because of their natural talents. In light of the conclusions above, personal desert in itself cannot serve as the ground for justifying inequalities. The only room for desert or merit lies in a just set of rules or regulations created impartially behind the veil of ignorance. So, Olympic athletes deserve the medals they receive if they and others abide by rules created independently of desert considerations. If such rules are created in accord with Rawls's procedure, then not only can a mild form of desert exist but inequalities can also exist. Athletes may receive a disproportionate number of scarce benefits in a free-market economy because such inequalities in the long run benefit society and the disadvantaged.

Simon (1991) is uncomfortable with this reasoning because it minimizes the idea of desert and could lead to conditions in which respect for persons is undermined. In particular, in a Rawlsian view, athletic talent might be considered community property to be developed and expressed independently of the interests and choices of the individual athlete. This, of course, would be disrespectful of people as autonomous agents. Should all seven-footers be compelled to play basketball? Should we not acknowledge the efforts to excel and the improved performance of one athlete over another when they both possess similar natural abilities?

Inequality of results is often a consequence of personal abilities and assets some people wish to develop and others recognize, without the added necessity of creating benefits for all and improving the lot of the disadvantaged. Simon (1991) suggests that perhaps within a Rawlsian society there is some room for individual merit in order to retain respect for persons. Based on this amendment, elite athletes are justified and deserve to be disproportionately rewarded for their natural abilities, but they should also recognize that their personal assets are fortuitous and that if they are being rewarded by society, they have an obligation to those worse off, a conclusion that results from behind the veil of ignorance.

In addition to Simon's (1991) misgivings about aspects of Rawls's (1971) theory, other criticisms have been raised as well. Rawls, of course, advocated a liberal society in which a premium on fairness and equality exists. This also happens to be the kind of society Rawls lives in, and so he seems to be speaking from an ethnocentric and biased position (Palmer, 1991). This criticism can be extended because some claim Rawls's original position is not neutral but assumes a liberal, individualistic view of society. Rawls provided no sound arguments to reject other social arrangements (e.g., a theocracy, where religious tenets are the foundation of political and social structures) that some might choose even behind the veil of ignorance (Bowie & Simon, 1977).

Another criticism is the special kind of self-interest Rawls (1971) assumes people would adopt, which tends toward playing it safe in case one ends up unlucky. If the stakes were high enough to become extremely wealthy, let us say, some might decide to take their chances and risk being a pauper in the original position (Raphael, 1981). An additional criticism goes as follows: If complete ignorance of one's own interests and identity is required, then signers to Rawls's social contract are not legally bound. No contract can ask its signatories to forego all knowledge of themselves, and so the contract must be deemed invalid (Palmer, 1991). Finally, Rawls has been criticized for not protecting individual rights where the redistribution of benefits and burdens will require undue state interference. Rawls's theory works only because it is assumed that social goods are heaven-sent, when they are really produced historically through the resourceful efforts of individuals. In other words, social goods belong to people, and treating them as if they did not is a violation of people's rights (Beauchamp, 1991).

This ends our discussion of an egalitarian theory of justice, which has much to recommend despite its weaknesses. In the next subsection, we will focus on a libertarian perspective that relies heavily on the protection of people's rights and directly challenges some egalitarian ideas.

Key Concepts	
comparative	desert
distributive justice	egalitarian
entitlement	equal outcomes
equal treatment	equalitarianism
equality of opportunity	ethnocentrism
justice as fairness	liberty
meritarian	needs and abilities
original position	primary goods
prudent self-interest	retributive justice
scarcity	Simon's critique
social contract	veil of ignorance
violation of rights to social goods	

Libertarian

Unlike the egalitarian perspective in which justice as fairness involves equal opportunity so that those disadvantaged can gain greater equality, libertarians in the main do not hold to such a premise. A libertarian asks only that fair procedures, rules, and regulations be in place in society to ensure that people have the freedom to make social and economic choices as they please. Any attempt to restrict people's liberty in this regard is deemed unjust. Creating conditions whereby people can freely control their lives to pursue their own interests leads to the just distribution of benefits and burdens. Those who are more industrious and contribute more to their own success and to that of society rightly deserve to be rewarded more than others who contribute less. The rights of liberty, happiness, property, and such are taken seriously by libertarians, who would prefer minimal government intervention in the lives of citizens.

> Libertarians want fair procedures, rules, and regulations in society to give people freedom; they see any restriction on people's liberties as unjust.

There are, of course, objections to the libertarian account of social justice, and these will be raised later in this subsection. Once again, however, there is a well-known contemporary spokesperson for this position, and we will turn to his thought to explain further the libertarian view.

As a challenge and alternative to Rawls (1971), Nozick's (1974) compelling work called *Anarchy, State, and Utopia* follows traditional and more recent views of libertarianism. Nozick begins with a critique of the anarchist's position that "no state has legitimate authority over its citizens" (Minton & Shipka, 1990, p. 462). Essentially, the state interferes in the lives of people through the principle of the right to command. For example, it can tax people and compel them to go to war. For anarchists, the state violates individual rights (suppose one does not want to pay taxes or go to war) on the basis that it provides protection for its citizens. Nozick reasons that the anarchist view is incorrect, because anarchy would still result in some grand protective agency emerging and operating as a state-like entity. Nozick concludes that anarchy would logically create a "minimal state" that can be defended as just (Palmer, 1991).

No state, whether socialist or capitalist in nature, should try to reach a just society by redistributing benefits and burdens. A state's only mandate is to ensure that people have an absolute right to liberty so they can make social and economic decisions in the most free and unencumbered way possible. Some theories of justice (e.g., utilitarianism) employ end-state goals whereby the distribution of benefits and burdens is determined in a nonhistorical way. Society might be better off if the rich were forced to share their wealth with others, but for historical reasons (e.g., if such wealth was acquired legally and legitimately), people cannot morally make these demands (Bowie & Simon, 1977). Similarly, if a state were to follow some patterned formula for redistributing benefits and burdens, it would always lead to some infringement of a person's liberty.

Because Nozick (1974) is critical of nonhistorical end-state principles and patterned formulae employed by some theories of justice, he proposes an entitlement theory of justice (Beauchamp, 1991). This theory refers to some basic rights contained in three main principles related to the acquisition, transfer, and rectification of goods or "holdings." Nozick borrows ideas of ownership from John Locke, a 17th-century moral and political philosopher, and claims that "Locke views property rights in an unowned object as originating through someone's mixing his labor with it" (p. 174). So, in the 17th century, explorers in North America could cross the Mississippi, set up a camp, and claim all the territory before them for France, England, or Spain. This kind of original acquisition, however, can worsen the situation for others, like native peoples. Because resources like land are scarce, Nozick agrees with Locke's proviso that acquisitions can occur as long as they do not worsen circumstances for others and some sort of baseline situation is maintained.

In addition to acquiring holdings, a person has a right to transfer personal goods if this transfer is done in a legal and legitimate way in accordance with the above disclaimer. So transactions such as selling, purchasing, gift giving, and inheriting are certainly appropriate in a minimal state. Finally, one has the right to defend one's holdings in the event they come under harm and to exact punishments against those who are guilty of such harmful practices. In order to seek rectification in such instances, the libertarian demands that the state intervene, and this is the only area where it can do so (Palmer, 1991).

It is clear that the above three principles and their related rights work optimally in a free-market, capitalist society. When pure procedural guidelines are followed in the latter areas and basic rights are upheld, then social justice can prevail. There is also recognition that ownership and monetary inequalities will exist in the minimal state. Despite the proviso Nozick (1974) introduces, he defends such inequalities by saying they are unfortunate, but not unjust (Palmer, 1991). Intuitively, one might find Nozick's libertarian view harsh and unsympathetic to the plight of those less fortunate. Some critics object to his ideas on these grounds. In the remainder of this subsection, a number of criticisms will be raised against the libertarian position, and a sport-related example will be discussed.

One of the main criticisms against Nozick's (1974) brand of libertarianism is the premium he places on economic rights. By doing so, he restricts the notion of individual rights, which can include the right to decent education, health care, environment, living standard, and the like (Bowie & Simon, 1977). Further, Nozick does not provide an argument to claim economic rights supercede noneconomic rights. He merely presupposes the former are absolute, and this is an arbitrary move on his part. Moreover, in most of Nozick's transactions, he presumes that those involved are on an equal footing. In the real world, however, acquisitions and transfers often occur between parties who have different levels of power and wealth. Justified outcomes may still be unfair even though power and wealth are acquired legitimately (Beauchamp, 1991).

Another criticism against the libertarian view relates to the meaning of "original" acquisition. How can one possibly determine when and where such an acquisition took place? Wars fought over territory do not resolve this problem, and merely looking back through history leads to an unclear and unhelpful regress (Palmer, 1991). Another area that is vague is Nozick's (1974) proviso that ownership not worsen the situation of others below a baseline level. First, to suggest such a baseline logically means that some rights must be given up to support this "safety net." This then would undermine Nozick's absolute and firm stance on noninterference when it comes to individual liberty. Second, Nozick sometimes suggests that the only situation in which people might be worse off is one that leads to their death (Bowie & Simon, 1977). Other than that, ownership can extend to impoverish the lives of others, and again, this might be unfortunate, but not unjust. Many of us would not tolerate such a lack of concern for others and would find it difficult to claim this is just.

The above criticisms are sufficient to reveal that libertarianism contains some serious flaws and shortcomings. Nevertheless, the wide attention given to Nozick's (1974) work by way of criticism also suggests the importance of his ideas. By way of closing this subsection and in light of the above discussion, a sport-related example will be taken up.

Once again we will turn to Simon (1991), who discusses the distribution of basic benefits of sport. Unlike scarce benefits such as fame and fortune, basic benefits refer to goods available to all sport participants. Whereas scarce benefits are ex-

Benefits to Sports Participants

Fun

Health

Improved skills

Teamwork

Challenge

clusionary (not everyone can acquire fame and fortune), basic benefits are nonexclusionary (everyone has access and can acquire these goods). Given this distinction, Simon asks whether or not all persons have the same right to the basic benefits of sport. The latter issue centers the idea of positive rights and liberty.

Positive rights establish that people are obligated to provide the basic benefits of sport to those who wish to pursue and enjoy these goods. This obligation must be manifested in concrete actions, and it usually means some cost is involved, monetary or time or personal effort. So a positive right to participate in sport with opponents who supply challenges means that some people would be obligated to become opponents. Suppose the state were to guarantee the latter; then this would surely violate the liberty of those individuals designated as opponents. Libertarians at this point would argue that such interference is unjustified, and the redistribution of the basic benefits of sport, therefore, undermines individual liberty.

Simon (1991) objects to the libertarian critique on two fronts. First, even though one cannot claim a positive right to ensure opponents, there may be other positive rights claims that are justified. So, to maintain a decent standard of living, people may have right to basic education, including physical education where the benefits of sports are enjoyed. Thus, the rejection of one basic benefit of sport as a positive right does not mean that all such benefits need be rejected. Second, the libertarian insistence on noninterference when it comes to individual liberty is suspect. Because the libertarian does permit a protection agency to ensure personal liberty itself is maintained (the minimal state), then he or she acknowledges that some social support system is valuable. The latter is a positive rights claim that obligates citizens to support the protection agency. If this is the case, then perhaps other positive rights claims (like basic education), which create social obligations, also ensure individual liberty. Despite these criticisms, Simon admits that the libertarian critique of positive rights warns us about the intrusive nature of these claims and that entitlement to the basic benefits of sport is not a clear-cut issue.

Key Concepts

acquisition

anarchist's position

disregard for persons

economic versus noneconomic rights

liberty

minimal state entitlement

"original" acquisition

positive rights

rectification of goods

"safety net"

scarce and basic benefits of sport

theory of justice

transfer

> Libertarians hold that people can best serve their own interests when left alone—that is, without interference from others or the state.

The libertarian view of social justice presented above places a premium on individual freedom and autonomy. In the next subsection, justice from a utilitarian perspective will be examined. Because utilitarianism as an ethical theory was taken up earlier in this chapter, the following short discussion will focus on the justice themes of this view.

Utilitarian

It was earlier shown how acts of injustice could result from a utilitarian calculation in which the consequences of behavior are a foremost concern and decisions are made in order to achieve the greatest good for the greatest number. Criticisms of traditional, act and rule utilitarianism were raised because, in each version, situations could arise in which basic principles of justice were violated. For example, there could be instances in which one should lie, cheat, steal, or kill if one or more of these acts produce a greater level of general happiness. Moreover, if two courses of action lead to identical utilitarian consequences and one happens to involve cheating, there are no criteria to recommend one of these forms of behavior over the other. Finally, establishing rules that prohibit objectionable conduct, like lying, stealing, and cheating (because in general they lead to more harm), often requires the attachment of exceptions to such rules and, eventually, the creation of a quagmire of complicated rules.

These general criticisms may not directly reveal injustices related to the social distribution of benefits and burdens, the main topic of this section. Therefore, the remainder of this subsection will consider only utilitarianism and issues related to just distribution.

Some sense of equality is contained in the idea of distributive justice, yet for most utilitarians there is a greater emphasis on the interests of the community rather than on those of individuals. That is, society is overvalued whereas individuals are undervalued (Beauchamp, 1991). As a result, the distribution of benefits and burdens may result in unjust practices. Frankena (1973) writes,

> It still may be, however, that they [utilitarians] distribute the balance of good over evil produced in rather different ways; one action, practice, or rule may, for example, give all the good to a relatively small group of people without any merit on their part. . . while the other may spread the good more equally over a larger segment of the population. In this case, it seems to me that we should and would say that the former is unjust and wrong and the latter morally preferable. (p. 41)

If cases of unjust distribution can arise on a utilitarian calculation, then conflicts can arise between utility and justice (Raphael, 1981). It may also mean that utility alone is insufficient to determine the best way to distribute benefits and burdens, and so nonutilitarian principles of justice would have to be attached to a utilitarian approach. John Stuart Mill, a progenitor of utilitarianism, recognized this conflict between utility and justice and addressed the problem in no uncertain terms. Essentially, he claimed that justice itself is part of the principle of utility and everyone has a right to be treated justly (Beauchamp, 1991). When one considers making decisions about what to do by weighing the potential consequences of one's actions, one is in fact establishing the most just alternatives. Because the desires and wants of each person are treated equally in a utilitarian analysis, justice becomes a moral right of every person. Therefore, a society's ideas about justice are served by and are a part of a utilitarian account (Bowie & Simon, 1977).

Critics of this argument, which declares justice is dependent on utility, point out that it only holds in hypothetical situations in which equality between persons and a just distribution can be worked out. In the real world, however, a cost-benefit analysis could recommend actions or programs that in fact result in unbalanced distributions, such as a health care system that denies access to disadvantaged members of society (Beauchamp, 1991). Earlier and later rule utilitarians can at least respond by saying that short-term or one-time cost-benefit analyses may pose the preceding difficulties. If this is the case, then alternatives or modifications to rules that govern fair distribution of and access to programs and actions are needed. This means that in some versions of utilitarianism, egalitarian principles can be introduced as rules to ensure the widest and fairest possible distribution of some benefit (Frankena, 1973). The critic might say now that the value of equal distribution is right or just in itself and is not just a utility-maximizing factor, even if the former happens to result in the latter. In this way the utilitarian can always claim justice relies on utility, but the connection between equal distribution and utility-maximization is contingent, and so the utilitarian endorses this relationship on a relatively weak foundation.

To illustrate the latter point, suppose funds are available to improve the athletic locker-room facilities at a university. The funds may be used to greatly improve either the women or men's locker rooms or to moderately improve both. Suppose also that the men's facilities are larger than the women's and that they are used more extensively, thereby requiring more funds for improvement and upkeep. On a utilitarian calculus, there might be a strong case to channel the funds to renovate only the men's locker room and forego improving the women's facilities. Suppose, however, that a more equal distribution does indeed maximize utility so that the funds should be used to moderately improve both locker rooms. If the latter was decided, the main reason would not be because it is more just or fair or deserving for women to have comparable decent facilities; it just so happens that this pattern of distribution results in greater utility. For some, this kind of reasoning might not seem right because justice can and should be considered independently from utility. That is, some things are right or just in themselves.

> Utilitarianism is often the foundation for corporate and public policies because of its ability to remove feelings, intuitions, and hunches from moral considerations.

As stated previously, utilitarianism is a powerful ethical theory and is typically employed in the establishment of corporate and public policies. It is a rational approach for determining right and wrong, and it seeks to remove feelings, intuitions, and hunches from moral considerations (Rachels, 1986). On the other hand, utilitarianism does face a serious challenge from principles of justice that are accepted as strong foundations for creating a just society. For this reason, many contemporary moral philosophers accept some of the basic tenets of utilitarianism but attach other nonutilitarian principles to it.

Key Concepts

community versus individual interests

equal distribution and utility maximization

utility and justice

There is another prominent view of justice that differs radically from those considered above by suggesting that a form of socialism, or even communism, is the best type of social arrangement. Contained in this political idea is a theory of justice attributed to Karl Marx (1818-1885), whose thought dramatically influenced the course of world events in the 20th century.

Marxist

To understand a Marxist theory of justice, even in brief, requires a minimal comprehension of Marx's worldview. Therefore, this subsection will initially outline some general themes before treating specifically the topic of justice.

Like his predecessor Georg Wilhelm Frederich Hegel (1770-1831), Marx believed that human history progressed toward the realization of some greater good and overall improvement. Unlike Hegel, who viewed this progression as idealistic, Marx was a committed materialist concerned with actual, empirical facts. He held that change and advancement must occur in the real world and there were social scientific principles that governed the evolution of human societies (Perry, Chase, Jacob, Jacob, & Von Laue, 1989). The main laws that guided human affairs were connected to economic and technological means that structured and ordered people's lives. Therefore, in every age, material conditions created particular social and political arrangements. So, machine-powered factories spawned the Industrial Revolution, which dramatically altered the social lives of those who lived in growing cities. The limited modes of production in the Middle Ages resulted in the feudal system, in which peasants worked for the nobility under generally harsh and oppressive conditions. The efforts of all individuals were thus interconnected historically as products of their social environment (Palmer, 1991). Marx's scientific understanding of human societies then is based on what is known as *historical materialism*.

According to Marx (Marx & Engels, 1848/1948), human history also unfolds as a struggle. In most of this history, there has always been a small group, usually the wealthy and upper class, who controlled the means of production. Relationships like those of the master and slave, the lord and serf, the capitalist and laborer attest to the historical reality that economic power generally remained in the hands of the few. Those in power primarily served their own interests and they established the dominant ideas of the day, thus creating a certain reality for all members of society. Usually, this reality became altered when economic conditions changed or social stability was weakened, or both. For example, a Marxist would explain the abolishment of slavery in the United States, in part, because technological innovations and methods became more efficient than human labor, and political thought was divided. Because the interests and power of the ruling class differed from the majority working class, there has always been conflict between these groups. Marx hoped to see societies progress so that the majority's interests would be served in a classless social structure.

As Marx interpreted the social conditions of 19th-century Europe, he noted another important development. His critique of capitalism tried to demonstrate that the worker was no longer organically connected to that which he produced as he had been in previous eras. Most factories and industries operated more efficiently when labor was divided, and so the worker was compelled to engage in menial, piecemeal tasks. Ultimately, the laborer experienced and became estranged or alienated from the fruits of his labor and from himself (Marx & Engels 1848/1948; Matson, 1987). The worker was dehumanized, exploited, and by necessity had to sell his labor to the capitalist for subsistence wages under the poorest working conditions.

Marx saw a tremendous injustice under these conditions. He believed that human beings sought freedom to express their natural, creative, and productive selves and that capitalism stifled and perverted these pursuits (Melchert, 1991). He also predicted capitalism was doomed to failure as a matter of course as were earlier socio-economic structures. His ideas about how and what to replace capitalism with have left an indelible mark on the history of the 20th century. What is the just society that he envisioned?

The inevitable destruction of capitalism would be precipitated by two main events. There would be a wide polarization between a much smaller wealthy, ruling class and the vast majority of laborers. The majority would then become poorer, embittered, restless, and inevitably desperate to improve their condition. Once this occurred, the masses would instigate a revolution to overthrow the existing government and the capitalists, abolish private property, control the means of production for themselves, and create a new social order (Marx & Engel, 1848/1948). There would no longer be any classes; the state would no longer protect the wealthy, and there would be a fair distribution of goods and services. A Marxist theory of justice would then be introduced to establish a just society.

At least three main principles are part of this theory. First, the needs of people would be divided between genuine or true needs and false needs (Palmer, 1991). Genuine needs are based on the real nature of human beings as biological and social creatures. Food, shelter, clothing, education, health care, love, and creative needs are examples of true needs. False needs are artificial desires for luxury items, wants that set some people apart as privileged, or desires created whose main purpose is to earn profit. Clearly, a just state would ensure that true needs are fulfilled, whereas false needs are exposed and done away with. Second, all resources, methods of distribution, and forms of production would be publicly owned and democratically controlled. Finally, each worker would choose his or her profession or vocation based upon his or her desire and ability. Marx envisaged no specific social roles in the classless society. Each person could act upon her or his talents and creative aspirations because there would be no strict divisions of labor. Individual potential and needs would be identical to social, community needs. As Marx and Engels (1848/1948) put it, "In place of the old bourgeois society, with its classes and class antagonisms, we shall have an association, in which the free development of each is the condition for the free development of all" (p. 31).

The Three Principles of Marxism

1. Needs are separated into two categories, genuine and false.
2. All resources are publicly owned.
3. Each worker chooses a profession based on desire and ability.

Justice in a Marxist society amounts to a total restructuring of people's economic and social lives. The implications of a classless society would ensure a fair distribution of goods and services and of benefits and burdens. There are, however, a number of drawbacks to Marx's theory of justice. First, he paints a rather optimistic picture of human nature such that people are genuinely cooperative, not selfish and competitive (Palmer, 1991). The Marxist response to those who hold the latter view is that they conceive human beings only through alienated lenses because they live in alienated cultures. In many instances, however, human history and experience have shown people to be both cooperative and competitive, and there is no strong evidence to say our basic nature is captured by one or the other expression.

Second, one could question the distinction between true and false needs. When do genuine needs become exaggerated so as to declare them false? Who is to make this decision? Here, individual freedom and interests would be curtailed at the expense of community interests. For example, if one wanted to produce a more efficient, spacious automobile as a matter of need, the classless society might deem such car as a luxury. It would seem then that Marx's insistence that collective and personal interests become identical undermines individual autonomy. Personal preferences would be obliterated because they would actually be social preferences. This raises a related criticism: Why should the meaning of the good life, the just society, be predicated on working-class ideals? Do laborers know the real meaning of life any more than other groups of people? Is there such a meaning? These questions point to some specific difficulties with Marx's theory of justice (Palmer, 1991).

Finally, if Marx's economic and social principles are indeed scientific and contain predictive value, then few of his speculations have materialized. There have been numerous Marxist revolutions around the globe since the 19th century, and many occurred in unlikely countries resulting in oppressive regimes (Perry et al., 1989). In recent years, the collapse of most socialist and communist countries appears to be a triumph for Western capitalist, democracies. Many theorists and historians have tried to explain the so-called failed attempt of the Marxist social experiment. It would take us too far afield to discuss these explanations, but suffice it to say, human history has not ended, and there are certainly weaknesses in Western sociopolitical structures. Perhaps at another moment in history, under different conditions, and with certain modifications, some manifestation of Marx's theory of justice will occur.

This ends our exposition of various theories of justice. Each theory disclosed a number of distinct principles and assumptions about creating a fair means to distribute social benefits and burdens. Some theories were more radical than others were; some have had a profound influence on world affairs; and others have yet to be realized in practice. In a number of the above discussions, reference was made to individual rights. The latter will be the topic of the final section of this chapter, and it will be a relatively short section.

Key Concepts

class conflict

classless society

critique of Marxist justice

estrangement or alienation

destruction of capitalism

genuine and false needs

historical materialism

means of production

modes of production

public ownership

The Concept of Rights

The issue of rights is often central to ethical theories because rights place demands on others as obligations or as noninterference with people who declare rights. *Human rights, natural rights, liberty rights, inalienable rights* are part of the language of rights. Generally, rights guarantee certain freedoms or a particular way one is to be treated by others, an institution, or the state (Beauchamp, 1991). Rights also have a strong, but not necessary, connection to power and interests. If one claims a right to something, it can mean that one possesses a certain amount of power or one is securing a particular interest (e.g., having the right to vote). Some rights have no power or interest component attached to them. Native peoples may have rights and an interest to recover parcels of land, but because of past treaties, they have no power to do so.

For some, rights are viewed as entitlements. That is, the latter are rights to something and are held as claims against others (Beauchamp, 1991). For example, when one exercises one's right to privacy, one also claims that others not infringe on that right. Two types of entitlements are described by Bowie and Simon (1977) when they assert, "Legal rights are entitlements that are supportable on legal grounds, while moral rights are entitlements that are supportable on moral grounds" (p. 58).

> Though rights entitle people to something, they also
> set restrictions or limitations.

Many people reasonably understand the idea of rights as described above because it is part of our language and everyday reality. However, the subject of rights is a relatively new area in moral and political philosophy. Before the 17th century, people were obligated to the king, the lord, the Church, and the like, and rights were not a consideration in political thought. With the Enlightenment, and specifically, the American and French revolutions, rights became and have been a significant topic in moral and social philosophy. The philosophical debate surrounding rights is lengthy, difficult, and implicated in many particular issues. In the remainder of this section, we will only discuss the idea of obligations and then identify several kinds of rights to gain a basic, general understanding of rights.

Rights and Obligations

We have already seen in the subsection on deontological theories the important role duty plays in ethical considerations. Similarly, the notion of obligations has a special relationship to rights. As Wheelwright (1959) indicates, "The idea of a right is logically correlative with idea of specific duty, or obligation" (p. 223). For example, if one has a right to speak, then others have an obligation to allow one to speak. If one has a right to privacy, then the police have an obligation not to barge into one's home without justification. Because there is usually a logical connection between rights and obligations, propositions involving rights can be translated into obligation statements, and vice versa (Beauchamp, 1991). The previous examples then can be reversed to read the obligation clause first and then the rights clause. According to Urban (1930), there are at least three senses in which rights and obligations are related.

The first sense refers to legitimate claims one makes to a right that establishes a corresponding obligation on others. If one legally acquires a piece of land, then others are obligated to acknowledge this ownership and not challenge this possession. Here, there may be legal grounds that create both rights and obligations.

Another sense of rights and obligations focuses more so on the individual. Owning a tract of land does not necessarily mean that one can do anything at all on one's property. A right to ownership also means that one has an obligation to develop the property appropriately within the law and in consideration of others. If one wishes to build an addition to one's home, city ordinances and bylaws must be followed, and often neighbors must be notified and agree with the type of improvement. Rights, therefore, sometimes carry personal obligations in acknowledgment of the law and others.

Finally, although rights tend to imply obligations, some theorists argue the reverse is not always the case. This means that there may be types of obligations that cannot be translated into rights claims. Even though, morally speaking, one may be obligated to give charity, one cannot claim charity from others as a matter of right. Charity seems to be the kind of gesture based on a personal standard, and so the obligation established here is of a special type beyond strict moral guidelines. This has led some to distinguish between *perfect* and *imperfect obligations* (Beauchamp, 1991). Legal rights, for example, imply perfect obligations, whereas some moral rights imply imperfect obligations. One drawback with this distinction is the difficulty by which to determine each type of obligation. Still, the idea that some obligations cannot be characterized as rights claims is an important feature to keep in mind as we next examine several types of rights.

Key Concepts

entitlement

freedom and treatment by others

individual emphasis

legitimate claims

obligations not as rights

power and interests

rights and duties

Kinds of Rights

Because a number of different rights have been mentioned already, it would be useful to briefly identify and describe them. The classification of rights developed by Beauchamp (1991) will be the basis of this discussion because he provides the most extensive list of different rights. The first kind of right and the most easily recognizable is a *moral right*. These are rights claimed by individuals by virtue of their nature as moral beings (Urban, 1930). Moral rights are determined by a system of moral principles and theories. "Punishing" someone who violates a moral right may involve not legal sanctions, but perhaps shame and public censure. The right to an abortion versus the right to life debate is one glaring example of a rights issue with deep moral sentiments and "punishments."

Legal rights are determined by a system of laws. Although there is usually a close link between legal and moral rights, there need not be. Some laws guarantee or deny rights that are immoral in themselves (e.g., the system of laws under apartheid). Legal rights tend to be more definitive than moral rights because the former are established in writing, have been tested in the courts, and are historically related through precedent cases (Wheelwright, 1959). Legal rights are also embodied in the workings of the state to uphold, protect, and enforce these rights. Appeals to the state by individuals and groups can determine whether legal rights and their corresponding duties have been protected or violated. Under a system of law, punishments for breaking legal rights are generally more severe than the violation of moral rights. Because these two types of rights are often indistinguishable or the former is viewed as an extension of the latter, both legal and moral penalties for rights violations can be similar. The main point is that laws, decreed by the courts and the state, establish legal rights and they are linked, but not necessarily so, to moral rights.

Another kind of right emerges from documents like the U.S. Constitution or the Declaration of Independence, which declare certain rights as absolute. So the rights to life, liberty, and property are sometimes seen as inalienable or absolute rights that no countervailing conditions can supercede, but can the preceding rights or any others be deemed absolute? If the right to life were an absolute, then no wars would be justified, one could not kill in self-defense, and capital punishment would be inconceivable. Many special circumstances can be raised where so-called absolute rights are overruled on moral and legal grounds (Wheelwright, 1959). For this reason, *prima facie* rights perhaps better describe what we mean by rights like life, liberty, and property. That is, if there are competing demands or conditions when considering these rights, then the claim one actually makes is a *prima facie* right (Brandt, 1959). Only in the absence of any conflict is one able to claim an absolute right (but, again, the latter is extremely difficult to establish). For this reason, the state may interpret or amend basic rights to accommodate special conditions. *Prima facie* rights, therefore, are tentative because they are claimed until overridden by other competing claims.

The provisional nature of exercising rights sometimes leads to conceiving of rights as fundamental and derivative (Beauchamp, 1991). This distinction was suggested above when legal rights were described as extensions of moral rights. Urban (1930) accepts this approach because he sees both civil and political rights as extensions of moral rights. *Civil rights* would provide citizens protection to exercise two species of moral rights, physical rights (life, liberty, and property) as well as mental activity (freedom of thought, of religion). *Political rights* would provide the means for citizens to create favorable social conditions to exercise the preceding moral rights. Beauchamp (1991) adds to this discussion by indicating that some rights are originally created and others flow from them (e.g., the right to an adequate standard of living is original), whereas other rights refer to bodies that possess certain powers to create laws and policies (e.g., a state legislature). Many fundamental and derivative *rights* are determined by basic social needs. For example, health care, food, shelter, clothing, and other necessary items required for a decent standard of living are often criteria for determining which rights are fundamental and which are derivative. In many instances, the distinction between these rights helps to establish public policies and corrective methods when dealing with social programs.

Rights involved in the development of social policies and programs usually consider the final two categories of rights, known as positive and negative rights. *Positive rights* refer to claims so that receiving certain goods and services improve one's welfare, whereas *negative rights* refer to one's liberty such that others are not to interfere with one's liberty (Beauchamp, 1991). Because of the correlation between rights and obligations, a negative right simply means others are obligated to leave the rights bearer alone. Negative rights as noninterference rights are generally contained in various documents that set out to protect certain freedoms and liberties that people wish to exercise.

A positive right, however, means others are obligated to provide the rights bearer with some particular good or service. We have already seen some implications of positive rights for sport in the libertarian subsection in this chapter.

Beauchamp's Classification of Rights

Moral rights—claimed by virtue of human nature

Legal rights—determined by law

Prima facie rights—named absolute by an authoritative body

Civil rights—provide for the exercise of physical and mental freedom

Political rights—freedom to create favorable social conditions

Positive rights—intended to improve welfare

Negative rights—delineated by what cannot be done

The main question there was, if basic benefits of sport can be claimed as a positive right, is it reasonable for society to assume this burden? It was clear in that discussion that positive rights are generally more difficult to deal with. Both positive and negative rights then must be identified to know what sort of obligations these claims have against others.

This concludes not only our discussion of rights but also the lengthy exposition of major ethical theories. Each section, in this and the previous chapter, has tried to convey to the reader different and complicated ideas and themes within moral philosophy. Although the accounts provided here are by no means exhaustive, the reader has been exposed to some of the most prevalent ethical theories in contemporary mainstream philosophy. Two final subsections will close this chapter.

Key Concepts

fundamental and derivative rights

inalienable or absolute rights

legal rights

moral rights

positive and negative rights

prima facie rights

Pluralism and Selecting a Theory

Once individuals understand and appreciate the variety, limitations, and advantages of ethical theories, they must still confront the issue of choosing a theory or make ethical decisions that have different theoretical assumptions. This choice is not an easy one. Each of the theories and concepts presented in chapter 3 and here has particular flaws and weaknesses. How then is one to act according to any given theory?

The question of selecting an ethical theory is itself problematic. Does it mean that one is entirely committed to a specific theory or that a single theory must be implicated in every moral situation? To answer yes to these questions leads to a rigid, inflexible approach, and such a posture is likely unreasonable and impractical. In many instances, ethical conflicts do not permit the application of a solitary theory. These dilemmas often have numerous conditions attached to them, special exceptions, unclear motives, unpredictable outcomes, and a host of other extenuating circumstances. To suggest that a single theory can account for and deal with all contingencies surrounding a particular moral problem is likely asking for and expecting too much.

There is also a hidden and unfounded bias in trying to adhere to one ethical theory. Someone who lives by just one set of ethical precepts is sometimes described as on solid ground, unswerving, and deeply committed. In some cases, such devotion can lead to untenable and sometimes immoral acts (e.g., the strict deontologist who never lies and tells a known killer the whereabouts of a potential victim). The notion that no alternative points of view have merit and that one's own position is exclusive and ideal also seems to be unreasonable. For these reasons at least, some contemporary moral philosophers have advocated a kind of pluralism when it comes to choosing "a theory."

Moral pluralism asks that one develop and accept elements of several ethical theories. Commenting on this multidimensional approach, Beauchamp (1991) writes,

> The virtue of a philosophical pluralism is that it cheerfully acknowledges
> a wide variety of moral conflicts, recognizes the extraordinary range of
> disagreement in contemporary moral philosophy, and tolerates different

traditions without attempting to force them into an artificial unity. (p. 296)

Being committed to diversity and eclecticism may seem to some as a sign of weakness and uncertainty. To others, like the authors here, adhering to pluralism demonstrates strength, insight, and sensitivity.

Moral pluralism extracts and combines the best parts of various ethical principles, placing issues in perspective and encouraging critical thought.

Another way to understand pluralism involves the idea that numerous values are needed to realize the good life (Kekes, 1993). Values that are personally, socially, and morally praiseworthy should be somewhat coherent toward the fulfillment of the good. In this sense, what counts as a worthwhile value, the relationships between values, and the need for moral and amoral values are relevant issues. Pluralism both describes features of the good life and evaluates differing values toward the achievement of that life. It also acknowledges that there are conflicting values, yet the good life must steer a coherent course through such inevitable controversy through compromise and occasional loss. The giving up or alteration of values, however, is understood to be an acceptable dimension of pluralism in comparison with its positive attributes. Of these worthy characteristics, Kekes writes, "For the plurality of values enriches the possibilities for our living good lives, increases our freedom, motivates us to assert greater control over the direction of our lives, and enlarges the repertoire of conceptions of life that we may recognize as good" (p.12). Pluralism in general and moral pluralism in particular, therefore, offer the broadest conceptual framework by which to live good lives and judge ethical problems. The remainder of this section will outline two such pluralistic approaches.

Rachels (1986) presents a multifaceted moral theory by asking the question "What would a satisfactory moral theory be like?" He begins his answer by suggesting that such a moral theory should be without hubris, a kind of inflated or false pride. For too long, human beings have exercised their power and will over their environment, other creatures, and fellow beings in a morally superior manner. Even though we are rational creatures who can articulate reasons for our actions and be consistent in our conduct, we have not yet overcome serious disagreements, conflicts, injustices, and other difficulties. Rachels (1986) identifies three basic ideas to overcome hubris: (a) impartiality, (b) fair rules that serve everyone's interests, and (c) modest caring for others. He adds to these components the concept of responsible agency, which maintains that human beings are free to make choices and that treatment toward others should be returned in kind. When these elements are combined, the fundamental principle of morality without hubris is that "we ought to act so as to promote impartially the interests of everyone alike, except when individuals deserve particular responses as a result of their own past behavior" (Rachels, 1986, p. 143).

This formulation incorporates utilitarian and Kantian ideas. There are consequentialist considerations here, as well as the requirements to remain impartial and treat others as ends. To test his moral theory, Rachels (1986) turns to the area of justice and fairness. We have noted that utilitarianism can lead to injustice when it comes to punishment, and it can lead to treating people as means. Rachels' theory, therefore, takes care of these flaws by insisting on its Kantian dimensions of impartiality and respect for persons. Utilitarianism also finds it difficult to deal with the issue of desert. By focusing on the outcomes of certain actions and their overall social good, what people deserve is rarely an issue. On Rachels' account, however, personal agency, effort, and past actions can lead to justifiable unequal treatment. So, people should be promoted because they have worked hard, not because the promotion provides overall benefits for the company or natural endowments and abilities, like intelligence and physical appearance, should be rewarded (in the Rawlsian sense). In the area of fairness and justice then, morality without hubris is able to provide more plausible answers to concerns that single theories find problematic.

Rachels himself (1986) is the first to admit that his moral theory is a modest attempt to account for the nature and interests of human beings and the ways they confront and view moral issues. Still, this example of moral pluralism provides a satisfactory and sound approach when dealing with ethical problems. Zeigler (1984, 1990) is a leading sport and physical educator who also recommends a pluralistic ethical approach that sport managers and others ought to seriously consider.

In brief, under Zeigler's (1984) view, three major philosophical positions are brought together to create a step-by-step procedure for making ethical decisions. From Kant, Zeigler borrows the idea of universalizability to demonstrate that one's ethical judgments need to be consistent. To ensure that the consequences and outcomes of one's moral actions are considered, Zeigler turns to Mill and the two versions of utilitarianism (act and rule utilitarianism) addressed previously. Finally, ideas on intention, virtue, and voluntariness are appropriated from Aristotle to understand the nature of motivation and blameworthiness within moral behavior. It is Zeigler's (1990) contention then that all three positions must be applied when making ethical judgments, and he calls this procedure a "triple-play approach" (p. 276). Although Zeigler then superimposes the above steps on various legal arguments, for our purposes, it is sufficient to note that he adopts a variety of sources toward the formulation of moral decisions. Choosing ethical theories then is not an insurmountable task as long as one recognizes the strengths and weaknesses of one's selections, and one can apply them to concrete situations intelligently.

Key Concepts

eclecticism

moral pluralism

morality without hubris

pluralism and values

the "triple-play approach"

Summary

This chapter set out to introduce and explain two major ethical precepts, namely, theories of justice and the concept of rights, and it also discussed the notions of pluralism and choosing an ethical theory. In the first instance, four theories of distributive justice were examined. The egalitarian view was concerned with the issue of equality. One important version of this theory introduced by Rawls was explained at length. His method of taking an original position and operating behind a veil of ignorance tried to ensure people were treated equally and given equal opportunities and that the disadvantaged were helped. The libertarian perspective insisted that justice require little or no interference in the people's affairs. People are entitled to exercise their liberty unencumbered, and if inequalities emerge, this is unfortunate, but not unjust. A utilitarian approach is often employed in justifying social programs by calculating both the costs and benefits and the overall good such programs provide. Finally, a Marxist view of justice explained that people have historically been engaged in a class and economic struggle. Consequently, laborers have been alienated from their work and themselves, and the only way they can overcome their plight is to engage in a social and political revolution and create a classless society where their creative selves can flourish.

The second theoretical section discussed the idea of rights. After defining rights, the special relationship between rights and obligations was considered. The section closed by briefly describing several different types of rights. It was shown how the notion of rights operates on a number of levels and in a variety of circumstances.

The chapter ended with a short comment on selecting a theory. After a brief critique of the selection process, moral pluralism was offered as a coherent and more complete approach toward choosing "a theory." Because many of the theories and ideas discussed in this chapter and the previous one will be referred to in Part III of this text, the reader will have more opportunities to learn how the above principles apply in concrete situations.

Questions for Consideration

1. Describe Rawls's "original position" and "veil of ignorance" expressions and explain how his theory is an egalitarian one.

2. How does Nozick's minimal state compare with Marx's classless state?

3. Why might utilitarian reasons not convey a sense of justice when distributing benefits?

4. For each type of right described in the section on rights, show how obligations are related in each case.

5. What is meant by moral pluralism? Describe how this notion relates to the selection of an ethical theory when faced with an ethical problem.

PART II:
PERSONAL AND PROFESSIONAL ETHICS

Chapter Five

Personal Ethics—
Rights and Responsibilities

Chapter Objectives

• To understand responsibility for actions by those associated with sport, namely the manager in all capacities as well as the consumers of sport, including the fans and participants

• To establish an understanding of the concepts of regard and respect for all associated with sport

• To understand the need to perpetuate the ethic of 'fair play' in all aspects of sport and in conjunction with constitutive and proscriptive rules

• To recognize professional obligations of the sport manager and be able to apply ethical principles regarding responsibility of all those involved in sport

Who is responsible for ethical and unethical behavior in sport? **Everyone is responsible**. Ethics is not optional, a condition that thus places the responsibility on all those associated with the sport industry, including all spectators and fans. Sometimes it is difficult to separate the responsibilities of the players, fans, media personnel, coach, sport manager, sport director, sport businesses, and so forth. Although each individual or organization contributes something different to the sport setting, the moral expectations of each situation should be the same in terms of professional and ethical behavior. The examples presented here and subsequent ethical expectations for each are not restricted to only one specific role. The reader should pay particular attention to the sharing of responsibilities for fair play and ethical behavior in the sport setting.

Terms of Responsibility

Social responsibility is the legal and moral responsibility we have to ourselves and others.

Corporate social responsibility is directly related to the social contract that exists between the business of sport and society.

The *social contract* refers to the obligations, duties, and relationships between organizations (or institutions) and people that affect social welfare.

Business ethics mandates that individuals or organizations act in accordance with the rules of moral philosophy.

In their research, Bredemeier & Shields (1995) point out that character development and fair play (i.e., sportsmanship) have served as the desired outcomes of sport programs at all levels. At least this has been the case in the early stages of learning about sport competition such as in physical education classes or youth sport programs. On the other hand, some college and university sport programs, and professional sport in particular, have been challenged to uphold the "good sportsmanship" and positive character development model. These behaviors have become an ethical challenge for players, fans, and sport managers, thus leaving the consumers of sport with models of behavior that are not acceptable in our society. Violent acts in sport as well as violations of conference and NCAA rules, other forms of cheating, acts of character defamation, and criminal actions seem to be at their peak, at least in professional sport. What is tremendously bothersome is that the individuals who are committing unethical acts and those who allow such acts to occur may or may not be aware of the harmful effects of their actions and are not disciplined to an extent equal to the oppressive nature and violence of their actions. All too often, acts of violence in a sport or unethical behavior on the part of the coach or spectators is dismissed as merely a part of the game. Thus, such actions take the form of needed intimidation to establish dominance or strategy and tactics and become acceptable.

It is not unusual for us to witness either in live action while in attendance at a sporting event or watching a televised version, a multitude of rule violations that are actually blatant acts of violence. These occur in professional ice hockey and football primarily, but not exclusively. The pseudo-sports of wrestling, roller derby, and "tough-man" contests, although not actually considered within the definition of true sport because their outcomes are predetermined, but passed off by the media as sport, have as a component the "acting out" of violent acts in the name of real sport competition. It is for these reasons that we have sought out sports as the primary activities for learning these behaviors. Counteracting such behaviors is difficult, but not impossible. Returning sport to its positive mode of character development and fair play need to be our goal. According to Butler (2000), "competitive sports is neither inherently positive nor negative in terms of character development. Depending on how competitive sports programs are conducted, they can either teach students to lie, cheat, and steal, or they can promote positive behaviors" (p. 32). This statement then becomes a challenge to all of us in sport management. How will we each proceed? Will we accept the obligation to be responsible for our actions, to be committed to fair play, and to follow such a commitment, no matter what sport management position we hold?

Commercialization has been blamed for much of the unethical behavior on the part of those associated with sport, including the consumer. It may not be the commercialization that is bad, but rather how the decisions are made that affect the promotions and resulting revenues. In other words, once the results of commercialization are considered to be more important than the individuals (athletes) involved in the sport, then our moral values are subsequently challenged (Lumpkin, Stoll, & Beller, 1999). The concepts of massification and commodification as discussed in the previous chapters must be used here as a foundation for understanding the degrees and importance of competition and success (winning) in a capitalist society.

Rules in Sport Competition

Using the examples presented by the categories of constitutive rules, proscriptive rules and sportsmanship (fair play) rules in sport competition will give insights into what may be considered control measures for restricting the behaviors of players, coaches and spectators. *Constitutive rules* are legislated by a sport-governing body (specific sport organizations and such groups as the AAU, NCAA, NAIA) and address those rules that apply to how the game should be played. Such rules were developed in an effort to equalize competition, regulate the numbers of players and length of the game, and determine eligibility of players. These rules also indicate what a player may and may not do, such as degrees of contact, place and positions on the field, and holding. Obviously, the actions are specific to the game being played. Violations of such rules result in a punishment of sorts (e.g., a foul, violation, advantage to the other team, or disqualification). Eligibility also falls under constitutive rules in that the academic status, recruiting, and financial aid, for example, are regulated by the particular sports organization.

For Reflection . . .

Can you imagine a team turning back a victory on a goal which was scored by a breach of ethics—a rule. The team said they just did not want to win that way and a rematch is subsequently rescheduled. In another instance, a professional tennis player calls a let against himself in an effort to maintain the rules. Is using your own judgment in making calls during a competition acceptable to your coach, teammates and opponents?

Proscriptive rules were designed to eliminate violence at all levels of sport. In an effort to keep players from seriously injuring other players, these rules stipulate that the body and equipment may not be used as weapons against opponents. The control of physically violent acts in sport is mandatory. If some of the same violent actions that take place in sport took place in public realms outside of sport, the individuals would be arrested, fined, and/or imprisoned for assault, intent to injure, or even kill the other person. Thus, by imposing rules and the punishments that coincide with the violations of such rules, it is hoped that the violent acts will lessen.

Rules of sportsmanship (fair play), are associated with maintaining the spirit and letter of the rules. The behavior of each participant determines the inherent quality of the game. As participants, we establish honor as individuals by upholding the rules out of regard and respect for ourselves and the welfare of our teammates and opponents. These rules, which were developed to prevent violent behavior and all other ethically questionable behavior, should be considered within rules of sportsmanship and fair play (Lumpkin et al., 1999).

Gough (1997) noted that "the greatest opportunities for sportsmanlike conduct arise where there are the greatest opportunities for unsportsmanlike conduct" (p. 9). This statement offers each of us a challenge to self-check and to reflect on our current behaviors and future actions as a sport manager or sport participant.

In his article "Fair Play: Respect for All," Butler (2000) noted that according to the Canadian Commission for Fair Play, "fair play is developed by demonstrating 'respect' toward all individuals, regardless of their role, at all times in the competitive sports environment" (p. 32). Fair play is further defined as a way of behaving that emanates from self-respect and includes the following:

1. honesty, straightforwardness, and a firm and dignified attitude when others do not play fairly;

2. respect for team members;

3. respect for opponents, whether they are winning or losing, stemming from an awareness that an opponent is a necessary partner in sport, to whom one is bound by companionship in sport; and

4. respect for the officials, which is displayed through positive efforts to cooperate with them at all times. (Butler, 2000, p. 32)

In Brief . . .

Ethics for the sport manager, sport participants, and spectators are not optional

Constitutive rules guide the specific play of the game.

Proscriptive rules prohibit actions which intentionally harm another player.

Sportsmanship rules refer to the player being honor bound to follow the spirit and letter of the rules.

Fair play constitutes respect for all individuals regardless of their role in the competitive sports environment.

While there are numerous situations and individuals with whom the sport manager must interact, only a few are noted here such as other sport managers, athletic directors, athletes, coaches, media personnel, and spectators and fans. Using these positions as examples, one can undertake the task of analyzing the ethical responsibilities associated with each.

The Sport Manager

Being responsible for one's intentional personal and professional actions and behaviors as a manager within the context of sport requires personal reflection and exploration from the ethical perspectives presented. Ross (1989) pointed out that responsibility refers to a general project or task for which an individual is accountable or answerable. According to Becker (1973), the concept of responsibility "is the notion expressed to explain the concept of agency that is invoked for the attribution of praise or blame, the assignment of obligations and duties, and the actual sanctioning associated with the practice of holding people responsible" (p. 128). The social institution of sport and the individuals who serve as managers of such programs are certainly not exempt from being responsible, as has been indicated in this text.

Constitutive rules guide the specific play of the game.

Proscriptive rules prohibit intentionally harmful actions.

Sportsmanship rules bind the player to the spirit and letter of the rules.

Fair play constitutes respect for all individuals in the competitive sports environment.

As questions of moral behavior are raised in the business setting, it is important that corporations and especially sport businesses be thought of as social enterprises, the existence and decisions of which are justified insofar as they serve public or social purposes (Dahl, 1975). Dahl further explained that the corporation cannot be considered only as a profit-making enterprise, "We the citizens give them special rights, powers, and privileges, protection, and benefits on the understanding that their activities will fulfill purposes" (pp. 18-19). This indicates that there is a contractual relationship between business and society and that the nature of the contract is explicit. Bowie and Duska (1990) explain that "the corporation must not only benefit those who create it; it must benefit those who permit it (namely, society as a whole)" (p. 113).

Applying ethical principles regarding the responsibility and behavior of all those involved in sport including players, coaches, and spectators, Eitzen (1988) introduces ethical principles that represent the ideals of sport and our professional obligations to the institution of sport and those who participate. These principles include

1. Athletes must be considered ends and not means.

2. Competition must be fair.

3. Participation, leadership, resources, and rewards must be based on achievements rather than on ascribed characteristics.

4. The activity must provide for the relative safety of the participants. (pp. 17-30)

Acknowledging and protecting the rights of others are key factors within ethical behaviors. It is the right of the athlete to be treated fairly and with respect and dignity by all those involved with the sport program. In the spirit of fair play, opponents should not resort to willful injury or other means of intimidation. The rules of the game, coaching, and equipment should provide for the welfare of those participating. The perception exists that the concepts of coercion and social control of athletes reign high in many American university NCAA Division IA athletic programs, due to the emphasis on success and winning. Sport administrators must be certain that the philosophy of their programs is consistent with ensuring the rights of those involved.

The corporation must benefit those who create it and permit it—that is, all of society. This responsibility is defined by an explicit contractual relationship between businesses and society.

Fair competition in sport incorporates the involvement of physical prowess that necessitates that the contestants not take part in cheating or artificially enhancing their performance in order to give a team or an individual an unfair advantage. Actions that violate the spirit of the sport are considered unethical.

Equal opportunity and equal access to sport must be ensured by those sport managers who deal with this setting. The participants of sport should be determined by ability and motivation rather than by the discriminatory factors of gender, race, ethnicity, sexual orientation, social class or disability.

The Athletic Director

The athletic administrator carries the responsibility for ensuring that the athletic programs are philosophically sound, academically founded, financially solid, and ethically managed. This responsibility includes personnel, resources, facilities, development, and all athletic programs that come under the athletic director's purview.

In Brief . . .

Responsibility refers to a general project or task for which an individual is accountable or answerable.

A contractual relationship exists between businesses and society and the nature of the contract is explicit.

The corporation must benefit those who create and those who permit it—society as a whole.

Acknowledging and protecting the rights of others are key factors in ethical behavior.

Areas of ethical behavior to which the sport administrator must pay particular attention include

1. promoting equal opportunity in major and minor sports for girls/boys, women/men in regard to meeting the needs, interests, and abilities of students, practice and competitive facilities, equipment, travel and per diem, recruitment, coaching, and financial assistance based on athletic ability (grants-in-aid);

2. scheduling teams that do not create a mismatch;

3. hiring coaches on criteria other than solely win-loss records;

4. regarding the "win-at-all-costs" philosophy as not acceptable behavior;

5. banning team physicians and athletic trainers associated with the care of the athlete from administering painkilling drugs to players so that they may continue to play when injured; and

6. banning athletic trainers or others responsible for the care of the athlete from dispensing performance-enhancing drugs.

Protection of the players is an utmost consideration by athletic coaches, trainers, and administrators. Not only must the health and safety of athletes be a consideration, but it must also be ensured that athletes neither act nor be coached in ways that have as the intent to harm an opponent or teammate. Still another question open for ethical debate concerns those sports in which the intent is to injure the opponent (e.g., boxing) or sports that encourage such conduct in which the intent is to injure the opponent (e.g., fighting in ice hockey).

Because the rules of sport provide an equal base for all who participate, these rules are considered binding to all, but ethical standards or practices are advanced, indicating how individuals ought to behave rather than how they actually do behave. Unethical practices do occur and are considered to be widespread. Therefore, if everyone or every team takes part in unethical practices, are such practices justified? Although illegal recruiting practices, transcript tampering, and anabolic steroid use, for example, do occur, these instances still deviate from the intended contest and thus violate the spirit of the rules. The gaining of a competitive edge in the ways noted are violations of the rules, not strategies of the game. Players are no longer on an equal footing in these instances and are no longer striving together in context. Rather, they are engaging in unethical behavior. Such conduct also undermines the integrity of the sport in general.

The Athlete

Once again, the responsibility for all ethical decisions and practices is shared among those who are associated with sport and physical activity. *Sportsmanship* (the term) or *fair play* (the concept) are commonly associated with ethical behavior in sport. It is concerned with both the written as well as unwritten rules of competition. The definitions of these terms are not associated only with the athlete. Fair play and sportsmanship include spectators, opponents, coaches, athletic directors, and everyone else associated with any sport setting. Sportsmanship or fair play ensures that the play will be fair, safe, and within the rules. People are all too familiar with the numerous violations of what is termed "unsportsmanlike conduct" in the forms of unnecessary roughness, placing the opponent at an unfair disadvantage not within the rules, and general unruly behavior.

Although aggression is to be controlled through the rules of the game, its encouragement by coaches, administrators, and trainers alike must be restrained to avoid violent outbreaks. The violence that may occur in sport as a result of coaching techniques, fan encouragement, or reactions within the game is condoned within the contest, and what is literally illegal in American society is difficult to discern. The violence and brutality of boxing and ice hockey are legitimized within the boundaries of the ring and the ice. Certain actions outside these realms are condoned by neither society nor the legal system.

Normative cheating is an illegal act that is accepted as part of the game and therefore ignored or punished minimally. *Deviant* cheating is an illegal act that is unaccepted.

Eitzen (1981) identified two forms of cheating in sport, namely, normative and deviant. *Normative* cheating includes illegal acts that are accepted as part of the game. These actions either are ignored or receive minimal penalties. *Deviant* cheating, on the other hand, is an illegal act that is not accepted. Drugging a race-horse, tampering with equipment, and accepting bribes are examples of deviant cheating. The resulting punishment is greater for these actions. Although these are grave offenses, Eitzen (1981) expresses a concern for normative cheating and how it violates ethical principles, but is still accepted. He and others offer the following examples of normative cheating:

1. intentional fouls in all sports (In basketball, the intentional foul at the end of the game in order to create an opportunity to obtain the ball is currently considered a strategic move, but a foul with the intent to injure a player is not acceptable);

2. intentional pass interference in football;

3. basketball players pretending to be fouled;

4. basketball players coached to bump the lower half of a shooter's body because it is assumed that referees are more likely to be watching the ball and upper half of the shooter's body;

5. offensive linemen in football coached to use special but illegal techniques to hold or trip the opponent without detection;

6. use of any loopholes in the rules to take unfair advantage of opponents;

7. wetting the nets in basketball to prevent the fast break;

8. "doctoring" the home field in baseball by digging up or watering the base paths or putting sand in the takeoff areas (A fast team can be slowed down by these techniques.);

9. application of a substance to the baseball by pitchers;

10. "corking" the baseball bat (The bat is hollowed out and the wood replaced with various substances to make it more powerful; Bowyer, 1982, pp. 308-309); and

11. Curving the blades of ice hockey sticks beyond the legal limits to make them more effective (Axthelm, 1983; Bowyer, 1982; Ostrow, 1985).

The normative form of cheating exists within sports as well. In football, ice hockey, and basketball (which is supposed to be a noncontact sport), violent play occurs, but usually no penalty is assessed. It seems that in these sports, such actions are socially rewarded, and the intimidating, hitting, and gang-tackling are part of the strategy. Crowd-pleasing violence in the form of fights is also a tactic condoned by those coaching, playing, and marketing sports. Sport has thus become a spectacle for entertainment purposes as opposed to true competition and fair play. Some individuals feel sport is a rather boring contest without the added violent displays.

Key Concepts

crowd-pleasing violence

deviant cheating

normative cheating

The Coach

The coach is a moral agent, but all too often the ethical behavior of coaches is questioned. In their quest for successful teams and the benefits and rewards associated with winning, some coaches violate recruitment and eligibility rules and use violent motivational techniques. The basketball coach may sometimes taunt the referee so that he or she will call a technical on the coach in order to motivate the team. Although this is a strategy of coaching, it is nonetheless a violation of the rules.

Intimidation used by coaches in order to motivate the player and elicit the athlete's best ability may be considered a moral issue if the action is intentional and constant. Intentional intimidation by coaches must be explored as an area of ethical concern. Numerous accounts of intimidation by coaches have been reported by athletes during practices and games. These include, but are not limited to, angry yelling at the athlete, cursing the player(s), throwing objects (sometimes at the athlete), pushing or hitting the player, and grabbing a face mask or jersey.

Sexual harassment by coaches is a serious moral issue noted by male and female athletes alike at all levels of sport participation. Such incidents are unethical, intimidating in nature, and play on the power relationships established with players by coaches. The reporting of such actions by the players is necessary to protect the welfare of the athlete. Steps should be taken by athletic administrators at all levels to educate coaches and athletes about sexual harassment and the procedures for reporting cases.

Unethical Coaching Behavior to Consider

1. Intimidating athletes with physical or verbal abuse
2. Treating athletes in a dehumanizing manner
3. Encouraging the use of performance-enhancing drugs
4. Encouraging cheating in any form on the part of the athlete
5. Neglecting the educational goals of athletic programs
6. Not reporting violations by coaching peers
7. Not self-reporting violations to the NCAA
8. Intimidating and not respecting officials, umpires, referees
9. Sexually harassing athletes

Coakley recommended to the United States Olympic Committee Coaching Symposium that a coaches' code of conduct be developed (cited in Nielsen, 1994). He indicated that the highest priority for a coach is establishing relationships with athletes that can assist the athlete in positive ways. Initially, coaches must establish expectations for what they consider to be appropriate conduct for the athletes and personnel in their charge. By establishing such expectations, coaches will have to balance the external expectations or those outside influences, which are so great, with their own in order to be able to develop a code of ethics.

Coakley also identified those barriers or contradictions that hinder the development of a code of ethics for the coach. First of all, the issues associated with ethics are sensitive ones and are difficult to approach. Then, too, there are many contradictory aspects to this area. Sport is often seen through various sets of moral lenses different from those used for other situations in society. Much more is permitted to occur in sport than is allowable elsewhere in society. For example, some coaches are able to get away with physically and psychologically abusing players. However, if the same type of maltreatment occurs in the classroom or other workplaces, such action is unacceptable and may lead to very different consequences (Nielsen, 1994).

The Media

All forms of the media permeate human culture. We are constantly bombarded with information from newspapers, movies, video games, the Internet, television, and billboards, for example. Everything we are exposed to from media images helps to form our values and influence our thoughts about our world and how we think about society locally, nationally, and globally. According to Coakley (2001), "Our lives and our social worlds are clearly informed by media content, and if the media didn't exist, our lives would be different" (p. 351). The print media include newspapers, magazines, books, catalogues, trading cards, and programs from sporting events, for example. In addition, billboards, bumper stickers, and advertisements outside of the standard newspaper or magazine are also included among print media. Electronic media include television, radio, film, video games, the Internet, and any publications generated by computers. Also included in electronic media are any messages we receive through audio and video transmissions.

Together, such media provide information, interpretation, and entertainment. It is important to keep in mind that the images we receive are selected and, in the case of specific entertainment, skewed. The content we ultimately see, hear, or read is always filtered or edited and re-presented by those in control of media outlets (e.g., producers, program directors, editors, writers, sponsors, commentators, and Internet providers). These individuals provide us with information, entertainment, and interpretation based on their focus on any one or combination of the following goals: (a) making profits, (b) shaping values, (c) providing a public service, (d) guiding their own reputations, and e) expressing themselves technically, artistically, and personally. Therefore, ethics again becomes a question of how individuals carry out such goals and with what intent. Because the media are subject to power relations among individuals and corporations, the emphasis placed on each of the goals may be different given the situation. Nonetheless, the dominant ideologies in society as a whole influence the foci of the media and the values of a given situation (Coakley, 2001).

Many place blame on the media for unethical behavior regarding sport. The glorification of violence in sport is often used to promote events. Some children choose the individuals at the heart of this type of action as role models. As children observe and act out their hero's violent actions, they intentionally or unintentionally injure or even kill their siblings and friends. The introduction of the Jumbotron® and televisions in the stadiums and arenas has allowed us to revisit previous plays and focus our attention on specific action. Slow motion and continuous viewing of plays that are particularly violent are considered to create a more violent response from fans (Eitzen, 1988).

The ethical role of the media with regard to the promotion and reinforcement of negative stereotypes regarding racial minorities and women raises question. Misrepresentation or the lack of representation of women in sport magazines is abundant, resulting in the primary focus on female athletes that emphasizes their physical appearance, dress, makeup, jewelry, and husband and family, rather than their athletic skills and abilities (Eastman & Billings, 1999; Weiler & Higgs, 1999). Not only has language or terminology become an important issue in the perpetuation of stereotypes regarding gender and the media, but the concepts of femininity and masculinity and how they are interpreted, socially constructed, and perpetuated also are called into question. It is not uncommon to find sexist language and demeaning comments made in the media when references are made to girls and women in sport. For example, "she plays like a man," or "for a girl in this sport, she is attractive." During broadcasts of the recent Winter Olympics in Salt Lake City, the events in which males participated were referred to as men's events, whereas distinctions were made in events in which females participated. For example, commentators referred to women's bobsled, but ladies' figure skating, and often, the female participants were referred to as girls by those covering the events. The male competitors were never referred to as boys, nor were the male figure skaters referred to as gentlemen. The U.S. Women's World Cup Soccer Champions "were described as the '(middle-class, white) girls next door' and 'babe city' " (Coakley, 2001, p. 370). Although such references may not appear to be an issue, this language perpetuates demeaning, unequal treatment of women. As a result, questions arise regarding the ethical coverage of women in sport.

Advertising receives much criticism from an ethical standpoint. The use of sexual images of females in advertising sporting equipment, clothing, and events (in addition to the swimsuit issue of *Sports Illustrated)* invites ethical questioning. As the media's function of promoting and perpetuating values in society is taken into consideration, the objectification and sexualization of women's bodies for the purpose of advertising becomes a legitimate question. The mere claim that "sex sells" may be insufficient to justify this particular issue.

More women's sports are televised than ever before, but only those that emphasize grace, balance, or aesthetics. By contrast, male sports on TV emphasize bulk, height, and strength.

The coverage of women's sports in televised media has increased throughout the 1990s, but such coverage is still only around 15% of all television sports programming. This coverage, however, has been limited to those sports emphasizing grace, balance, and aesthetics or those attributes consistent with traditional gender ideology and images of femininity (Duncan & Messner, 1998; Jones, Murrell, & Jackson, 1999). Men's sporting events that are covered primarily "emphasize bulk, height, physical strength, and the use of physical force and intimidation to dominate opponents—all qualities consistent with traditional images of masculinity," according to Coakley (2001, p. 371).

Although the patterns of media representation of race and ethnicity in sports have not been as clearly defined as they have been for gender, the media also influences society and how we make sense of race and racial stereotyping. In more recent years, the racial stereotyping of athletes in the media coverage has somewhat diminished, but has not totally subsided. Media representations of blacks in the United States appear to be more sensitive to the numerous racial and cultural diversity issues. However, Hawkins (1998) observed that the representations of black men in newspapers and television coverage are primarily in stories and programs related to sports, entertainment, and crime. The tendency to depict black men in particular as fearsome, angry, and potentially violent individuals still permeates some media outlets. In addition, disproportionate numbers of stories regarding the theme of "poor black athlete who makes good" seem to consistently appear in the print media as well as focus on that individual's material possessions in comparison to those of white athletes. According to Dufur's "Race logic and 'being like Mike': Representations of athletes in advertising, 1985-1994," as cited in Coakley (2001):

> Research is needed on this issue, but there is a chance that more white people perceive individual black male athletes presented as fearsome, angry, and potentially violent as representative of all black men than perceive fearsome, angry and potentially violent white male athletes as representative of all white men. (p. 374)

Race logic is the assumption that one race, (i.e., whites) are superior to other races. How the media interpret and report particular stories can either support or reject the race logic and stereotyping that is used by some individuals in our society. A commentator or journalist may refer to the physical capabilities of the black athlete in deference to mental capabilities. These and other racist beliefs are the result of race logic and the general stereotyping that has occurred in our society. Coakley (2001) further pointed out that whiteness, unlike blackness, does not become an issue when white males are depicted as violent or associated with violent crimes. At the same time, journalists must be careful to avoid the concept that our society is free of racial discrimination because of the representation of blacks in sport.

Ethnicity poses similar issues within the media representation of athletes of Asian, Native American, and Hispanic descent as well as other cultures. As with the black athlete, stereotypes regarding ethnicity and nationality are often referred to by journalists and associated with the individual's success or failure in sport. The Asian athlete may be descsribed as intelligent, self-disciplined, and machinelike, indicating that their cognitive skills are superior, whereas Latinos have been described as emotional, moody, and hot-tempered. It is critical that media representatives learn about ethnicity, ethnic relations, and the actual cultures, histories, characteristics, and social experiences of different people rather than rely on unsubstantiated stereotypes based in race logic. The relationship of these issues with ethics again points to the responsibilities that media personnel have to the general public and to the true representation of those individuals about whom they are reporting (Coakley, 2001).

Another area very much associated with the media, but often overlooked because it is tied to the marketing of sporting events, is the concept of mascots and who they represent. Although mascots for sport teams may have been chosen to depict aggressive, warlike themes, the groups who are represented (usually Native Americans) are actually demeaned. Mascots may have been chosen to honor individuals, yet the interpretations used to depict groups of people are manifested in racist caricatures (Cleveland Indians), racist names (Redskins), actions (tomahawk chop), ceremonial dances, costumes, and chants (not authentic, choreographed, and considered to be mocking Native Americans), and warlike music to encourage a crowd (not authentic and produced by "Hollywood" for scenes in movies) that degrade individuals rather than respect and honor them. The video *In Whose Honor* brings to light these issues and tells the story of Charlene Teeters, a Native American graduate student at the University of Illinois. Ms. Teeters was raising her children in Native American traditions and ceremonies, but upon taking them to a basketball game and encountering Chief Illiniwek, a "made-up" Indian chief, she and her children were horrified and considered the mascot as demeaning and dishonoring her ethnicity, culture, and traditions. Sport and our media representations of what sport represents in our culture must be considered and expressed with regard and responsibility for everyone.

Gambling in sport is another area rich with unethical motives and practices, yet it has a long history and association with sports. The media have been accused of legitimizing gambling in sports because such media report point spreads, information, and advertising, all of which make gambling more accessible. In those states where gambling is illegal, the media would be supporting this activity through providing such information. Therefore, the corruption of sport is thought to occur to some degree, because of the practice of gambling and its relation to the media.

Key Concepts

ethnicity

mascots

objectification

sexualization

stereotyping

The Spectator/Fan

The individual as a sports spectator or fan also has a responsibility for ethical behavior during sport contests. Sportsmanship applies to all individuals associated with the contest, not just players. During certain sport events, team sports in particular (e.g., football, baseball, basketball, ice hockey, softball, soccer), as spectators, we are able to yell, scream, and cheer in an effort to give support to our team(s) or to express our feelings to umpires and referees. Such behavior is, in fact, encouraged to motivate the players. However, in other sports such as golf and tennis a more controlled demeanor is required of the spectators so that the competitors may concentrate on their performance without interference or distractions by those observing. The history of these and some other sports, imbedded in the concept of "genteel" games in which gentlemen participated, is perpetuated, and the rules of sportsmanship are honored and considered sacred. Thus, fan reactions and responses are contained. In these instances, cheering and applauding are allowed only at specific times, generally after a point is scored an advantage is obtained by a player, or in the case of an excellent play worthy of praise. Of course, the differences noted here are also those differences regarding the nature of contact and noncontact sports.

The publicized violent behaviors by spectators at sporting events have made our society more aware of violence at all levels of sport. Players as well as coaches and umpires have even been the victims of violent crowd behaviors. In some contests, these individuals are escorted off the field or court by police officers and other personnel who offer protection. Parents of youth sport participants have attacked each other at games and practices, resulting in injury and death. As well, there have reported incidences at youth sport events of game officials' being violently attacked.

Crowd violence at sporting events has taken several forms. One is centered on the *contest* itself, in which intense rivalries heighten fan spirits, creating antagonistic situations among fans from opposing teams. The intensity of the game is much higher when what is at stake is considered, such as a championship, for example. If a crowd perceives that the referees or officials influenced the outcome of a game by unfair calls, they too are targets for violence. Another factor that may contribute to violence associated with the game itself is how the spectators perceive the actions of the players. Smith (1983) noted that if spectators perceive the actions on the field as violent, they are more likely to take part in violent acts either during or following games. The promotion of a particular game or sport event is also a factor that may create a violent situation. The responsibility now extends to the promoters and media personnel and how they choose to market the sporting events.

A second form of violence is imbedded in the *social and political issues* within a community, state, or nation. History, racism, ethnic oppression, unemployment, and social class issues are but a few examples. Because sport is considered a mirror of society, each of the issues that occur in our society is also present in sport. Although sport as entertainment may for a moment take our minds off social issues, it also calls attention to such oppression. For example, at one extreme, ticket prices for sporting events are so high that an average family cannot attend the event whereas at the other extreme, some individuals are enjoying the luxury of viewing the game from corporate boxes. This, among other inequities, creates a vivid distinction and area for tensions. As Coakley (2001) noted, "When tension and conflict are intense and widespread in a community or society, sport events may become sites for confrontations" (p. 197). The gang element (whether organized around race, ethnicity, or class) in some U.S. cities would use the sporting events as grounds for contestation. The soccer hooliganism that occurred at soccer matches in England is a result of the class conflict in that society. As a result of alienation of disenfranchised working-class men in England and Europe, the influence of professionalization and commercialization of society as well as soccer has created tensions and violent acts at these sporting events.

> When the media uses violent images to promote a sport event, spectators may perceive violence during the event, making them more likely to behave violently.

A third form of violence is manifested in what is termed *celebrato*ry violence. This is probably the least understood form of behavior, and some have difficulty understanding that tearing down goalposts following a victory in football is not merely exuberant behavior or a demonstration of loyalty to a university. It is violent behavior. A more serious problem arises when the destruction moves outside the stadium and into the community and involves those individuals who did not attend the game. It is at this point that such actions will involve legal violations and subsequent punishments (Coakley, 2001).

In some team sports, crowd behavior that interferes with the progress of a game such as throwing objects onto the field or court and heckling the referees, umpires, or players is punishable by expulsion from the game and/or awarding an advantage or points to the opposing team. Another problem among fans presents itself when individuals are not respectful of others and stand up for extended periods of time, thus blocking the view of those behind them. Antagonism and frustration are the results of this situation, creating animosity, harsh words, and arguments. It is important that sport managers, particularly those in charge of game-day operations and stadium/arena safety, consider the various possible dynamics.

Potential Problems for Sport Managers to Consider

1. History or relationship between teams and spectators
2. Location of the event (home field, opponent's field, or neutral site)
3. Importance of the game (regular season game, championship)
4. Crowd composition (gender, age, race, ethnicity, social class)
5. Alcohol/drug consumption by spectators
6. Size of the crowd
7. Importance of the event for the spectators (identity with regard to race, ethnicity, class, local, regional, club)
8. Crowd-control strategies (guards, police)

(Coakley, 2001)

Summary

Key Concepts

alienation

celebratory violence

commercialization

hooliganism

This chapter discussed the ethical responsibilities of the sport manager when dealing with athletic administrators, athletes, team coaches, and media personnel. Specific issues within each of the positions were noted, among which was the recurrent theme of regard and respect for others and the personal ethical responsibilities one assumes as a sport manager. In addition, the ethical responsibilities of the athletes and spectators/fans were also reviewed. An important point regarding the specific responsibility for ethical sport programs as a part of everyone's personal responsibility was emphasized. Constitutive, proscriptive, and sportsmanship (fair play) rules were explored as well as how they fit in to the ethical analysis of sport and those individuals responsible for sport.

Questions for Consideration

1. How would you go about developing your own personal ethical standards?

2. How would you incorporate your personal ethical standards into the organization of which you are in charge?

3. Who else in the organization is responsible for ethical behavior?

4. What are the ethical responsibilities of the athletic administrator, coach, and athlete?

5. With what ethical issues should media personnel be concerned?

6. What are the ethical responsibilities of the sport spectator/fan?

Chapter Six

Professional Ethics and Social Responsibility

Chapter Objectives

- To define and understand the concepts and value of social responsibility, corporate social responsibility, the social contract and business ethics

- To examine the relationships between social responsibility and the values of the family and the organization

- To gain an understanding of the features of the ethical profile

- To recognize the need for social responsibility within sport management settings

Recognition of ethics and social responsibility has increased in recent years as the call for accountability on the part of all those associated with the management of sport has been made abundantly clear. Incidences of illegal and immoral actions in all sport settings have emerged to the point that some factions of society have made efforts to call those in charge to take responsibility and improve situations. As a sport manager, learning to adopt a social consciousness leading to a commitment of being socially responsible is paramount to the execution of one's job. Developing a social consciousness and being socially responsible assists sport managers with the creation of a sound professional philosophy and subsequent ethical action.

Within athletic programs at the college and university level, the certification program initiated by the Knight Foundation Commission on Intercollegiate Athletics (1991) and carried out by the National Collegiate Athletic Association (NCAA) is one example of how issues of responsibility and accountability have been addressed. The Knight Commission report called for the presidents of colleges and universities to assume the sole responsibility for their athletic programs. This means that although athletic directors may be in charge of programs, it is the president with whom the ultimate responsibility rests. As academic integrity, financial integrity, governance issues, and the commitment to equity are explored within the athletic departments of educational institutions, it is obvious that ethics and social responsibility are at the forefront of this movement for accountability.

Another example is the responsibility of a professional sport franchise to a city or community. The owners of sport teams, the individual players, and the managers who oversee such programs need to be aware of these commitments.

The concept of *social responsibility* is inextricably intertwined with one's values, beliefs, and actions. We are free to make certain choices, but must also be personally responsible for those choices and decisions. Taking responsibility and being accountable for our actions are not always simple tasks. Looking beyond how our choices and decisions benefit or disadvantage us is crucial to being socially responsible. Questions regarding the nature of the complex relationships between sport, society, and the formal organizations of sport are raised within the concept of social responsibility and require the close attention of sport managers whose positions require responsible actions.

Referring to the importance of social responsibility, Chelladurai (1999) noted that the three imperatives that drive the concern with human resource management include profitability, changes in the values and awareness of the workforce and customer base, and social responsibility. He explained that

> Social responsibility includes the reliability, trustworthiness, and integrity of the individual, as well as the individual's moral and legal accountability to self and others.

> organizations as agencies of society are beholden to society, which includes the human resources of the organizations. Thus, when an organization institutes effective human resource practices to enhance the quality of life for their human resources, they also are contributing to the society as a whole. (p. 14)

Chelladurai emphasized the importance of social responsibility and the critical need for sport managers to consider this concept in all phases of their duties.

Another concept related to social responsibility is that of *corporate social responsibility*. This indicates that social responsibility is directly related to the social contract that exists between the business of sport and the setting or society in which it operates. The *social contract* refers to those accepted obligations, duties, and relationships between organizations or institutions and the people that relate to the corporate impact on the welfare of society. This makes the social responsibility of sport, as with any business, a significant part of the social contract (Steiner, 1972). Within the social contract, profit maximization and social involvement are not necessarily mutually exclusive concepts. It is possible for these goals to coexist. Recently, businesses in general have given much attention to employee welfare, support for minorities, consumer satisfaction, community improvement, and environmental protection. It has also been noted, however, that such emphases have not had a unified collective impact on public opinion. The reason for this may be attributed to the fact that these objectives are not explicit and do not appear to fit into an overall plan with the organization.

Within management planning, the objectives selected by the organization, in some cases, relate to social awareness and social responsibility. Nonprofit organizations are based on such awareness and on the awareness of actual needs of society such as the providing of shelter, food, and clothing for the homeless, or, in the case of sport management, offering sport programs for those who do not have access to them. In the case of for-profit organizations such as professional and intercollegiate sport, the mission, purpose, and objectives may not reflect the concepts of social awareness and social responsibility. This does not mean, however, that they could not do so (DeSensi, 1998).

Lawson (1999) stated in his article "Education for Social Responsibility: Preconditions in Retrospect and in Prospect" that "all of the helping fields face the necessity of confronting this topic and the issues it implicates as a new century dawns" (p. 116). The field of sport management is not exempt from social responsibility. It is incumbent upon those in our profession to be responsive to this need. Education for social responsibility needs to be a part of the academic preparation for all sport managers, but it must be undertaken by socially responsible and responsive educators. The structures, cultures, missions, goals, and conceptions of ethical practice in sport management require what is referred to as *field integrity* (Lawson, 1999). Field integrity includes the commitment by educators, students, and most importantly, practitioners of sport management to have a firm mission for socially responsible education and practice.

A distinction exists between corporate social responsibility and *business ethics*. Although social responsibility is directly related to the social contract, ethics, on the other hand, mandates that individuals or organizations act in accordance with the rules of moral philosophy. Both social responsibility and business ethics seem to lead to the same end, but may at times be different in their approach. Both have been regarded as outside or external to strategic planning processes in corporate codes of ethics. Such codes seem to be directed more toward those issues that influence profit than toward social responsibility or the concerns of society. Ethics presents more specific demands than does the concept of social responsibility, thus providing a base or foundation from which to function. Both concepts, however, are subject to problems of interpretation by the public as well as by those within an organization. This particular problem could perhaps be eliminated by a carefully designed mission statement that would clarify the intentions of the organization.

The concept of the business or the sport setting as being amoral, that is, neither moral nor immoral, is misconceived. North American society must go beyond such thinking. The realities within capitalistic democracies suggest that all businesses and their leaders must be held accountable in a moral and ethical sense for their behavior. According to DeGeorge (1986):

> . . .the breakdown of the Myth of Amoral Businesses has been signaled in three fairly obvious ways: by the reporting of scandals and the concomitant public reaction to these reports; by the formation of popular groups, such as the environmentalists and the consumerists; and by the concern of business, as expressed in conferences, magazine and newspaper articles, the burgeoning of codes of ethical conduct, and so on. (p. 4).

Because businesses or, in this case, sport organizations, are a human activity, they have been and will continue to be evaluated from a moral point of view. There is no way business can escape its moral role by referring to its nonhuman nature. The business or corporation is also a legal entity with individuals as its legal agents and owners. Both the sport organizations and the individuals who work within this setting are judged by society to be liable for the behavior of its agents.

Once again, social responsibility and ethics can be successfully integrated if such concepts become a part of the mission of the organization. It is necessary for social responsibility and ethics to be a part of the core values that should permeate the entire organization, its planning process, and the implementation of all phases, including organizing, leading, marketing, etc., of the corporate setting.

From a business ethics perspective, Robin and Reidenbach (1987) pointed out that the concept of the business organization is created by society and its agents and, therefore, must meet the expectations of that society or "pay the price in consumerist and antibusiness legislation" (p. 49). If the expectations are transferred to ethical theory, it is possible to use them in the development of organizational values. Robin and Reidenbach further noted that social systems utilize aspects of both deontology and utilitarianism in the formulation of their laws and social policies: "In the United States, cost/benefit analysis, a principal component of utilitarianism, is a tool of major importance in policy making at the national, state, and local levels. Further, the concept of capitalism has strong roots in utilitarianism" (p. 49). It should also be noted that individual rights are protected at all the levels of government, as noted in the Declaration of Independence (e.g., inalienable rights), the Bill of Rights of the U.S. Constitution, and the Charter of Rights in Canada. Thus, we utilize a blend of the two philosophies. However, even these are subject to evolutionary change in our society. Robin and Reidenbach (1987) expanded this thought further by stating:

> One problem is to determine how to treat this blend of philosophies. . . deontology, . . . derived from "duty" is fundamentally concerned with the individual and tends to dominate our thinking when the plight of individuals is deemed serious. Even when reasonably sound arguments about the "greatest good for the greatest number" can be made on one side of an issue, the deontological arguments on the other side tend to dominate if individual's "rights" are seriously impaired. (p. 50)

Basic Family Values	Basic Organizational Values
Caring for nuclear family member (e.g., husband, wife, children)	Caring for the organization family (e.g., employees, management, stockholders)
Caring for close relatives (e.g., grandparents, aunts, uncles)	Caring for integral publics (e.g., customers, creditors)
Being a helpful and friendly neighbor	Being a helpful and friendly corporate neighbor
Obeying the law	Obeying the law
Being a "good" citizen in the community	A portion of the organization budget is allocated for philanthropic purposes
Protecting and caring for the family's home and land	
	Protecting and caring for the physical environment on which the organization has an impact

Figure 6.1. Parallels between basic social responsibility values of the family and the organization.

From "Social Responsibility, Ethics, and Marketing Strategy: Closing the Gap Between Concept and Application by D. P. Robin and R. E. Reidenbach, January, 1987. *Journal of Marketing, 51*, p. 51. Copyright 1987 by the American Marketing Association. Reprinted with permission.

From a social responsibility perspective, it is suggested that the organization attempt to establish a similarity or parallel between the problems it faces and the problems faced by an average family. Figure 6.1 represents these parallels.

As Figure 6-1 illustrates, the structure of caring relationships among members of a nuclear family can transfer or extend to caring for the organization's employees, management, and stockholders. In the organization, the consumer or client is in a situation similar to that of a close relative. Although caring for a close relative is important and ranks higher than caring for neighbors and friends, it is still not as important as caring for members of the nuclear family. Customers should receive considerable concern that goes beyond the concept of simply not doing anything that would harm them. Social responsibility then has been given a prominent position as a much needed ethic within these institutions.

Social Responsibility in Intercollegiate Athletic Programs

Whereas professional sports for men in particular have set the standard for college and university sport programs, positive and negative outcomes have been experienced. The power structures as well as the players as labor are themes that permeate both professional and college or university athletic programs. Such programs have lost credibility as these similarities are evidenced. Revenue production for athletic departments may in fact be the ultimate concern for schools whereas the NCAA purports to represent educational programs and concerns for athletes and member institutions. It has been said that athletic programs in educational institutions are primarily a business and the bottom line has been more important than the welfare of the athletes. Sound foundational ethical standards can more readily be established if the organizations that are responsible for sport in school settings acknowledge the similarities and differences (i.e., the production status, the emphasis on the win-loss record, and the need to increase revenues) (DeSensi, 1998).

The focus of social responsibility in these cases needs to be the welfare of the athlete and his or her education. Athletic programs at the college and university level seem to be in a paradox in that the programs attempt to please conflicting social groups such as players, alumni, administrators, and the NCAA. In addition, those individuals responsible for the programs seem to be attempting to balance the educational model of athletics with the business model. These two models need not be mutually exclusive and can serve as an ethical "check" on the ethical standards of the organization. An honest effort by the athletic administrators and coaches to put the athlete at the center of the program is a move toward academic integrity and ethical excellence.

> College athletic programs must first consider the athletes when making ethical decisions.

During the 1990s a certification program was established within the NCAA. This venture would be considered an important action of social responsibility. As part of the reform agenda of the NCAA, the Presidents Commission, the NCAA

Council, and the Knight Foundation Commission on Intercollegiate Athletics developed a certification program for NCAA Division I institutions. This program was instituted in order that member institutions would be accountable for their current practices involving academic integrity, financial integrity, governance, and commitment to compliance and equity (i.e., gender, race, ethnicity, and equity along a number of lines regarding athletes, athletic staff, coaches, assistant coaches, graduate assistants, and nonathletes). The process began with the institution's preparing a self-study in which the areas noted above were explored. Participation in the study included campus faculty, administrators, athletics personnel, athletes, and graduate and undergraduate students. After the self-study is examined by the NCAA Review Team, an external peer review team composed of three to five members who are experienced educational and athletics personnel then visits the campus to verify and evaluate the self-study. After a time, the institution is informed of its certification or of areas that must be improved to achieve certification. The NCAA Committee on Athletics Certification (Hemphill, 1983) indicated that the benefits of such a process include self-awareness, affirmation, and opportunities to improve. *Self-awareness* pertains to the open nature of the self-study to the public and informing the campus about the athletic program's goals, purposes, and how it supports the institution's overall mission. Affirmation is achieved by noting the facets of the program that deserve recognition and praise. Opportunities to improve are noted by revealing issues and problems and offering potential solutions for improvement.

Social Responsibility in Professional Sports

As new sport franchises in various professional leagues develop across the country, or as franchises move from one city to another and millions of dollars are spent on demolishing older stadiums and arenas to make way for new structures, the issues regarding social responsibility again emerge. What is the responsibility of a sport franchise to a city or community? Given that some professional team owners may have no knowledge of sport and consider their teams investments or toys that they can sell, buy, and manipulate, the team owner may be interested only in the power structures of business rather than concerned with socially responsible actions regarding the team and the city or community. Flint and Eitzen (1987) explained this concept:

> Because sport is still categorized as simple play, the power of wealthy capitalist owners can be overlooked as simple aberration or eccentric pastime. Although the meritocratic recruitment arguments are held high by the owners as well as the participants (players or consumers), little attention is given to the contradictory fact that owning a team is not based on merit but on enormous wealth. (p. 25)

Numerous questions regarding the complex relationships between society, sport, and the formal organizations of sport may be raised within the context of social responsibility, but the questions do not stop here. They extend into the concepts of power, corruption, and ownership, for example, and create even more ethical concerns. Hemphill (1983) emphasized that profit maximization has taken precedent at the professional level of sport and that sport management and labor have sacrificed public interest in favor of monetary self-interest. Questions regarding the public interest in sport, the responsibility of the franchise owner to the community, and the revenue generation potential of teams need to be addressed. Do owners of teams consider the consumers of sport individual human beings who hold allegiances to family, community, school, and hometown team? Do owners consider how the decision to move a franchise will affect these individuals? Is consideration given to the fact that a city depends on the revenue generated by a sport franchise? The sport team owner has three indirect obligations to the community: (a) franchise location stability, (b) quality of team performance, and (c) unpredictability of performance outcome. The sport spectator should expect the demonstration of a relatively even competition in that the outcome is uncertain and some degree of team roots whereby broad-based identification, loyalty, and support can be generated. At the minimum, these obligations need to be considered by the franchise owner(s) to ensure the needs of the public and a profitable outcome for the team.

The direct or legal obligations of the sport franchise owner include (a) obligations to other owners in terms of abiding by the competitive restrictions in the production and marketing of the sports product; (b) obligations to the broadcasting networks with regard to the sale of broadcasting rights and the provision of the sports product; (c) obligations to the athlete with regard to individually negotiated salary contracts; (d) obligations to the collective-bargaining agreements between players' associations and leagues for the provision of sport labor; and (e) obligations to the public in terms of facility leasing, construction, or renovation agreements and safety. In addition, the direct obligation to the league promoters and public is a provision of the sports product.

The Sport Team Owner's Community Obligations

1. Franchise location stability
2. Quality of team performance
3. Unpredictability of performance outcome

Social Responsibility and Sport and Fitness Clubs

The social responsibility of the sport and fitness club is the obligation of the owners and managers have to their consumers or clients. Among these obligations are to provide a clean and safe environment, qualified or certified trainers/instructors to ensure safe practices in exercise prescription and adherence, safe equipment, honest evaluation of performance and stress tolerance, flexible hours of availability, appropriate facilities and equipment for women and men, fair membership costs, information concerning the risks of the activities, adaptability to the changes in society, programs and accessibility for all populations, and general concern for the well-being of the clientele. Although some of these points such as the safety regulations may be legal requirements, meeting the clients' needs and concern for their well-being is socially responsible and is linked to mutual trust and goodwill among all involved in this business setting.

Summary

This chapter has reviewed the concepts of social responsibility, corporate social responsibility, social contract, and business ethics. In an effort to show how social responsibility can be understood and generated within a sport setting, Robin and Reidenbach's parallels between basic social responsibility values of the family and the organization were utilized. Specific examples were presented regarding social responsibility for college and university athletic programs, professional teams, and sport and fitness clubs. Emphasis was placed on balancing the concepts of serving the public interest and maximizing profit rather than sacrificing the public interest to increase revenues.

For Reflection . . .

Consider a sport management position you hold/will hold and envision your social responsibility in that position. What information will you rely on from the organization to ensure that you will carry out these responsibilities?

Questions for Consideration

1. How can we distinguish between corporate responsibility and business ethics?

2. What is the relevance of social responsibility for the sport manager?

3. How is it possible for a sport franchise to develop a balance between maximizing profits and serving public interests?

4. What is the difference between social responsibility for nonprofit and for-profit organizations?

Chapter Seven

Models and Codes of Ethics

Chapter Objectives

- To identify the purposes and functions of codes of ethics

- To make explicit the need for codes of ethics

- To present the components for a code of ethics

- To note the limitations of ethical codes

- To provide samples of codes of ethics

Professional organizations, educational institutions, athletic programs, businesses, and sport organizations, as well as the government and the practices of law and medicine have established ethical guidelines, sometimes referred to as codes of behavior, codes of ethics, or moral frameworks, that employers and practitioners are bound to follow. Although moral expectations of behavior extend from the vision and mission statements of these organizations and are directly related to the services provided, the manner in which those services are fulfilled by employees and practitioners is often called into question. The Ethics Resource Center in Washington, D.C., indicated that over three quarters of America's major corporations have developed and periodically update their codes of ethics (Nielsen, 1994). Those individuals entering the professions of business, law, and medicine are now required to take courses in ethics during their academic preparation. According to the NASPE/NASSM Guidelines for Curriculum in Sport Management (NASPE/NASSM Joint Task Force, 1993), the study of ethics also is required of those preparing to enter the field of sport management. Such information is most pertinent to those in sport and specifically sport management. Although the study of ethics pertaining to each of the areas noted above is important, it is imperative that organizations not only establish meaningful guidelines, but also be certain that those guidelines are well known, publicized, and enforced.

The Need for a Code of Ethics

As with any other profession, control of the practice of sport managers is important. Although a sport manager was

- admitted to an academic program to prepare to become a sport manager;

- studied the content of sport management, including ethics;

- took part in practica/internships;

- passed the appropriate examinations; wrote research papers;

- engaged in the research of a project, thesis, or dissertation;

- graduated from a college or university; and

- joined the appropriate professional organizations that govern one's practice,

there can be no guarantee that all sport managers will behave ethically in the position for which they are hired. However, based on past questionable and unethical practices in business, industry, sport, and government, both responsibility and accountability are much needed. A code of ethics then serves as a means to guide, motivate, and monitor the performance of sport managers in the ethical delivery of the services of the organization. Expecting high standards of behavior can anchor performance evaluations from individual organizations as well as from the profession as a whole.

Decades ago, when codes of ethics were introduced in businesses, they were concerned with points of etiquette rather than with substantive issues that the organization faced. The 1960s and 1970s, however, brought to the forefront concerns for the rights of the consumer and the challenge to professional paternalism. It seems all professions have encountered mistrust on the part of the public and have had their practices questioned. Professions have to undertake self-scrutiny to reevaluate their practices and the social contract that exists between them and society. The manner in which public interests are served continues to be a formidable question (Jennings, Callahan, & Wolf, 1987).

The question that perhaps should never arise, but at this point often does, is "Why should businesses act in a moral manner?" Statements such as "sound business ethics means good business practices" or "it pays to be moral," are often the responses given to such inquiries, but Bowie and Duska (1990) explained that "the corporation should be moral because acting morally is in the interests of the corporation. Moral behavior. . . on the part of the corporation . . . is simply rationally prudent behavior" (p. 111). In the midst of this discussion, another question is raised: Why should companies that are forced by consumers to focus on the short run be concerned with long-term morality? Souvenir touting for special short-term sport events or those associated with pop culture go in and out of business quickly as the event comes to an end or as the interests of society change. Often, such fly-by-night businesses are not looked upon favorably either by consumers or by more legitimate businesses. Such groups consider such behavior profitable, but not moral. According to Bowie and Duska, what is needed is something similar to that which is in existence in general society—a combination of law and morals. Those companies regarded as respectable make certain that the stockholders and the consumers are aware that the products and/or services provided are neither shoddy nor imperfect, that the workers are treated fairly, and that the company is making an effort to assist with the problems of society. For those organizations not regarded as respectable, there is a conflict between the socially responsible behavior, or the demands of morality, and the demands of prudence or self-interest (Bowie & Duska, 1990).

> Respectable organizations advertise the fact that their product undergoes quality control, their workers are well-treated, and they are involved in the community.

Zeigler (1992) pointed out that professionals involved with sport management will "increasingly have obligations to the public, to their profession, and to their clients" (p. 9). In addition, the sport manager's conduct and ethical responsibility to society must give consideration to laws, individual freedoms, equal opportunity, right to privacy, and the overall welfare of individuals for whom the professional is responsible.

The Philosophy Academy of the National Association for Sport and Physical Education (NASPE) also cites the need to develop a strong code of behavior in a profession. The academy indicated that as professionals they take an active role in their organization and serve and promote the discipline and practice of sport and physical education. The position of these professionals is that they are responsible for the integrity of the profession and that they strive to "embody values, virtues, and standards of excellence appropriate to teaching, coaching, research, and other sport and physical education professions" (Code of Conduct for Sport & Physical Educators, 1999-2000, p. 8). The commitment on the part of these professionals then is to uphold social responsibilities and ethical duties to others.

When the areas of sport management in which a code of ethics could be implemented are explored, coaching emerges as a primary example. Coakley (cited in Nielsen, 1994) pointed out the need for codes of ethics for coaching. One major purpose of such a code is basically to let all others know what to expect from the individual as the coach. Athletes are much more attuned to cases of abuse from coaching staff and have used reports of such actions in pursuing legal action and the subsequent removal of coaches from their positions.

Sexual harassment and abuse are extremely pressing issues in women's sport, particularly when males are coaching female athletes. Complaints at major universities have been brought against male coaches regarding harassment of female athletes. Whereas it is asserted that athletes may idolize coaches, romantic attraction for some seems inevitable. Acting on the attraction between an athlete and coach is unethical, counterproductive, and professionally inappropriate. Such an act abuses the power that coaches have by virtue of their role, distracts the athlete from game-related tasks, may cause the athlete to misinterpret certain behaviors as sexually motivated, and may cause the coach to lose objectivity in making decisions relating to the athlete. Many coaches' careers depend on the performance of the athlete(s), which may influence the coach to take advantage of athletes' time and physical well-being. Still other reasons for developing a code of ethics for coaching involve how coaches will ensure the safety of their athletes and what their beliefs are regarding the emphasis on training and winning. Nielsen (1994) indicated that

> . . . while a code [of ethics] cannot necessarily provide answers to all of the issues. . . it can (and should) provide guidelines in ambiguous situa-

tions when what is ethical or proper is not clear. . . . A code also helps to reinforce correct conduct and establish parameters to discourage improper behaviors. (p. 4)

Coakley (cited in Nielsen, 1994) recommended that a code for sport be a joint effort between a governing body and its coaches. His suggestion was that the United States Olympic Committee (USOC), in conjunction with its sport-governing bodies, draft codes of conduct for both coaches and other adults who control and sometimes benefit emotionally or materially from the performance of children. It would also be up to the USOC to develop, implement, and enforce such a code.

The Ethics Resource Center assists groups by reviewing, assessing, developing, and implementing codes of ethics as related to the conflicts and issues of individual organizations. This is precisely the responsibility that the USOC and other sport-governing bodies must take if such codes are to be meaningful and successful.

Nielsen (1994) suggested that the code of ethics for coaches should (a) have as a base the social and physical development of all athletes; (b) stress the importance of a cooperative rather than command style of coaching; (c) be closely aligned with a mandatory education and credentialing program for coaches; (d) be enforced by a sport-based regulatory agency such as the USOC; (e) undergo aggressive publicity to athletes and their families and be included on bulletin boards, locker-room walls, and other places visible to athletes; (f) cover a variety of areas; and (g) serve as a list of goals and guidelines for coaches.

It is crucial that a code of ethics for coaches address what athletes desire from their coaches. Coakley (as cited in Nielsen, 1994) reported that competence, approachability, fairness and consistency, confidence, motivation, personal concern, and support are what athletes between the ages of 12 and 20 years of age look for most often in their coaches. Although this age-group is not the only one sport managers will serve, this study offers interesting information regarding ethics, the athlete, and the coach.

In the United Kingdom and Canada, codes of ethics are developed by governmental agencies that regulate sport and coaching. The British Institute of Sports Coaches has established both a code of ethics and a code of conduct for coaches. This code of ethics is regarded as a series of guidelines rather than instructions. Nielsen (1994) pointed out that one example from this code indicates that "the good sport coach will be concerned primarily when the well-being, health, and future of the individual performer and only secondary with the optimization of performance" (p. 5).

The code of conduct put forth by the British Institute is intended to be more specific and provides guidance in the implementation of the principles in the code of ethics. Regarding the concept of commitment, this code of conduct reads

> When coaches enter into a commitment with an employer, with a team or with an individual performer, the nature of that commitment should be specifically agreed.

What Athletes Expect From Coaches

Competence

Approachability

Fairness and consistency

Confidence

Motivation

Personal concern

Any such contract or terms of reference should be set out in writing and include. . .

The time commitment involved and an indication of the expected outcome of the coaching. (Nielsen, 1994, p. 5)

The British Institute includes the codes in its coaching certification programs with the expectation that coaches will follow them. There is also a formal complaint procedure giving individuals or organizations the opportunity to file a complaint against a coach within the context of the codes. Because the coach is encouraged to develop a personal code of conduct and the athlete(s) and coach realize the expectations, there is an opportunity for the athlete(s) and coach to have a prosperous relationship.

In the United States, very few sport organizations have well-developed ethical codes for coaches. Because there is no American institute of sport coaches, like the ones in Britain or Canada that oversee this responsibility, an ethical code has been slow in developing or is nonexistent. The USOC, which oversees amateur sport in the United States via the Amateur Sports Act of 1978, is currently in the process of developing a code of conduct for coaches that might possibly be adopted by each national sport-governing body.

Key Concepts

ethical codes of conduct

moral frameworks

professional paternalism

sexual harassment

Purposes and Functions of Codes of Ethics

Codes of ethics serve different functions in different settings. For example, some codes serve the *self-interests of professional groups* in that the code helps to give legitimacy to the organization or field (Bowie & Duska, 1990; Callahan, 1982; Fraleigh, 1993), and a code of ethics for a profession promotes a social objective by noting the ideals of the profession. In a sense, the code serves as a public relations tool because it publicly states that an organization promotes a social objective, and therefore, it is a profession, and its members are ethical. The ideals of a profession or field are often imbedded within the code of ethics, thus leading the public to believe that the organization is credible and that its members behave in an ethical manner. D. Callahan (cited in Fraleigh, 1993), stated that another self-interest function of codes of ethics is that "they help establish a profitable monopoly of skills." In turn, the economic well being of the profession is established. "The monopoly over a skill then, serves as a means of assuring predictable high quality service" (Kultgen, as cited in Fraleigh, 1988, p. 14). This particular situation indicates that although there is a profitable monopoly over a certain skill, there is also autonomy or autonomous control established over who is admitted to the profession as well as over any disciplinary sanctions. The self-interests of professionals and the interests of clients are served in this case.

> The code of ethics can be a public relations tool—it advertises a profession's social conscience.

The function of *serving the interests and welfare of clients or students of professionals* is accomplished through the code of ethics by regulating the "relationships between the individual professional and clients or students in sensitive areas such as confidentiality, informed consent, conflicts of interest, and fair fees, thus providing useful guidance for practitioners" (Kultgen, 1988, p. 85). The concept of professional adequacy is also an area in which the interests of clients or students are served. In other words, if the code is specific, a basis for disciplinary action can be established, and the threat of such action may serve as a deterrent for unethical behavior (Kultgen, 1988; Mishkin, 1988). If codes of ethics are utilized as the basis for professional education, the self-interests of clients as well as those of the profession are served.

Another function of codes of ethics is that they can *serve society or public interests*. By specifically stating the public duties and responsibilities of the organization or profession, service to society is rendered. In the legal profession, *pro bono* services are considered public duty or responsibility. The providing of expertise to the public is also a way to serve society. The sport manager and fitness professionals, for example, are able to share with policy makers and appropriate public officials their intellectual and technical expertise on issues and public policies regarding their respective areas (Fraleigh, 1993; Jennings et al., 1987).

Lastly, the function of *serving two or more groups* (i.e., professional groups, clients, and society) occurs when the previously noted functions expand beyond their boundaries. For example, autonomy that serves the self-interest of the profession also serves the clients' or students' interests by the production of high-quality service.

Bayles (as cited in Fraleigh, 1993) noted that the public duties of professions extend beyond the boundaries of their immediate values and include governance by law, freedom, protection from injury, equality of opportunity, privacy, and welfare. Further, those standards required in life removed from the profession include justice, respect for the rights of others, and beneficence. It is precisely these points that, according to Jennings et al., (1987), provide for the moral dimension of a profession and ultimately public trust.

According to Ulrich (1997), a code of ethics is a distinguishing characteristic of a profession, and the profession and practice of sport management is no exception. The consumer of sport in whatever form it takes (fitness clubs, college or university sport, LPGA), because of its entertainment value, may not readily acknowledge the "professional" status of sport management and may be more easily convinced that law, medicine, and sales, for example, are more likely to need a of a code of ethics. Nothing could be farther from the truth. The rules of sports dictate not only how to play the game, but also the expectations of the players regarding fair play. Some but not all sports also indicate unacceptable behavior of the spectators to the point that if such behavior occurs, the team or teams is penalized.

In order to regulate fairness and honesty in the manner in which the vision, mission, and subsequent delivery of the product of the organization is carried out by all those involved, Bowie and Duska (1990) recommended that ethical principles and codes be developed that members of the organization are expected to follow and that will be enforced. Explicit moral guidelines can facilitate a means by which individuals in the organization can

> Explicit guidelines can help to ensure that a company conducts business with fairness and honesty.

compare themselves and each other to an organizational standard and monitor their own behavior. A code of ethics may also be used to assist individuals and motivate them to respond in an ethical manner. The motivation to act ethically may result in part from the fact that all individuals in the organization operate within a particular moral code.

Advantages of a Code of Ethics

—Motivates ethical action through peer pressure

—Provides stable and permanent guides to right and wrong actions

—Provides guidance in ambiguous situations

—Controls the autocratic power of employees

—Specifies the social responsibilities of the organization

—Serves the interests of the business or organization itself

Businesses depend on confidence and trust. The establishment of a sound vision, mission, and subsequent code of ethics, if followed, adds to the legitimization of the organization and authenticates or attests to its credibility and that of its employees. Providing and maintaining public trust are critical. Thus, the code of ethics would ensure that those involved with a particular sport business would behave according to the moral actions put forth in the code and that these actions would be beneficial to the public and the business as a whole.

Sport managers can use codes of ethics as a guide to moral excellence as they fulfill their obligations to the public, the profession, and their clients. In turn, these codes will legitimize the field of sport management as a whole.

Elements of a Code of Ethics

Codes of ethics are probably the most visible sign of the ethical philosophy and beliefs of a company, business, or organization. For the code to have meaning, it must clearly state its basic principles and expectations and focus on potential ethical dilemmas that could be faced by members of the group. Most important, it must be enforced. The code should also be developed and accepted by the employees before it is mandated that they abide by it. Stead, Worrell, & Stead (1990) recommend that although it is the manager's responsibility to tend to the content of the code, it is critical that the code itself be developed by as many of the employees or organization members as possible in an open atmosphere in order to be effective. To ensure successful institutionalization of a code of ethics, Stead et al. (1990) recommend that communication of the code occur at all levels within the organization, that it be distributed to new employees as part of their orientation and selection, and that seminars on the codes be conducted so that open discussion can occur on its meaning and implementation.

Codes of ethics vary in breadth and depth. Some may be statements or creeds that concisely state the ideals of a profession or organization. Creeds, according to Zeigler (1989), "are general and less confining to the professionals concerned" (p. 40). Although they identify the ideals of a profession, Fraleigh (1993) indicated that creeds also allow adaptability and interpretation by autonomous professionals. As the ideals of the profession are identified in this type of document, so is the profession or organization's value to society. By noting the ideals, a sense of trust is established as well as the common values for members, which serves as a foundation for the professional education of those who aspire to the profession.

Other forms of codes may be longer, appropriate to the functions noted, and contain statements that denote disciplinary actions for violations of the code. Concerned with the ethical actions of professionals in sport management, the North American Society for Sport Management (NASSM) appointed an ad hoc committee to develop a creed. However, prior to the development of the creed, it is important to understand the nature of the membership and the purpose of this organization. As succinctly stated by Zeigler (1989), the purpose of NASSM reads:

> The North American Society for Sport Management is a professional association whose primary mission is to provide the leadership that will result in physically active lifestyle for all North Americans. NASSM members work in positions related to healthful physical activity, and we believe that such physical activity programs should be of high quality and should encourage regular participation.
>
> Developmental activities such as exercise, sport, dance, and play should be made available for average, accelerated, and special populations of all ages. As professionals, therefore, NASSM members are deeply aware of the need to stimulate participation in the appropriate kinds of physical activity by all North Americans, regardless of age, sex or level of competence. (p. 2)

Because it is important that creeds to be directly related to the purpose(s) of the organization, the NASSM Ethical Creed was developed and reads:

> Members of the North American Society for Sport Management live in free democratic societies within North American culture. As practitioners and scholars within a broad profession, we honor the preservation and protection of fundamental human rights. We are committed to a high level of professional practice and service. Our professional conduct shall b e based on the application of sound management theory developed through a broadly based humanities and social scientific body of knowledge about the role of developmental physical activity in sport, exercise, and related expressive activities in the lives of all people. Such professional knowledge and service shall be made available to clients of all ages and conditions, whether such people are classified as accelerated, normal, or special insofar as their status or condition is concerned.
>
> As NASSM members pursuing our subdisciplinary and professional service, we will make every effort to protect the welfare of those who seek

our assistance. We will use our professional skills only for purposes which are consistent with the values, norms, and laws of our respective countries. Although we, as professional practitioners, demand for ourselves maximum freedom of inquiry and communication consistent with societal values, we fully understand that such freedom requires us to be responsible, competent, and objective in the application of our skills. We should always show concern for the best interest of our clients, our colleagues, and the public at large. (Zeigler, 1992, p. 35)

The NASSM Ethical Creed was accepted in June 1989 at the Annual General Meeting of this organization. It incorporates the purposes and serves as a foundation upon which NASSM was founded.

Another example of a creed are the Principles of Medical Ethics of the American Medical Association, noted by J. C. Callahan (1988), which state, "A physician shall be dedicated to providing competent medical service with compassion and respect for human dignity" (p. 351). Although creeds are valuable and identify the ideals that may be central to a profession, they are not specific and do not offer directions regarding either violations or disciplinary action.

Kultgen (1988) pointed out that there are four basic elements that should be included in the document that comprises a code of ethics: (a) an ethical code, (b) model laws, (c) basic ideals, and (d) rationale. Each of these should also be related to a function that was previously discussed. The *ethical code* legitimizes a field and helps establish a monopoly of skill "by specifying noncooperation with noncertified or nonlicensed occupations" (Fraleigh, 1993, p. 16). By establishing common standards for all practitioners, high-quality service is guaranteed. Autonomy is also gained by establishing standards for admission to the profession, review, and discipline. By prescribing certain types of actions, acceptable relationships with clients are established. Although the code serves as a foundation for education and professional preparation, it also guides disciplinary actions by its prescription of how professional reviews will be carried out. Within the realm of providing expertise for policy makers, the code can make explicit public duties of a professional in a specific field and that generic to all professionals and pronounce the provisions relevant to the values of a liberal society such as privacy, equality of opportunity, protection from injury, and freedom (Fraleigh, 1993).

The *model laws* portion attempts to clarify and make effective specific elements of the code of ethics. Fraleigh (1993) stated that model laws recommended by a profession serve several functions:

> It can help regulate relations with clients by means of legal privacy rights, provide the base for judgments of adequacy and discipline, establish monopoly of skill by specifications for admission to practice, and assure some predictable level of competence. It can result in professional autonomy in crucial areas. And it facilitates education by informing aspirants where professional practice is affected by legal provisions as well as moral constraints. (p. 17)

Regarding the issue of model laws, Kultgen (1988) reminded us that it would be a mistake to have all elements of the code underlined by laws because it would restrict freedom, thus making moral duties legal obligations, but those laws that govern credentialing and licensure and that would protect the public against malpractice or incompetence are most appropriate.

The *rationale* section serves as a basis for interpreting the code. As it clarifies professional norms, it also expresses the sense of public as well as the profession and any issues that interfere with moral behavior are presented as well as ways to overcome such issues (Kultgen, 1988). Also noted in this section is the nature of the relationship of the profession to the values of a liberal society (i.e., governance by law, freedom, protection from injury, equality of opportunity, privacy and welfare; Bayles, 1981).

> **Key Concepts**
>
> ethical code
>
> ethical creed
>
> model laws

Organization of Codes of Ethics

Kultgen (1988) pointed out that the "basic ideal for an adequate code is that the provisions should provide an objective basis for major ethical questions confronted by the professional" (p. 240). Therefore, it is recommended that codes be organized according to *relationships*. Such relationships would include (a) duties of the individual professional to clients, students, employers, institutions, colleagues, the professional associations, public, and society and abstract principles such as truth and justice; (b) duties of employers and institutions to individual professionals and to the public and society as well as the abstract principles; and (c) duties of the profession and professional associations to the individual professional, to society, and to abstract principles. To illustrate this point, Fraleigh (1993) uses the code of the American Association of University Professors (AAUP) as an example. He noted that the AAUP "organizes its brief code around the duties of the professor to the discipline, to students, to colleagues, to the institution, and to the community" (p. 17). J. C. Callahan (1988) used as an example the code of social workers and pointed out that it shows the duties of the individual social worker to himself or herself as a social worker, to clients, colleagues, employers, the profession, and society.

Dill (1982) suggested organizing codes by *responsibilities*. Based on the responsibilities of the varying positions sport managers may hold, it is possible to list the responsibilities of the particular job or position and be certain each is addressed. In his research, Kultgen (1988) identified ways of organizing by *types of action*, which might include (a) competence or the objectivity and honesty of qualifications; (b) contribution to the body of knowledge by research and publication; (c) respect for autonomy embracing privacy, confidentiality, and trade secrets; (d) territorial rights of colleagues, which includes cooperation, giving proper credit, and fair competition; and (e) truthfulness in public statements.

> Codes of ethics should document the profession's ideals, ensure a sense of trust, and serve as a foundation for the professional education of those who aspire to the profession. They may be organized according to relationships, responsibilities, and types of action of Sport Managers/Organizations/Businesses.

Because no two organizations are exactly the same, the manner in which each represents its code will be different. The ways to organize a code of ethics are not limited to the categories previously noted; however, some organizations have found these categories helpful. Kultgen (1988) in his work discovered as many as 15 categories under classes of action It is possible to combine several of the categories discussed or to expand the categories as long as accounting of the multiple ethical issues of an individual in a particular profession.

Limitations to Codes of Ethics

Many individuals are quick to voice opposition to and negatively judge codes of ethics. Some objections note that codes of ethics are too broad and lack pattern or structure. Although ambiguities may be present in some codes, efforts toward interpretation and procedures for adopting interpretations need to be established. It is insufficient to claim *ambiguity* or lack of knowledge as a reason for not establishing a code of ethics. Actually, other language usages are often questioned and need to be interpreted. The *enforcement* of codes of ethics presents another issue. Without enforcement, the code will not be effective. Bowie and Duska (1990) stated that "a code of ethics without adequate enforcement is hardly a code at all. An effective code of ethics must be enforced and must have real penalties attached to it in order for it to bring about conformity" (p. 99). Participation in the development of the code of ethics presents another issue. If there is not participation by all employees as well as the public the organization serves, the code may be deemed unacceptable. The concept of codes of ethics as ideological *smokescreens* that mask the economic self-interest and social power of the organization is yet another criticism in addition to the lack of enforcement and *penalty* for violations (Jennings et al., 1987).

Another point that is made about ethical guidelines and codes of ethics for sport organizations includes the problem that what is considered the ethical way of doing things is not always conducive to coaches keeping their jobs. In NCAA Division I colleges and universities, coaches are generally fired if they do not produce winning teams. The challenge is to maintain a successful program while subscribing to ethical standards.

Chonko and Hunt (1985) explain that codes of ethics may be ineffective if they have not been integrated into the corporate culture. Codes that are developed and placed aside are worthless. The existence of ethical codes is insufficient to effect ethical behavior unless they are enforced.

Key Concepts

ambiguity

enforcement

penalties

Sample Code of Ethics

Professional organizations that deal with the study of sport and sport management have instituted codes, statements, and guidelines that define their ethical directions. Among such organizations are The North American Society for the Sociology of Sport (NASSS), the North American Society for Sport Management (NASSM), and the Youth Sports Institute. In addition to the professions of law and medicine, codes of ethics have also been written for sport organizations, coaches, teachers, and administrators. A Bill of Rights for Young Athletes, which outlined the rights for youths in sport was developed through the American Alliance for Health, Physical Education, Recreation and Dance (AAHPERD). Although the points in the young athletes' bill of rights served as guidelines noting the ethical parameters regarding participation in sport, a more specific code of ethics for coaches developed through the Youth Sports Institute (Seefeldt, 1979) was developed. This code reads as follows:

Code of Ethics for Coaches

1. I will treat each player, opposing coach, official, parent and administrator with respect and dignity.

2. I will do my best to learn the fundamental skills, teaching and evaluation techniques, and strategies of my sport.

3. I will become thoroughly familiar with the rules of my sport.

4. I will become familiar with the objectives of the youth sports program with which I am affiliated. I will strive to achieve these objectives and communicate them to my players and their parents.

5. I will uphold the authority of officials who are assigned to the contests in which I coach and I will assist them in every way to conduct fair and impartial competitive contests.

6. I will learn the strengths and weaknesses of my players so that I might place them into situations where they have a maximum opportunity to achieve success.

7. I will conduct my practices and games so that all players have an opportunity to improve their skill level through active participation.

8. I will communicate to my players and their parents the rights and responsibilities of individuals on our team.

9. I will cooperate with the administrator of our organization in the enforcement of rules and regulations and I will report any irregularities that violate sound competitive practices.

10. I will protect the health and safety of my players by insisting that all of the activities under my control are conducted for their psychological and physiological welfare, rather than for the vicarious interests of adults. (Seefeldt, 1979, p. 4).

The National Association for Sport and Physical Education has developed a code of conduct that is presented through eight principles for the discipline and practice of these fields. This code is to serve as a guide for both students and professionals in the broad range of study and application of sport and physical education. The opening paragraphs expressly note the services provided, the individuals who are to receive the services, and the responsibilities of the practitioners. This particular code notes an acceptance of responsibility for ethical practice and offers a framework for the resolution of ethical dilemmas. Although the code is not an exhaustive list regarding professional integrity, it serves as a good example.

National Association for Sport and Physical Education Code of Conduct

Sport and physical education practitioners value sport and physical activity's contribution to overall human development. They are committed to increasing, refining, and promoting knowledge that relates to the contribution of sport and physical education to overall human welfare across a lifetime of physical activity. Through proficient application of professional skills, they promote personal, professional, and social well-being in sport and physical education experiences, regardless of an individual's socioeconomic status, age, gender, race, ethnicity, national origin, religion, disability, or sexual orientation.

Sport and physical education practitioners realize that establishing and maintaining high standards is imperative for the discipline and its professions. They teach and coach relevant knowledge and skills by implementing best practices gained through appropriate qualifications and experiences. As a community of scholars and practitioners, they are dedicated to ongoing knowledge and skill development through involvement or interest in research projects that use accredited methods of critical inquiry. They take an active and supportive role in the various organizational structures that serve and promote the discipline and practice of sport and physical education.

Sport and physical education practitioners are responsible for the integrity of the profession. They strive to embody values, virtues, and standards of excellence appropriate to teaching, coaching, research, and other sport and physical education professions.

Sport and physical education practitioners are responsible for promoting a healthful community. They actively pursue professional goals, realizing the importance of their own and their fellow professional's commitment to uphold ethical duties and social responsibilities to others.

Sport and Physical Education practitioners:

1. maintain professional and personal standing through the highest standards of ethical behavior.

2. participate in, and encourage others to engage in, appropriate sport and physical education activities that contribute to overall human welfare across a life time of physical activity.

3. critically discuss and communicate with others what collective knowledge, and which shared practices, best embody the importance of sport and physical education to overall human welfare.

4. strive to achieve and maintain accepted standards of excellence in sport and physical education (i.e., National Standards for Physical Education, National Standards for Athletic Coaches, etc.).

5. attain relevant qualifications and experiences necessary to carry out professional duties and obligations with competence, honor, and integrity.

6. seek out and implement appropriate instructional methods that reflect best practice in teaching physical education and coaching sport.

7. engage in, or understand, valid research that furthers the scientific and non-scientific understanding of sport and physical education.

8. provide appropriate service to organizations that promote the value and importance of sport and physical education's contribution to overall human welfare. (Code of Conduct for Sport & Physical Educators, 1999-2000, p. 8).

Due to the unsportsmanlike conduct in youth sports, codes of ethics have been and are currently being implemented. Such codes are not for the young players, however, but for the parents of the children. In Jupiter, FL, if parents wanted their child or children to play on one of the Jupiter Athletic Association Teams, the adults had to watch a video on sportsmanship and then sign a code of ethics that included a pledge that stated: "I will remember that the game is for youth—not adults—and I will do my very best to make youth sports fun for my child" (Kultgen, as cited in Fraleigh, 1988, p. 85). If this code is broken, the individuals are banished from the association's games for up to a year.

National Athletic Trainer's Code of Professional Practice

The responsibilities of the athletic training professional are monumental. These individuals constantly deal with the protection of the welfare of the athlete and must not only be certified or qualified to carry out their duties, but must maintain high ethical standards in order to ensure the safety of each individual. The following National Athletic Trainer's Code of Professional Practice emphasizes these ethical principles.

1. Athletic trainers should neither practice nor condone discrimination on the basis of race, color, sex, age, religion, or national origin.

2. Athletic trainers should not condone, engage in, or defend unsporting conduct or practices.

3. Athletic trainers should provide care based on the needs of the individual athlete. They should not discriminate based on athletic ability.

4. Athletic trainers should strive to achieve the highest level of competence. They should use only those techniques and preparations that they are qualified and authorized to administer.

5. Athletic trainers should recognize the need for continuing education to remain proficient in their practice. They should be willing to consider new procedures within guidelines that ensure safety.

6. Athletic trainers should recognize that personal problems may occur, which may interfere with professional effectiveness. Accordingly, they should refrain from undertaking any activity in which their personal problems are

likely to lead to inadequate performance or harm to an athlete or colleague.

7. Athletic trainers should be truthful and not misleading when stating their education, training, and experience. (National Athletic Trainers' Association, 1990, p. 341)

The Code of Ethics of the North American Society for Sport Management

(accepted by NASSM, June, 1992)

The following canons or principles, arranged according to category or dimension, shall be considered by the sport manager in the performance of professional duties:

Category I: The Professional's Conduct as a Sport Manager

a. Individual Welfare. The sport manager should hold paramount the safety, health, and welfare of the individual in the performance of professional duties.

b. Service Where Competent. The sport manager should perform services only in areas of competence.

c. Public Statements. The sport manager should issue public statements in an objective and truthful manner, and shall make every effort to explain where statements are personal opinions.

d. Solicitation of Employment. The sport manager should seek employment only where a need for services exists.

e. Propriety. The sport manager should maintain high standards of personal conduct in the capacity or identity of the physical and health educator.

f. Competence and Professional Development. The sport manager should strive to become and remain proficient in professional practice and the performance of professional functions.

g. Integrity. The sport manager should act in accordance with the highest standards of professional integrity.

Category II: The Professional's Ethical Obligations to Students/Clients

a. Primacy of Students'/Clients' Interests. The sport manager's primary responsibility is to students/clients.

b. Service as Agent or Trustee. The sport manager, when acting in professional matters for employer or student/client, should be a faithful agent or trustee.

c. Rights and Prerogatives of Clients. The sport manager should, in considering the nature of the relationship with the student/client, make every effort to foster maximum self-determination on the part of the students/clients.

d. Confidentiality and Privacy. The sport manager should respect the privacy of students/clients and hold in confidence all information obtained in the course of professional service.

e. Fees. When setting fees for service in private or commercial settings, the sport manager should ensure that they are fair, reasonable, considerate, and commensurate with the service performed and with due respect to the students'/clients' ability to pay.

Category III: The Professional's Ethical Responsibility to Employers/Employing Organizations

a. Commitments to Employers/Employing Organizations. The sport manager should adhere to any and all commitments made to the employing organization. The relationship should be characterized by fairness, nonmaleficence, and truthfulness.

Category IV: The Professional's Ethical Responsibility to Colleagues/Peers and to the Profession

a. Respect, Fairness, and Courtesy. The sport manager should treat colleagues with respect, courtesy, fairness, and good faith.

b. Dealing with Colleagues' Students/Clients. The sport manager has the responsibility to relate to the students/clients of colleagues with full professional consideration.

c. Maintaining the Integrity of the Profession. The sport manager should uphold and advance the values and ethical standards, the knowledge, and the mission of the profession.

d. Development of Knowledge. The sport manager should take responsibility for identifying, developing, and fully utilizing knowledge for professional practice.

e. Approach to Scholarship and Research. The sport manager engaged in study and/or research should be guided by the accepted convention of scholarly inquiry.

Category V. The Professional's Ethical Responsibility to Society

a. Promoting the General Welfare. The sport manager should promote the general welfare of society.

b. Community Service. The sport manager should regard as primary his/her professional service to others. He/she should assist the profession in making information and services relating to desirable physical activity and health practices available to the general public.

c. Reporting Code Infractions. The sport manager has an ethical responsibility to society in that minor and major infractions by colleagues should be reported to the appropriate committee of the professional society (when and where such mechanism exists).

(Chelladurai, 1999, p. 42)

The codes of ethics cited above in their current form, may not adhere to all of the points recommended for content, but they are nonetheless statements intended to ensure ethical behavior and are worthy of exploration in all business/organizational structures with deal with sport and/or the product of sports.

Sanctions for Violation of Codes of Ethics

Although the Academy of Management, the North American Society for Sport Management, and the National Intramural and Recreational Sport Association have created codes of ethics for their association members, in these organizations, no equivalent exists to those sanctions that might be enforced for the violation of ethical codes in the legal or medical professions. That is, at this time there is no formal disbarment or loss of license, for example (Chelladurai, 1999).

One of the major criticisms of codes of ethics is that they state how one ought to behave within an organization or business, but rarely are directions provided for the reporting of violations, nor are punishments or sanctions set forth for code violations. In many cases, the self-regulatory function of codes has not been effective (Fraleigh, 1993). The detection and punishment of those who violate the code need to be addressed. As with the concept of due process, a procedure needs to be put in place by which the accused is informed of the charges as well as gains the opportunity to rebut the charges. Punishment for violations may take the form of sanctions that may be imposed internally by a particular business or educational institution or externally by a professional organization.

Russell (1991) summarized the types of internally imposed sanctions that have been more frequently reported:

1. verbal reprimand;

2. letters of reprimand (may or may not be part of an individual's permanent record);

3. monitoring of current and/or review of previous research or work;

4. salary/promotion freeze;

5. restriction of duties;

6. termination of work on a particular project;

7. reduction in title;

8. separation from workplace with or without loss of benefits; and

9. fines.

Those sanctions that may be imposed externally may include

10. revocation of licenses, certifications, accreditations, and publications;

11. letters to parties who have been offended;

12. discontinuance of service to outside agencies;

13. release of information to agencies, the profession, newspapers, superiors;

14. referral to legal system for further actions;

15. fines; and

16. penalties by ruling bodies (e.g., NCAA).

Often, with certain violations of codes of ethics, various forms of rehabilitation are recommended. Because there is such an emphasis on winning and success, repeat offenses may occur. The existence of the code itself is insufficient. If offenses are to be eliminated, a mentoring system that includes the education and training of individuals within the organization or business may be required.

> Employee input should determine how a code of ethics is developed, accepted, and instituted. Then the code must be enforced by the organization according to the sanctions detailed in the document.

Summary

This chapter presented the needs, purposes and functions of codes of ethics. In addition, the organization of and components for a code of ethics were discussed, and examples were provided. It is important to realize that as strong as the need is for codes of ethics in professions, organizations, and businesses, the numerous limitations must be taken into consideration. It may be impossible for the code to encompass all possible ethical violations. In this case, a periodic evaluation of the code is necessary by members of the organization in order to update and cover issues that may have occurred. Regardless of the limitations, the development of an ethical code is warranted.

Questions for Consideration

1. Provide a rationale for the need for codes of ethics in the varying fields of sport management.

2. What is the value of organizing your code of ethics according to relationships, responsibilities, and actions?

3. What are the limitations of codes of ethics, and how can these be addressed?

4. What procedures would you use to have the greatest input from your personnel in developing a code of ethics for your organization?

5. How would you incorporate a code of ethics into a sport management setting?

PART III:
SPORT ETHICS APPLIED

Chapter Eight

Ethical Responsibilities and the Functions of Sport Managers

Chapter Objectives

• To review the concepts of planning, organizing, leading, and evaluating as functions of the sport manager

• To examine the relationship between ethics and each of the functions of sport managers

• To explore ethical concerns within various sport settings

In his text *Sport Management: Macro Perspectives*, Chelladurai (1985) discussed planning, organizing, leading, and evaluating as the four main functions of management. He indicated that these functions are inextricably intertwined with each other as well as with the concepts of ethics and personal, social, professional, and organizational responsibility within the management setting. The focus in the behavior approach to management includes the relationship between the tasks to be accomplished, the individuals involved in the process, and that which brings them together. Although planning is concerned with what is to be achieved and how it will be achieved, organizing, leading, and evaluating are concerned with who will be carrying out the specific tasks and in what organizational configuration, the motivation to be used to encourage production, how well the individuals carry out the task, and the overall effectiveness of the outcome. Chelladurai (1985) further pointed out that ethics and adherence to ethical standards are of the utmost importance in the workings of these relationships. Integrity and responsibility are to be established and maintained within each process and extend to the activities that are carried out and the individuals responsible for each task, program, and activity of the organization.

Other scholars, among them Mullin (1980) and Leith (1983), have described the functions of the manager as including those of planning, organizing, leading, and evaluating, but also add the concepts of controlling, staffing, motivating, communicating, and decision making. For the purposes of this chapter and in consideration of all the functions a manager performs, controlling, staffing, motivating, communicating, and decision making are considered within one or more of the major roles of planning, organizing, leading, and evaluating. For example, decision making and communication are assumed to take place in each of the four functions.

Planning is the process of establishing goals for individuals and scheduling their activities. As managers assign members of the group a specific goal, they expect each member to complete the goal within a specified time period. This is the foundation and most basic of the four functions of the manager. Although planning entails decision making, it is difficult to separate these two concepts from each other, but information regarding ethical decision making is covered in another section of this text (Chelladurai, 1985, 1999). Quarterman and Li (1998) further explained that planning involves identifying the organizational goals to be achieved and developing and implementing strategies to achieve the goals. For example, if there is the prediction of an increase in the enrollment in a private sports club for the coming year, planning for the club to be opened longer hours to accommodate the increased enrollment would be required (p. 109).

Because the planning process involves defining objectives, strategies, and policies, ethical standards and principles emerge from the outset and become the basis upon which the organization or project is founded. The decisions that are made regarding the planning process fit within the parameters of the identified seven-step model, which includes

(a) setting objectives,

(b) identifying constraints,

(c) generating alternatives,

(d) specifying performance criteria,

(e) evaluating alternatives,

(f) selecting alternatives, and

(g) preparing a formal document as needed (Filley, House & Kerr, 1976).

Integrity of the organization is maintained through professional standards of behavior or professional ethics. In addition, personal ethics as well as social responsibility would be considered in the setting of the objectives stage of the model. This is exemplified as individuals or organizations, or both, consider the areas of profitability, growth, market share, productivity and efficiency, leadership, client satisfaction, and social awareness in relation to the objectives and goals of the organization. The way in which each of these points is undertaken relates back to the primary objectives and is bound by the mission and philosophy of the organization.

An organization's ethical standards help it to maintain integrity.

In the process of generating alternative courses of action within the planning process, various constraints or restrictions may occur. These include, but are not limited to, those that are biological, authoritative, physical, technological, and economic in nature. Such constraints may hinder the progress of the plan; thus, the manner in which each of the alternatives is evaluated should follow an established set of criteria in order for the best choice to be made. Although creativity and the development of new ideas should be encouraged, attempting to develop and try new approaches may lead decision makers to set aside the task of interpreting constraints and thus lead to placing greater emphasis on the task or goal at hand, rather than on the ethical concerns relating to the process and product. For example, barriers encountered during planning, such as budgetary constraints, may necessitate the use of products of an inferior quality in order to meet production deadlines.

Problems that may arise in the organizational goals as well as a lack of information may limit one's rational and potentially one's ethical approach to planning. Maintaining a rational perspective should be a primary goal within the process (Chelladurai, 1985).

Organizing

Quarterman and Li (1998) explained the function of organizing as "dividing the organization into work units and subunits so their efforts will mesh and fulfill the overall objective" (p. 109). Fink, Jenks, & Willits (1983) pointed out that organizing is the arrangement of people and tasks to accomplish the goals of the organization. Specifically, the task of organizing delineates the relationships between the tasks and the individuals who are to perform them. The principles associated with organizing include (a) specialization, (b) span of control, (c) departmentalization, (d) unity of command, and (e) responsibility and authority. As sport managers incorporate these principles associated with organizing into the sport setting, they are basically setting up a decision-making process that will allow the most qualified individual to make the decision based on the best available information. Again, the close connection between ethics and decision making is brought into the functions of the sport manager with the task and responsibilities of organizing. The placement of the proper responsibilities with capable individuals takes on new meaning as one's capabilities are evaluated and judged appropriate or inappropriate according to the task at hand.

Using the setting of the private sport club as with the planning process, an example of the task of organizing could be explained by the following: "After conducting an assessment, the general manager establishes a work unit for teaching golf at the club. A full-time coordinator is appointed who will coordinate three teaching pros and a new golf course with an adequate budget" (Quarterman & Li, 1998, p. 109).

What is intended through proper organizing is that the relationship between the individuals and the tasks to be completed will be efficient and free from harmful friction. The function of organizing requires the combination of conceptual, human, and technical skills on the part of the sport manager. Conceptual skills are considered the ability of the manager to envision the organization as a whole as well as the relationships among all of its parts. An entire organization may be made up of several entities; thus, being able to conceptualize the "whole" organization and its interactions with the other entities is critical to being able to work within the organization. Interpersonal or human skills are needed in order for the manager to work with others and to coordinate group and individual efforts toward the established goal. Being able to perceive potential problems and use good interpersonal communication skills (both oral and written), combined with techniques of resolving conflict, is critically important for the sport manager. Technical skills are also needed within all of the manager's functions. Specialized skills, knowledge, tools, techniques, and resources are considered to be technical skills. The preparation of budget reports, marketing techniques, computer knowledge, and other resources that give a unique perspective to the task at hand are examples of such skills. Conceptual, interpersonal, and technical skills are needed in different ways and in varying degrees within sport management positions, but are required at some level in all positions (Quarterman & Li, 1998).

Important Managerial Skills

Philosophical relativism—There are no universal values or morals.

Conceptual skills—the ability to envision the entire organization and the relationships between each of its parts

Interpersonal skills—the ability to interact and communicate effectively with others

Technical skills—field specific knowledge and resources

Leading

It is within the function of leading that our personal and social responsibilities are assumed as sport managers. Leading is the task of motivating individuals to move toward a desired goal. Motivation is presented by Chelladurai (1985) as the basis of the function of leading. With the proper knowledge and understanding of the motivational factors that affect both the leader and followers, the process of leading can more effectively be carried out. In the case of the private sport club, the leading function is implemented by the manager who wishes to influence the employees to perform their jobs with excellence as they move toward attaining the desired goals and objectives of the organization. Therefore, the general manager encourages the golf teaching pro to prepare weekend course packages for local executives who have expressed an interest in learning golf skills. In this process, the general manager indicates that a new rewards system will be in place for the support staff in the form of flexible benefits, merit pay, or profit sharing, for example (Quarterman & Li, 1998).

Personal and social responsibility must be assumed in order to understand the relationship between the behavior and needs of the follower and the task to be accomplished. On a human level, regard and respect for others, no matter the diversity of the group, are paramount. Good leadership invites mutuality and reciprocity in the personnel relationships between peers, superiors, and subordinates. The sport manager is responsible for bridging the gap (if one exists) between the goals and mission of the organization and those of the individual working within the system in order to maintain the integrity of the goals sought. Once again, the skills associated with leading are relevant to the functions of organizing, planning, and evaluating as well.

Evaluating	Chelladurai (1985) stated that "evaluating is defined as the process of assessing the degree to which the organization as a whole and various units and individuals have accomplished what they set out to do" (p. 171). Quarterman and Li (1998) noted the concept of controlling (as part of evaluating) as "monitoring progress against goals and objectives derived from planning; evaluating performance to determine if the goals were met as planned" (p. 109). In our private sport club, the general manager, after a period of time and careful observations and monitoring of the progress of the new golf program, meets with the coordinator to share the strengths and weaknesses of his or her evaluation and discusses ways to make improvements or to make the program more attractive to bring in new members. An evaluation of the personnel may be a part of the observation and evaluation phase.

The manner in which the organization, its units, and individuals are evaluated is an extremely important aspect of the sport manager's responsibilities. The evaluation of an employee should be based on the job description and specific criteria regarding expectations of the employee in order to ensure that the evaluation is equitable and fair. In addition, the day-to-day tasks of the job performed should be noted (Clement, 1991). It is vital that multiple input be given from diverse perspectives within the organization regarding the employee. The perspectives of superiors as well as subordinates with whom the individual works should serve as input for an effective evaluation process. Because organizational effectiveness and individual performance are evaluated based on prescribed criteria, obtaining the needed information to judge adequately the effectiveness of any facet of the organization or individuals within the organization, or both, is crucial. That information must also be shared with those involved in the organization in a manner that maintains the integrity of the process and the dignity of the individual being evaluated.

Evaluation without feedback is undesirable. The manner in which the feedback is shared with the employees should follow prescribed legal and ethical standards regarding evaluation. The results should be made available to the employees and discussed with them personally. A due-process system should also be in place in the event the employee wishes to present an opposing position or alternative explanation to the evaluation. Employees must be afforded the opportunity to overcome any critical remarks noted in an evaluation, and proper monitoring of this situation must occur. The entire process of evaluation should be carried out in a manner that protects the rights of the employee (Clement, 1991).

> In order to be effective, evaluations must be followed by feedback.

Another type of evaluation, *job feedback*, is addressed by Hackman and Oldham (1980) and can be relied upon by the individual employee and, in some cases, the supervisor. Job feedback is described as "the degree to which carrying out the work activities provides the individual with direct and clear information about the effectiveness of his or her performance" (p. 80). Job feedback is immediate in that as the task is being performed, the employee realizes that the approach or decision is or is not working, or after reflecting on the performance of a particular task, the employee realizes that there would have been better ways to carry it out.

In such cases, job feedback could lead to a self-evaluation. The key in these instances, however, is to make immediate changes so that the corrections may be made to achieve the desired outcome.

Ethical Considerations and Functions of Sports Managers

The ethical and social responsibility of those involved with the functions that have been discussed includes examination, evaluation, and efforts to connect the mission and goals of the organization with those of the people working with the organization in order to maintain integrity. This effort in and of itself is not a simple one and requires much authentic dialogue on the part of those involved. When different sport settings are addressed in conjunction with the functions of the sport manager, the following must be considered:

1. level of sport (e.g., Olympic, recreational, professional, sport for special populations, and sport in educational institutions);

2. mission and goals of the organization or sport program;

3. values, beliefs, and goals of the leaders and followers within each setting;

4. available resources (e.g., funding, personnel, facilities, equipment);

5. programs and services offered within each setting; and

6. current and potential consumers/clients of the program(s).

Once the sport manager has an in-depth understanding of the previous points, ethical responsibility for planning, organizing, leading, and evaluating can then be realized in a more complete context.

At each level of sport, a consideration of all individuals who wish to participate must be included (i.e., those working as sport managers as well as consumers of programs and services offered). An approach that may assist the sport manager to focus on such issues is a concept suggested by Hums (1990). She recommended that we think about social participation and accountability, work, human rights, peace and justice, and world populations. Hums's recommendation serves as a guide to sport managers as it encourages us to think beyond the confined functions as they are connected to a more global perspective of those functions and how broader interpretations can be implemented. A more detailed analysis of the concept suggested by Hums will be taken up in chapter 11.

Key Concepts

evaluating

human rights

leading

motivating

organizing

peace and justice

planning

social participation and accountability

world populations

Moral Dilemmas in Sport Settings

Following are examples of moral and ethical issues as related to the concepts discussed in this chapter.

1. Daphne is responsible for the planning of a building project for a new sports arena. Expenses for this project are extremely high. One of her bosses, in this case, the general manager for the team that will use the facility, is insisting on better locker-room facilities and a more respon-

sive playing surface that will help prevent injuries to his athletes. Activists from an organization promoting better accessibility for the disabled are demanding more wheelchair ramps and viewing areas for the mobility impaired (even though the minimum building-accessibility guidelines are already being followed as required by law); otherwise, they will take their case to the "court of public opinion" and picket the facility—something the facility's management team wants to avoid.

One day the general contractor walks into Daphne's office and says, "I've heard about your problem trying to please everybody at once." She nods, silently marveling at how her problems have become public knowledge. "You know," he continues, "for no extra money, I can provide all the upgrades that are being demanded."

"How?" she asks.

"As long as you don't ask how I'm going to do it." He brings his finger to his lips and winks.

Daphne's mind races through the options suddenly made available. She assumes he may use less adequate building materials than originally called for in the bid, but she isn't sure. She peers quizzically at him, and he reads her mind. "Well, there may be a few less bathroom stalls," he says, "and the spectator seats may not be as comfortable as originally hoped. Anyway, let me know if you're interested, okay?" He turns and walks out of her office, leaving her to imagine all the stress that will be mercifully lifted off her shoulders.

What issues are involved with this scenario and what would you do?

2. How should the organizer of an intramural program, handle the following situation?

Past performance in both the intramural coed basketball and men's ice hockey leagues has involved numerous incidents of violent play, improper player conduct (including foul language and obscene gestures), eligibility violations, and abuse toward officials. Just last year, for instance, a hockey referee (after an admittedly questionable call) was sent to the hospital when a stick "accidentally" hit him in the face and fractured his nose.

On the other hand, tempers can and do get heated in competitive sports, and hockey is a violent game in its own right. Furthermore, few players have requested any changes to the program, except the hiring of better officials, and fan attendance has dramatically increased, bringing in much-needed money from concession sales. This extra income helps draw better referees through an increase in salaries and also funds a woman's recreational racquetball league—which will hopefully help silence the incessant demands from the Women's Center on campus for fewer men's or coed activities and more strictly women's activities.

Given the situation, what organizational reforms, if any, should be implemented to curtail and eliminate these unfortunate behaviors? If reforms are implemented, should they differ in the case of men's sport as opposed to women's sport? How will these reforms affect the program? Is reform even necessary—or the organizer's responsibility?

3. As manager of the New Body Health and Racquet Club, Siddhanta noticed that some employees are not performing up to club customer-service standards. Some take too many breaks, others leave work early and arrive late. A few have become less than courteous to the patrons. It is an embarrassing situation, especially when some of the club members have angrily approached you about these incidents, complaining that their high monthly fees should be able to pay for a decent staff. "After all," they gripe, "our dues pay your salaries."

Siddhanta has been meaning to deal with the situation, but he has been preoccupied and frequently absent from the club—visiting school administrators, politicians, day-care providers, tutors, and lawyers. His son Mark was suspended from middle school for carrying a weapon on school grounds. A ludicrous charge, he raves, considering the weapon was a wood awl, provided by the shop teacher so Mark could finish his project at home. But the school administrators insist he intended to use it as a weapon, and the school district's zero-tolerance policy cannot make any exceptions.

One day at the club, while Siddhanta is preparing discipline procedures for the ineffectual employees (including one who is being laid off), the club owner calls him into the office. Once in the office, he complains that Siddhanta has been away from his job responsibilities too much, leaving work early and arriving later than he should. In fact, the club members have been complaining about his ineffectiveness in dealing with their concerns.

Siddhanta apologizes, but explains that he has personal difficulties of his own. The owner sympathizes, but reminds him that there are members here who have problems as well. "Problems," he emphasizes "the members pay me to pay you to fix." The owner sits back in his chair and asks him to come up with a plan to rectify all the problems facing him and the club.

How should he respond? How should he address and improve his own performance, as well as that of the employees who demonstrate unsatisfactory work? How should he balance the needs of his family with the needs of his employer? What leadership concerns and issues pertain to this example?

4. As head football coach of NCAA Division I Eastern State University (ESU), Coach Bob Montgomery posted a winning record in each of his 10 previous years at ESU. This year, however, with a fairly young squad, his record fell to 4 wins and 8 losses, much to the disappointment of fans, students, faculty, and school administrators. Applica-

tions for enrollment are down this year, ticket sales are lagging, newspaper editorials are becoming more and more vitriolic, the athletic director gave him a poor formal evaluation, and representatives from the alumni association have already spoken to the university president about Bob's coaching abilities.

With the prospect of the team's performance in the coming year looking bleak as recruitment progresses more poorly than expected, what was once secure has now become uncertain. Bob is concerned for his future as a head football coach. Naturally, this new and very real possibility of unemployment has caused a great deal of stress in his private life. With substantial debt, a recently purchased home, and a wife expecting twins in a couple of months, Bob has spent many nights listening to his wife cry herself to sleep.

One day, Coach Montgomery receives a call from the ESU president asking that he come to her office the following morning. After 10 years, he thinks he knows the president and believes her to be a fair and compassionate person. Perhaps if he reasons with her, he can salvage his position and his future. What will he say? Can he argue that his poor evaluations were not fair? Might he argue that the criteria for evaluation were insufficient or simply erroneous? How might he reply to the special interest groups demanding his removal? Or should he just accept the inevitable and tender his resignation, eliminating any messy fight to save his job and assuring a good reference when he begins looking for a new position?

Ethical Analysis

The following discussion analyzes the ethical dimensions and implications of the third scenario above (New Body Health and Racquet Club) to demonstrate how moral principles relate to a given case. Readers should try to analyze the other examples and draw their own conclusions and resolutions to any particular problems.

In general, the third case involves the role of the manager and the functions of dealing with personnel. It is clear from this example that employee performance is poor, and this could have a negative impact on club members and the success of the club itself. Rectifying problems with employees is a delicate matter because the sources of the problems are not always apparent. In this case we know that the manager is having problems at home, but in some cases that will not be clear, and issues in personal lives or in the workplace can be monumental. Some issues that lead to poor job performance are private matters that people just do not want to reveal and talk about.

On the other hand, the behavior of the manager in this case is relatively no different from that of the employees. The main issue here may not be what the employees are experiencing, but a lack of leadership and integrity shown by the manager. Employees may feel that if the manager is displaying a poor work ethic, then it is acceptable to live up to that standard. The owner, however, perceives the situation much differently and would want the quality of performance for all employees, including the manager, to improve significantly. Under these circumstances, the owner might insist that the manager alter his or her behavior to set an example for the rest of the employees. Initially, the owner might be able to identify the personal and work-related problems of the manager and try to encourage the individual to make concrete changes in behavior. If specific goals and regular follow-up evaluation sessions could be established and implemented, then this might be a good first step toward significant improvements. The owner might also specify a time period to realize these changes and attach particular consequences, including termination of the manager or of others in this process.

Like the owner, the manager has a mandate to supervise and access employees under her or his change. In this situation, the manager might proceed by showing concern for each individual in order to identify the problems shared by all employees. Having genuine interest in the well-being of others, treating others as ends and not means, and maintaining an impartial view toward others could be some principles to follow in trying to resolve the issue in this example. These principles refer to some aspects of the deontological ethical theories discussed in earlier chapters.

The application of the moral guidelines suggested above to the present case may require that the manager meet each employee privately to discuss, in a constructive way, the reasons for the poor job-related behavior. The meeting should be staged in a comfortable, nonthreatening setting to ensure that a mutual understanding of the problems is reached. Once the meeting with each employee has taken place, the manager could try to locate any common concerns that were raised in the discussion.

Let us assume that the main problem was a lack of incentive and motivation on the part of the employees because such a lack was perceived in the manager's conduct. If the manager could propose that employees help decide on strategies and standards to change their working conditions, this might create greater enthusiasm among employees to fulfill their duties. Moreover, the manager could provide assurances, through periodic evaluations, so the manager's own performance would also meet acceptable levels. Here is the possibility of a mutual, interactive process being implemented where impartiality, respect for others, and fair treatment exist at three levels of management.

Summary

This chapter discussed the functions of the sport manager in relation to the ethics. When the functions and roles of the sport manager are considered, ethics is not something that should slip away or be considered in another category or as a second or third thought when one assumes responsibilities in sport management. The theory and practice of ethics in regard to planning, organizing, leading, and evaluating should be ever present. The need for ethical practices in sport management should be at the foundation of the sport manager's responsibilities, beginning with the planning process and permeating each of the other functions.

Questions for Consideration

1. In which of the functions of the sport manager do you envision potential violations of ethical behavior?

2. What steps would you take to ensure integrity within each function?

3. Is the concept of "Sport for All" a reasonable expectation in our society given the differences in interests, abilities, and opportunities?

4. Do specialized sport events (e.g., the Gay Games, Highland Scottish Games, Maccabean Games, Senior Games, Good Will Games, and the Special Olympics) contribute to the concept of "Sport for All?"

Chapter Nine

Ethical Decision Making

Chapter Objectives

- To examine decision making in sport

- To introduce models of ethical decision making

- To explore ethical decision making in sport settings

- To understand the concepts of moral insensitivity and moral callousness

Making a decision is a judgment or a choice between alternatives (Drucker, 1966, p. 143). Because decision making involves judgment, it is important that the sport manager be certain that the judgment is founded in ethics and that the decision is arrived at having considered the implications of ethical and unethical behavior. Decision making is rooted in philosophy, specifically in the areas of logic and reason and of ethics and moral judgment. The philosophical treatment of these is normative, indicating arguments on how one *should* think and act. Descriptive models of logic in decision making are utility or probability based, and much has been done to expand such theories into examples of actual reasoning processes. This work has been integrated into business research. Normative theories of ethics are difficult to put into descriptive form, thus indicating to us that perhaps this process should move *from* the examination of the outcomes of decisions and *toward* the examination of the processes used by individuals, whereby choices are made from a number of possible outcomes (Strong & Meyer, 1992).

According to Chelladurai (1985), decision making permeates all management activities, is closely allied with the managerial function of planning, and involves making choices or the best choice from the alternatives generated within the planning model. Within this process, the goals to be achieved are identified, alternatives are generated and evaluated against the established criteria, and the best alternative is chosen. Rationality plays an important role in this process and affects the selection of the best means to achieve a goal and the selection of the goal itself. Thus, decision making is a cognitive and moral process as well as a social one.

Because more information may be generated from a group than from one person, it may be wise to include members of the organization in the decision-making process. Given the importance of identifying goals for the organization as well as carrying out all the phases of the planning process, it is obvious that the amount of colleague interaction and shared information is critical and will require ethical and moral considerations. The degree to which the sport manager involves others in the organization in decision making varies. Not seeking input from others or employing the autocratic style, involving one or a few members in the organization in the decision, consulting everyone, or allowing the entire group to make the decision are the degrees of interaction that may occur.

The classic work of Vroom and Yetton (1973) that denoted ways to involve group or organization members in decision making has been termed by Chelladurai and colleagues as *decision styles*. These include

(a) Autocratic I (AI), in which leader makes decision on own based on available information;

(b) Autocratic II (AII), in which leader obtains needed information from members and makes decision on own (The leader may or may not explain the problem and members do not have a role in the decision);

(c) Consultive I (CI), in which leader shares problem with relevant members on an individual basis, takes their input into account, and makes decision on own;

(d) Consultive II (CII), in which leader shares problem with all members as a group, takes their input into account, and makes decision alone;

(e) Group II (GII), in which leader shares problem with group, allows group to generate and evaluate alternative solutions and arrive at consensus solution. [The leader role is that of chairperson (Chelladurai, 1993; Chelladurai & Arnot, 1985; Chelladurai & Haggerty, 1978; Chelladurai, Haggerty, & Baxter, 1989; Chelladurai & Quek, 1995).]

There are advantages and disadvantages to each of these degrees of input. If a sport manager is autocratic in decision making, it does not mean that this is negative, evil, or immoral in and of itself. There are times, in fact, when this style of decision making may be recommended. For example, the maturity of the group will affect the decision to be made as will the amount of information to which subordinates have access. This process is more time-consuming and may be divisive if the group is not cohesive or if there are conflicts among its members. Another factor to consider under autocratic decision making is that the group understands and accepts the decisions made by the leader—this is an advantage. Without this understanding and acceptance, carrying out the decisions in an effective manner may not occur. Participatory styles of decision making, however, do allow the flow of information to occur with less likelihood of hidden agendas being involved. Of course, this may not always be the case. Consultative and group forms of decision making have a greater possibility for higher rationality, understanding, and ownership of the decisions, as well as the possibility of having the decisions carried out in a more collegial and efficient manner. Some may consider the participatory process a more ethical approach to decision making because of the nature of the openness, the sharing of information, and the allowing others to contribute, thus giving the individuals in the group the sense of ownership for the decision. As a result, the process is likely to contribute to the positive nature of the individual's job and ultimate satisfaction among the members of the organization (Chelladurai, 1999).

Models of Ethical Decision Making

Using the concepts and theories discussed in the first part of this text, in addition to what is proposed in the second part is an appropriate basis upon which ethical choices in decision making could be based. To add to this, the work by Josepheson (1992) is suggested as a potential way for sport managers to explore ethical and moral obligations in decision making. In this approach, the areas of character are proposed for the sport manager to explore her or his ethical foundations. The areas of character include

1. trustworthiness (includes honesty, integrity, promise keeping, and loyalty);

2. respect;

3. responsibility (includes accountability, pursuit of excellence, and self-restraint);

4. justice and fairness;

5. caring; and

6. civic virtue and citizenship.

It is suggested that adherence to these areas will serve as a personal guide to ensure that decisions will be of an ethical quality. Although this process may sound as if it is a simple recipe to follow, much consideration must be given to the process of evaluating and choosing among alternatives. The choices involved must also be consistent with ethical principles. It is recommended that in making either professional or personal decisions, one must be aware of and eliminate unethical options and then select the best ethical alternative. Due to the competing values and interests involved in making ethical choices, the process is rather complex. Economic, social, professional, and other pressures usually intervene in the process, resulting in confusion and a question of employing the correct ethical decision.

Unethical decisions and improper conduct are often aligned with larger problems; that is, failing to perceive the ramifications and implications of certain actions and conduct as well as failing to express the moral convictions in one's behavior. Our focus may be on the end, such as increasing revenue in sport organizations or events, rather than on the promotion of an ethical ideal and how we should go about pursuing that goal in our conduct. The employment of problem-solving skills and sound reasoning is necessary to bring to fruition a union of ethical theory and practice. An evaluation must take place in terms of the integrity of the information that is at hand and upon which the decision is to be based. In addition, the ability to create alternative goals and ways to achieve them must be employed in order to eliminate unethical decisions. Foresight is also critical. The ability to envision the consequences of behavior is a skill the sport manager must develop. Evaluating the potential for risk and harm to others as a result of a decision or action is the social and moral responsibility of the sport manager (Josepheson, 1992).

Based on the work of Cavanaugh (1990), gathering facts for the decision to be made; incorporating the concepts of utility, rights, and justice; and considering overriding factors produce a model of ethical decision making that could be utilized by the sport manager. *Utility* refers to the aim of organizational goals in satisfying the constituencies of the organization. The goals should be attained as efficiently as possible by minimizing external costs imposed upon others, and employees should use every effective means to achieve organizational goals without jeopardizing them or entering into situations in which personal interests conflict with the goals. *Rights* refer to those individual rights regarding life and safety, truthfulness, privacy, freedom of conscience, free speech, and private property. Individuals have the right

(a) not to have their lives or safety unknowingly and unnecessarily endangered;

(b) not to be intentionally deceived by another, especially regarding what they have a right to know;

(c) to do whatever they choose outside working hours and to control information about their private lives;

(d) to refrain from carrying out any order that violates those commonly accepted moral or religious norms to which they adhere;

(e) to criticize conscientiously and truthfully the ethics or legality of corporate actions as long as the criticisms do not violate the rights of others in the organization; and

(f) to hold private property, especially as this right enables individuals and their families to be sheltered and to have the basic necessities of life.

Justice includes fair treatment, fair administration of rules, fair compensation, fair blame, and due process. Individuals similar to each other (e.g., in respect to job level and responsibilities) should be treated similarly. Those who differ in regard to the jobs or positions they hold should be treated differently in proportion to the differences between them. Rules should be administered consistently with fairness and impartiality. Individuals should be compensated for the cost of their injuries by those who are responsible for the injuries. Individuals should not be held responsible for matters over which they have no control, and the right to a fair and impartial hearing is required when an individual believes that personal rights have been violated. The following model by Trevino portrays these components.

Figure 9.1 Ethical Decision Making

Gather Facts for the Decision

Is the action acceptable according to the three ethical criteria?

1. Utility—Does it optimize benefits?
2. Rights—Does it respect the rights of those involved?
3. Justice—Is the action fair?

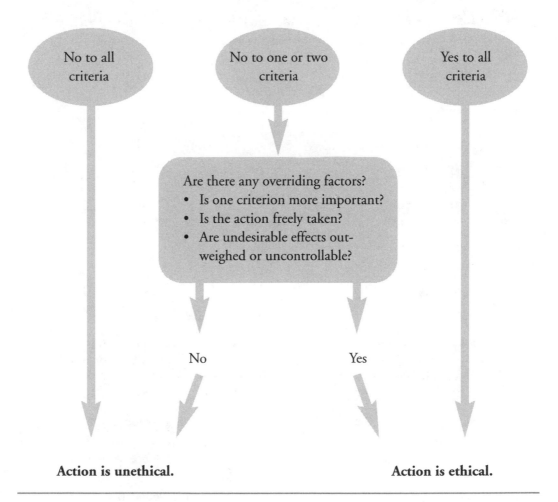

Action is unethical.   **Action is ethical.**

Flow diagram of ethical decision making. Reprinted by permission, from G. F. Cavanaugh, 1990, *American Business Values,* 3rd ed. (New York: American Management Assoc.), p. 195.

Trevino (1986) pointed out in the model above that decision making proposed by Trevino (1986) takes into consideration the concept of corporate and social responsibility that was covered in the introductory chapter to this text. Keep in mind that social responsibility refers to the moral, legal, or mental accountability on the part of individuals for oneself and others. Trevino's model indicates that there is a relationship between an individual's moral development and his or her ethical decision-making process. Moral development as presented by Kohlberg (1987) and Gilligan (1982) was also covered in an earlier chapter.

Figure 9.2 Managerial Decision-Making Model of Corporate Responsibility

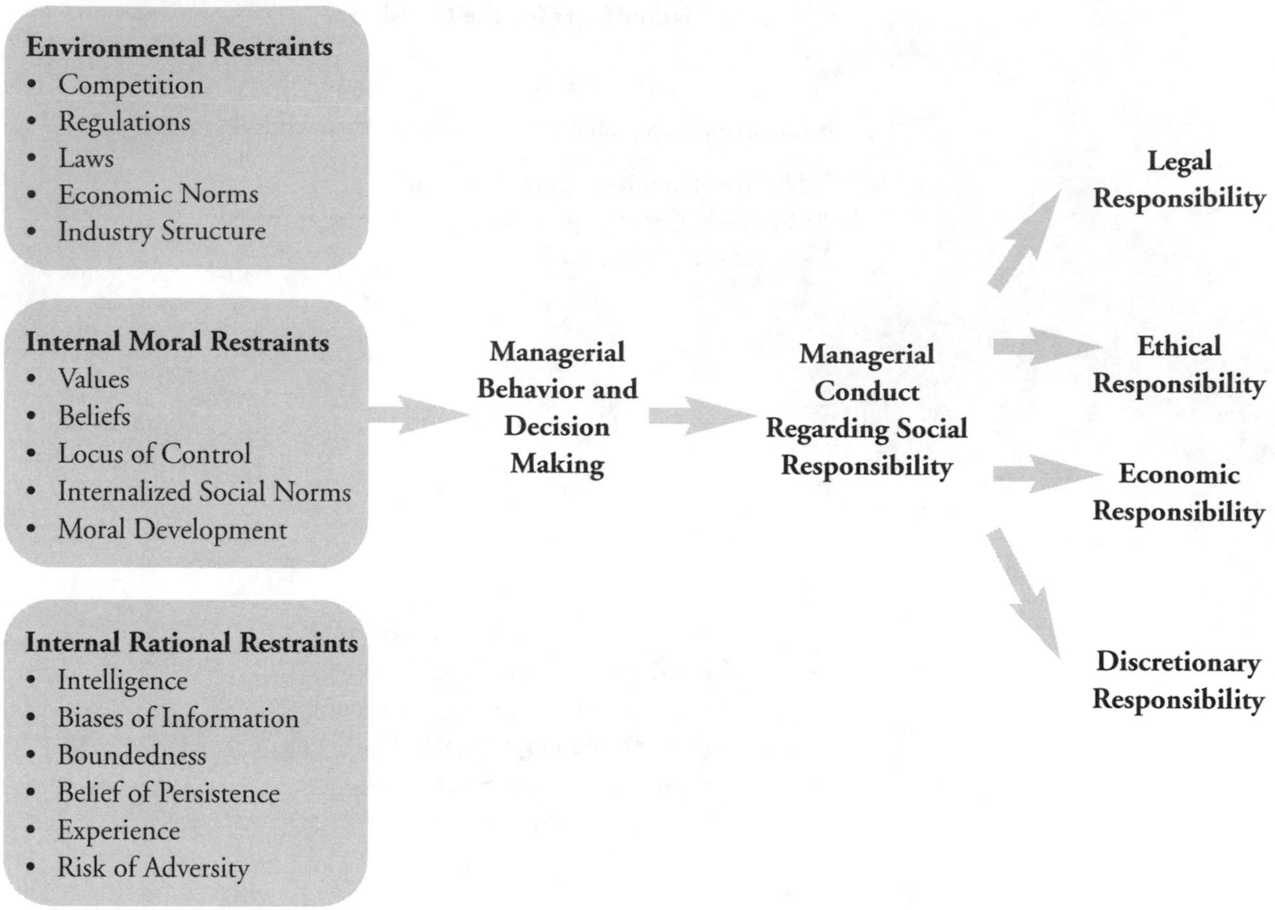

Environmental Restraints
- Competition
- Regulations
- Laws
- Economic Norms
- Industry Structure

Internal Moral Restraints
- Values
- Beliefs
- Locus of Control
- Internalized Social Norms
- Moral Development

Internal Rational Restraints
- Intelligence
- Biases of Information
- Boundedness
- Belief of Persistence
- Experience
- Risk of Adversity

Managerial Behavior and Decision Making

Managerial Conduct Regarding Social Responsibility

Legal Responsibility

Ethical Responsibility

Economic Responsibility

Discretionary Responsibility

(Trevino, 1986) From "An Integrative Descriptive Model of Ethical Decision Making," by K. C. Strong and G. D. Meyer, 1992. *Journal of Business Ethics, 11,* p. 90. Copyright 1992 by Kluwer Academic Publishers. Reprinted by permission of Kluwer Academic Publishers.

Trevino (1986) pointed out that environmental restraints such as competition, laws, and social norms; moral restraints such as values, beliefs, social norms, and moral development; and internal rational restraints such as intelligence, experience, and boundedness influence managerial behavior and decision making. Managerial conduct regarding social responsibility is also influenced as the setting and its responsibilities to clients are examined in the context of legal, ethical, economic, and discretionary responsibility.

Within the study of moral development and ethical decision making, both theory and research by Kohlberg (1963, 1970) and Gilligan (1982) were previously discussed in chapter 2, but there is a need to recall that information at this point. Noted are the stages of moral development, and what is indicated is that the postconventional stages of moral development can solve conflicts that lower-level stages cannot because critical moral thinking is more developed in the higher stages.

The progression of Kohlberg's stages of moral development can be followed in Figure 9.3

Figure 9.3 Kohlberg's Stages of Moral Development

Stage	What Is Considered to Be Right
Level One: Preconventional	
Stage One—Obedience and punishment orientation	Adherence to rules to avoid physical punishment. Obedience for its own sake.
Stage Two—Instrumental purpose and exchange	Following of rules only when it is in one's immediate interest. Right as an equal exchange, a fair deal.
Level Two: Conventional	
Stage Three—Interpersonal accord, conformity, mutual expectations	Stereotypical "good" behavior. Living up to what is expected by people close to you.
Stage Four—Social accord and system maintenance	Fulfillment of duties and obligations to which you have agreed. Upholding of laws except in extreme cases when they conflict with fixed social duties. Contribution to the society, group.
Level Three: Principled	
Stage Five—Social contract and individual rights	Awareness that people hold a variety of values; that rules are relative to the group. Upholding of nonrelative values and rights regardless of majority opinion.
Stage Six—Universal ethical principles	Following self-chosen ethical principles. When law violate these principles, action in accord with principles.

Figure 9-3. Kohlberg's Six Stages of Moral Development. Adapted from "Moral Stages and Moralization: The Cognitive-development approach." By T. Lickona (Ed). 1969, *Moral Development and Behavior: Theory, Research, and Social Issues*, pp. 34-35. Copyright 1969 by Holt, Rinehart, and Winston. Reprinted with permission.

What is indicated in Figure 9.3 is that at the lower end of moral development, Level I or the Preconventional Level (Stages 1 and 2), the individual is focusing on self and survival or obeying rules to avoid punishment or is using the rules only when they are instrumental to the individual. In the Conventional or second level (Level II) of the model (Stages 3 and 4), the individual is subject to what is considered the expected good behavior and to the fulfillment of obligations. The third level or Principled level (Level III) of moral development (Stages 5 and 6) finds the individual being socially responsible, obeying rules as social contracts, and upholding rights in the spirit of majority opinion. This level also indicates a responsibility on the part of the individual for choosing appropriate ethical principles.

Kohlberg's findings indicated that men developed to the higher stages of moral development and women only developed to Stage 3 of his six-stage model. Kohlberg concluded that women were viewed as inferior to men in their moral development and moral reasoning, and only when women entered into some form of activity traditionally identified as male activity could they recognize the inadequacy of this reasoning and progress to the higher stages of Kohlberg's developmental sequence. Because Kohlberg used only males in his 1969 study, those qualities found in women, known as *expressive qualities* (although not by Kohlberg), were seen as inferior to the instrumental qualities expressed by males. Critics of this work indicated that because Kohlberg's research was done only with male subjects, the information should not be generalized to both males and females because to do so would be problematic. Basing female reasoning and behaviors on a male model raised questions and served as a motivation for more research. As a result, the research undertaken by Gilligan (1982) and then Belenky, Clinchy, Goldberger, and Tarule (1986) narrowed the gap that seemed to exist between women's and men's moral development. Rather than being viewed as inferior, women's moral reasoning is now viewed as a *different* developmental process.

In her work *In a Different Voice,* Gilligan (1982) pointed out that the disparity between women and men is due not to the inferiority of women 's ability to reason, but rather to a misinterpretation of the research. Gilligan's work on moral reasoning and moral development has raised questions and needed dialogue regarding women's experiences in this literature. Questioning the male biases inherent in Kohlberg's moral-reasoning hierarchy, Gilligan proposed an alternative that brought the perspectives of women to the forefront. Gilligan's (1982, 1988) proposal that an ethic of caring may be a valuable contribution to research in ethical development offers another approach to gender and moral development and decision making. Gilligan's research is inclusive of the experiences of women and projects a perspective known as "women's voices." Her model includes the concepts that women's moral judgments develop from a concern for survival to a focus on goodness as seen through the eyes of others and finally to an understanding of care and responsibility for self and others. The three stages of this model offer a more complex understanding of self and others. Moral decisions for women are not based on abstract principles, but instead are grounded in the context of relationship. Decisions about conflict and morality are made with the other in mind and in relation to the situation. Moral decisions are contextual in nature.

The feminine concept of a morality of understanding is different from that of men, which is a morality of rights. Women's morality has been based on the ideal of connection rather than on the men's ideal of separation.

> Women's construction of the moral problem as a problem of care and responsibility of relationships, rather than, as one of rights and rules, tied the development of their moral thinking to changes in their understanding of responsibility and relationships. . . . Thus, the logic underlying an ethic of care is a psychological logic of relationships. . . . (Gilligan, 1982, p. 73)

Wright (1988) pointed out that according to Gilligan, one of the greatest conflicts for women is between responsibility and selfishness. In the moral evolutionary pattern, this conflict between selfishness and responsibility is continually reevaluated. The most reasonable context for resolving moral conflict is understanding and care.

The transitions through Gilligan's (1988) levels of moral development, as seen in Figure 9.4 begin with Level I, in which survival and one's own desires and needs are primary. Transition to the next level involves the conflict between selfishness, the concern with one's own desires and needs, and responsibility to others. Here the issue is the integration of responsibility and care. In addition, connection with others is highly valued. Also on this level, the concept of women's voice is clear; one's self-worth is based on caring and responsibility for others, and self-sacrifice is seen as the highest value.

Stage Description Level I Survival and primary needs foremost concerns; silence exemplified Level II Conflict between own needs and caring for the needs of others; attempts toward integration; discovering one's voice; issues of self-worth and self-sacrifice significant gaining strength from ability to care Level II Conflict between selfishness and self-sacrifice; responsibility toward others; concept of hurting and nonviolence; contextual considerations relevant; balancing own needs and others' needs realized as internal judgment.

Stage	Description
Level I	Survival and primary needs are foremost concerns; silence exemplified
Level II	Conflict between own needs and caring for the needs of others; attempts toward integration; discovering one's voice; issues of self-worth and self-sacrifice significant gaining strength from ability to care
Level II	Conflict between selfishness and self-sacrifice; responsibility toward others; concept of hurting and nonviolence; contextual considerations relevant; balancing own needs and others' needs realized as internal judgment.

Figure 9-4. Gilligan's Ethic of Care.
Developed by J. DeSensi and D. Rosenberg based on Gilligan (1982). Adapted from C. Gilligan (1982). *In a Different Voice: Psychological Theory and Women's Development.* Cambridge: MA: Harvard University Press.

Transition from the second level of Gilligan's model to the third centers on the conflict between self-sacrifice and responsibility to oneself. This transition to visualizing oneself and one's ideas as worthwhile and valid produces a moral crisis involving the concept of selfishness. At this point women begin to question the idea of self-responsibility in relation to selfishness and the question of whether responsibility should also include being responsible for oneself as well as the other. Gilligan pointed out that the central moral problem for women involves the conflict between self and other. On this level, women realize that not only do they have a responsibility to others, but they also are responsible for themselves. During Gilligan's second level or the development of moral states, women envision their strength coming from their ability to care for another. This stage relates to the typical societal stereotypes for women, and women judge themselves on what others (society, males, and other groups) have to say about them.

In the transition from Level II to Level III, the concept of selfishness emerges again. The self-sacrifice issue also arises. Women at this point begin to realize that their own needs are also important and that a morality of care must also include caring for themselves. A point of conflict here is the emergence of the concept of hurting. The conflict of choosing whom to harm is solved by the introduction of the value of nonviolence. One is not to cause harm to another or to oneself. The principle of nonviolence governs all moral decisions, and self and the other are seen as equally valid and important. During conflicts between the self and the other, one has to decide who would be the victim. The decision in these cases is contextual and based on the best possible outcome that would benefit all involved. Again, the idea of a morality of relationship that is based on connectedness rather than separation emerges. Realizing that one's own needs have equal value with the needs of the other, women have to choose between self and other.

> It is precisely this dilemma, the conflict between compassion and autonomy, between virtue and power, which the feminine voice struggles to resolve in an effort to reclaim the self and to solve the moral problem in such a way that no one is hurt. (Gilligan, 1982, p. 71)

At Level III, women realize that they have choices and that it is possible to be responsible for others and themselves. The goodness of women no longer comes from outside sources or external societal judgment, but is grounded internally in the idea of truth or one's own judgment of intentions and consequences of one's actions. Conflict still exists on Level III between self and other in the form of a dilemma of whom to hurt, but the issue between selfishness and responsibility has been narrowed within the concept of nonviolence.

Gilligan's (1982) three levels of transition in women's moral development lead from the initial concern towards oneself, to caring for others, to responsibility for caring for others and oneself. The issues of moral development for women involve self-worth in relation to others, acceptance of the power to choose, and acceptance of responsibility to choose oneself as well as others (Wright, 1988).

There are still issues however, that must be addressed. If we compare and contrast Kohlberg's "male" model of moral reasoning and Gilligan's model of "female" moral reasoning, we then have the problem of "categorizing individuals into extreme types without considering the complexities of gender influences with moral reasoning and behaviors" (Gill, 1994, p. 261).

The research of Belenky et al. (1986) on women's epistemologies or women's ways of knowing, using interviews with women from diverse backgrounds, brought up similar questions regarding women's perspectives. This work at the time was thought to have incorporated nontraditional methods (interviews) and different ways of knowing to the research, by having women with diverse backgrounds participate in developing this knowledge.

Using the research of both Gilligan and Belenky et al., Bredemeier (1984) went beyond Kohlberg's work and incorporated the concepts of caring and responsibility into the making of moral judgments. Gill (1994) discussed the research by

Bredemeier and her colleagues and noted that in order to encourage moral development through sport and physical activity, young people need to be challenged by opportunities for autonomous thinking about values, exposing them to alternative views and providing opportunities for dialogue, negotiation, and balance of moral conflicts (Bredemeier, 1984; Bredemeier & Shields, 1987; Weiss & Bredemeier, 1990). Using the same methods noted above, moral development can also be encouraged in other settings as well.

Decision Making and Sport Management

Key Concepts

environmental restraint

Gilligan's ethic of care

internal moral restraints

internal rational restraints

Kohlberg's six stages of moral development

moral callousness

Sport offers many challenges that often require professionals to look inward and examine the consequences of their actions. These choices and decisions affect not only the decision maker, but also others. With the models that have been presented in this chapter, we are challenged to think through our own moral development and decision-making processes.

In his discussion of ethics, Kretchmar (1994) indicated that the issues of moral sensitivity and moral callousness develop from our lack of caring. Moral sensitivity involves the ability to identify moral dilemmas and, in turn, exhibit a concern about them. On the other hand, moral callousness involves lesser care, concern, and moral sensitivity. Kretchmar used the example of how during a girl's soccer game, the players themselves stopped the play when a player was injured, exhibiting a spontaneous gesture of concern for the welfare of the injured player. Much of the time, we observe sport participation that involves intimidation, violence, cheating, and lack of concern for the welfare of other players. We have developed moral callousness regarding these issues.

Kretchmar's example of moral sensitivity and moral callousness offers a practical viewpoint of possibilities within our behavior in the sport setting. Additional characteristics that compare and contrast good and bad ethics or moral behavior include (a) concepts such as self-control and rationality versus recklessness and emotionalism, (b) a sense of fair play versus a win-at-all-costs attitude, (c) patience versus opportunism, (d) courage to stand by one's values in the face of difficulty versus an unwillingness to let extraneous values stand in the way of success, and (e) altruism versus survivalism. These comparisons make clear the points to be considered as one explores one's own intentions and subsequent behavior within sport.

Symptoms of Moral Callousness

1. Frequent appeals to the fact that "everyone is doing it" (Therefore, how could it be wrong?)

2. Inability to distinguish between what is a part of the game and what is not (If there are no penalties in the rulebook for behavior x, behavior x must be a part of the game.)

3. Difficulty in telling morally sound strategy from win-at-all-costs trickery (Some blatant rule breaking is now referred to by TV commentators, for example, as "shrewd strategy.")

4. A sense that if one is not caught, nothing wrong happened (Whatever works is right.). (Kretchmar, 1994, p. 239)

Further situational examples of moral and ethical issues are noted in the following scenarios. What is the right thing to do?

1. As an athletic director of a small school district in the Midwest, you have come to the conclusion that the funds allocated to your sports program are insufficient to maintain the quality of performance you and the community desire. Uniforms are old and bulky, equipment is unsafe, and facilities are crumbling. Your program is an embarrassment to the school administrators, the school board, and the athletic conference, each of which is questioning your abilities as an administrator as well as the school's future within the athletic conference.

   In response to this critical situation, you gather a group of interested parents and local business leaders, one of whom is a wealthy beer distributor who offers to help raise money. His proposal is that you conduct a sanctioned softball tournament at the local park for the surrounding area. At this tournament, you will sell beer to the participants and the spectators. Seventy-five percent of the beer sales will be given to your athletic program if the distributor is the exclusive vendor and he is permitted to place signs in the park to promote his products. There is a potential to raise over $15,000 in the venture; some of that total will come from tournament fees team will pay and the sales of various softball and sports paraphernalia, but the bulk of the money will come from selling beer (which is not illegal off school property). If all goes well, the distributor will donate an additional $1,000 to your program.

   While considering the offer and the possibility of an infusion of $16,000 into your coffers, you recall that just last year four of the school's students died in a car accident with a drunk driver. Rumors spread quickly, though, that at least one of the students killed smoked marijuana prior to the collision. However, the rumors, persistent as they were, remain unsubstantiated. With $16,000 the school district's reputation and perhaps your job at stake, what would you do?

2. You have just been hired as the assistant manager of the New Body Health and Racquet Club, an exclusive, privately owned fitness center. During your first day on the job, Phyllis Williams, the club manager, brings you into her office. In her office awaits Norm Muscoli, the club owner, to discuss an issue that has suddenly arisen. It recently became known to him (through private contacts he wishes not to divulge) that one of the club members, a suspected homosexual, has just been diagnosed with AIDS.

   "Do you know how devastating this could be to the club's membership roster?" he exclaims. "If it becomes known that a queer is running around the club spreading his infection everywhere, I'd be sued, the club would go out of business, and we'd all be out of work."

   You try to delicately explain to Ms. Williams and Mr. Muscoli that HIV is a hard virus to catch—for instance, the chlorine in the pool water can kill the virus—and that casual contact won't harm anyone. Your response only agitates the pair.

"Hey, you know these kind," Ms. Williams replies. "You know how they share razors, needles, and everything else."

The two reiterate how devastating this situation could be to the membership levels. They further inform you, in no uncertain terms, that though no established policy exists for such a case, you work at a private club and, therefore, are legally able to forbid this member from using the locker room, pool, and fitness areas. Essentially, you can revoke his membership without any legal repercussions.

As you about to leave the office, Mr. Muscoli promises you a hefty bonus for taking care of this problem quickly and quietly. He strides over to you, opens the door, and shakes your hand.

"You're young and you're smart," he says, "and you have a long future to look forward to with this company as we expand. I'm sure you will do the right thing."

The office door closes behind you, and you walk away wondering what the right thing is for you to do.

3. In a few moments, you are to speak at the press conference concerning the newest recruit to the men's basketball team. As the new sports information director for the athletic department, it is part of your duties, yet this engagement won't be a pleasant one. You know the topic of discussion will shift quickly to the NCAA reprimand—a subject that kept you awake all night.

Less than two weeks ago, a local radio news report came out with a story claiming that two years ago, prior to your school's winning the national championship, the NCAA issued your athletic department a reprimand for a serious yet unspecified infraction committed by the basketball team. Initially, you wanted to deal with the issue and put it aside as quickly as possible, but when the local papers contacted you, you decided to approach the athletic director before issuing any statement.

Much to your surprise, the AD made it clear that the matter was not to be addressed publicly. The sportswriters and editors have become increasingly upset and suspicious at your failure to return their requests for information since their initial contact. In retaliation to your reticence, the sports editors have refused to print a growing percentage press releases from the athletic department. Your reputation with the local media rapidly has eroded.

A couple of days ago, to make matters worse, a partial list of infractions was somehow leaked from the NCAA and printed in papers all across the country. After an hour and a half of fielding inquiries from seemingly everyone and everywhere in the world, you instructed your secretary to screen all calls. During a hastily arranged meeting the following afternoon, the AD repeated his mandate that you discuss nothing.

Alas, the moment has arrived! It is time to climb the podium and face a slew of aggressive and antagonistic faces, each with burning questions you have been told not to answer. What do you do? How do you handle this crisis? How do you balance the public's right to know with your department's stone-faced silence—all the while your credibility and job hang by a thread?

4. As the director in charge of a youth sports league, you learned that one of the coaches, Ms. Vinnie Gagner, has been unusually hard on her team. She demands that the players strive only to excel and that they strictly follow her rules and commands, all the while emphasizing winning as the only important objective of the game. It also has come to your attention that Ms. Gagner has embarrassed several players by yelling at and belittling them in public when they committed mistakes on the field. Furthermore, a number of players have been purposely benched, due to low skill levels, even though they pay the same entry fee as every other player in the league.

Once the name of the coach was mentioned, however, you cringed; Ms. Gagner has the most successful team in the league—a team that will be traveling to the state championship tournament in a few weeks. Her team is also sponsored by one of the largest monetary contributors to the league. This company likes her, likes her winning ways (which is good publicity), and is quick to support her coaching methodology if she is ever accused of being overbearing. "Winning takes sacrifice," said the company spokesperson, "and the sooner these kids learn that, the sooner they will be successful in their own lives."

You have interviewed several members of the team in question to get their perspectives on the coach. Though all of the players admit that Ms. Gagner is tough, and a few of the players do resent her harsh treatment, most enjoy being on the best team in the league and accept being benched occasionally as a necessary part of the game and their team's overall success. "We're team players," one of the players said, "and if staying on the bench is what it takes for the team to win, then we should have to do it, shouldn't we?"

Another one of the kids actually told you it was better to sit on the bench for a winning team than on to be on the field for a losing team. "Winners get things losing teams don't," said the child. "For example, losers won't stay over at a motel during the state championship tournament."

Finally, in a brief conversation you had with Ms. Gagner at the end of her last game, she commented that she does what she does for the sake of the community. Seeing your puzzled look, she went on to explain that losers are avoided, whereas winners bring people together. "Winning teams," Ms. Gagner argued, "pack stadiums full of people ready to share in the glory of victory and to enliven their otherwise mundane lives."

In a few minutes, the league committee will assemble in your office, and this coach is on the agenda. What do you say to the committee about the parental complaints? Should you say anything at all? Is Ms. Gagner violating any moral or ethical principles? Does this coach's behavior need improving? Will the fact that she is a woman have any influence on your decision?

5. As interim director of women's athletic department at the university, your duties should have been fairly routine. The search committee is finalizing its selection for a new AD, and a vote should take place by the end of the month. Besides the department runs on autopilot for the most part.

However, disturbing reports have been forwarded to you by members of one of the few women's varsity teams on campus coached by a male. The reports indicated that the coach was becoming too intimate with certain team members. He had been making explicit sexual advances toward some athletes, and he had also threatened the team status of some individuals if they did not comply with his requests.

You proceeded to discretely interview members of the team and were shocked to discover the magnitude of the situation. A few athletes complained vehemently of his innuendoes and harassment. They described being "flashed" in the coach's office and propositioned into performing various acts, all the while being threatened with losing their starting positions and scholarships. They rebuffed his advances and, predictably, they are no longer in starting positions.

Dealing with this issue seemed straightforward initially; yet, it quickly grew into a more confounding situation. Most of the other athletes on the team claimed to be unaware of any improprieties between the coach and their fellow teammates. The worst they said about the coach was that he seemed very affectionate—but in a way a father might act towards a daughter. Moreover, when asked about the few athletes that were harassed, most admitted the coach was being hard on them, but probably because they weren't putting out enough effort—wishing instead to spend more time with themselves and their friends. In fact, only a month ago, those players started becoming very confrontational with the coach.

Now, what do you do? How can you know whether the accusations are truthful rather than retaliatory, and how do you begin determining that? You aren't even sure if it is your place to make these inquiries. Shouldn't this be handled by the student disciplinary council or perhaps the courts? Should you talk to the coach? Would that even help? Or maybe you could just wait and pass the problem on to the new AD. After all, a few more weeks won't make that much of a difference.

6. With a beaming smile on your face, you lean back in your big leather

athletic director's chair and reread the glowing editorial about you in the local paper. According to the editors, you hit a home run when you hired your newest coach, having convinced him to give up his assistant coaching position with a top ten team to head up your team's program. The fact that the new coach is black also helps your department's affirmative action numbers. The coffee is hot, the room is cool, and you think everything is going your way—that is, until Mr. Deniger, the new coach, storms into your office, complaining about the rampant racism in town.

Mr. Deniger goes on to describe the discriminatory treatment he has suffered from the moment he took his new position. As part of his employment perks and benefits package, you told the new coach he would be given a membership at a local country club. Because this perk was traditionally provided to all the previous coaches and is currently being provided to all the head coaches and yourself, you felt secure in mentioning it—though you have no real authority to offer memberships to the club. In this case, however, Mr. Deniger has not been offered a membership. In fact, when he called the club inquiring about beginning his membership, he was told that the memberships were not automatic and that his name had been turned down by the club's nominating committee. You tell Coach Deniger to give you a few days to find out what is going on.

You call the club and talk to the nominating committee chairman, Mr. Ray Syst, about the situation. You ask why Mr. Deniger, of all the coaches, was not offered an automatic membership. Mr. Syst replies first that you should never have given the impression that memberships were rubber-stamped by the country club and the athletic department, and second, that Coach Deniger isn't of the right character for this club.

"What are you talking about, Ray? What is this talk about character all of a sudden?"

"The club feels that Mr. Deniger's presence would have a detrimental effect on our membership. Some of our more vocal and wealthy members expressed their opinion that Mr. Deniger was not the right kind of member for the Club. You understand, don't you?"

You understand and threaten to withdraw yourself and all the other coaches from the club in protest.

Mr. Syst replies, "That is your prerogative." However, he informs you that some of your coaches were among those who wanted Coach Deniger excluded.

You next threaten to go to the papers with the story.

Again, Mr. Syst says that is your choice, but that you should also consider all the alumni and booster money at stake—much of which comes from other members of the club and their companies—if word of this situation reaches the media. You can't help but pause to think of what might happen to your department's finances, your recruitment budgets, and your job with that big a loss.

"What if Mr. Deniger himself decides to tell his story to the press?" you ask.

"If you can't control someone like him," the committee chairman replies, very slowly and laden with innuendo, "perhaps we ought to reconsider your membership to this club."

Mr. Syst hangs up the phone. You crumple into your big AD's chair wondering how you will ever keep Mr. Deniger from telling the press about this. You further wonder how you will explain the situation to your new coach. You then start wondering about your coaching staff and who among it dislikes minorities. Last, you wonder how your family might react to not having the prestige of a club membership anymore.

You spend a lot of time wondering, but what do you do?

7. As facilities manager, you look over your recent handiwork. The new bleachers has been installed, the locker room has been updated with a whirlpool™ and carpeting. You were even able to purchase for the restaurant a new hot dog rotisserie. Although you wish you could have done more, at least now the Alpine Ice Rink can accommodate the influx of media and spectators and the understandable demands of your hometown pride and joy—skater Patina Glace, the next U.S. and World Champion.

Still, you sigh in frustration as you look out over the ice from your office window. Patina was in your office, and she wasn't satisfied. She screamed at you because you failed to provide, among other things, a private locker room for her. You replied that the ice-rink budget was severely limited even before the improvements. You have done what you could.

"That's not enough," she countered. "I have serious concerns about my safety, and I don't think you're dealing with them right."

You groaned when you heard that line—a relative nonissue until 1994. The Tonya Harding-Nancy Kerrigan debacle has created constant headaches at all the facilities training elite skaters. Patina continued her outburst, preventing your mind from wandering off to other topics.

"Apparently you don't care about all the crazies out there who would do anything to get to me."

As you tried to daydream, you asked yourself how one fluky aberration could have instigated so much fear and paranoia in the skating community?

"I have millions of dollars in endorsements on the line, and you sit there impotent and lazy, telling me that you can't afford to keep me safe."

Was it all about money? Was it all about winning? Perhaps the rising demands of competition require increased sacrifices and risks on and off the ice? Or maybe, it was just bitterness. After all, Harding was the National Figure Skating Champion in 1991, but almost no notoriety or endorsements followed from the triumph. She was eighth in the world in 1994, but rarely is her name mentioned now without people flinching from disgust.

"You know, there are other skating rinks in other cities that would pay anything to get a skater like me on their ice. This podunk town means nothing to me except as a good image booster. More and more, however, it's getting in the way of my advancement."

The fact that Tonya Harding was permitted to skate throughout the inquiry process certainly didn't do anything to discourage other would-be champions from considering all their options. On the other hand, what else could the USFSA have done?

"So, either you give me the necessities I need to train with, or I'll take my skates somewhere else and you can try to pay for your nice new carpeting with no one around to see it."

You remembered, however, what happened after the Olympics. The USFSA banned Harding from the sport and stripped her of her 1994 U.S. Championship title because she supposedly approved of the attack before it happened. The committee's statement remained fresh in your mind. Harding's actions as they related to the assault on Nancy Kerrigan evidenced a clear disregard for fairness, good sportsmanship, and ethical behavior—this from a group of people who presumed her guilt based on evidence never mentioned or cross-examined within a court of law.

"Are you listening to me?!"

You stared at Patina, a young girl who has been skating at your rink for over 10 years. Suddenly, you hardly recognized her.

Ethical Analysis

The following discussion will analyze the ethical dimensions and implications of the fourth example above to demonstrate how moral principles relate to a given case. Readers should try to analyze the other examples and draw their own conclusions and resolutions to any particular problem.

Ethical concerns in the area of adult-organized youth sports are particularly pervasive and serious for a number of reasons. First, there is a distinct power imbalance among the parties involved at this level of sport, namely, that between adults and children. Adults have a great capacity to assert their authority and impose their values upon children. Second, children do not always have the same ability to reason and understand issues at the same level as adults, yet children may not be treated with this in mind. Third, children usually have fewer opportunities to speak and be heard around adults to effect the change deemed appropriate. As is often the case in adult-organized activities and institutions, the individuals directly involved in the activity (the children) are the least able to make changes within the activity, whereas those further away from the activity (from coaches to league officials to administrators at the national headquarters) are increasingly capable of making changes. Finally, adults often neglect to consider the genuine interests of children and may be too wrapped up in satisfying their own goals and ambitions. In each case, adults must behave based on a clear understanding of what is in the best interest of the child. However, what makes being an adult difficult is dealing with the uncertainties and ambiguities of selecting which among many options are in the best interests of children. These are but a few important considerations one should try to keep in mind as the discussions turn to the youth sport example.

Youth coaches can be a difficulty for league directors if the process for selecting coaches does not contain certain safeguards. For example, league rules could insist that an individual who wishes to coach be required to have an approved coaching certificate. This requirement might indicate that coaches have had some specific training and sensitivity in handling particular youth problems, yet it in no way guarantees any improvement in coaching quality. If a sound selection process had been established and implemented, then some of the problems with the coach could have been avoided altogether. The league director (either you or the former one) may have made a bad original judgment in accepting the services of Ms. Gagner. So despite her success and support from her team members and her sponsor, she was perhaps not sufficiently qualified, or she possessed poor communication skills, or she couldn't relate to youth very well.

> Although requiring a coaching certificate makes the selection process easy and quick, certifications should not replace a personal evaluation of a coach's ability.

As the example indicates, however, Ms. Gagner was already part of the league and you must deal with that individual. As part of the decision-making effort, the likely place to begin is to make sure you have adequate relevant information related to the coach's actions, the team policies, and the experiences of the players under this coach. Some type of investigation is, therefore, required. The coach should be informed about what you have heard, and she should know that an inquiry is being conducted. The gathering of information should be carried out discreetly by speaking to team members, other coaches, parents, officials, and the coach in question. We would advise that an open meeting to gather information is inappropriate because of the likely undue hardship such a forum might cause with children present. Once a sufficient amount of information has been collected, which you appear to have done, some basic moral principles can be employed to assess the case and draw relevant conclusions.

From an ethical standpoint, a utilitarian approach might be useful because this view makes explicit reference to the ideas of paternalism, that is, acting or deciding on behalf of others in their best interest. In this case, children are not usually mature and rational enough to fully understand their own physical, emotional, and cognitive needs and abilities, and so adults generally make decisions on their behalf, especially in areas where safety and protection are involved.

Your foremost concern as league director has to be the welfare of the participants. If the information gathered clearly indicates that children are being harmed physically or emotionally by the coach in question, then this must be brought to her attention immediately. Unfortunately, as stated above, one of the most difficult tasks of an adult is to decide which action is in the best interests, and in this case, the best interests of the children as a group. So, even though some of the children are upset with Ms. Gagner's coaching style, clearly not all are upset; some of her players and supporters find her actions consistent with fielding a winning team and enjoy the perks of success. Furthermore, any ethical decision must be made in conjunction with a realistic understanding of the requirements and necessities of league management and perpetuation. The main monetary backer of the league is an ardent supporter of Ms. Gagner, and loss of this money could jeopardize the league's stability and risk the livelihood of the other children playing on other teams. So, in this situation, the league has two concurrent, yet conflicting, concerns: the welfare of the participants and the continuous functioning of the league.

If you decide to discipline the coach, an explanation must be presented so she and her supporters understand the breach of serious and basic moral guidelines. Surely, it could be argued, no child should be publicly embarrassed in front of others, or even in private, and a youth sports league should not be an environment to condone or permit such behavior. The point should be emphasized that every child in the league is to be treated with dignity and respect, no matter what the coach has in mind.

If the league is primarily for recreational purposes, then principles of fairness and equity may be a concern. If the coach is explicitly violating league rules and objectives that ensure equal playing time for all participants, she should allow one practice session per week, and place a premium on participation rather than on winning. Of course, this rejects some of the participants' own views that being a part of a winning team is better than just playing. You will need to be very careful in explaining to the children that universal participation is more important than winning, especially when the objective is that sport is to win.

Also, if the coach is circumventing league regulations, then perhaps her dismissal is warranted. This would be a delicate choice, considering the amount of money that would be lost, leading to a drop in facility and equipment availability. Money could be raised in other ways like increasing player or sponsor fees to make up the loss. But is it fair to place additional financial burdens on people and businesses who essentially did nothing wrong and have, at best, mixed opinions about her coaching? There may also be a public backlash against you for dismissing the only coach in the league capable of bringing one of the community's teams to the state championships. She might fight the dismissal, arguing that she is quite capable of making rational decisions on behalf of her players and that you are in no better position to know what is in the best interests of the children than she is. Any justification for dismissing Ms. Gagner would have to carefully consider all these ramifications.

On the other hand, perhaps you can convince the coach to pledge to change her behavior in the future. In other words, are her humiliation tactics necessary to develop a successful team? You might suggest to her that she enroll in a youth coaching workshop and learn alternative coaching pedagogy. Team practices and contests could be monitored by league representatives, parents, or other coaches in order to enhance her coaching quality and ensure that no further problems arise and that concrete changes are being developed. You might suggest that a second coach with equal authority be part of the team to temper any excessive tendencies. Finally, you could mention that Mc. Gagner listen to the needs of the players and parents about team goals, ways of practicing, and methods of rotating players in and out of games so that players are treated as decision makers as well.

Summary

In this chapter the responsibilities associated with decision making were discussed. Styles of decision-making styles and ethical decision models were presented in an effort to remind the sport manager of his or her ethical responsibilities in this area. Josepheson's (1992) character approach to decision making, which involves trustworthiness, respect, responsibility, justice and fairness, caring, and civic virtue and citizenship, was suggested as a personal guide to ensure decisions will be of an ethical quality. Cavanaugh's (1990) model involving the criteria of utility, rights, and justice was presented as a way to evaluate the ethical or unethical nature of decisions. Using moral development (Kohlberg and Gilligan) as a basis for ethical decision making, Trevino's (1986) model showed how environmental restraints, internal moral restraints, and internal rational restraints affect managerial behavior and decision making and the subsequent managerial conduct regarding social responsibility. Kretchmar's (1994) term *moral callousness* captures the idea of our moral insensitivity to moral issues associated with sport and ethics in sport. These models and approaches will assist us as we attempt to make sense of the moral dilemmas and analysis presented in this chapter.

Questions for Consideration

1. Based on the theories presented in this chapter, can you identify and critically examine your own decision-making process in the scenarios presented?

2. In what settings is an autocratic decision-making style more effective than a participatory style?

3. Which models or parts of the models presented can you incorporate into your own decision-making style? How will different settings affect your decision-making style?

4. What incidents of moral sensitivity and moral callousness have you observed in the sports or sport management settings in which you have participated?

5. What is the value of Cavanaugh's concepts of utility, rights, and justice in ethical decision making?

Chapter Ten

Ethics and Sport Marketing

Chapter Objectives

• To explore the obligations of sport organizations to the consumer

• To discuss ethical issues related to sports marketing

• To present models for analyzing ethical decisions in marketing

• To explore ethical decisions in advertising

• To examine ethical dilemmas in sport marketing

Western society is founded on capitalist economic principles; thus it is not, at its foundation, bad to make money in modern society. The manner in which this is done, however, the type of power used, and how the individuals, the action has coerced, disadvantaged, or in some way negatively influenced others are often questioned. Success in capitalistic society is driven by terms such as the bottom line and the almighty dollar. Financial survival and success are primary objectives. Concerns along these lines are associated with rivalries with competitors, the power of the present suppliers, the power of the consumers, the power of substitutes, and barriers to entry (Brooks, 1994).

> Sport managers must offset profit seeking with socially responsible legal and ethical behavior.

It has been noted that marketing is the function within businesses that is most often charged with ethical abuses (Dubinsky & Loken, 1989). Marketing abuses within the business world and in sport have been brought to the attention of the public eye and as a result, there is increased attention on the part of the consumer. With the increase in public scrutiny regarding marketing practices, producers of goods and services, and those selling sport merchandise, sport marketing plans have been instituted that are more closely derived from and associated with the mission statements of organizations.

The definition of marketing is broad and complex and includes numerous activities. Pride and Ferrell (2000) defined marketing "as a process of creating, distributing, promoting, and pricing goods, services, and ideas to facilitate satisfying exchange relationships with customers in a dynamic environment" (p. 4). Pitts and Stotlar (1996) noted sport marketing as "the process of designing and implementing activities for the production, pricing, promotion and distribution of a sport product to satisfy the needs or desires of consumers and to achieve the company's objectives" (p. 80).

Pride and Ferrell (2000) distinguished between a definition of marketing and the concept of marketing. They consider the marketing concept to be "a philosophy that an organization should try to satisfy customers' needs through a coordinated set of activities that also allows the organization to achieve its goals" (p. 10). Although the satisfaction of customers may seem like an obvious focus now, that has not always been the case. Pride and Ferrell pointed out that the marketing concept has evolved from a production orientation to a marketing orientation. From the 1850s to 1900, the orientation was on production; from 1900 to the 1950s, sales took over as the orientation, and from the 1950s to the 21st century, the focus has been on a marketing orientation. This marketing orientation requires the generation of the organization-wide market intelligence that pertains to current and future customer needs, dissemination of the intelligence across departments of the organization, and organization-wide responsiveness. In other words, the marketing orientation means being responsive to the dynamic needs and wants of the consumer (Pride & Ferrell, 2000) We would add to this the imperative need to be responsive to the diverse nature of the consumer.

Marketing in and of itself is complex, but as Blann (1998) pointed out, sport marketing is even more complex because of the uniqueness of the sport product. Sport is unique and distinguishes itself from other products in that (a) it is intangible and subjective; (b) it is inconsistent and unpredictable because of different factors associated with team members (e.g., injuries, team momentum, weather); (c) it is perishable, and thus advanced sales of tickets are important; and (d) consumers/spectators become emotionally attached to sport teams (e.g., fanatics/fans) and want to identify with the team by purchasing licensed products with team logos.

The elements associated with marketing create what is known as the *marketing mix*:

1. product—a tangible good or object, a service, or intangible quality that satisfies the consumers' wants or needs;

2. price—the value of the product and costs consumer agrees to pay for the product (According to Blann, 1998, when the benefits obtained from a particular product exceed the costs associated with it, the consumer believes there is value in the product.);

3. place—distribution channels where the consumer may obtain the product; and

4. promotion—methods and techniques of communicating information to motivate consumer to purchase the product.

The sport marketer uses the above noted marketing mix in different ways. In other words, based on the goals of the organization and market fluctuation, for example, these elements may be manipulated in various ways to carry out the mission of the organization and the specific marketing plan. It is at this particular place that ethical issues are encountered by the sport manager working in marketing (Blann, 1998; Pitts & Stotlar, 1996).

We are assuming that readers already have knowledge and background in the components of sport marketing; therefore, it is not the intent of this chapter to give a complete overview of marketing and marketing strategies in sport management because readers have probably studied that information in previous courses. Rather, the objective here is to identify the ethical concerns and ethical decision making regarding the marketing of sport.

Emphasis has been given to the development of a marketing plan for the purpose of linking it to the mission and core values of the organization to ensure that marketing, promoting, and selling will be carried out in socially responsible ways (Blann, 1998; Pitts & Stotlar, 1996).

This point is further explicated by Blann (1998):

> A sport marketing plan derived from and consistent with the mission statement and core values is necessary to ensure that marketing, promoting, and selling will be done in socially responsible ways. Viewing marketing as a means of honest communication that creates a distinctive and socially responsible image of a sport product is the best way to position a sport product in the market. Sport marketers who are proactive will achieve the promise of the marketing plan because their actions will be socially responsible and will help fulfill the mission of the organization. (p. 182)

In Brief . . .

Sport marketing includes designing and implementing activities for the production, pricing, promotion, and distribution of a sport product to satisfy the needs or desires of consumers and achieve the company's objectives. The *marketing plan* involves linking marketing activities to an organization's mission and core values to ensure socially responsible behavior.

When one uses the steps in developing a sport marketing plan originally presented by Pitts and Stotlar (1996) and adapted by Blann, it is expected that within each phase, social responsibility based on a sound ethical foundation will be implemented. The following diagram illustrates these steps:

Figure 10.1 Developing a Sport Marketing Plan

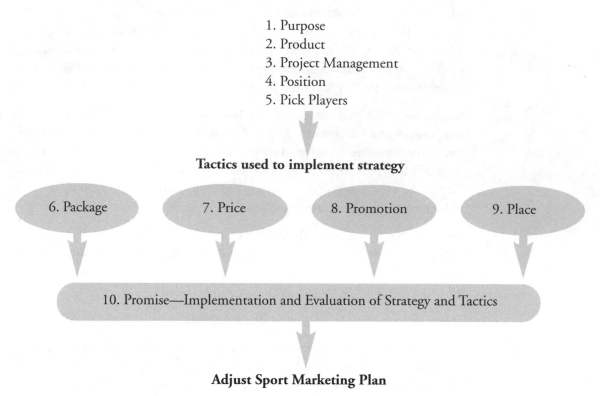

1. Purpose
2. Product
3. Project Management
4. Position
5. Pick Players

Tactics used to implement strategy

6. Package   7. Price   8. Promotion   9. Place

10. Promise—Implementation and Evaluation of Strategy and Tactics

Adjust Sport Marketing Plan

Adapted by Blann (1998), with permission from *Fundamentals of sport marketing,* by B. G. Pitts and D. K. Stotlar, 1996, p. 81 (Morgantown, WV: Fitness Information Technology, Inc.) and cited from "Sport Marketing," by W. Blann, 1998, p. 173, *Contemporary sport management,* ed. J. B. Parks, B. R. K. Zanger, and J. Quarterman (Champaign, IL: Human Kinetics).

Obligations to Consumers

When questioning whether or not businesses have responsibilities to their customers or consumers, it would seem that based on the general principle of fairness, businesses do in fact have responsibilities. Consumers' expectations of businesses include receiving quality goods that are safe and reliable products. This is the case whether the goods are tangible or considered services. When investigating the ethical basis of our expectations, we must realize that we are free to choose either to buy a product or not to buy it. Generally, one is not coerced into the decision to "buy." This would mean that the buyer determines the quality, safety, and reliability of the product. Using the phrase "let the buyer beware" takes on considerable meaning here. Because one possesses the freedom to choose and purchase a product, one is basically agreeing with the concept that one does not need to be protected from the company that produced the product. People are reasonable consumers with the freedom and wisdom to choose for themselves. Bowie and Duska (1990) pointed out that the concept of caveat emptor, or "let the buyer beware," is morally flawed in that it places the total responsibility on the consumer and none on the producer of the goods. It would seem that the prudent thing to do would be to make safety and reliability the joint responsibility of the consumer and producer. Because it would be impossible in today's society for consumers to research the safety and reliability of all products they are interested in buying, joint responsibility may not make sense. Therefore, the businesses are

Key Concepts

marketing concept

marketing mix

marketing plan

required to take on more of the responsibility for safety and reliability. Consumer advocate groups serve as additional watchdogs in this process, but the ultimate responsibility is with the company producing the product. The concept of *strict liability* is imputed to producers of goods, meaning that they are responsible for unintended and undetected defects in their products.

<table>
<tr><td>

In Brief . . .

Consumers' expectations of businesses include receiving safe and reliable products. Product safety and reliability is the joint responsibility of the consumer and the producer.

</td></tr>
</table>

Considering the potential of how a new marketing mix might entice the consumer to take part in the product or exchange, the marketer needs to consider if he or she will take advantage of consumer weaknesses such as ignorance or lack of interest. How the marketer's strategy and actions will influence the effectiveness of the marketing plan needs to be considered along with how the strategy will influence individual consumers. Social responsibility and ethical questions arise from such situations (Robin & Reidenbach, 1985).

Ethical Decision Making in Marketing

As noted previously, ethical abuses in marketing seem to have been commonplace in businesses and in sport settings and are visible and noticed by the general public. Deceptive advertising, fictitious pricing, incongruence of product quality with personal philosophy, exploitation of consumers, and misrepresentation of minority groups are but a few of these incidents. Dubinsky and Loken (1989) pointed out that the potential ethical misconduct in marketing occurs within the following areas and positions: (a) ethical issues confronted by marketing managers, marketing researchers, advertising personnel, purchasing personnel, field and retail salespersons, and retail store managers; (b) consumers' perceptions of various marketing practices; and (c) nonbusiness professors' and marketing practitioners' beliefs about the appropriateness of applying marketing principles to social issues and ideas.

Several models have been developed for studying ethical decision making in marketing. Ferrell and Gresham (1985) prescribed a multistage contingency model of the variables that influence ethical decisions in an organizational environment. This model comprises three antecedents of ethical decision making, specifically, individual factors such as the employee, significant others within the organization or setting, and the opportunity for action.

In a similar effort, Hunt and Vitell (1986) developed a model for situations in which the individual views a particular behavior or action as having ethical content. This view possesses four constructs: (a) personal experiences, (b) organizational norms, (c) industry norms, and (d) cultural norms. Each of these constructs is considered to influence ethical decision making through its moderating effect on perceived ethical problems, perceived alternatives, deontological and teleological evaluations, ethical judgments, and intentions.

As an alternative to the models offered by Ferrell and Gresham (1985) and Hunt and Vitell (1986), Dubinsky and Loken (1989) suggest another framework for ethical decision making in marketing. This model is rooted in social psychology and approached from the theory of reasoned action. This theory assumes that individuals are rational, that they use available information when deciding how to behave, and that their behavior is under volitional control. This model is represented in Figure 10.2. The components of the theory include intention, determinants of intentions, attitude toward the behavior, determinants of attitude toward the behavior, and determinants of subjective norm.

Intention is the individual's subjective probability that he or she will engage in the behavior. The intention to perform or not perform the behavior is the immediate determinant of behavior. *Determinants of intentions* include the individual's attitude toward the behavior of interest and the subjective norm. *Attitude toward the behavior* refers to an individual's judgment concerning whether engaging in a certain behavior is good or bad. When an individual more favorably evaluates performing a behavior, he or she is more likely to intend to perform the behavior. The *subjective norm* (i.e., one's family, coworkers, or superiors) enters into this explanation. The individual's perception of whether others who are important to the individual think he or she should or should not engage in a certain behavior affects the behavior. In other words, the more an individual perceives that important others think he or she should engage in the behavior, the more likely the person intends to do so. It is concluded then that performing some ethical or unethical behavior may be a function of attitudes or subjective norms. *Determinants of attitude toward behavior* are based on the individual's salient behavior beliefs and outcome evaluations. To further explain, behavior beliefs are considered one's salient beliefs that performing a certain act will lead to specific consequences or outcomes that will be positive or negative. For example, with fictitious pricing, one's salient belief may be that this act will increase sales volume or will incur ill will among customers. The outcome evaluations include the person's evaluation about whether each outcome produced from the behavior of interest is good or bad. In this example, the markets would view increasing sales volume in a positive light, but view negatively the concept of ill will among customers. When it is perceived that a particular behavior generates mostly positive outcomes, the individual will have a favorable attitude toward that behavior. *Determinants of subjective norm* are determined by an individual's normative beliefs (belief that certain groups or individuals think a certain behavior should be performed) weighted by the motivation to comply with specific important others.

Applying this model to ethical decision making in marketing, Dubinsky and Loken (1989) stated:

> Moving from right to left [on Figure 10.2] the theory espouses that the immediate determinant of engaging in ethical/unethical behavior (or action) is one's intention to perform the behavior. Intention is influenced by the individual's attitude toward the behavior and/or subjective norm (i.e. perceived social influence/pressure placed on the individual to perform or not to perform the behavior). Attitude is determined by one's salient behavioral beliefs about the outcome associated with performing the behavior and evaluations of those outcomes. Subreferents think he or she should engage in the behavior and motivations to comply with there referents. (p. 85)

For example, a potential referent from top management such as an athletic director may want an unbiased presentation of the results of a research project involving graduation rates of athletes. If the people doing the research and writing the project report believe this is what the athletic director actually desires, then they are more likely to engage in behavior that will achieve this end. Motivation to carry out this task in an ethical manner is reflective of the referent's desire to have the study done in an honest and forthright manner. Thus, the subordinate will carry out the task to the extent that the significant other wishes.

One advantage to the model proposed by Dubinsky and Loken (1989), as interpreted by some, is that it does not assume the individual perceives the behavior as having ethical content. This is in contrast to those models suggested through deontological and teleological philosophy, which require that the person see the situation as containing ethical content. These authors further explained:

> . . . the cognitive components underlying behavior in the theory of reasoned action are considered independently of whether the behavior is perceived as ethical or unethical . . . In fact, for many ethical behaviors in which marketers are interested, individuals may be unaware of a behavior's ethical content; that is, its "rightness" or "wrongness" may not be salient. (p. 89)

This is exemplified by a salesperson in a sporting goods store who has a positive attitude toward giving gifts to customers because of the favorable consequences of giving away gifts, not because the behavior is perceived as ethical.

Figure 10.2 Model for Analyzing Ethical Decision Making in Marketing

Behavioral Beliefs (bl)
Likelihood that ethical/unethical behavior leads to certain outcomes

Outcome Evaluation (Nbi)
Goodness or badness of outcomes of ethical/unethical behavior

Normative Beliefs (Mci)
Likelihood that referents think individual should/should not perform ethical/unethical behavior

Motivation to Comply (Mc)
Motivation/willingness to acquire to referents

Attitude Toward Ethical/Unethical Behavior (Ag)
Individual's evaluation of behavior

Intentions to Engage in Ethical/Unethical Behavior (Bi)
Subjective likelihood that individual will engage in behavior

Subjective Norm Toward Ethical/Unethical Behavior (SN)
Individual's belief that significant others think individual should/should not perform behavior

Ethical/Unethical Behavior (B)
Relevant behavior of interest

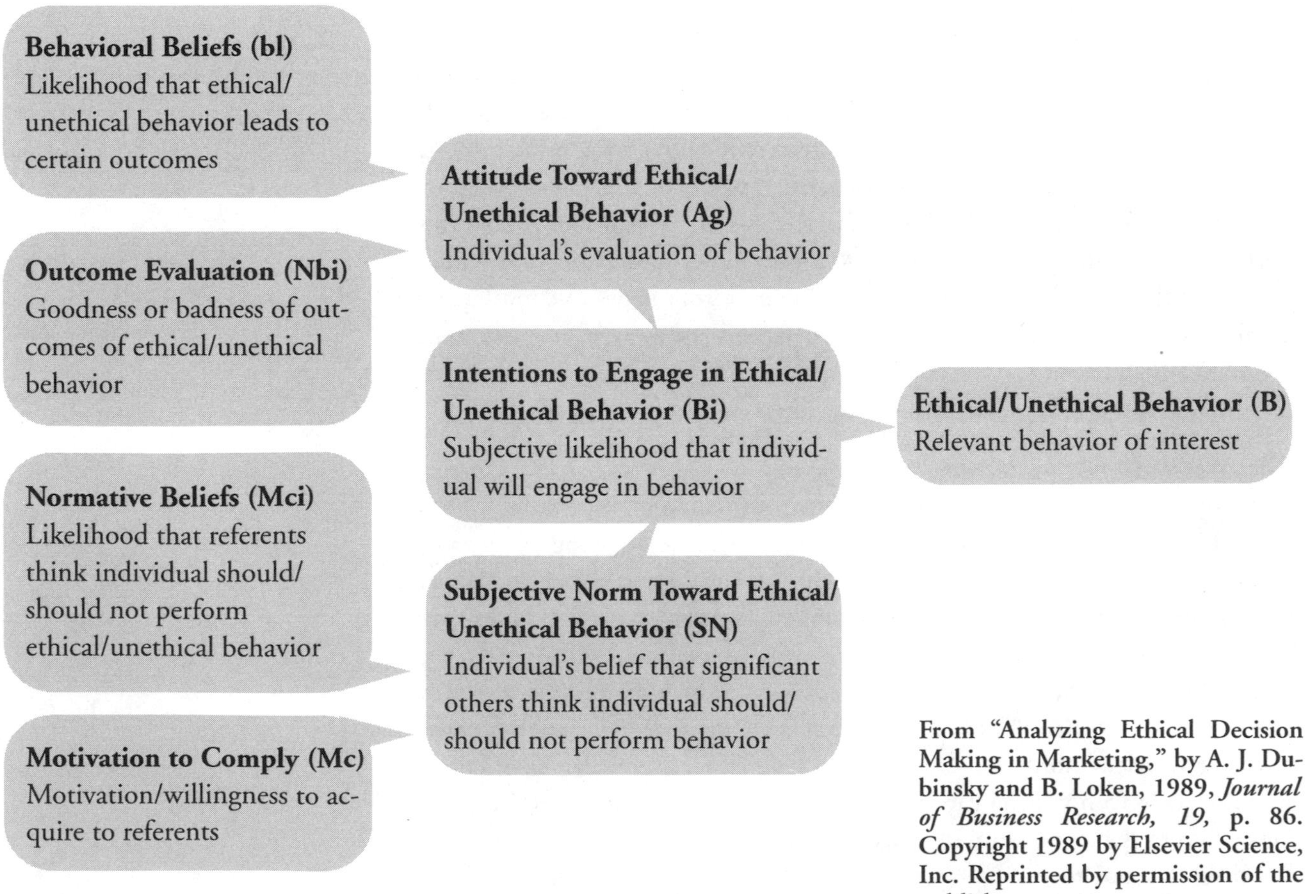

From "Analyzing Ethical Decision Making in Marketing," by A. J. Dubinsky and B. Loken, 1989, *Journal of Business Research, 19,* p. 86. Copyright 1989 by Elsevier Science, Inc. Reprinted by permission of the publisher.

Laczniak, Burton, and Murphy (1999) presented a model by which to analyze sport marketing ethics. Although this model is from the area of decision making in general, it is not limited to this area and has strong affinities to decisions made regarding sport marketing. The model is presented in stages represented by the following questions:

1. Is there a problem?

2. What issues can be identified that relate to the problem?

3. What stakeholders are affected by the issue?

4. What organizational mechanisms can assist in solving the problem?

5. What solutions are available to solve the problem? (Laczniak & Murphy, 1993)

Is there a problem? Using the traditional marketing-mix variables such as product management, pricing, and promotional strategy, questions regarding certain practices in sport marketing may be raised. Because sport marketing is such a fast-growing competitive entity, an ethical audit of the practices is appropriate and professionally responsible. Without such an audit, Laczniak et al. pointed out that there may be a lower credibility for sport-related marketing and an increase in public cynicism regarding professional or Olympic-level sport, for example. They further noted that there may be a "reduction in the brand equity of the sport affiliated with the questioned marketing practice" (Laczniak et al., p. 44) If issues such as fighting and increased violence in sports in addition to dilemmas such as Olympic site selection, which has plagued the International Olympic Committee, are not dealt with, sport will be much less desirable as a mass-marketing vehicle. Additionally, the reputation that sport marketers are manipulators and cheaters interested only in the bottom-line or "win-at-all-costs" does not help those marketers who are, in fact, concerned with ethical practices. Other issues such as the individual athlete's behaviors, practices, and moral judgments also affect marketing. How this individual and his or her behavior is used in the marketing of a sport raises value questions and moral judgments that reinforce the notion that such behavior cannot be separated from issues of ethical analysis simply because professional sport is considered entertainment. It is incumbent upon academicians and sport marketing practitioners to review current practice and provide insight into eliminating those tactics that may be unethical.

What marketing-mix issues relate to the problem? In regard to product issues, the names of teams, logos, and mascots, the question that must be posed involves the extent to which sport franchises contribute to social stereotyping by the use of certain team names, logos, and mascots (e.g., Washington Redskins, Fighting Illini, Florida State Seminoles). The use of Native American names and mascots has been found offensive to the culture resulting in college and university teams such as Marquette, St John's, Stanford, and Syracuse changing their team names. The Cleveland Indians baseball team, however, continues to use the cartoon character of the smiling, red-faced Indian chief. This particular representation does not seem to honor, but to demean. The name the Washington Bullets was considered to depict violence in a city that has a high per capita murder rate and was thus changed to the Wizards. These and other such examples raise ethical questions that need to be further explored by those responsible for the name selection, representation, and marketing.

Another issue within the product area involves the professional athlete and the responsibilities inherent in the role of public personage, in other words the athlete's responsibility to serve as role model. The noted case is that of Charles Barkley, who publicly indicated that "I ain't no role model" and further noted that he had no "personal responsibility to provide a positive image or behavioral ideal for young people" (Laczniak et al., 1999, p. 46). The primary ethical question concerns the extent to which such role-model obligations should be specified by league rules and individual performance contracts, and the degree to which nonperformance in failing to meet such role-model expectations should result in financial fines and/or nonparticipation penalties for the athletes involved. Further, are morals clauses in endorsement contracts desirable?

Changes in team colors, uniforms, and logos are considered another product-related issue. Along with these changes comes the pressure on fans of all ages to purchase the newer styles to remain current and up-to-date with the team changes. The ethical question that must be posed is whether such changes are implemented in order to increase the merchandising potential of such items as caps, shirts, jackets, and other team paraphernalia.

Ethical practices regarding the pricing of tickets, athletic apparel, and stadium and arena concessions are other important issues that affect the spectators and fans. Although sport was supposed to be something everyone in society could rally around, doing so has become almost impossible for a majority of the lower- and middle-class market. For the most part, high ticket prices for sporting events have excluded many individuals and now seem to be available to accommodate corporate America in the form of giveaways for corporate entertainment. A contradiction arises when we consider that although the lower and middle class have been priced "out of the ball park," the professional team jackets, shoes, and other apparel are target marketed to these groups.

> In the past, sporting events brought Americans of all backgrounds together. Recently, rising ticket prices have discouraged attendance by lower and middle class people.

In the case of college and university sport, an ethical issue is raised regarding season tickets. It is becoming a practice that to qualify for season tickets for men's football and men's and women's basketball, fans must make a substantial donation to the university and to the athletic departments specifically, in order to qualify to apply for season tickets. Are such pricing strategies discriminatory? Many would respond, "Yes."

Promotional issues in sport marketing seem to raise numerous ethical questions. Such incidences would include the sponsoring of professional or other sporting events by producers of alcoholic beverages and the advertising of beer in television commercials associated with sport. Given the increase in underage drinking and deaths related to alcohol consumption and driving, the responsibility for the messages this type of promotion has must be explored. The effects of such advertising and sponsorship on the broad age range of children and college-age individuals who are watching sport events must be raised, and the linkage of alcohol advertising and auto racing must be ethically questioned.

Deceptive advertising campaigns are also considered under ethical issues within sport marketing. Deceptive advertising occurs when products or services are advertised, but the truth in the advertising of the product is either nonexistent or expanded. In other words, what is available is not what was advertised or is not available for the price noted. Deception in advertising is difficult to define because not all falsehoods are deceptive in advertising. Some of the deception may be considered to be "harmless bluffing" by those responsible for advertising. Michael Jordan does not jump as high as he does because he is wearing Nike shoes, and Sheryl Swoops does not play with the skill she does because she is wearing Nike shoes, but the product advertisers would like consumers to believe this is the case. Therefore, if individuals purchase the particular shoes, they believe they not only will jump like Michael Jordan and play like Sheryl Swoops, but also will play the game of basketball with the same skill and finesse that these individuals exhibits. The thing is, such advertising works. The public responds, the products are purchased, and consumers are not considered to be hurt by the exaggeration or harmless bluffing associated with the advertising of the product. In fact, deception is considered by some advertisers to be "part of the game of advertising" or taken in the "commercial sense." Although purchasing the shoes may make consumers feel they can play the game like Sheryl Swoops and Michael Jordan, in actuality what has been purchased is a bit of confidence and style. This may be considered harmless advertising. Is it?

> Inaccurate statements about product cost, amount, and quality are considered deceptive advertising.

Deceptive advertising involves the use of false statements or inaccurate information related to cost, amount, and quality of the product. The cost of items is obviously significant, but when something is being sold for less than the "manufacturer's suggested price," the idea is conveyed that it is a bargain. Since there is no proof of the manufacturer's suggested price, in this instance, there is potential for deception. Packaging techniques make it appear that buyers are getting more for less simply because of the manner in which the item is packaged. It is wise to check the weight and contents of packages. Quality of a product is another factor that is often represented in a deceptive manner. If superior quality is offered at a low price, it is recommended that close scrutiny of the product occur prior to purchasing the item.

Everyone is hurt by deceptive advertising and harmless bluffing, but those most susceptible to such techniques are children, the uninformed, the less educated, the poor, and the ill. These individuals are considered vulnerable; they may put their faith in the advertised product, be ultimately hurt by the deception, and suffer the wrath of false advertising. Too often, individuals purchase products that are not what they expected. Deceptive advertising is not persuasion, but manipulation that violates the principle of maintaining respect for others.

One criterion that could be applied in the case of deceptive advertising is that of "public openness," which indicates that a public practice is not deceptive when the business acknowledges the rules under which it is operating. If the consumers know that there is bargaining potential in a setting and that the price on the item is not the actual price, then there is public openness. Deception enters the picture when there is action indicating one set of rules and there are behaviors indicative of another set. When the rules of the advertising practices are known, then the public is more likely to accept the consequences of various business practices (Bowie & Duska, 1990).

Another issue that comes under the heading of deceptive marketing and has ethical implications is the pervasive use at the professional and collegiate levels of sport of women cheerleaders and dancers who are minimally dressed and performing suggestive or erotic routines. Regarding these issues, Laczniak et al., (1999, pp. 48-49) pose the following questions: Is this a negative role model for young girls to follow? Does the meaning come across that women should be used as entertainment for sporting events rather than to be the participants in them? Does this set up women as sex objects, thus making them more likely to be targets of domestic violence?

What stakeholders are affected by the issue? O'Sullivan and Murphy (1998) pointed out that various groups, among them athletes, teams, fans, agents, and governing bodies of sport, are influenced by the marketing techniques of sport organizations. A familiar issue to some, yet one that is ethically questionable and often found around sporting events, is *ambush marketing*. Defined by Sandler and Shani (1989), ambush marketing is "a planned effort by an organization to associate itself indirectly with an event in order to gain at least some of the recognition and benefits that are associated with being the official sponsor" (p. 11).

As the sport manager examines the impact of a decision on a wide range of people or groups, this is known as stakeholder analysis. The primary stakeholders are those with a formal, official, or contractual relationship with an organization. These include sponsors of the event, official corporate sponsors, athletes taking part in the event, and fans in attendance. The rights of each of these individuals must be considered in the stakeholder analysis. *Secondary stakeholders* include those in the media, the general public, and other companies such as nonsponsors and nonambushers, as well as activist groups (Carroll, 1993). Another category of stakeholder known as the *indirect stakeholder* exists. That is, nonsponsoring companies or "ambushers" that do not have a contractual relationship with the event and its sponsor and yet have well-established and well-planned actions. (Sandler and Shani, 1989). Fans viewing televised broadcasts or listening to radio broadcasts of events are also considered indirect stakeholders as well as the targets of ambush-marketing efforts. Others included as indirect stakeholders are sports agents representing athletes, coaches, and broadcast announcers.

In reference to ambush marketing and the stakeholders, Laczniak et al. (1999) stated:

> Decision makers need to be aware of these stakeholders and their potential impact on the event. Although the focus should largely be on primary (including indirect) stakeholders, the media and their investigative

reporters can influence the general public with negative statements about any international event. Ignoring public sentiment and the views of companies that might be potential sponsors in the future will likely have a long-term detrimental impact. Interestingly, although many sport organizations rely on media coverage to serve as a 'free' marketing arm, they are unprepared when those same media investigate disturbing practices. (p. 49)

Coverage of the site award to Salt Lake City for the 2002 Winter Olympics and the scandal regarding bribery and gifts to Olympic officials are examples of the importance of secondary stakeholders.

Meenaghan (1994) defined ambush marketing as "the practice whereby another company, often a competitor, seeks association with the sponsored activity without payment to the activity owner . . . " (p. 77). He further noted that

ambush marketing occurs when another company, often a competitor attempts to deflect some of the audience's attention to itself and away from the sponsor. . . . because such activity reduces the effectiveness of the official sponsor's promotional efforts while simultaneously denying the activity owner potential revenue, there is reason to question the morality of this type of competitive practice. (p. 77)

Meenaghan (1994) provides the following as the most common methods of ambush marketing:

1. Sponsoring the Broadcast of the Event—a company other than the event sponsor sponsors the broadcast of the event (this may be a legitimate sponsorship opportunity in and of itself).

2. Sponsor Subcategories within the Event and Exploit this Investment—ambusher sponsors a lesser element associated with the event and exploits the association through major promotional activity.

3. Purchasing Advertising Time Around Replays of the Competitor's Event—the buying of advertising time in slots around television replays of the event. This denies a competitor the full benefits of their event or broadcast sponsorship.

4. Engage in Major Nonsponsorship Promotions to Coincide with the Event—using mainstream media advertising or 'below-the-line' promotions to achieve marketing communications objectives during the event

5. Other Ambush Strategies—the suggesting of involvement with an event such as using photography of places which may be recognized, or staging sequences from the same sport as the background in advertising and coinciding with the event; the giving away of licensed souvenirs or trips to the event which may suggest the sponsorship involvement. (pp. 80-82)

Although some may believe that ambush marketing is a major ethical infringement, others believe it is a creative marketing strategy. It is suggested that the determinants of these actions be subjected to ethical analysis through the exploration of the company's intentions and motives.

What organizational mechanism can help solve the problem? As was covered in chapter 7, ethical creeds, codes, and value statements can be extremely helpful in avoiding ethical pitfalls in sport organizations. Such mechanisms when they address marketing specifically, may offer promise in regulating some of the issues discussed in this chapter. Ethical statements, codes, ethical audits, and institutionalization of ethics oversight in sport advertising are but a few of the examples offered by Laczinak et al. (1999) in order to improve ethical standards. They also indicated that

(a) working from a guiding philosophy of the organization,

(b) dealing with the issues central to the business,

(c) communicating the ethical statements to internal and external stakeholders,

(d) publicizing or posting ethical beliefs for the public to see,

(e) revising the document periodically to meet the changing world issues,

(f) living or practicing the ethics document, and

(g) enforcing or reinforcing the code within the organization will contribute to moral excellence.

What solutions are available to solve the problem? It is advocated that ethical reasoning (as discussed earlier in this text) be implemented to identify ethical issues, select ethical standards, and apply the standard to specific situations. The analysis of various ethical theories (also covered earlier in this text) can also apply here. For example, within deontological theories, the use of Kant's categorical imperative might offer a solution; that is, basically, that a situation should be treated as we would wish all situations with similar context to be treated. In addition to these suggestions, Laczniak et al. (1999) also suggest that the TV test be implemented. If as a sport manager one would be comfortable in truthfully explaining the motivations for one's actions or decisions to a TV audience, then the action may be ethical (p. 51).

The previous models and discussions may be helpful as one explores potential unethical behaviors in sport marketing. Understanding one's responsibility to one's organization, clients, and oneself in relation to these behaviors is critical. As readers contemplate the examples presented in this chapter, it may be helpful to know that such issues are not new. They have been around for some time. In studies in which marketing managers were asked to list the ethical issues that posed the most difficult ethical or moral dilemmas for them, the following were included:

(a) bribery,

(b) fairness,

(c) honesty,

(d) price,

(e) product,

(f) personnel,

(g) confidentiality,

(h) advertising,

(i) manipulation of data, and

(j) purchasing (Chonko & Hunt, 1985; Hunt, Chonko, & Wilcox, 1984).

Marketing researchers have had major concerns regarding

(a) research integrity;

(b) fair treatment of outside clients;

(c) research confidentiality;

(d) marketing mix and social issues;

(e) personnel issues;

(f) fair treatment of respondants;

(g) fair treatment of others in company;

(h) interviewer dishonesty;

(i) gifts, bribes, and entertainment;

(j) fair treatment of suppliers;

(k) legal issues; and

(l) misuse of funds.

The primary ethical concerns here dealt with balancing the demands of the corporation against the needs of the client.

In Brief . . .

Ethical decision-making models in sport marketing allow you to examine your decisions in light of the responsibilities associated with marketing. *Organizational goals* are necessary to determine and maintain the product-consumer relationship.

The sport manager constantly deals with the issues surrounding marketing. If the points made regarding responsibility are employed, the sport manager is responsible for knowing not only the components of the product with which he or she is associated, but also the true needs of the consumers and knowledge of how the product can truly meet those needs. The manner in which the behaviors and activities associated with obtaining this knowledge and bringing the product-consumer relationship together necessitates ethical decision making. Responsibility extends not only to individuals with whom one is working, but also to the product and organizational goals. In an effort to sell the product to the consumer, it is easy to lose sight of one's own personal and professional goals as a sport manager and the needs of the consumer. The ethical sport marketer will be cautious of such pitfalls.

Key Concepts

ambush marketing

deceptive advertising

multistage contingency model

1. As promotions director for a minor league baseball team, one of your responsibilities includes planning an event day for this year's July 4th home game. After discussions with your staff, and interviews with local business leaders to gauge the feasibility of the plan, you have decided to put several ideas into action. During the preceding month, you advertised that the first 500 youths under age 12 who attended the game will receive free baseball caps. There will also be a 7th-inning-stretch raffle to give away a television, a video recorder, and a digital camera. Finally, a spectacular fireworks display will be held following the game.

On the morning of game day, however, one of your staff meekly informs you that only 250 caps have arrived; that Pat's Electronics store, which was to donate the raffle prizes, was robbed the night before and no longer has the merchandise; and that the threat of rain makes the fireworks program tenuous.

You hastily assemble your staff for an emergency meeting hoping for solutions, but every solution has its own associated problems. Concerning the hat shortage, one of your staff proposes that they be given away as usual. "Think about it," he says, "who's going to know the difference between 500 and 250 hats? I mean, it's not as if they're going to count them all." Another staff member argues for hat rain checks, but you worry that that would make you and team look incompetent.

As for the raffle, there is not enough petty cash to cover the costs of purchasing the electronic equipment elsewhere. When you ask whether another store would donate prizes for the game, your staff questions why another store would donate products in the name of Pat's Electronics—the store advertised for the last several weeks.

"We could pass the hat," one of your student interns suggests.

No one laughs.

As for the fireworks, you discover from another member of your staff that the pyrotechnics team is now balking at coming to the game. "Not only is it dangerous to operate fireworks display in the rain," she tells you, "but the fireworks company doesn't want a large portion of its stock ruined by exposure to inclement weather."

As if things couldn't get any worse, one of your staff glibly remarks that you should all perhaps be praying for rain. "After all," he says, "if the game is rained out, everything we have talked about and worried about will be moot."

How should you deal with these seemingly disastrous and unavoidable problems in light of marketing techniques and social responsibility? How will your decisions affect your future marketing techniques and social responsibility? How will your decisions affect your relationship with your staff, the team, and the community?

2. "Please have a seat, Ms. Goodwin."

Karin Goodwin was usually accustomed to pressure. Throughout her college career, her reputation was built on her flawless drives, pinpoint chip shots, and pressure putts on the final few holes. It was this tenacity that propelled her through the LPGA qualifying tournaments and into the professional ranks. As a pro, she had such phenomenal first-year success that she was named Rookie of the Year. Because she was young, attractive, photogenic, and an excellent speaker, a sports equipment company quickly offered her a multimillion dollar contract to endorse its new line of clubs, clothes, and other golf accessories, an offer that she eagerly accepted.

This all happened just last year; and she was on top of the world. Now, however, the pressure is almost unbearable. Only last weekend the company owner, while watching the LPGA Seattle Open, happened to notice Karin using another brand of golf clubs and not wearing the company's logo on her attire. A few terse phone calls later, she finds herself sitting in the company president's office to discuss this situation.

"Ms. Goodwin, let me get to the point," he begins. "Your behavior last weekend was alarming and raised many questions about your suitability as one of our spokespersons. We do not pay you to wear another company's clothing or use another company's products on national TV. Was there a problem with the equipment? We do have several custom sets, designed to fit your exact specifications, ready and available in case of an emergency. Was the clothing uncomfortable? Were the shoes too tight? We could have manufactured any jacket, pants, socks, whatever—anything just for you. But you didn't ask. That makes us very skittish.

"Now, what you do on your own time, in the privacy of your own home, is your own business, and that's fine with us. But in public, we own your clothing, we own your clubs, your umbrellas, your tees, and those fuzzy animal head covers you like so much. Everything seen by your fans, your enemies, and the media will have our logo emblazoned upon it—even your panties, if you are so inclined to exploit your attributes that way."

Karin shivers at the way he leers at her.

"Remember, Ms. Goodwin," he goes on, "for the duration of your contract with this company, the moment you step outside your house door, we own you."

Karin's mouth dries up. Though a brilliant golfer, her business skills are undeveloped and the endorsement game is new to her. She realizes too late that she ought to have brought along her lawyer or her manager. It is a mistake she'll never make again.

"Ms. Goodwin," the company president continues, "I've done all the talking so far. Perhaps you would like to explain yourself. I'm a reasonable man, and if you have a good reason for breaching your contract, I'm willing to cut you some slack—call it just an honest mistake from a naive young girl—and we can each go back to what we do best. No hard feelings. So tell me, why did you so egregiously violate your contract?"

What does Karin say? Do you feel Karin actually breached her endorsement obligations? Does the company in fact "own" her? How would you have broached the subject with Karin, her manager, or her lawyer? How might the conversation have gone differently had either of her representatives been present? What possible explanation can you provide for her odd display during a nationally televised tournament?

3. SportsCo has been very successful in the past decade specializing in producing balls and other rubber-based sports equipment, and as marketing director, you are quite proud of your company's reputation as a manufacturer of high-quality equipment at very reasonable prices. You readily admit, however, that the bulk of the credit should go to the company's buyers, who have been able to find excellent, yet low-priced overseas suppliers.

Unfortunately, your buyers have reported back that the company's current supplier, a large rubber company in South America, is planning to corner the market in raw materials, thus creating an artificial shortage and driving up the price of rubber. You cringe at the potential negative impact this will have on the company's prestige, but the buyer also mentioned that he has located a second source of rubber—still inexpensive but, unfortunately, of much lower quality.

In anticipation of spiraling costs in a year's time, the company board of directors decided to purchase the lower-quality rubber. You immediately prepared and sent to the company president sample press releases in anticipation of the flood of complaints due to the sudden rash of inferior products that the company will be selling. Later that same day, the CEO of the company, Mr. Gommer, contacted you to see him in his office ASAP.

"I admire your honesty," Mr. Gommer states, "but we will not be informing anyone—neither our retailers, nor our customers—of our change in materials. We are still using rubber. And as far as the consumer is concerned, rubber is rubber; quality between producers is not that much different to warrant this kind of public information program."

This is nonsense. From your experience in the rubber industry, you know that there is a wide difference between rubber products. The manufacturing process is filled with numerous stages that must be carefully monitored: Limits on the exposure to light, the right balance and combination of chemicals and compounding agents, the proper temperature and duration of vulcanization. Even the overuse of reclaimed rubber can accelerate material deterioration causing premature failure. It becomes a safety issue, and you mention this to the CEO, who now leans forward in his seat, wearing a scowl.

"You are in no position to tell me how rubber is manufactured. I've been in this business since you were an infant—having worked my way up all the way from assistant calendar operator."

You squirm in your seat shrinking from Mr. Gommer's withering gaze. Having adequately humbled you, he goes on.

"There is more to this than simple safety! You may or may not realize this, but our overemphasis on quality is not paying off. Our shareholders have been clamoring for increased profit margins for the past half a dozen quarters, and our stock prices have plateaued. Finding this alternate supplier is a boom.

"Why, you ask? We will be able to continue supplying retailers with low-priced sports equipment; yet now, our profits will be greater. For as the rubber supply dwindles, and other companies are raising their prices, we'll raise our prices as well, of course. After all, we must remain competitive; we don't want to appear as if we're using cheap materials. The rise in prices will send our profits soaring, and our shareholders will be happy.

"As for the customer, our reputation will convince him or her that any perceived shortened life span of the product will be illusory. Our market share will remain high for quite a while. You know that brand loyalty is a powerful force in the marketplace. People still buy American cars, for example, despite their poor overall repair history."

The CEO leans back in his chair and continues in a more relaxed manner. "Don't worry. Everything will be fine. We'll weather the storm. In fact, our company will come out stronger than before. Now, return to your office—unless you have something else to say."

Do you?

Ethical Analysis

The following discussion will analyze the ethical dimensions and implications of the third example above to demonstrate how moral principles relate to a given case. Readers should try to analyze the other examples and draw their own conclusions and resolutions to any particular problems.

Marketing generally refers to how products are moved from a producer to a consumer. Ethical considerations are raised in this area of management because sometimes the marketing practices of producers are questionable. Producers may not honestly inform the consumer about the product, or the product itself may be faulty, and such information may be withheld from the consumers by the producer.

The sports equipment manufacturer in this case is obviously more concerned about maintaining his profit margin than maintaining the quality of his products. His sole interest is not to be encumbered by a possible increase in the price of the rubber he needs to manufacture his products. Further, he is willing to sacrifice quality to ensure he does not experience losses in the future. On the face of it, some of these judgments may be sound from a business perspective; they are not, however, from marketing and ethical standpoints.

There is nothing inherently wrong or morally questionable if a manufacturer decides to produce a lower-quality product. In this case, this might be a wise move; perhaps it is the only way the manufacturer can stay in business. On the other hand, there are other features of this case related to marketing that point to several areas that are morally objectionable.

In selling his products to retailers, the manufacturer neglects to inform his buyers that they are receiving inferior goods compared to what they have previously received. Because poor raw materials have been used, the quality, endurance, and standards of the products have likely deteriorated, perhaps to the point at which certain retailers would not buy the goods. The manufacturer, therefore, is being deceptive and acting in an unethical manner by not informing retailers that the goods they are now receiving are below the standards they have come to expect. By withholding this information, the manufacturer is doing himself a disservice because in all likelihood, the genuine quality of the products will be discovered in a short period of time and lead to returns and cancelled orders.

The withholding of vital quality changes from safety regulators in relation to the production process is not only unethical but may also lead to serious legal problems. Most sports require the strict use and maintenance of equipment to ensure high standards of safety are in place. In the case of a manufacturer, it would be exceedingly irresponsible and unconscionable to produce equipment where safety is not a foremost concern. No physical activity participant should exercise or engage in sport with a fear that serious equipment failure will occur as a result of a manufacturer's neglect for safety. When injury to a participant does occur where equipment failure is involved, manufacturers are often named in negligence suits. In this case, the producer knowingly refrains from notifying safety officials and organizations about the lower quality of his products and thereby tries to avoid the implementation of new standards tests.

Finally, the use of the same packaging for the products is another fraudulent and unethical marketing technique related to the previous point. If the same boxes and instructions are still being used when the products themselves are inferior to those produced in the past, then incorrect and potentially harmful information is being conveyed to consumers. Moreover, there may be safety information, warnings, and safe-use advice, which may pose a threat to users if they incorrectly handle the "new," poorer-quality products. Here, the manufacturer may directly be the cause of some type of damage linked to consumers, because they would be the primary users who would read labels and instructions in order to benefit from the products.

> Unethical marketing practices can involve producers and retailers, producers and safety regulators and organizations, and producers and consumers via unsafe packaging.

In this one case then, there are three separate areas in which unethical marketing practices can occur. They can involve producers and retailers, producers and safety regulators and organizations, and producers and consumers via unsafe packaging. Ethical principles linked to social justice would be important to apply here because there is an obvious element of one person or company influencing the lives of many others in some potentially harmful manner. Ideas referring to impartiality, social good, state interference, liberty, and many other notions could be implicated in assessing this case. The theories of justice discussed in an earlier chapter should, therefore, be reviewed before any specific application is carried out.

Summary

Increased attention has been directed toward sport marketing practices resulting in sport businesses' and companies' paying closer attention to their obligations to the consumer. In this chapter numerous ethical violations regarding sport marketing are pointed out. It is imperative that attention be given to such behaviors. Also in this chapter, marketing is defined and differentiated from the concept of marketing. The elements of marketing mix and a marketing plan are presented, and obligations to the consumer are discussed. Ethical decision making in marketing is specifically addressed, and models by Ferrell and Gresham (1985), Hunt and Vitell (1986), Dubinsky and Loken (1989), and Laczniak et al. (1999) are discussed in detail. Close attention has been given to Laczniak, Burton, and Murphy's (1999) model and those practices most closely related to potential ethical issues were brought out. These included: (a) marketing mix—team names and mascots, the professional athlete and responsibilities regarding public personage, ticket pricing, athletic team apparel, deceptive advertising, and the objectification of women as part of the sporting event; (b) stakeholders—primary, secondary, and indirect stakeholders and ambush marketing; (c) organizational mechanisms to help solve problems; and (d) solutions available to solve problems. Although issues regarding integrity in sport marketing are not new, it is important that readers recognize the dilemmas posed and the potential consequences of the behaviors that they choose. It is their responsibility to protect and ensure the integrity of the practices in sport marketing.

Questions for Consideration

1. What are the most critical areas of abuse in marketing that are evident to you?

2. What approaches can be used to overcome the negative impressions regarding sport marketing in our society?

3. What are your responsibilities as a sport manager regarding the concept of marketing?

4. What steps would you take to ensure truth in advertising?

Chapter Eleven

Human Resource Management

Human resources management, sometimes referred to as personnel management, "refers to practices that employers use to recruit, develop, reward, maintain, retain, assess, and manage individual workers and groups of workers." (Slack, 1997, p. 233) To provide sport organizations with a qualified, effective, harmonious, diverse, and satisfied work force, certain factors must be considered. Among these factors are hiring, training and development, evaluating performance, compensating employees, ensuring they are satisfied in their job, and possibly working with labor groups. The ethical practices associated with each of the factors noted above involve individual responsibilities to the organization and obligations to employees and must be given close attention.

Ethical Concerns Regarding Staffing Needs, Job Description, Recruitment, Interviewing, and Hiring

After staffing needs have been determined for a particular sport organization, specific jobs descriptions and specifications are determined. The positions are then advertised, and the recruitment process is undertaken. The job description is a written statement explaining the duties, working conditions and other aspects of the job. This statement offers a profile of the job. The job specification explains the demands of the employees and the human factors required. This includes education, training, experience, and physical and mental demands (Werther, David, Schwind, Das, & Miner, 1985).

Good Managers Must Consider

Hiring, Training and Development, Performance Evaluation

Employee Compensation, Employee Satisfaction, Labor Groups

Although the categories noted within the job description may vary among institutions or organizations, this basic information is generally included. The ethical responsibility of the employer at this stage is the honest representation (i.e., responsibilities, qualifications, and other information) of the position to be filled.

Hopefully, recruitment for a position will generate a pool of qualified applicants and involve locating, identifying, and attracting applicants interested in and qualified for the position. Recruitment is done through (but not limited to) personal contacts, advertisements, internal searches, job fairs, or private employment agencies. The size of the organization or agency will determine the range and breadth of recruitment. Recruitment, depending on organizational size, may be as narrow as an internal or local search to nationwide or even international (Slack, 1997).

The breadth of advertisements regarding the position in order to reach all qualified applicants must be broad. That is, the position should be advertised in all places where individuals will see the advertisement and, if interested, apply for the position. This means that all outlets for publication of the job should be tapped. Publications of professional organizations, the organizations themselves, or specific places that employ individuals appropriate to the position at the local, district, regional, and national levels should be tapped in order that individuals of diverse backgrounds will have access to the information regarding the search.

> **Job Descriptions Include**
>
> 1. Position title
> 2. Purpose of position
> 3. Specific responsibilities
> 4. Work schedule or time frame of appointment
> 5. Required qualifications
> 6. Desired qualifications
> 7. Information regarding salary (e.g., commensurate with qualifications/ experience or a salary range)
> 8. Information about the organization
> 9. Instructions on how to apply and submit recommendations

In some sport management settings, a selection or search committee may be used. The committee may have representatives from several departments within a large organization or consist of representatives from the specific area in which the individual is to be hired. It is these individuals who will aid not only in the recruitment, but also in the review of candidates' applications, and they will take part in the selection for the interview process and the ultimate selection of the candidate. In smaller businesses and organizations, there may be only one individual who is responsible for each of these tasks. In any case, the same ethical and legal considerations apply.

Hiring is the selection of an individual from the pool of qualified candidates who applied for the position. Qualified candidates are those who meet the required qualifications stated in the job description. Chelladurai (1999) noted that this process is complicated because of the need to "forge a fit between the individual and the job as well as a fit between the individual and the organization" (p. 141). Although the individual-job fit is achieved through the job description, specifications, and advertisements, the individual-organization fit (e.g., needs, attitudes, and values of the person and values and culture of the organization) will require checking the letters of reference and biographical background as well as conducting interviews. It is at this point that personal judgment will need to be used. It is important to remember that personal judgment is a human phase. Personal biases regarding age, race, ethnicity, sexual orientation, gender, religion, politics, and all other forms of diversity may surface at this point. The process, as

Chelladurai pointed out, must be free of discriminatory practices. Not only is this an ethical consideration, but it also is a legal one. Laws govern the requirements that organizations must follow in hiring practices, but the sport manager must be aware of personal biases and questions that may be directed to candidates that may be irrelevant to the job.

> The best job candidate will fit well with the organization, in addition to having the necessary qualifications.

Another ethical consideration that emerges at this point is truthfulness. Both the candidate and those representing the organization are required to be truthful in the information they reveal to each other. In other words, although the candidate should not overstate nor falsify his or her qualifications or experiences, or both, those representing the organization should not misrepresent the organization or position in any way (Chelladurai, 1999). There have been many incidents in which a candidate has been hired for a position, but when the individual arrives on the job, the responsibilities have changed, or the job title, salary, or benefits are different.

Interviewing candidates (face-to-face) will help to compare candidates with each other and to determine if the candidate is capable of meeting the requirements of the job. Depending on the financial situation of the organization, several individuals are invited to interview for the position. Interviews may range from a few hours to several days, given the specific position and organization. Structured and unstructured interview processes may be used; that is, having each candidate respond to the same questions or having an open-ended question-and-answer exchange with the candidate, committee, and selected individuals from the organization. In some settings, the candidate may be required to give a short presentation, but is notified of this in advance.

Following the interview process, the committee evaluates each candidate and meets to discuss each individual and make its selection. Once again, ethical issues may arise among the committee members regarding the concept of diversity when comparing the qualified individuals and making the final selection.

In Brief . . .

To provide the sport organization with a qualified, effective, harmonious, diverse, and satisfied work force, the sport manager must seriously consider ethical practices regarding individual responsibilities to the organization and obligations to employees.

Government Regulations Related to Hiring

Although the law and ethics do not always coincide, ethical considerations regarding fairness are certainly a part of the government regulations in connection to staffing procedures. These are summarized by Chelladurai (1999). It is wise for the sport manager who has the responsibility of hiring personnel to be familiar with the ethical implications as well as the laws and executive orders:

1. Age Discrimination in Employment Act (1967): Forbids discrimination against individuals between 40-70 years of age.

2. Americans With Disabilities Act (1990): Provides for increased access to services and jobs for persons with disabilities.

3. Civil Rights Act (1978): Allows women, persons with disabilities, and persons of religious minorities to have a jury trial and to sue for punitive damages if they can prove intentional hiring and workplace discrimination.

4. Equal Employment Opportunity Commission Guidelines (1978): Created by the 1964 Civil Rights Act, this commission investigates and eliminates employment discrimination against certain groups of individuals (e.g. women and African, Asian, Hispanic, and Native Americans).

5. Equal Pay Act (1963): Forbids sex-based discrimination in rates of pay for men and women working in the same or similar jobs.

6. Immigration Reform and Control Act (1986): Prohibits hiring of illegal aliens.

7. Older Workers Benefit Protection Act (1990): Provides protection for employees who are more than 40 years of age regarding fringe benefits and gives employees time to consider an early retirement offer.

8. Pregnancy Discrimination Act (1978): Requires pregnancy to be treated as any other medical condition with regard to fringe benefits and leave policies.

9. Rehabilitation Act, as amended (1973): Forbids discrimination against persons with disabilities and requires affirmative action to provide employment opportunities for persons with disabilities.

10. Title VII, Civil Rights Act (1972): Forbids discrimination based on race, sex, color, religion, or national origin.

11. Vietnam-Era Veterans Readjustment Assistance Act (1974): Forbids discrimination in hiring disabled veterans with a 30% or more disability rating, veterans discharged or released for a service-connected disability, and veterans on active duty between August 5, 1964, and May 7, 1975. (Chelladurai, 1999, p. 142)

Although the above are derived from the law, they legally as well as ethically protect the rights of individuals in our society.

At-Will Hiring and Affirmative Action

Hiring issues and affirmative action are additional concepts that emerge in the management of personnel. The classical point of view regarding the concept of hiring indicates that the best qualified individual was hired. This is considered to be the best market value. A concept known as employment at will is a practice utilized in publicly-owned companies or businesses. This concept is interpreted by businesses as an issue of liberty. In other words, the employer can hire whomever he or she wishes, allegedly, in order to get the job done. At-will hiring is rarely public knowledge. Still, many individuals are hired under this concept, and specifically most part-time employment falls into this category (Bowie & Duska, 1990; Clement, 1991).

> As business becomes public in the sense that its stock is sold on the open market, or there are stockholders other than just the owner, the business needs to be operated in conformity with the primary principle—to make a profit. That means hiring the most qualified in the sense of those who will serve the company best. (Bowie & Duska, 1990, p. 59)

Employment at will is often not compatible with the goals of maximizing profits and productivity. At-will employment often results in various forms of nepotism; individuals may be hired not for their qualifications, but in the name of family loyalty. Not hiring the best qualified, in essence, hurts the business. Historically, the at-will principle has served to exclude individuals because of their race, sex, nationality, sexual orientation, or religion even when they are qualified to do the job. Such exclusion is indefensible both economically and ethically.

A publicly-owned business that uses the at-will principle is operating legally, but not ethically.

Out of Title VII, Civil Rights Act (1972), the concept of affirmative action emerges. Affirmative action requires that available jobs be made public and accessible on an equal basis for all qualified persons. An often misunderstood concept, it was intended to give equal opportunity to minorities to apply for positions. A misconception regarding affirmative action is that it requires businesses and organizations hire unqualified personnel. There are numerous people of diversity qualified for jobs who have been overlooked in the job market due to a history of discrimination. By making available jobs public and accessible on an equal basis for all qualified persons, the pool of qualified candidates is broadened for businesses and organizations. "Historically speaking, if human beings acted etchically, equal opportunity and affirmative action policies would not be necessary."

According to Bowie and Duska (1990), two types of affirmative action should be considered: weak and strong. Both types of affirmative action are warranted within society. The weak type requires that jobs be advertised and announced to everyone, including minorities and women. Not only must the job opportunities be announced, but there must also be an equal opportunity to compete for the job. The principle of equal opportunity is noted by Bowie and Duska (1990):

> . . . persons with the same ability and talents who expend roughly the same effort should have roughly the same prospects of success. Race, religion, sex, and family background should not be relevant to one's success or failure in the competitive struggle. (p. 60)

Under strong affirmative action, a member of the disadvantaged minority may be selected for a position over another candidate with relatively equal qualifications.

In this sense, the minority status is viewed as a "plus factor." This in no way means that an unqualified individual will receive the job. Further comments are made on this issue by Bowie and Duska (1990):

> There is a deontological justification for strong affirmative action in terms of compensatory justice. There was harm done in the past because of racial and/or sexist discrimination. Individuals from disadvantaged minority groups were hurt and consequently they should be recompensed. Besides this deontological argument there is the utilitarian argument that the integration of all groups into the society is an important goal, and thus preferential hiring is an effective means to their integration. We leave unsettled the equally utilitarian argument that preferential hiring is counterproductive because it causes more resentment, racial hatred, and strife than it alleviates. (p. 63)

This issue takes on even greater meaning when the responsibility of businesses is explored. A disputable point is whether businesses have a direct responsibility to promote general welfare or solve the issues and problems of sexism and racism in our society. Government, on the other hand, does have the responsibility to promote general welfare and establish justice and, therefore, could oblige other systems in our society, such as education and business, to devote their power and resources to alleviating social injustices.

In Brief . . .

A business that uses at-will hiring practices operates within legal boundaries, but such practices are ethically questionable. *Affirmative action* requires that available jobs be made public and accessible to all qualified persons. *Weak affirmative action* makes minimal efforts to providing equal opportunity to compete for a job. *Strong affirmative action* means that a person with minority status is hired even though another candidate has equal qualifications. Hiring the minority is considered a plus-factor, and the individual is regarded for the value and strengths he or she brings to the organization.

Orientation, Training, and Evaluation

According to Slack (1997), the employer is responsible for the orientation, training, and evaluation of the employee. As a part of the socialization process, the new employee goes through an orientation that may cover a multitude of information regarding the organization including day-to-day operations, employee benefits, and review of the employee handbook. Such orientations assist new employees with critical information and understanding of their responsibilities and the manner in which those responsibilities are to be carried out. Orientations may take the form of lectures, videos, facility tours, and review of handbooks including safety regulations and requirements. Included in orientations should be a review of the ethical code of the organization and its relationship to the vision and mission of the organization. The expectations of employees in regard to the code should also be addressed. Depending on the type of sport organization one enters and the nature and level of one's sport management position, orientations may take different forms. Nonetheless, they are an important part of the employee's career and a legal and ethical responsibility the employer should take seriously.

> During orientation, employers are ethically responsible for making sure both ethical and legal information is communicated and understood.

Training is designed to "improve an employee's skill level, knowledge base, or experience, or to change their attitude about aspects of their work situation" (Slack, 1997, p. 240). With the onset of new technology and equipment related to specific job responsibilities, additional training of the employee in certain cases may be mandatory. As new equipment is added to a training room or as diagnostic testing devices are updated and computer technology is upgraded, training in the use of these devices is important from an ethical and in some cases a legal standpoint. Slack discussed that training occurs on three levels: organizational level, job level, and individual level. The organizational level may involve new strategies or technology. At the job level, a change in a specific task for which one is responsible may require additional training. At the individual level, certain managers may require the acquisition of skills such as conflict management, interpersonal communication, or supervision. In each of the examples cited, the employer is again responsible for providing such training. Training in the way of protecting the welfare of the employee may also be provided; that is, workshops and training on issues such as diversity or sexual harassment.

Evaluation or performance appraisals of the employee are a critical responsibility that should be carried out with the utmost integrity and sensitivity. Such appraisals determine the extent to which the individual employee or the employee's workgroup is contributing to the overall purpose of the sport organization (Slack, 1997). The evaluation also contributes to the enhancing the effectiveness and efficiency of sport organizations by guiding management in making decisions about promotion, compensation, merit, and other rewards. Through performance appraisals, employees who are not working up to the required standards are identified.

There are a number of ethical issues related to the evaluating of employees that must be acknowledged. First, the evaluation must be relevant and contain criteria associated with the job responsibilities. Second, the appraisal should be reliable in that as others use the instrument, it should yield similar results. Third, the appraisal instrument and system should have the support of the organization's members. Feedback is critical. Without sharing the evaluation results with the employee, the performance appraisal is useless. Not only should the employee's strengths and weaknesses be shared with the individual, but also ways in which she or he could improve and an indication of resources available to help the employee improve should be provided.

The sport manager may implement various instruments for performance appraisal. Written feedback based on observation, critical incidents reports, and rating scales are but a few examples. A self-evaluation form filled out by the employee may also provide the employer with important information regarding the individual's perspective on his or her performance. If there are consistently low performance appraisals of an employee, clearly communicating this information to the individual is extremely important, and records should be maintained in all instances. To gain a broader picture of the organization and the performance of all of its employees, it would be appropriate for subordinates to evaluate superiors as well as superiors evaluating subordinates. The coach is evaluated by an athletic director (and in some instances on win-loss records alone), but rarely is the coach evaluated by the players with whom she or he works so closely. In institutions of higher education, obviously professors evaluate students, and most often, students evaluate faculty, but how often do the faculty evaluate deans, and do deans have the opportunity to evaluate provosts or presidents? The concept of evaluation as a function of the sport manager and ethical implications were also discussed in chapter 8.

Performance Evaluations Should:
—Be relevant to a particular job
—Be consistent
—Be approved by the organization's members
—Be followed by feedback

In Brief . . .

The *orientation, training, and evaluation* of employees is a legal and moral responsibility of the sport manager. Furthermore, it adds to the welfare of the organization and its clients. *Employer evaluations* that are accompanied by individual performance feedback can enhance both the employer's performance and the success of the organization.

More Recent Issues

Slack (1997) emphasized that much time has been spent on the part of the employer on the recruitment, selection, hiring, and evaluation of employees, but changes in our society have brought other issues to the forefront. The numerous ethical and legal responsibilities on the part of the employer for the employee have expanded as moral and social responsibility and legal aspects are better understood. More recently, employee stress, drug and alcohol abuse, and sexual harassment have been noted as areas of concern for the sport manager.

Recognizing, understanding, and acknowledging the causes as well as the negative outcomes of constantly stressful situations for sport managers are paramount to his or her welfare and the welfare of the organization. Slack (1997) suggested that interventions be used in these cases such as redesigning an individual's job, giving attention to employee workloads, establishing a career counseling program, and offering stress management and time management courses as well as opportunities for recreational breaks to assist the employee in lowering stress levels.

Drug and alcohol abuse is on the increase in high-stress working environments. The sport manager has the responsibility to organize programs to help staff identify drug and alcohol abuse and offer support to employees through rehabilitation programs. The individual responsibility does have a large impact in these cases, but the legal and moral responsibility on the part of the sport manager for safety in the workplace, in the production of the product or service, and for the employee is crucial.

Sexual harassment is another area for ethical concern for the sport manager. It is illegal and is defined as repeated verbal or physical abuse of a sexual nature. Further, it may be "graphic commentaries on the victim's body, sexually suggestive objects or pictures in the workplace, sexually degrading words used to describe the victim, or propositions of a sexual nature" (Slack, 1997, p. 248). In addition, sexual harassment indicates a quid pro quo situation, or something for something. In other words, if sexual submission does not occur, there is the threat that this will affect the individual's employment in some way (e.g., salary, promotion, duties). It is important that employees be informed of the organization's ethical stand on this issue and that its leaders not tolerate this type of behavior. The sport industry has had its share of sexual harassment incidents, and sport managers who are now being educated in professional behaviors are well informed of the severity of sexual harassment. Certain actions can be taken to attempt to avoid sexual harassment and include the establishment of a policy against such behavior, developing procedures to be followed on how to handle sexual harassment complaints, informing employees of the nature of sexual harassment as well as the legislation, and including this information in orientation programs with new employees and training sessions with current employees.

In Brief . . .

Drug and alcohol abuse affect the employee and the employer, making them the ethical responsibility of the sport manager. Employee orientation and training should address the legal and ethical ramifications of these issues. *Sexual harassment* is illegal and unethical. Employees should be informed of what constitutes sexual harassment, the potential punishments for the behavior and how to report incidences of sexual harassment.

Obligations to Employees

When one considers the employer-employee relationship, it is necessary to examine the rights of each. Whereas it has been established that employees have certain rights, which include due process in hiring and firing, fair wages, and respect of their privacy, then it is the employer's moral obligation to ensure these rights. Bowie and Duska (1990) pointed out that questions regarding the conflict between employer and employee rights may arise, requiring a decision to be made between the conflicting positions. In the sport setting, it is the manager's responsibility to decide between the conflicting positions. This task is undertaken by first acknowledging that employee-employer relationships should be contractual. They involve an authority-subordinate relationship, thus opening up greater potential for abuses of power within the relationship. Actually this relationship should be consistent with laws of moral custom and free from coercion and fraud. The individual who is desperately in need of a sport management position may be exposed more to various forms of subtle coercion than will individuals who have skills that are highly marketable. It is the freedom of the employee that is jeopardized, necessitating the careful examination of one's contract conditions.

The employee's rights to liberty, privacy, and a fair wage should be explicit within the contract. Regarding the right to liberty, Mill (1859/1956) wrote more than a century ago:

> The sole end for which mankind are warranted individually or collectively in interfering with the liberty of action of any of their number is self-protection. That the only purpose for which power can be rightfully exercised over any member of a civilized community, against his will, is to prevent harm to others. His own good, either physical or mental, is not a sufficient warrant. (p. 13)

Based on Mill's explanation, once the hierarchy of power (i.e., relationship) and responsibility (i.e., task or job to be accomplished) between the employer and employee has been established, then the employer does not have the right to interfere with the employee's freedom unless there is either harm or evidence of potential harm to the employer, company, or work setting. The most widely used example here is drug use. In the broadest view, if the drug use does not bring harm to the work setting (i.e., the employer, product, consumer), then what the individual chooses to do in private life should not be of concern to the employer. Using the concept of harm associated with the sport organization is still another approach to this issue. If there is potential harm to the setting present, then violations of the individual's liberty may be necessary to prevent harm to the company, corporation, or business. Because businesses have been known to control or regulate employees' behaviors regarding dress, family, and social life, for example, then any action that the employer feels may negatively affect the profit of the organization harms the organization and could potentially be restricted (Bowie and Duska, 1990).

There is a close relationship between the employees' right to liberty and their right to privacy. In the drug-use example cited in the discussion of liberty, the right to privacy arises. The issue of privacy has received much attention in regard to the drug testing of athletes. Is such testing an invasion of an athlete's privacy? Why are coaches and athletic administrators not tested as well? The same questions arise with the Olympic athletes. Why not test all who are connected in any way with the Olympics? Why single out athletes? Regarding this point, Bowie and Duska (1990) stated that

> . . . some defenders of the market point out that the really important aspect of the market is that it allows us to do business without being hampered by irrelevant considerations such as the beliefs, personal habits, politics, race, sex, or other behavior and ideological idiosyncracies of the person we are doing business with. (p. 89)

When this same concept is applied to the employer-employee relationship, it could be concluded that as long as the product that one is interested in purchasing is able to be delivered and its quality is not hampered because of drug usage, the drug issue is not relevant and any probing into an employee's private life in this case is not justified. On the other hand, the relationship between the employer and employee extends beyond the simple market explanation. Rather, it is considered a long-term relationship wherein the employee becomes an agent or representative of the employer. In this case, it is difficult not to pay attention to certain behaviors if they do, in fact, impinge on the job responsibilities or put the company, organization, and possibly the consumer at risk. If businesses are to operate ethically and within the law then

> . . . business activity should conform to the laws and basic moral norms of society. Once this background condition is understood, a business cannot restrict the freedom of an employee when that restriction requires the employee to perform some act that violates either the law or a basic moral norm. of society. An employee cannot be ordered to falsify experimental data relating to product safety or to discriminate against a fellow employee on the basis of race. The fact that the falsification of the data or the discrimination would improve profits is irrelevant. (Bowie & Duska, p. 91)

The right to fair wages brings up issues such as the employer's treating the employee as a human being with dignity and respect, not taking advantage of the employee, and not using employees as means to specific ends. As ethical behavior is considered, within the right to a fair wage, dependency and autonomy are concepts that should be explored. Enlisting Kant's (1785/1959) second imperative of never using another human being merely as a means to an end is a good approach here. It is important for the employee to retain autonomy and keep in mind that the concept of reciprocity of use prevails. If, however, the equality changes and one party becomes more dependent, the relationship that was freely entered into changes drastically. In other words, if the employee desperately needs the job, then his or her bargaining position becomes weak, and manipulation and coercion may occur on the part of the employer. In this instance, management would be able to increase profit by paying what the market would bear at the expense of the employee. It is no wonder that unionization and minimum wage laws were enacted.

Key Concepts

affirmative action

at-will hiring

employees' rights

sexual harassment

strong affirmative action

weak affirmative action

Moral Dilemmas in Sport Settings

1. Two faculty members are retiring from the sport management department as of next fall. You, as head of the faculty search committee responsible for finding the two replacements, have advertised the future vacancies in several major professional publications. However, you also know that the university is undergoing a financial review, and austerity measures may be implemented. With this in mind, you inserted a clause in the advertisement indicating that the positions were contingent upon budgetary approval.

   At the time during the course of the search and hiring process when your committee came up with the short list for interviews, the sport management department faculty were informed that one of the positions could be offered only on a temporary 9-month basis, and the other could no longer be offered as a tenure-track position. Fortunately, the interview invitations have not yet been sent, so you decided to insert the new information in the letters.

Dr. Dee Jonissy, the department head of sport management, has caught wind of your intention and called you into her office. You enter and have a seat; once the pleasantries are dispensed with, Dr. Jonissy starts.

"Are you nuts? You know how hard it's going to be for us, especially now with the budget cuts, to get quality scholars. If you tell our candidates about the change in funding, do you have any idea what that's going to do to the quality of our applicant pool? The top candidates will be dropping out faster than our basketball players after their fourth year of eligibility. The best applicants will take their searches elsewhere, and all we'll have left are the desperate ones, the ones who can't get real jobs, the ones all the other departments' searches turned away. It will do nothing for our regional reputation and the accreditation board if we hire mediocre assistant professors to replace the quality professors we lost. And won't that look great—having our students taught by second-rate academicians."

You remind her that somebody must replace them. Anyone picked from the pool will be fairly green. Dr. Jonissy shakes her head.

"The pool will be less green if we don't tell them about the changes," she says. "Get the quality candidates on to the campus. We'll show them around and woo them with our facilities and research opportunities. Trust me. They'll be so happy to get an interview that once they arrive, the news about the position changes won't be so hard to swallow.

"Besides, it may all be moot anyway. Rumor has it that the cuts won't be as severe next year; we'll be able to get our funding returned and convert these positions back to permanent, full-time tenure-track positions."

You have heard the rumor as well, but you have little faith in it. Rumors have a way of enhancing a reality other people wish to see, whether or not there is any truth to them. You also know that according to university policy, all reclassified positions are to be treated as new vacancies and, therefore, must be advertised and a new applicant search must take place. The new hires have no guarantee that they will have a job the following year.

You express your disdain at Dr. Jonissy's ill-treatment of the applicants. Her face hardens around a frozen smile as she scrutinizes you.

"Think of our students," she says. "Those are the people you should really be worried about, not some faceless stranger. My students are the most important variable in this ethical equation—as they should be to you—and I will do everything I can to keep them uppermost in any decision I make. They pay good money to get a good education, and I couldn't live with myself if the education we provided was insufficient in assuring them a good career in the field of sport management. We shouldn't be in business if we can't offer a good return on their investments.

"But no matter," she says, calming down, her face softening, "you're in charge of the committee. Do what you wish. But remember who your loyalties ought to rest with."

What will you do?

2. "Of all people, why did Coach Dixon have to do this?" you say to yourself. As principal of Weatherby High School, you've known and respected Coach Bill Dixon for the past 5 years and have seen and heard nothing but exemplary reports about his behavior, his conduct with students, his professionalism, and his character during his physical education classes and his coaching. The fact he was a bachelor never seemed to bother anyone, except maybe the female students of the school with their crushes.

However, in just a few short minutes, everything has turned upside down for the school, the community, and you. While chaperoning the end-of-the-year athletes' formal, you saw Bill arrive with a male friend. The way the two men interacted with each other soon made it clear that Bill and his friend were a gay couple.

As you debate with yourself on whether or not you should deal with the situation, Vice-Principal Lauren marches over to Bill and pulls him away from his partner and towards you. You blanch and look for a place to hide. This is not the time or place, but within moments the two are upon you.

Immediately Ms. Lauren speaks up. "You need to deal with this situation."

"Don't you think it would be best to leave this for tomorrow?" suggests Coach Dixon.

Before you can reply, however, Ms. Lauren interrupts. "No! There are children present, and they need to know that we can address this problem quickly and efficiently."

"What problem?" asks Coach Dixon. You see Ms. Lauren's face redden as she turns to face him, fully ignoring you. Standing aside from the two, you opt to stay out of their argument for the time being and just listen.

"You're gay," she says. "Isn't that enough? And a gym coach, for goodness sake—with all those boys under your responsibility." Her body visibly shivers from the thought. "You know you won't be working here much longer."

"You know," Coach Dixon responds, "I do have tenure."

"Yeah, sure, but this is a special circumstance—" Ms. Lauren responds.

"Oh, but incompetent teaching isn't? It is well known to this school's faculty, its students, and the community that one of our teachers throws tantrums and chairs, hides in his office to eat lunch, and could curse the paint off the wall—all during class time! The kids hate him and learn nothing; yet still he teaches. How incompetent does a teacher have to be to get fired?"

"Are you claiming that because this teacher has tenure, there's nothing that can be done?"

"I on the other hand, having done nothing like that—possessing instead a stellar string of evaluations in my file—need to now worry about employment? Haven't you seen the movie *In and Out*? It's about—"

"I don't care about that, Bill," she interrupts. "Your teaching skills are not what is being questioned."

As the voices of the two arguers rise, a small crowd of students and parents gathers and surrounds the three of you.

"This isn't the movies," Ms. Lauren continues. "There are real boys and real girls in this school who are affected by everything you say and do. The way you speak, the way you dress, the way you grade the class—all have an impact on our students. Your very presence in the classroom is a moral and ethical statement. And unlike the movies, happy endings are not so clear-cut here. We don't get two hours to solve all our problems and make the world fall into place. There are people in this community that find your lifestyle disgusting, and they are the ones we have to answer to."

"But incompetent teachers are fine?" Coach Dixon retorts.

"I told you your competence is not in question; it's your moral choices."

Coach Dixon waves his hand in Ms. Lauren's face. "It is my choice, is it not, to live my life in the way I think it ought to be lived? You have no business speaking for the entire community simply because you've prejudged my lifestyle and found it distasteful. Is that what the fundamentalist church you go to teaches you?"

Ms. Lauren's jaw drops in horror at Coach Dixon's statement. With a predatory twinkle in his eye, Coach Dixon goes on.

"You didn't think I knew who puts those little flyers in the teacher's mailboxes. But, of course, you have tenure as well."

"How dare you insult my beliefs," Ms. Lauren rails back, knocking aside his hand and shoving her face into his. "My religious beliefs and morality are not the problem here. Your beliefs and moral stance are, and you would do best not to deflect the issue. Education always has and always will have the responsibility to the community and to the students to maintain the moral high ground. Isn't that right?"

Vice Principal Lauren quickly swings around to face you. So does Coach Dixon. Suddenly, all you can hear is your heartbeat speeding up as Ms. Lauren, Coach Dixon, and everyone else in the room stares expectantly at you waiting for a reply.

What do you say? Should Coach Dixon's private life be an issue in the school? Should Ms. Lauren's private life be an issue? To whom should the school answer to, if anyone? Does the fact that Coach Dixon is a physical education teacher and coach have any special relevance?

3. A position is available for an assistant director for the Meadowvale Recreation Department, and as director it is your job to find someone to fill for this position. So, you have spent the last couple of weeks interviewing, and the list of suitable candidates has been shortened to three people: a white male, a black male, and a white female. Each possesses comparable, if not equal, qualifications and experience.

The recent memo from the mayor's office is certainly not making the choice any easier. It said that the selection process for all city positions must be sensitive to the demographic makeup of the current staff and clientele. What does this statement, a wonderful example of politicalese, mean? Does it mean that you should continue current staff demographic levels, or does it mean that you should increase diversity away from current levels? Although a subtle change in policy, this does seem to be a clear and conscious move away from the strict proactive affirmative action procedures of the former mayor—a policy that has led to your staff's being represented mainly by black male and female employees.

You considered ignoring the memo and selecting the white female for the position. After all, based on your experiences in the health club industry, if all things are equal it is an unwritten rule to hire women because a higher percentage of female clients will discuss their weight problems with women than with men. Still, you hesitate. You contact the mayor's office for some clarification, explain your problem, and your choice for the position. The deputy mayor, a white male in his forties, commends your choice.

"That's exactly what we're looking for," he says, "more diversity within our staffs. It will demonstrate to the community that we are not locked into this flawed notion of quotas." He does suggest, however, that you ought to consider the male candidate more thoroughly. Before he hangs up the phone, he says that based on your forward-thinking management style, he will try to get your department extra funding, but he won't have any information for you until after you have made your selection.

Sitting back in your chair, you realize you have no idea how your staff has interpreted the new policy. So you call into your office your staff directors and tell them the situation. To your dismay, they unanimously interpret the policy as keeping the demographic levels the same. The clientele is mostly minorities, and a black male in a management position would go a long way in providing a good role model for the community and for its young black men.

So what do you do? How do you interpret the needs of the community and staff in light of their racial and ethnic backgrounds? Should race even be an influencing factor in the hiring decision?

Ethical Analysis

The following discussion will analyze the ethical dimensions and implications of the first example above to demonstrate how moral principles relate to a given case. Readers should try to analyze the other examples and draw their own conclusions and resolutions to any particular problems.

Hiring is an essential, often first-step, component of personnel management. In many places of employment, especially governmental and other public-sector agencies, there are strict hiring procedures that must be followed when searching to fill vacant positions. In some institutions, specialized officers oversee the hiring process within departments to ensure that laws and rules are followed and fair hiring practices are implemented. In the case under consideration, several questions may be asked about the hiring procedure from a moral perspective. For example, does the contingency clause in the ad provide a fair warning to candidates that the position they are applying for will indeed be available? Should applicants be informed when there is a status change in the position for which they have applied? At what point in the hiring process should this change be conveyed, if at all, to the applicants? What moral obligation(s) does the employer have to the prospective candidates? How much information can or should be reasonably provided to the applicants? How much individual initiative should be expected by the applicant in the hiring process?

In answering these questions, we will forego dealing with any legal issues even though there may be moral concerns attached to unlawful conduct. Although inclusion of the contingency clause appears to be a legal safeguard for the employer, its application may not be broad enough to cover certain moral demands. For instance, Dr. Jonissy and other members of the sport management department could reason that if one of the full-time positions reverted to a temporary nine-month appointment, each candidate in the pool of applicants still has the potential to secure the remaining full-time appointment. Once the selection is made to hire someone for the full-time position, then a second individual would be chosen from the same pool and offered the temporary job with an explanation as covered by the contingency clause. This sort of reasoning would seem plausible to Dr. Jonissy and the administration.

The question that seems to be debated is whether all the applicants should be told in advance of making any firm decisions that the status of one of the positions has been altered. Following this line of thinking, it is obvious Dr. Jonissy feels no need to convey this information to the candidates before the committee makes its selections. In effect, she and the department are withholding information from all of the candidates—information that the applicants might judge important. Why might this information be significant? Some applicants might prefer to withdraw their names from the pool once they learn that there is the potential to be offered a temporary, limited appointment—the very possibility Dr. Jonissy fears. Perhaps these candidates have no intention of applying for a 9-month job, even on the possibility that this might occur.

Other complications are likely connected to such a case as well. Usually when a department advertises two positions, the job descriptions of each are different, or certainly the needs of the department are likely different. This often means that the department is planning to hire two individuals with dissimilar profiles and qualifications who can work in a specific area of a program. In the case before us, there is no indication that the department is required to disclose which of the two positions might be preferred as the full-time appointment. In other words, candidates would not know, for instance, that the department has prioritized the hiring of a sport manager on a full-time basis, rather than hire a full-time person in another area. Once again, withholding the status-change information, which might reveal the preferred ranking of positions, appears to deny these individuals knowledge to make an informed decision. Treating applicants in this way is morally wrong.

A deontological perspective that demands other people be treated with utmost respect and dignity, only as ends and not as means, could be a useful ethical guideline to follow here. Although Dr. Jonissy and the sport management department have probably covered their tracks from a legal standpoint, on moral grounds, they should immediately make available to all the candidates the status change of one of the positions. Otherwise, the applicants are indeed being duped and exploited, contrary to deontological principles and common decency.

> No one should be deliberately misinformed or denied access to information when crucial life and career decisions are at stake.

The preceding remarks are especially relevant for anyone who has entered or will enter the job marketplace where the expression "timing is everything" is commonplace. Job applicants need to be informed about working-condition changes immediately as related to a specific position so they can concentrate their search efforts in a more efficient manner. They need to know whether to eliminate certain positions from their lists of potential jobs and remove as many unnecessary contingencies as they can. If prospective employers neglect to provide applicants with certain information so these decisions can be made by candidates, valuable time may be wasted, anticipated commitments may not materialize, the reputation of the department may be jeopardized, and both the employer and applicants may become part of a situation in which distrust and suspicion are prevalent.

Of course, this distrust is limited only to the individuals involved in the deception. Unless all of the candidates are in contact with each other, such distrust will remain individualized. A department may not suffer that much public relations damage.

Are Dr. Jonissy's concerns valid as well? Are not her desires to maintain the quality of her program at least equally legitimate, if not more so? In fact, cannot the deontological argument be made from the standpoint of her relationship to her students? By not trying to acquire the best possible instructor for the students, would Dr. Jonissy then not be treating them with less concern than the applicants? Should she then inform her students that the new instructor may be of markedly inferior quality and with that information determine whether they wish to remain a student in the department?

In the final analysis regarding this case, Dr. Jonissy has a moral obligation to inform job applicants of any status change related to specific positions as the applicants take the initiative to determine the job status. Open, honest, and forthright dealings with applicants ensure that the hiring process not only conforms to legal standards, but also values the balance between moral interests. Without establishing such a relationship, the employer, organization, or department may undermine its own integrity.

Summary

This chapter explored the ethical practices related to the issues of staffing, job descriptions, recruitment, interviewing, and hiring personnel. Eleven government regulations related to hiring were presented, and the importance of the knowledge regarding these areas was stressed. The concepts of at-will hiring and affirmative action were presented. Strong and weak types of affirmative action denoted how organizations may consider the equal access to jobs. The importance of orientation, training, and evaluating the employee was stressed, and the ethical implications of these areas explored. The more recent issues of stress, drug and alcohol abuse, and sexual harassment in the sport management setting were presented, and the importance of the employer responsibilities regarding the awareness and action to prevent these issues was considered. Obligations to employees regarding conflicts and the rights to liberty, privacy, and fair wage were discussed using Mill's and Kant's considerations of these issues.

Questions for Consideration

1. In what ways would the concept of hiring at will be advantageous?

2. What instances of weak or strong affirmative action have you experienced?

3. Were the rights of liberty, privacy, and fair wages extended to you in jobs you have held?

4. What types of evaluation have you experienced in jobs you have held?

5. Have you experienced education/training/workshops in jobs you have held regarding diversity, sexual harassment, drug/alcohol abuse, or stress management? What were these like?

Chapter Twelve

Governance and
Legal Aspects of Sport

Chapter Objectives

• To identify various sport governing bodies

• To explore the concept of governance and sport

• To discuss specific laws and their relationship to ethical theory

This chapter will present a brief overview of the governance and legal aspects of sport and their relationship to ethics. Each of these areas is important in its own right. Therefore, it is imperative that sport law and governance aspects related to the sport manager be taken up in classes that are separate from that of ethics in order to give specific attention to each of these areas and to gain the knowledge and understanding needed to effectively engage in the management of sport.

Governance

An important issue often raised by sport scholars is society's is concern with who should have the ultimate governing power for sport in our nation, states, districts, and educational institutions. Unlike some other nations, the United States does not have a formal minister of sport for sport participation at any level. The U.S. Congress, however, did pass The Amateur Sports Act of 1978, which created the United States Olympic Committee (a nongovernmental body), which serves as the organizing body for amateur sports. This Act also protects athletes from exploitation by self-interested sport-governing bodies. It should be noted that the Amateur Sports Act was revised in 1998 to have the USOC support and fund paralympic athletes. This revision gave disabled athletes opportunities to participate in elite amateur sport—an opportunity previously denied to physically challenged individuals.

Another issue of governance deals with the laws or policies that have been established in order to safeguard the public order, ensuring that sport programs that are publicly funded are open to everyone. In the United States, Title IX is an example of this regulation. It was intended to promote gender fairness in educational institutions. In Canada, the organization that regulates high-level sports, Sport Canada, established a policy on women in sport that puts forth strategies that ensure equity and fairness throughout the country (Coakley, 2001).

Intercollegiate athletics falls within the amateur sport category, but governing bodies that oversee this area only govern intercollegiate athletics and not any amateur events outside educational institutions. A number of governing bodies exist that promote and supervise intercollegiate athletics. A few of these governing organizations are noted below.

The National Collegiate Athletic Association (NCAA)

Whereas the Amateur Sport Act governs competition among amateur athletes in the United States, the National Collegiate Athletic Association (NCAA) governs women's and men's sport competition at the college and university levels. The NCAA and its various internal subcommittees, which include compliance and ethics, operate within their own purview and oversee the numerous institutions within their scope. Based on the size of the financial base, number and types of sports offered, focus of the program, and existence of athletic grants-in-aid for example, which notes only a few of the criteria, educational institutions are classified as Division I, II, and III within the NCAA (Abney & Parks, 1998).

Basically athletic programs within the NCAA Division I category are those institutions considered to be generators of significant revenue. These programs are highly competitive yet are considered entertainment; they include football and men's basketball and offer full grants-in-aid based on athletic ability. The institutions within this division are attempting to achieve national and regional recognition. There may be different ways such programs are financed. For example, gate receipts, television broadcast revenues, licensing revenues, private donations, and student fees may constitute some of the ways these programs are financed. NCAA Division I is further divided into Divisions I-A, I-AA, and I-AAA. Again the classification criteria may vary.

NCAA Division II institutions are attempting to achieve regional prominence and offer grants-in-aid, but not to the extent Division I institutions are able to give such awards. The primary difference between Division III schools and the other divisions is that participation is the primary goal. Grants-in-aid are not offered to the athletes for their athletic abilities, and they remain much like any other student with regard to admission, academic advising and scholarship opportunities (Parks, Zanger, & Quarterman, 1998).

The NCAA has power at the level it serves, and there is considerable national attention paid to the governance of intercollegiate athletics. The weekly publication of *The Chronicle of Higher Education* features an entire section on athletics that consistently informs readers of the governance policies and procedures of the NCAA and violations by its member schools as well as the subsequent sanctions imposed by the NCAA. Although the NCAA oversees its member institutions, the *primary responsibility and control* of athletic programs is with the educational institution itself, specifically, the president and those athletic administrators who are directly responsible for its programs. This includes governance, compliance, and most certainly concerns of an ethical nature.

Institutional control has been of a rather elusive nature, especially in the NCAA Division I institutions. As a result, the Knight Foundation Commission on Intercollegiate Athletics (1991) was formed and consisted of college and university presidents who were to study athletic programs in NCAA member schools. After a year's study the commission published a document known as *Keeping Faith With the Student-Athlete: A New Model for Intercollegiate Athletics*. The members of the commission recommended reforms that were to bring athletic programs back into compliance with traditional values and principles of higher education. The reforms noted the following: (a) presidential control, (b) academic integrity, (c) financial integrity, and (d) independent certification. This was known as he "one plus three" model. What was proposed included that presidential control (the "one") was responsible for and directed toward the "three," or academic integrity, financial integrity, and independent certification. The institutional self-study reports, which were to be submitted to the NCAA prior to a visit by a certification committee to review such documents and interview college and university personnel to verify the reports, included a section called "commitment to equity." This rounded out the total report and indicated how the welfare of the student-athlete was instituted as well as that of the nonstudent-athletes, in other words, what benefits were extended to student-athletes that were not extended to nonathletes. This was only one of the parts of the commitment to equity. Others included, but were not limited to, diversity (race, gender, ethnicity, etc.) of coaching staff and personnel, salaries of coaches, and dining and training facilities for all athletes. Also reviewed within the report to the Commission is the mission of the college or university, mission of the athletic program, athletic program goals, and outcomes.

Each of the categories of the Knight Foundation Commission report (Knight Foundation Commission on Intercollegiate Athletics, 1991) relates directly to the integrity of the athletic programs and the welfare of the student-athlete. The need for attention to these areas was referred to by Eitzen (1988) in a previous chapter and has been elaborated upon by Abney and Parks (1998):

> The Knight Commission further stated that the dignity of the student-athlete should be maintained; that the health, welfare, and safety of student-athletes should be the primary concern of the administrators; and that all student-athletes, regardless of race, gender, or sport, should be treated fairly and should reap the educational benefits of the institution. This principle is a departure from the highly publicized emphasis on revenue generation and win-loss records, particularly in big-time programs. Clearly, the commission considered the student-athlete to be at the center of the program and expected institutional leaders to ensure that this philosophy was implemented. (p. 125)

Presidential control mandates that president of the institution exercise the same control over athletic programs that she or he does over all other university programs. This includes all others associated with the athletic programs such as the board of trustees, athletic directors, boosters and alumni. *Academic integrity* is concerned with the admission policies for the student-athlete. No athletes should be admitted unless they can be expected to graduate; once admitted, they must be making progress toward graduation, and graduation rates of both student-athletes and other students should be comparable. *Financial integrity* indicates that all financial transactions will be under the auspices of the university and includes equipment, shoe and clothing contracts, booster clubs, and athletic foundations.

Athletic departments are permitted to use institutional funds, which affirms the legitimate role of athletics on the campus (Abney & Parks, 1998). *Certification* indicates that those NCAA programs that award financial aid for athletic ability will be audited on academic and financial integrity.

There is a commitment to social responsibility being met with the Knight Foundation Commission report (Knight Foundation Commission on Intercollegiate Athletics, 1991) and the certification process. As the NCAA and individual educational institutions take part in the self-study required for certification as well as the follow-up visit by a peer group to examine the self-study and talk with people associated with the athletic programs, there is a sense of establishing (a) self-awareness, by opening the self-study to the public and educating the campus about the athletic program's goals, purposes, and how the program supports the institution's overall mission; (b) affirmation, by revealing parts of the athletic program worthy of praise; and (c) opportunities to improve, by revealing problems within the athletic program and identifying solutions for improvement (DeSensi, 1998; NCAA Committee on Athletics Certification, 1993).

Conferences

Within the college or university sport setting, conferences exist that govern their member institutions. Examples of current conferences include the ACC (Atlantic Coast Conference), SEC, (Southeastern Conference), SWAC (Southwestern Athletic Conference), the Big Ten Conference, the Ivy League Conference, MEAC (Mid-Eastern Athletic Conference), and the Pennsylvania State Athletic Conference. At the conference level, rules for competition are established, and the oversight of conference championships takes place.

The National Junior College Athletic Association (NJCAA)

The NJCAA governs the junior-college level of athletics by promoting and supervising programs that are in conjunction with the educational objectives of junior colleges. Although not much is heard about this national governing body, it nonetheless oversees numerous athletic programs nationwide and has been in existence since 1938.

The National Association for Intercollegiate Athletics (NAIA)

The NAIA governs four-year and upper-level two-year colleges and universities in the United States and Canada. The NAIA athletic programs are similar to those found at the Division II level of the NCAA. This organization has been in existence since 1940 (Lessig & Alsop, 1990).

Conference Functions Include

—Communication within and beyond the membership

—Scheduling

—Officiating

—Crowd control/contest management

—Compliance with and enforcement of rules and regulations

—Eligibility of student-athletes

—Television contracts

—Informational services

—Merchandising/sponsorships

—Surveys of members

—Fostering collegiality among member institutions

—Record keeping

(Kinder, 1993)

The National Small College Athletic Association (NSCAA)

This organization was formed in 1966 and is dedicated to promoting athletic opportunities for smaller (fewer than 1,000 students) accredited colleges in North America. The primary goal of the association is to develop equitable opportunities for intercollegiate athletic competition for the student-athletes of its member schools on district and national levels.

The National Christian College Athletic Association (NCCAA)

The NCCAA began in 1968 and provides a Christian-based organization that functions uniquely as a national and international agency for the promotion of outreach and ministry and for the maintenance, enhancement, and promotion of intercollegiate athletic competition with a Christian perspective. The NCCAA consists of two Divisions (I and II). Division I includes Christian schools, and Division II includes Bible colleges. The intent of this organization is to produce winners in the "game of life." The organization holds the beliefs that athletics are a means to an end, not the end in themselves, that the process is as important as the performance, and that the student-athlete is more important than the program.

Amateur Sports

Coakley (2001) pointed out that amateur sports do not have owners, but do have an association with commercial sponsors and governing bodies that have control over sanctioned events, rules, and athletes. The governing bodies are considered to be nonprofit, but they do utilize event revenues to keep their organization running and to maintain power over amateur sports. Although there are centralized sport authorities who oversee amateur sports in some countries, they work in conjunction with national governing boards (NGBs) of individual sports and have control over sanctioned events, rules, and the athletes. For amateur sports not connected with colleges and universities, the United States Olympic Committee (USOC) is the controlling organization. NGBs are responsible for regulation within specific sports.

Individual NGBs have depended on corporate sponsorship money throughout their history. This money pays for operating expenses, the events themselves, and the training of athletes. Corporate sponsorships are sought by the NGBs and/or the athlete, in exchange for advertising and/or wearing the company's logos, clothing, and shoes as well as use their equipment. Sponsorships may take various forms; even colleges and universities now have contracts with various companies such as Adidas, Nike, and Converse, for example.

The ethical issues surrounding the amateur athlete are numerous and connected with the economic benefits to the corporate sponsor and the athlete. Although visibility of the corporation is the key, an economic recession could mean the decline or elimination of some sponsors. The circumstances under which and the degree to which the athlete wishes to be a spokesperson for the "interests of international corporate capitalism in the world" has to be taken into consideration from the perspective of amoral values (Coakley, 2001, p. 337).

Although what has already been presented does not by any means exhaust each of the levels of sport, organizations governing youth sport as well as senior competitions must also be considered. Participation in these activities even differ along skill levels. That is, there is opportunity for youth sport competition at the recreational level as well as at the elite level (e.g., National Alliance for Youth Sports, American Youth Soccer Organization). The same is true for seniors who wish to participate in sport. The master's level of competition in certain sports is available to seniors, as well as competitions such as the Senior Games. The organizations that provide opportunities for specific sports and levels of competition for youth and seniors are the governing bodies for these competitions.

Professional Sport

Professional sport is "any sport activity or skill for which the athlete is compensated for his or her performance. Compensation can be in the form of salary, bonuses, reimbursement for expenses, personal services contracts, or any other forms of direct payment." (Sutton & Gladden, 1998, p. 243) Governing bodies in professional sport regulate the competition between professional teams and include such organizations as the National Basketball Association NBA, the National Football League NFL, and the National Hockey League NHL. Divisions according to location (e.g., east, central, west) and/or National and American Leagues in Major League Baseball as well as other breakdowns that occur within professional sport. The Ladies' Professional Golf Association (LPGA) and the Professional Golf Association (PGA) are also examples of professional-level governing bodies. Each sport at this level has its own structure and system of governance. According to Sutton and Gladden (1998), this includes (a) a league commissioner; (b) board of governors or committee structure composed of team owners; and (c) central administration, which negotiates contracts and agreements and assumes responsibility for scheduling, licensing, coordinating publicity, and advertising on behalf of the team.

International Sport

Governing bodies such as the International Olympic Committee (IOC), the National Olympic Committee (NOC), and the Local Olympic Organizing Committee (LOOC) as well as the members of the International Sport Federations (IFs), National Sport Federations (NSFs and NGBs), and Local Organizing Committees regulated international competition. More recently, the Professional Sport Organizations (PSOs)—(league, franchises tours and circuits), Professional Players' Unions and Athlete Representatives (PPUs and PARs), the Court of Arbitration for Sport (CAS), and sport organization and event sponsors (SO and ESs) were added to the mix.

The need for the additions to the international governing bodies was precipitated by issues of (a) corporate sponsorships regarding professional basketball players playing in the Olympic Games and (b) drug testing. Some of the basketball players had contracts for sponsoring one line of clothing and were wearing the apparel of another company. One athlete (Michael Jordan) covered the Reebok insignia with a U.S. flag because he had a contract with Nike. The drug-testing issue

Key Concepts

amateur sports act

international sport

Knight Foundation Commission

NAIA

NCAA

NCCRA

NJCAA

NSCAA

paralympics

professional sport

arose in 1992 when Butch Reynolds challenged the Olympic drug-testing procedures, claiming that the urine sample had been tampered with and the analysis was flawed. The right of an athlete to sue an international sport federation for the right to compete in the Olympic Games was the primary issue in this case. "The court held for Reynolds and threatened to freeze IAAF sponsorship money from U.S.-based corporations to force the IAFF to fulfill its obligations of a compensatory award." Thoma and Chalip (1996) noted that

> The issues created in this situation and the results of a successful legal action served to pressure international sports federations to join with the IOC to support the authority of the Court of Arbitration for Sport (CAS) to mediate sport-related disputes that cross national boundaries. (cited in Fay, 1998, p. 286)

The International Paralympic Committee (IPC), the National Paralympic Committee (NPC), and Local Paralympic Organizing Committee (LPOC) are parts of a governing group as well at the international level. The Paralympic Games are held usually 2 weeks after the Summer and Winter Olympic Games and include athletes with physical and sensory disabilities. From an ethical standpoint, these games denote inclusion and provide an opportunity to integrate athletes who are differently abled into the elite level of national and international competition.

Legal Aspects

The areas within sport law are so numerous and expansive, it would be impossible to address each one independently. Therefore, an overview of certain legal aspects and their interrelationships with ethics will be presented. The law determines what is right and wrong and good and bad, which may give the impression that anything that is legal is therefore ethical. In reality, it may be difficult to achieve both legal and ethical outcomes. For example, at one time, it was legal to own slaves, but it was certainly not a moral action. The law includes certain rules that govern behavior. Failure to abide by these rules result in civil or criminal penalties, or both. Several laws with which the sport manager needs to be familiar were noted in chapter 11 dealing with personnel (e.g., Americans With Disabilities Act, Title IX). Other legal areas the sport manager may face include tort law, antitrust law, constitutional law, labor law, criminal law, and licensing laws. This list is not all-inclusive, but includes an example of the breadth of laws sport managers may encounter.

> It is important to remember that an action that is legal is not necessarily ethical.

In Brief . . .

The *governance* provided by specific sport organizations helps to protect the rights of participants at all levels of sport, as well as to uphold ethical and legal standards.

Regarding legally related issues, Hums (1990) brought up the following points:

1. Does one uphold the law because one has to, or because it is in the best interests of one's constituents to do so?

2. Does one provide a minimum standard of care so that one does not get sued or so that participants have the safest environment possible?

3. Is Title IX enforced because one fears losing federal aid or because one truly believes in equal access to opportunities for women? (p. 7)

These questions further indicate the interconnectedness of ethics, moral action and the law.

Tort Law

Based in deontological ethical theory, negligence within tort law deals with a private or civil wrong or injury suffered by an individual as a result of another person's conduct. Negligence is an individual's failure to act as a reasonably prudent person would act in a similar situation. If an individual failed to act in an appropriate way, based on the relationship with the injured party, a wrong may have been committed. The remedy for a wrong of this type may be compensatory (monetary) or punitive (beyond the costs of injury) damages (Miller & DeSensi, in press).

Certain elements constitute negligence and include duty, breach of duty, proximate cause, and resulting injury. Duty is based on the relationship an individual has with another (e.g., teacher-student or coach-athlete), voluntary ssumption of a duty, or duty imposed by a statute. Breach of duty indicates that an individual did not perform an act as a reasonably prudent person would, either not doing something or doing something improperly. Proximate cause is the linkage between the individual's duty and the resulting injury. Assumption of risk, comparative negligence, missing any one of the elements of duty, not meeting procedural guidelines, and governmental or other types of immunity can serve as possible defenses for negligence.

Because deontological ethical theory focuses on duty and responsibility for the other person, the focus and concern in this case is on the person who was injured. There is not, however, an issue in the case of negligence of the greatest good for the greatest number as teleological ethical theory purports (Miller & DeSensi, in press).

Intentional torts include issues with which the sport manager should be familiar. Intentional torts are characterized by intent to commit a harmful act. Assault and battery fall within intentional torts. Invasion of privacy, infliction of emotional distress, and defamation are a few of the other issues that compose this area. The invasion of privacy is an issue that has been linked with drug testing in sport. Four types of invasion of privacy (intrusion, disclosure, commercial misappropriation, and false light intrusion) exist within the law. Intrusion and disclosure require that the individual has an expectation of privacy and society recognizes this expectation as a legitimate privacy claim. False light intrusion involves the defendant's making known information that taints the perception of the plaintiff. Commercial misappropriation occurs when an individual tries to make money by using someone else's likeness or name. Defamation is a false negative statement that is negligently made by an individual and that results in damage to another person. Defamation is further divided into libel (the publication of a defamatory nature by writing) and slander (written defamatory statement[s]). Deontological ethical theories appear to emerge within the content of intentional torts. Individual rights and the concept of duty are paramount within tort law. Right and wrong within the deontological concept of duty is determined by just that, rather than the outcome or effects of behaviors in a situation that is prescribed by teleological theories. Individual rights are also important regarding torts. The happiness of others is not taken into consideration in these cases, because the individual's human rights are to be protected.

Federal Legislation

Title IX (1972) and the Americans With Disabilities Act, as well as others, are important federal legislation associated with sport with which the sport manager should be familiar. Although these were covered in chapter 11, they bear repeating as important cases continue to emerge that affect sport and sport participation.

Title IX

Although Title IX was originally passed in 1972, there are still public educational institutions that do not provide equality of opportunity to participate in sport. Title IX indicates that "no person in the United States shall, on the basis of sex, be excluded from participation in, be denied the benefits of, or be subjected to discrimination under any educational program or activity receiving federal financial assistance. Equity is measured in institutions receiving federal financial aid in the United States by a three-prong test. That is, an educational institution is in compliance with Title IX if it meets any one of the following tests: (a) proportionality, (b) history of progress, and (c) accommodation of interest."

Proportionality test. The institution must demonstrate that sport participation opportunities for each gender are substantially proportionate to its full-time undergraduate enrollment. "If 49% of the students are female, no less than 44% and no more than 54% of the student-athletes should be female. A 5-percentage-point deviation from exact equality is determined to be within the law" (Coakley, 2001, p. 215).

History of progress test. Schools must show that there is a history and continuing practice of expanding its athletic programs for females. Showing progress for the last 3 years is the most crucial point within the 'history of progress' test. This time frame indicates a point of integrity regarding the institution's plans. Other benefits and opportunities related to equity are evaluated here. These include

(a) equipment and supplies;

(b) scheduling of games and practice times;

(c) travel and per diem allowances;

(d) opportunity for coaching and academic tutoring;

(e) locker-room, practice, and dining facilities and services;

(i) publicity and recruitment procedures, and

(j) support services (clerical and administrative).

Accommodation of interest test. The institution must show that its programs and teams have fully accommodated the interests and abilities of individuals of the underrepresented sex. The school has to prove that the underrepresented group (male or female) of students do not have the ability or interest to sustain these opportunities or that a new women's team would not have opportunities to compete against other teams because no other teams are in existence (Coakley, 2001; Title IX of the Educational Amendments of 1972).

Coakley (2001) pointed out that those institutions within the law have met the "history of progress test." Good faith efforts have been shown over the past three years, but the changes must continue until one of the other two tests is passed. In cases where there are not documented changes, the school is required to meet the proportionality test. This particular test is dependent on numbers that are easy to measure and easily used in court cases when the other two tests have not been passed

From an ethical perspective, Title IX created a situation wherein the access and opportunity for underrepresented individuals in sport are supported. Yet controversy surrounds this legislation. The argument has been presented that equality of opportunity is necessary, but on what basis? There is the belief that there should not be equity in women's athletic programs due to the limited resources. The money must come from some source to support these programs. Limited acceptance of girls and women's sports by society indicates that there might not be the interest on the part of all girls and women that there is by a few, and Title IX challenges gender roles of girls and women in society. From a teleological perspective, the happiness of the majority, may in fact, not be supported here. Other sacrifices may have to be made on the part of those who do have the opportunities as well as the revenues; that is, men's and boy's programs may have to be limited or eliminated in order to provide for the increase in the numbers of girls and women who wish to participate in sport. The counterargument to this point, however, is that if all things had been equal from the beginning, Title IX would not be necessary, nor would any other legislation that favors the access and opportunity of underrepresented groups.

The Americans With Disabilities Act (ADA)

This act has permitted the access to participation in sport and sport settings by prohibiting discrimination in employment and in places of public accommodation. Title I of this act noted that if a differently abled person meets the essential job qualifications with or without reasonable accommodation, then that individual cannot be discriminated against. Also, Title III prohibits discrimination in places of public accommodation. Access must be provided in recreation/leisure facilities such as sport arenas and stadiums, fitness clubs/centers, and other places that offer sport participation. If changes to accommodate disabled individuals pose a threat to others or if undue hardship (financial or otherwise) is created by the needed changes, then participation may be denied. An individual would be considered under the Americans With Disability Act if she or he has a physical or mental disability that limits one or more of major life activities, a record of a disability, or a perception of possessing a disability. (Miller & DeSensi, in press)

This act, in addition to other laws incorporating the rights of individuals, was put to the test with the professional golfer, Casey Martin. Because of his disability, he requested that he be permitted to use a cart during PGA competition. Legally, he was permitted to do so. From the perspective of ethical theory, and deontology in particular, the best interests of the individual were considered and if the Golden Rule, Kant's categorical imperative, and other theories that involve acting out of duty were considered, this was a humane and fair decision. However, further questions emerge. Will every person hereafter want this same accommodation? Will this change the future of sport as we know it?

Other Legal Considerations

Although there is a multitude of potential legal cases that could be discussed from various ethical perspectives, it is not the intent of this chapter to go into depth in each area. Rather, it is important that the sport manager be aware of and understand the scope of legal issues and realize that if an individual's rights are violated, this may result in litigation.

Constitutional law. From the area of constitutional law, the issue of prayer in the schools as well as at sporting events can be challenged. The individual's rights regarding due process and the deprivation of life, liberty, and right to own property need to be understood within the athletic setting. Claims of due process may be brought on the regulations and constitutions of athletic institutions, conferences, and other governing organizations. Unreasonable search and seizure issues are brought up in relation to the drug-testing procedure of athletes.

Contract law. In the area of contract law, the morals clauses that are now included in professional athletes' contracts could be questioned. Can we actually require by contract that an individual act in ethical ways? Labor laws dictate the rules and regulations governing the relationship between labor and management. The rights, privileges, duties, and responsibilities of each are defined as collective bargaining in professional sport takes place.

Tort law. An extension of tort law would raise questions regarding the value and use of injury waivers. Although waivers do serve as an ethical way to share knowledge about an activity in which an athlete is about to take part, in no way do they morally or legally relinquishes an individual coach, teacher or trainer from acts of negligence.

Antitrust law. Knowledge regarding antitrust laws in relation to professional team sports is imperative. Because professional sports teams are composed of private economic entities that are operated as a business to make a profit, private economic power is controlled and regulated. At the intercollegiate level of sport, particularly NCAA Division IA, which is considered big business, antitrust laws pertain to the televising of sports. Involved with this legislation are the Sherman Antitrust Act and The Clayton Act.

In Brief . . .

Sport managers need to know the law as it relates to their specific position in order to avoid violating individual human rights and to best serve sport participants and consumers. Understanding the intersections of the law and ethics will help the sport manager avoid decisions that may lead to legal liability and unethical behavior.

Key Concepts

Americans With Disabilities Act

Antitrust laws

Constitutional law

Contract law

Title IX

Tort law

Although laws may be passed such as Title IX or the Civil Rights Act, this does not mean that these laws will automatically change the hearts and attitudes of individuals in society who oppose such laws. That takes time. What it does mean is that guaranteeing and protecting the rights of individuals is the ethical and moral thing to do. As the rights of individuals are protected by laws, they should also be protected by other individuals. If an individual has a right to privacy, for example, others must not interfere with that right. In other words, others are obligated to leave the rights bearer alone. Knowing our rights as citizens, athletes, students, and professionals is critically important to the sport manager. Therefore, it is imperative that further education regarding the law and ethics be undertaken.

By understanding the intersection of the law and ethics, sport managers can make sound ethical judgments that serve both the sport participant and consumers.

Moral Dilemmas in Sport Settings

1. You hustle into your boss's office. "Eric," you say, "we have a situation." As program director for the Meadowvale Community Center, you have received some unsettling news and want to discuss it with the center director, Mr. Eric Ostacolo.

   "What's the problem?" Eric asks, hardly raising his head.

   "There is a gentleman, Sam Stopier—"

   "Sam!" His head jerks up. "Yes, I know him. A wonderful athlete. A great runner. Too bad about that fluke fall. Paralyzed from the waist down, I hear. What a shame. Anyway, what does he want?"

   You explain to Mr. Ostacolo that Sam has always had an interest in physical activity, but because he is only mobile in a wheelchair, he has been denied many opportunities to pursue such interests.

   "I'm sorry to hear that."

   You continue that with the passage of the American With Disabilities Act, however, Sam must be reasonably provided with access and opportunities to participate in publicly funded and supported programs.

"Fine, but what does that have to do with us?"

You, at last, tell Mr. Ostacolo that Sam wants the community center to organize and run a wheelchair basketball league.

"We can't afford that." Mr. Ostacolo sits straight up in his chair and begins waving his arms as if he were shooing the idea out of his office. "Adjustable-height basketball rims, floor maintenance, not to mention the additional handicap facilities we'd have to install."

You remind Mr. Ostacolo that the center is publicly funded . . .

"I know that. We receive subsidies all up and down the government ladder."

. . . and is therefore mandated to abide by the statutes in the ADA.

"Well, I don't know about that. Too often these government bureaucrats ram legislation down our throats with no concern over who's going to foot the bill. It's all well and good to do the right thing, but any time our elected representatives get the urge to be righteous, guess who has to pay for their moral enlightenment?

"I mean," Mr. Ostacolo continues, "I can sympathize with the disabled when it comes to ramps and elevators—I'm all for accessibility—but I refuse to believe that anybody, simply because they are physically challenged, has a right to force us to provide a team for them to play on."

You point out to Mr. Ostacolo that his arguments are very similar to ones used to prevent women's access to sports.

"I know that. But don't you see the difference? Don't you see the slippery slope? First, we give women equal access to sports. Now, we are making accommodations to give the physically challenged the same access. What's next? A veteran's league? An ex-convicts' league? A mailmen-bitten-by-dogs' league? At what point do we say, 'I'm sorry, but we can't provide your special status any extra privileges to sports access?'

"If we had the money," he says, holding up and showing you the spreadsheet that was lying on his desk, "then the whole issue would be moot. We couldn't afford the referees, the facility upgrades, the equipment purchases. If Sam wants to pay for all this, great. But we don't have the money. I can hardly afford to run the programs we do have: aquatics aerobics, strength training, basketball and volleyball leagues, Tae Kwon Do, Aikido, Tai Chi, birthing classes, day care, after-school programs, and diet and weight-control classes. Geez, how much more do we have to do? How many interest groups are we already addressing? How many more will we need to satisfy?"

He pauses.

"You know," he says, "if we weren't already doing so much, people wouldn't expect so much more from us. Instead, they see us doing all these things and never consider the possibility that one more program could be all that much more difficult. Well, after a while, one more straw will break the camel's back."

Mr. Ostacolo sits back and remains quiet.

You bring up Sam once again. He rubs his forehead and lets out a deep sigh.

"Fine," he says, turning his attention back to his budget sheets, "he can have his handicapped b-ball league. Just let me know which of our other current programs he would like me to drop so I can use that money for his benefit."

2. Your job as a high-ranking representative for a nationwide sports-governing body is to certify college and university athletic programs. This involves ascertaining whether the institution is meeting specific standards related to financial integrity, academic integrity, equity, compliance, student welfare, and other similar concerns.

Today, however, the organization's president calls you into his office. He tells you that some information has reached his desk involving one of the schools currently undergoing certification review—Trampista University. Normally, the review process is fairly simple: Forms and questionnaires are sent to the school to be completed, and a review committee is sent to the site to inspect the facilities and files and to talk with those involved in the program. At this time, Trampista has completed and submitted all its forms to the organization and received an absolutely glowing report from the review committee. All that is left to do is review the materials and then submit a summary to the re-certification committee for approval.

The story the president tells you about the school, though, is nothing short of scandalous. The accusations consist of numerous documented recruiting violations, athletes receiving illicit gifts (like telephone calling cards and gifts provided by the athletic department and boosters), grade fixing, plagiarism, and on and on—each infraction worse than the previous one. The final transgression makes you physically ill; it accuses your review committee and entire certification office staff, including yourself, of accepting bribes to "overlook" these violations.

You sit flabbergasted, unable to speak after being indicted for something you didn't do. Fuming and insulted, you leap out of your chair, rip the report from the president's hand and read it. Immediately, you notice that the anonymous affidavits of supposedly eyewitness accounts originated with the individuals who work at another school—a school that has an intense ongoing rivalry with Trampista University, a school whose football team recently lost miserably to Trampista University.

You fling the paper back on to the president's desk and scoff at the report. You know your staff, you tell him, and you stand by their integrity. The president is impressed by your loyalty, but not by your acumen. He tells you that the head of the review committee just purchased a new BMW. Another member of your staff recently purchased a home that seemingly is considerably above her means to afford.

Dumbfounded, you say nothing, but your mind races to comprehend. The president sees your distress and gestures to you to sit down. He says he wants only one thing from you right now: to convince him that your methods of collecting information from the campuses under your charge, as well as your office's dealings with all compliance issues, are accurate and reliable, and that he should have every reason to disregard these accusations against Trampista University and sleep well that night.

What do you say?

3. You can't believe this is happening. As the first-year intramural director in charge of a large college intramural program, you have discovered that accident reports filed over the past several months by student organizers have been inaccurate, that some reports were altered weeks after the accidents occurred, and that some reports have disappeared. You became aware of this situation when one student brought up charges of negligence, and eyewitnesses confirmed details that were not on the specific report related to the episode. After checking further, you amass a large collection of other accident reports where false and exaggerated statements are evident. Soon your mind reels from the plethora of moral and ethical issues involved, as well as the legal liabilities you and the university face.

Realizing the endemic scope of the problem, you meet with your student organizers. You present them with all the materials you have uncovered and ask what they ought to do about the predicament. The group sits quietly, seemingly unaffected, and unanimously replies, "Nothing."

You never expected this response. You bring up all the eyewitness reports. How can they be ignored?

"Eyewitnesses are unreliable," says Jim, the volleyball director. "You must know that. They rarely agree on even basic information like height, weight, and clothing. Do you honestly expect them to understand, much less agree upon, the subtleties of physical injury? Besides, most of those eyewitnesses have by now forgotten they talked to you, especially with finals approaching."

The other coordinators nod in agreement. Once again, you can't believe such a conspiracy exists. Nonplussed, you ask why this way of doing things exists. One of the students, June DePort, stands up to speak for the group. You know her as a bright and charismatic exercise science major, and one of your best coordinators.

"Because you're new to the university," she begins, "let me explain how things have worked in the past. As you know, our program is funded by the university. What you may not know is that the less frequently injuries occur in the intramural program, the safer and better the program looks. The university then allocates more money towards it. Look at all the wonderful equipment we have for the students to use. Jim got new volleyball standards; Steve received new racquetball paraphernalia; we now have intramural fencing. And the referee stipends make your student employees, including us, some of the highest paid per hour on campus.

"Furthermore, and I'm sure I needn't have to inform you of this, better equipment reduces the likelihood of injury. Look at all the padding on the walls in the gym, for example. Do you think padding grows on walls? So what if we ignore a sprained ankle here and there? We've had no problems with the system so far, and in the long run it will lead to safer conditions for all students. Besides, most of the injured will be walking within a few days—no harm done. Don't worry about anything—we've been here longer than you. We know the drill. We talk to the injured students a few days later following the incident, ask them how they are doing, then toss their records. What the university doesn't know benefits all of us, and what benefits all of us benefits the students."

"Why do you want to open up a can of worms, anyway?" said Jim. "You'll just get us all in trouble, get the university in litigation for years, and get yourself unemployed."

What now? Were the students morally wrong to "doctor" the reports?

Ethical Analysis

The following discussion will analyze the ethical dimensions and implications of the third example above to demonstrate how moral principles relate to a given case. Readers should try to analyze the other examples and draw their own conclusions and resolutions to any particular problem.

Those involved in physical activity programs and institutions assume an additional responsibility to ensure the physical and emotional safety of participants. Instructors, teachers, and coaches work in an environment where participants can and do experience accidents by virtue of the distinct tasks, equipment, and demands required. Despite the inevitable, and despite the assertion that a participant who voluntarily engages in such potentially harmful activities takes upon him- or herself the responsibility of dealing personally with the injury if it occurs, in an increasingly litigious society every attempt must be made to ensure that safe equipment is used and safe practices are implemented and that when accidents do occur, sound guidelines are in place to treat accident victims in a responsible and respectful manner. A crucial part of the follow-up procedures following an accident is preparing an accident report. There should be a standard form for this report, and all physical activity employees should be familiar with when and how to complete this form. Clearly one of the most important features related to the accident report is that it contains accurate and precise information. Accident reports may be used as evidence in legal proceedings, and the individual who prepares the report must be made to realize this fact. To deliberately exaggerate, withhold, or tamper with vital information on an accident report can create severe legal difficulties not only for an institution, but also quite possibly for the person who completes the report. From a legal standpoint then, it is imperative that those who work in the physical activity profession recognize the seriousness of this document.

In the case under consideration, therefore, the college definitely has a legal obligation to produce and maintain accurate records when accidents occur. The student employees are likely considered representatives of the school because they are league organizers, but ultimately, the responsibility rests with you, as both intramural coordinator and employee of the college, to ensure that accident reports are not only completed, but also completed appropriately. All individuals under your charge must not only be informed of the contents of the accident report and of the procedures for gathering and entering the relevant information, but also trained to do so and evaluated on their competence. After all, any person who writes an erroneous report (whether purposely or not) can feign ignorance, blaming you for poor training and lack of follow-up evaluations. Of course as coordinator, you should also stress that every accident, no matter what a student worker thinks, must be acknowledged with the completion of an accident report. No one should risk making a judgment whereby a small matter later turns into a serious situation, and no record was kept of the initial incident. Student workers must be impressed with the fact that accident reports are essential and must be referred to as an accident in every circumstance.

However, though what ought to be done by you is fairly obvious, the perceptual nuances and moral positions held by your staff are anything but obvious. Sometimes, student organizers assess accident situations differently to justify or, at least, to condone such manipulation of reports. Perhaps some feel the need to protect themselves if they neglected to carry out some specific task, like mop up a dirty or wet gymnasium floor before or during an activity. Perhaps others might be led to believe that doctoring the accident reports protects the institution and that this expression of loyalty to the school/employer is an expected practice among student workers. Finally, some may have felt that certain accident situations were too trivial or unbelievable and created a more plausible and reasonable scenario or omitted the incident entirely.

It can be argued that none of these possible rationalizations is acceptable from a moral perspective in light of the above discussion. Not only were the students who doctored the accident reports morally wrong because they were only less than truthful, but they also placed others, mostly the injured victims, at greater risk. The latter might refer to significant information whereby medical decisions have to be made, and if such information was inaccurate, this could lead to some serious harmful consequences.

Furthermore, in this case, moral principles related to social justice, where again the decisions of a few have an impact on the lives of many, may be implicated. It could be argued that the paternalistic notions of these intramural employees is unforgivable in light of their relationship to their peers, to you, and the institution. The college likely has a policy or set of procedures to follow when accidents occur, and so these become the action guides that affect student participants. There may also be utilitarian grounds and calculations to determine the right course of action by demonstrating the costs and benefits involved in accident situations. When these factors are assessed together with the goals and objectives of the intramural program, then moral decisions may be upheld and supported by the college, the intramural coordinator, student workers, and physical activity participants.

Yet in this scenario, June, Jim, and their fellow organizers would be unimpressed by these moral positions. They would reject the claim that their questionable activities enhance risk, arguing that the additional money garnered from lower accident rates permits purchase of safer and better safeguarding equipment, improving safety in the long run. The notion of paternalism would be a nonissue because the organizers readily admit that they are acting with the students' best interests in mind, and such paternalistic behavior is a justifiable moral high ground—a high ground appropriated by all authority figures. These students see their behavior as benefiting not only the students who partake in the intramural activities, but also those who are employed to supervise them. This, in turn, may improve student satisfaction with the university, enhancing future recruitment efforts, fund-raising, and donations. Lastly, the utilitarian argument fails because there is no doubt that the organizers are acting with a utilitarian framework, in this case, by overlooking the injuries of a few to benefit the larger majority of students.

One solution might be to simply fire the current intramural crew and start over; yet this drastic decision would lead to a multitude of problems—everything from student challenges based on violations of due process to acrimonious and unchecked exposure of your department's history. In some ways, swallowing this bitter pill may be the quickest solution as well as avoid debating the issue.

Barring that, the only feasible alternative, perhaps, is to demonstrate to these students that their utilitarian moral foundation in untenable in this situation, in other words, that one of the moral issues in this case is whether it is more morally right to commit a wrong in the present in exchange for possible future, morally defensible benefits. Bertrand Russell, for example, argued that no present wrong can be excused for a possible future good, simply because there is no guarantee that a future good will ever come about. Such a flawed utilitarian position, he went on to suggest, simply gives power to tyrants and dictators where clearly rational and humane actions instead ought to prevail.

Although it may be difficult to explain to these organizers that their position is based on this type of faulty utilitarianism, considering their level of success, it needs to be impressed upon them that such a moral foundation does not provide an end point—a point at which current wrongs can cease because the future good has finally arrived. For instance, how much safety equipment is necessary to reduce injury to the lowest possible level? What is the goal? No injuries? Is that even possible? At what point does the continuation of wrongs outweigh any further future gains in injury prevention?

Essentially, the way the ethical situation has been framed by these students provides no ostensible end point; thus, their moral foundation is indefensible because it perpetuates unacceptable behaviors (like paternalism) that no longer have any utilitarian benefit.

Summary

In this chapter, issues regarding governance in sport organizations were presented. Several formal sport organizations were discussed as well as their responsibilities for the governance of specific levels of sport. The concept of NCAA certification was presented in an effort to show how the areas of academic integrity, financial integrity, equity, and governance in intercollegiate athletic programs as an ethical commitment to the athlete, fans, and educational institution can be carried out. Tort law and federal legislation including Title IX and the Americans With Disabilities Act were presented, and relationships were made to teleological and deontological ethical theories. Other areas including constitutional law, contract and labor law, and antitrust laws were briefly presented. The importance of sport managers' knowledge and understanding regarding governance and legal issues was emphasized.

Questions for Consideration

1. What will ensure that all sport organizations will protect the rights of the athlete as an individual and ethically carry out the mission of the organization?

2. To what degree are the laws that govern sport and society ethical?

3. Will certification of NCAA Division I athletic programs ensure that college and university athletic programs operate within ethical standards?

4. Is the governance of drug testing sufficient for Olympic and amateur sport?

PART IV:
WHAT LIES AHEAD

Chapter Thirteen

The Future of Ethics and Morality in Sport and Sport Management

Chapter Objectives

- To realize that sport managers must take responsibility for ethical behavior in sport settings

- To explore the future directions of sport and physical activity

- To present ways of educating for moral responsibility and action

- To suggest ways for achieving moral excellence

It is not our intent to predict the future, but rather, to reveal what is possible. Understanding the possibilities and probabilities will empower sport managers to make informed decisions regarding the ethical management of sport. Predicting the future of sport management ethics with precision is difficult at best, but the potential for bettering the way in which the management of sport occurs is a reality. For this to happen, individuals have to take responsibility—personal responsibility, moral responsibility, and social responsibility. Being responsible and accountable takes courage. Being ethical takes courage. That courage will lead us to the future of sound ethics in sport management.

Included among the individuals who must take responsibility and be accountable is YOU. In addition to you, every other sport management student (undergraduate and graduate alike), every professor involved in the education of future sport managers, as well as current sport managers, are the ones who must take on the responsibility of setting and maintaining high standards of moral excellence in sport settings. Together, we have the potential to create sport environments that will maintain moral excellence.

The Future of Sport

The demographics of our society are changing, and more individuals have access to and the opportunity for participation in sport, no matter the individual's skill and ability. Sport programs will increase, thus increasing the market for sporting goods and equipment and the development of other sport businesses. With these noted increases and development in sport and physical activity, the value that sport holds for individuals in society will be of a high quality. Thus, as the value of sport increases, what must be monitored and sustained are the rights and privileges of each individual as a consumer of sport and sport products.

Coakley (2001) identified several trends regarding the future of sport. These include a growth of power and performance sports and the growth of pleasure and participation sports. It is predicted that sports and athletes that exhibit power and performance will be the most publicized and most visible. Power, strength, speed, and aggressiveness will continue to be used as ways to push the human body to its limits to dominate opponents. As athletes are pushed to set records, train the body as a machine, and incorporate technology to perfect performance, only the best performers will survive in this elitist and exclusive setting. The hierarchy of the organization in power and performance sports features the athletes at the bottom of the structure who are trained, manipulated, and humiliated, in some cases, to produce a winning team worthy of sponsorships and monetary rewards. Out of the hard work, pain, efficiency, and test of competition, sponsors rely on the winning team to elevate them in the eyes of the consumer. The rewards tend to go to individuals in these sports who will maintain the cycle of power and performance sports as a valuable asset in our society. Others will, in turn, want to be associated with the winners of these contests. A growth of professional franchises is predicted as well as the development of new "rookie" leagues. The need for maintaining an ethical balance with the issues involved in power and performance sports is great. From balancing the interests of the participants with profits to maintaining the welfare of those who are spectators of these sports, maintaining an ethical balance is a monumental task. Marketing and advertising responsibilities will also need to be in line with moral concerns. Those who look to the future in this area tend to believe that this form of sport will be maintained. The need for ethical regulation and compliance for these types of sports will be mandatory for the future (Park, Zanger, & Quarterman, 1998; Pitts & Stotlar, 1996).

> Experts predict alternative sports that emphasize pleasure and participation will become increasingly popular and visible to the public.

Not all individuals, however, will see the need for power and performance sports because such sports may not be consistent with their values. As a result, Coakley (2001) indicated that alternative sports that emphasize pleasure and participation are predicted to become increasingly popular and visible to the public. Such sports will offer freedom, authenticity, and personal connections between the mind and body and the individual and the environment. Such sports and activities emphasize personal expression, enjoyment, growth, good health, and mutual concern and support for teammates and opponents. This type of sport will be of an inclusive nature. Personal empowerment as opposed to the domination of others will be the focus of these sports; and encouragement for democratic decision-making structures characterized by cooperation, sharing of power, and give-and-take relationships between coaches and athletes will be the norm (Coakley, 2001). Support for pleasure and participation sports will be slow but steadily growing, and a number of individuals of diverse backgrounds and abilities will seek the values of these sports. On the other hand, corporate sponsors will still be drawn to power and performance sports, but that does not mean there will be a place for sport that supports mutual respect.

With the growing concerns about health and fitness in our society, fitness clubs, health care and programs that emphasize improved health, fitness, and rehabilitation will be developing as well. Also predicted is the increase in participation in sport, fitness, and physical activities by young athletes, older people, females, individuals with disabilities, and lesbian, gay, and bisexual individuals. Growth is also predicted for youth sport, high school sports, and intercollegiate sports in the United States specifically, but there is no doubt that globally, sport is also in an increased growth pattern. Technological and media growth is also predicted. The impact of the Internet growth in sport is phenomenal. Thus, economic expansion will be a goal for numerous sport enterprises. Commercialism and consumerism will be a part of this expansion as will the concept of "sportainment" (e.g., WWF and WCW). With such a formidable increase in sport participation predicted, there is no doubt that the future will bring the need for ethical sport managers to take on the responsibilities of working in a variety of positions.

Education for Ethical Responsibility and Moral Action

Although the call for moral reform in sport has been loud and clear, in some instances, it has fallen on deaf ears; in other instances, individuals have responded. The practice domains of sport offer a primary ground for violations of moral responsibility, but also the hope one develops morally and expresses ethical behavior. The future holds the potential of moral training associated with the sport setting. Physical education classes, among others, offer this potential, but the real possibilities are within the competitive settings of sport at all levels. Few academic settings have provided an opportunity for students, and the athlete in particular, to examine values, beliefs, and behavior with regard to their practices, but athletes do have this potential opportunity if guided by teachers and coaches. The same is true for those preparing to be sport managers. Such examination and understanding of concepts regarding ethics and social responsibility are required of those preparing for a career in sport management. Moral excellence should be the foundation upon which the sport manager's academic preparation rests.

The possibility for the future of ethics includes academic courses, workshops, and specialized educational opportunities and interactions that directly address moral development, responsibility, and ethical behavior in all facets of sport. As students, athletes, coaches, teachers, and sport managers, we have a moral obligation to ourselves and others to accept the responsibility for fair play in our personal and professional lives.

At the University of Notre Dame, Brenda J. Bredemeier and David Light Shields (codirectors) have established the Mendelson Center for Sport, Character, and Culture. This particular center has been established to promote moral excellence. Through the components of *sport* (which includes concepts of body, play, competition, exhilaration, motivation, pain, challenge, sweat, grace, and power); *character* (including integrity, virtue, respect, honesty, fairness, courage, commitment, compassion, resilience, loyalty, and responsibility); and *culture* (including relationships, traditions, customs, norms, symbols, diversity, community, values, languages, and belief systems), the Mendelson Center promotes sport as a means for developing and expressing all facets of human excellence, especially moral character, and offers a broad reassessment of the role of sport in contemporary culture and the cultural values that shape sport participants' experiences. The Center strives to combine the research of social scientists, the wisdom of concerned sport practitioners, and the cultural influence of those associated with policy making, media, and successful athletes and coaches in order to move sport toward its full potential and to enhance positive character through this endeavor.

More specifically, the Mendelson Center for Sport, Character and Culture shares its mission with the University of Notre Dame to "create a sense of human solidarity and concern for the common good that will bear fruit as learning becomes service to justice." (Mendelson Center for Sport, Character, & Culture)

> ...the Center encourages sport participants, sport organizations, and educational institutions to embody those values and behaviors that promote social justice, such as valuing diversity, creating equal opportunity, and advocating for the disadvantaged. Furthermore, in recognition of the importance of sport in contemporary society, the Center seeks to offer critical analyses of the relationship between sport and broader culture, exploring both the possibilities and the limitations of sport's contributions to a more just and compassionate world.

> The Center envisions a sport culture that exemplifies and celebrates each participant's quest for excellence in all dimensions of life. This vision guides [the Center's] efforts in research, education, and service to promote social and moral development through sport. The Center is dedicated to fostering a sense of moral community within sport teams, and empowering sport participants to experience the joy and pride of striving for excellence with integrity. (Mendelson Center for Sport, Character, & Culture)

Efforts toward developing moral excellence are being made on the part of academicians as well as sport professionals and practitioners. With such efforts in mind, sound moral development in and through sport may be attainable. The future of ethics in sport management will be determined by all of us and with the work of professionals such as Bredemeier and Shields, it has the potential to be an attainable goal.

A significant step has been taken by Sharon Stoll, director of the Institute for Ethics in the College of Education at the University of Idaho, and Jennifer Beller, who serves as the Institute's associate director. After intensive study of moral values and critical reasoning with university athletes and coaches, Beller and Stoll (1993) have developed courses and programs that address ethical issues in sport. Their work on moral reasoning intervention with athletes has received acclaim. The College of Education Center for Research Theory and Service at the University of Idaho houses the program termed ETHICS* (ethical theory and honor in competitive sport). This program is committed to helping competitors, coaches, and administrators make ethical choices based on impartial, consistent, and reflective reasoning.

Another educational technique that has been developed is The West Point Fair Play Project (Butler, 2000). This project is based on a series of research studies involving the intramural program at the United States Military Academy at West Point. Once positive and negative behaviors on the part of the intramural participants were noted and compared with contributing factors to each, an educational program was developed. Positive behaviors were noted as (a) acknowledging opponents' good play, (b) assisting opponent in getting up, (c) shaking opponents' and officials' hands before and after the contest, and (d) accepting officials' calls even if questionable. Negative behaviors were considered (a) student coaches' working the officials, (b) players' questioning and arguing with the officials, (c) profanity, (d) unnecessary roughness, (e) trash talk, and (f) hitting bleachers in frustration. According to Butler (2000), sport programs can either teach students to cheat, lie, and steal or promote positive and ethical behaviors. The outcome depends on the way teachers and coaches teach about ethical behavior and conduct these programs. The West Point program began with educating students who were in the leadership roles through coaching and officiating workshops. Through dialogue, strategies were developed for promoting fair play principles. The student coaches were encouraged to (a) communicate to students that principles of fair play transcend sport and apply to life, (b) provide students with definitions of fair play and respect, (c) strike a balance between winning games and developing their players, (d) incorporate fair play and character development into their written coaching philosophy, and (e) review the details of the fair-play assessment system. The student coaches developed written plans for addressing the importance of fair play with players during the first team practice (Butler, 2000).

The second phase of the educational strategy involves a fair-play workshop that includes physical education teachers, student leaders, key administrators, team captains, and varsity and club coaches. The president of the Academy emphasized the importance of fair play on the playing field and in personal and professional life. The group then studied controversial sport scenarios and took part in discussing and analyzing the scenarios. This educational program is similar to that established by Beller and Stoll, but takes a different course. In an effort to couple the concept of fair play with winning and losing, a "fair-play" score was used in combination with the win-loss record. This system emerged as a direct result of the moral education approach and was used to make a positive lasting impact. The student officials for each game gave a postgame fair-play score for each team. The scoring included the following categories and points:

1. good behavior (10 points)—striving to win and playing aggressively while treating one's opponents and officials with respect and civility; no instances of behavior resembling lack of respect for the opponents, officials, opposing coaches, or the integrity of the game;

2. below-average behavior (5 points)—verbally or physically taunting an opponent or trash talking; disrespecting opposing team, opposing bench, officials, or coaches, or other behaviors such as unnecessary roughness, actions going beyond normal aggressive play, or self-directed frustration-induced profanity; and

3. unacceptable behavior (2 points)—berating and belittling officials or opponents; fighting, kicking, throwing, or directing profanity at officials, opposing players, or opposing coach.

Half-time fair-play scores were given to the coaches, and at the end of the season, league standings were reported for fair play as well as win-loss records. The league rankings were determined by the fair-play average plus the win-loss record. In addition, daily updated league standings were posted in a visible portion of the school on a daily basis to inform others of the fair-play scores and win-loss records. The results of this type of program were considered to be successful because the fair-play scores were considered to be equally important and the observed behavior was much improved (Butler, 2000).

Considerations for a Moral Future in Sport Management

At the initial level, a rethinking of the role all levels of sport play in our society is needed. An important reconsideration of sport in society is that of the role, value, and meanings associated with sport in educational institutions. One philosophical stance regarding sport in educational institutions noted by Arnold (1999) is that "sport, as a culturally valued practice, can be thought of as a competitive rule-bound physically demanding activity in which its internal goods and standards are pursued in a moral way for their own sake" (p. 48). He goes on to note that "whatever is done in the name of character development and moral education in school, the virtues and their cultivation clearly have a necessary and fundamental part in any program that purports to producing them" (p. 51). The question we must ask ourselves then is whether sport is truly used as a means to character development and moral education.

Although moral reform in sport has been the call from various sources, the individuals to whom this call has been directed do not possess the necessary background either in moral and ethical development or in social responsibility. Inappropriately or inadequately trained individuals in these areas could be a detriment to the management of sport. Thus, the critical need for sport managers who have a sound ethical philosophy and proven moral actions.

At the intercollegiate level of sport, Beller and Stoll (1993) pointed out that in order for meaningful reform to occur in the United States, the following must occur:

1. Primary participants (athletes) and secondary recipients (athletic directors, coaches, university administrators, and faculty) must be involved in dialogue concerning personal, program, and institutional values, beliefs, and goals.

2. The dialogue must be based in what Meyer and Pruzan (1993) state is an "ongoing, self-reflexive, and value-based" educational model.

3. All shareholders must be involved in the development, implementation, and continued evaluation of program and institutional values, beliefs, philosophies, and goals. (p. 4)

For the intercollegiate athletic program, the dialogue referred to above would center on the mission and goals of the program in conjunction with the values and beliefs of the shareholders.

The future for sport and the ethical and moral behaviors within these settings present some difficult challenges. Although Meyer and Pruzan (1993) indicated that educational systems should expand their capacity to redesign themselves in order to effective in serving the purposes of society and itself, all social systems, including sports, should take part in the exercise noted above. The self-designing system demonstrates that it has the ability to meet its own overall goal of contributing to its shareholders' values at any time. In addition, a contextually dependent situation is created in which the shareholders' values in relation to the system depend upon the design of the particular system. The self-redesigning system is in constant fluctuation between harmony, dissonance, harmony, and then dissonance again. The dissonance and harmony occur between the shareholder's actions and value and the shared values and goals of the specific sport program and the program's role within the mission of the larger social community (cited in Beller and Stoll, 1993).

It is evident how self-redesigning can occur within sport management. The top-down management style offers the best example. This particular model is paternalistic, indicating that those at the top know what is best for those at the lower levels. Top-down management has the potential not to acknowledge the worth of individuals, their values, and their importance within the organization. If the individual does not have the opportunity to take part in value-based, self-reflexive structure, then the overall operation, strategies, and goals of the organization will be diminished.

The revenue produced, win-loss records, graduation rates, and other award systems are insufficient upon which to ground value-based dialogue. Beller and Stoll (1993) pointed out that unless those associated with the administration of sport and those involved at other levels as well (e.g., athletes, spectators, and other participants) are involved "in an ongoing dialogue concerning values, beliefs, and program philosophies that lead to mutually acceptable visions and strategies, the system cannot develop a collective identity" (p. 14).

Reform in sport in terms of exploring one's personal values and beliefs, taking part in value-based dialogical interactions, and continually challenging one's values and beliefs in conjunction with the mission of sport programs and businesses is critical for the future of ethics in the field. Many within the sport community like the current status of sport and do not wish to see reform. Many are afraid to seek the challenge of change, even for moral excellence. How then does reform take place?

When sport in its current form is critically examined and challenged from various perspectives, it is necessary for the sport manager to look for the positive and negative influences of this environment. This includes (a) how individuals (participants and the public) are affected, (b) how the sports world is consistent with the values, issues, and problems of a multicultural and diverse society, (c) what value the sport brings to society as a whole, and (d) how moral excellence is achieved and maintained through sport.

Kretchmar (1993) made clear that

> ethics most fundamentally is about seeking and promoting the good life —about finding out what it is, celebrating it, and keeping it in focus. It is about pursuing values like truth, knowledge, excellence, friendship, excitement, and any number of good things.

> Ethics is also about compassion and sympathy—about making sure that the good life is shared with others who inhabit this planet with us. It is about caring for others, particularly those who do not have the position or power necessary to protect themselves or have their way. (p. 11)

This is the future of ethics in sport management.

Summary

This chapter emphasized the responsibility of future sport managers to take on the responsibility for maintaining ethical standards in light of the future directions of sport and physical activity in our society. The future of sport is ensured as access and opportunities for participation increase. The value of sport needs to be constantly reevaluated in human lives and in society as a whole as does its effect on human moral development. Those educators preparing individuals for careers in sport management, the students studying this area, and those already holding sport management positions are responsible for assuring that sport and those associated with sport maintain moral character. Ethical reform within sport will occur when self-reflexive dialogue among the shareholders takes place. This dialogue requires the discussion of personal values, beliefs, and goals in conjunction with program mission and goals. Models for moral education by Bredemeier and Light, Stoll and Beller, and Butler were presented in an effort to challenge the current status of moral behavior in sport settings. These models are considered ways of educating for moral responsibility and action in an effort to achieve reform and moral excellence.

Questions for Consideration

1. In what ways have sport experiences contributed to or hindered your own personal moral development?

2. In what ways can you ensure that you as a sport manager will take on social responsibility and maintain ethical behavior in your future work setting?

3. How can you gain additional education and training in ethics related to the sport management setting?

4. What is the potential value of the Mendelson Center for Sport, Character, and Culture, the ETHICS* program developed by Stoll and Beller, and the West Point Fair Play program developed by Butler?

References

Abney, R., & Parks, J. B. (1998). Intercollegiate athletics. In J. B. Parks, B. R. K. Zanger, & J. Quarterman (Eds.), *Contemporary sport management* (pp. 119-137). Champaign, IL: Human Kinetics.

Amateur Sports Act of 1978 (36 U.S.C. sections 371-396).

Americans With Disabilities Act of 1990, 42 U.S.C.A. § 12101 et seq. (West, 1993).

Arnold, P. J. (1999). The virtues, moral education, and the practice of sport. *Quest, 51,* 39-54.

Atkin, R. (1998, February 26). High and low marks on a sports racial report card. *Christian Science Monitor,* p. 14.

Axthelm, P. (1983, August 8). Psst, somebody may be cheating. *Newsweek, 122,* 74.

Bayles, M. D. (1981). *Professional ethics.* Belmont, CA: Wadsworth.

Beauchamp, T. L. (1988). Ethical theory and its application to business. In T. L. Beauchamp & Bowie, N. E. (Eds.), *Ethical theory and business* (3rd ed., pp. 1-55). Englewood Cliffs, NJ: Prentice-Hall.

Beauchamp, T. L. (1991). *Philosophical ethics: An introduction to moral philosophy* (2nd ed.). New York: McGraw-Hill.

Becker, L. C. (1973). *On justifying moral judgments.* London: Routledge & Kegan Paul.

Belenky, M., Clinchy, B., Goldberger, N., & Tarule, J. (1986). *Women's ways of knowing: The development of self, voice and mind.* New York: Basic Books.

Beller, J., & Stoll, S. (1993). *A praxeological assessment of the need for reform in United States intercollegiate sport through moral education.* Unpublished manuscript.

Billington, R. (1988). *Living philosophy: An introduction to moral thought.* London: Routledge.

Blann, F. W. (1998). Sport marketing. In J. B. Parks, B. R. K. Zanger, & J. Quarterman (Eds.), *Contemporary sport management* (pp. 171-184). Champaign, IL: Human Kinetics.

Blum, L. A. (1994). *Moral perception and particularity.* Cambridge, MA: Cambridge University Press.

Bommer, M., Gratto, C., Gravander, J., & Tuttle, M. (1987). A behavior model of ethical and unethical decision making. *Journal of Business Ethics, 6,* 265-280.

Bowie, N. E., & Duska, R. F. (1990). *Business ethics* (2nd ed.). Englewood Cliffs, NJ: Prentice-Hall.

Bowie, N. E., & Simon, R. L. (1977). *The individual and the political order: An introduction to social and political philosophy.* Englewood Cliffs, NJ: Prentice-Hall.

Bowyer, J. B. (1982). *Cheating: Deception in war and magic, games in sports, sex and religion, politics and espionage, art and science* (pp. 271-323). New York: St. Martin's.

Brandt, R. B. (1959). *Ethical theory: The problems of normative and critical ethics.* Englewood Cliffs, NJ: Prentice-Hall.

Brandt, R. B. (1967). Ethical relativism. In P. Edwards (Ed.), *The encyclopedia of philosophy* (Vol. 3, pp. 75-78). New York: Macmillan and The Free Press.

Branvold, S. (1996). Ethics. In B. L. Parkhouse (Ed.), *The management of sport: Its foundation and application* (2nd ed., pp. 149-163). St. Louis, MO: Mosby-Yearbook.

Bredemeier, B. J. (1984). Sport, gender and moral growth. In J. M. Silva & R. S. Weinberg (Eds.), *Psychological foundations of sport* (pp. 400-413). Champaign, IL: Human Kinetics.

Bredemeier, B. J., & Shields, D. L. (1987). Moral growth through physical activity: A structural/developmental approach. In D. Gould & M. R. Weiss (Eds.), *Advances in pediatric sport sciences,* (Vol. 2, pp. 143-165). Champaign, IL: Human Kinetics.

Bredemeier, B., & Shields, D. L. (1995). *Character development and physical activity.* Champaign, IL: Human Kinetics.

Brennan, J. G. (1973). *Ethics and morals.* New York: Harper & Row.

Brewer, K. B. (1997). Management as a practice: A response to Alasdair MacIntyre. *Journal of Business Ethics, 16,* 825-833.

Brooks, C. M. (1994). *Sports marketing: Competitive business strategies for sports.* Englewood Cliffs, NJ: Prentice-Hall.

Butler, L. F. (February, 2000). Fair play: Respect for all. *Journal of Physical Education, Recreation and Dance, 71,* 32-35.

Callahan, D. (1982). Should there be an academic code of ethics? *Journal of Higher Education, 53,* 334-335.

Callahan, J. C. (Ed.) (1988). *Ethical issues in professional life.* New York: Oxford University Press.

Carroll, A. B. (1993). *Business and society: Ethics and stakeholder management* (2nd ed.). Cincinnati, OH: Southwestern.

Cavanaugh, G. (1990). *American business values* (3rd ed.). Englewood Cliffs, NJ: Prentice-Hall.

Chelladurai, P. (1985). *Sport management: Macro perspectives.* London, ON: Sports Dynamics Publishers.

Chelladurai, P. (1993). Styles of decision making in coaching. In J. M. Williams (Ed.), *Applied sport psychology: Personal growth to peak performance* (2nd ed., pp. 99-109). Palo Alto, CA: Mayfield.

Chelladurai, P. (1999) *Human resource management in sport and recreation.* Champaign, IL: Human Kinetics.

Chelladurai, P., & Arnot M. (1985). Decision styles in coaching. Preferences of basketball players. *Research Quarterly for Exercise and Sport, 56.* 15-24.

Chelladurai, P., & Haggerty, T. R. (1978). A normative model of decision styles in coaching. *Athletic Administrator, 13,* 6-9.

Chelladurai, P., & Quek, C. B. (1995). Decision style choices of high school basketball coaches: The effects of situational and coach characteristics. *Journal of Sport Behavior, 17,* 276-293.

Chelladurai, P., Haggerty, T. R., & Baxter, P. R. (1989). Decision style choices of university basketball coaches and players. *Journal of Sport and Exercise Psychology, 11,* 201-215.

Chonko, L. B., & Hunt, S. D. (August, 1985). Ethics and marketing management: An empirical investigation. *Journal of Business Research, 13,* 339-359.

Clement, A. (1991). Sports law: Product liability and employment relations. In B. L. Parkhouse (Ed.), *The management of sport: Its foundation and application* (pp. 97-106). St. Louis: Mosby Year Book.

Coakley, J. (2001). *Sport in society: Issues and controversies* (7th ed.). Boston: McGraw-Hill.

Code of Conduct for Sport & Physical Educators. (1999-2000, Winter). *Academy action, 7,* p. 8.

Collins, D. (1987). Aristotle and business. *Journal of Business Ethics, 6,* 567-572.

Copi, I. M. (1982). *Introduction to logic* (6th ed.). New York: Macmillan.

Corlett, J. (1997). Political philosophy and the managerial class: Implications for the administration of sport. *Journal of Sport Management, 11,* 250-262.

Cornman, J. W., & Lehrer, K. (1974). *Philosophical problems and arguments: An introduction* (2nd ed.). New York: Macmillan.

Dahl, R. A. (1975). A prelude to corporate reform. In R. L. Heilbroner & P. London (Eds.), *Corporate social policy* (pp. 18-30). Reading, MA: Addison-Wesley.

D'Arcy, E. (1963). *Human acts: An essay in their moral evaluation.* London: Oxford University Press.

DeGeorge, R. R. (1986). Business ethics (2nd ed.). New York: Macmillan.

DeSensi, J. T. (1998). Philosophical foundations of sport. In J. B. Parks, B. R. K. Zanger, & J. Quarterman (Eds.), *Contemporary sport management* (pp. 49-65). Champaign, IL: Human Kinetics.

DeSensi, J. T., & Rosenberg, D. (1996). *Ethics in sport management.* Morgantown, WV: Fitness Information Technology, Inc.

Dill, D. D. (1982). The structure of the academic profession: Toward a definition of ethical issues. *Journal of Higher Education, 53,* 253-267.

Doig, J. (1994). Ethics and sport management. In L. Trenberth & C. Collins (Eds.), *Sport management in New Zealand* (pp. 264-275). Palmerston North, New Zealand: The Dunmore Press.

Donnelly, P. (2000). Young athletes need child law protection. In P. Donnelly (Ed.), *Taking sport seriously: Social issues in Canadian sport* (2nd ed., pp. 102-106). Toronto: Thompson Educational.

Drowatzky, J. N. (1993). Ethics, Codes, and Behavior. *Quest, 45* 22-31.

Drucker, P. (1966). *The effective executive.* New York: Harper & Row.

Dubinsky, A. J., & Loken, B. (1989). Analyzing ethical decision making in marketing. *Journal of Business Research, 19,* 83-107.

Duncan, M. C., & Messner, M. A. (1998). The media image of sport and gender. In L. A. Wenner (Ed.), *MediaSport* (pp. 170-185). New York: Routledge.

Eastman, S. T., & Billings, A. C. (1999). Gender parity in the Olympics: Hyping women athletes, favoring men athletes. *Journal of Sport and Social Issues, 23,* 140-170.

Eitzen, D. S. (1981). Sport and deviance. In G. R. F. Luschen & G. Sage (Eds.), *Handbook of social science of sport* (pp. 400-414). Champaign, IL: Stipes.

Eitzen, D. S. (1988). Sport and deviance. *Journal of Sport and Social Issues, 12,* 17-30.

Eitzen, D. S. (1993). Ethical dilemmas in sport. In D. S. Eitzen (Ed.) *Sport in contemporary society: An anthology* (4th ed., pp. 109-122). New York: St. Martin's Press.

Eitzen, D. S., & Sage, G. H. (1993). *Sociology of North American sport* (5th ed.). Dubuque, IA: Brown & Benchmark.

Ewing, A. C. (1953). *Ethics.* London: The English Universities Press.

Falikowski, A. F. (1990). *Moral philosophy: Theories, skills, and applications.* Englewood Cliffs, NJ: Prentice-Hall.

Fay, T. G. (1998). International sport. In J. B. Parks, B. R. K. Zanger, & J. Quarterman (Eds.), *Contemporary sport management* (pp. 277-291). Champaign, IL: Human Kinetics.

Feibleman, J. K. (1967). *Moral strategy: An introduction to the ethics of confrontation.* The Hague: Martinus Nijhoff.

Ferrell, O. C., & Gresham, L. G. (1985, Summer). A contingency framework for understanding ethical decision making in marketing. *Journal of Marketing, 49,* 87-96.

Filley, A. C., House, R. J., & Kerr, S. (1976). *Managerial process and organizational behavior.* Glenview, IL: Scott, Foreman.

Findlay, J. N. (1970). *Axiological ethics.* London: Macmillan.

Fink, S. L., Jenks, R. S., & Willits, R. D. (1983). *Designing and managing organizations.* Homewood, IL: Richard D. Irwin, Inc.

Fletcher, J. (1967). *Moral responsibility: Situation ethics at work.* London: Westminster Press.

Flint, W. C., & Eitzen, D. S. (1987). Professional sports team ownership and entrepreneurial capitalism. *Sociology of Sport Journal, 4,* 17-27.

Fraleigh, W. P. (1993). Codes of ethics: Function, form and structure, problems and possibilities. *Quest, 45,* 13-21.

Frankena, W. K. (1973). *Ethics* (2nd ed.). Englewood Cliffs, NJ: Prentice-Hall.

Freedman, W. (1987). *Professional sport and antitrust.* New York: Quorum Books.

Freeman, J. B. (1988). *Thinking logically: Basic concepts for reasoning.* Englewood Cliffs, NJ: Prentice-Hall.

Frey, J. H. (1994). Deviance of organizational subunits: The case of college athletic departments. *Journal of Sport & Social Issues, 18* (2), 110-123.

Galasso, P. J. (1988). Sport organizations and ethical concerns. In P. J. Galasso (Ed.), *Philosophy of sport and physical activity: Issues and concepts* (pp. 352-357). Toronto: Canadian Scholar's Press.

Garner, R. T., & Rosen, B. (1967). *Moral philosophy: A systematic introduction to normative ethics and meta-ethics.* New York: Macmillan.

Gill, D. L. (1994). Psychological perspectives on women in sport and exercise. In D. M. Costa & S. R. Guthrie (Eds.), *Women and Sport Interdisciplinary perspectives* (pp. 253-284). Champaign, IL: Human Kinetics.

Gilligan, C. (1982). *In a different voice: Psychological theory and women's development.* Cambridge, MA: Harvard University Press.

Gilligan, C. (1988). *A contribution of women's thinking to psychological theory and education.* Cambridge, MA: Harvard University Press.

Gough, R. W. (1997). *Character is everything: Promoting ethical excellence in sports.* Fort Worth, TX: Harcourt Brace College Publishers.

Hackman, J. R., & Oldham, G. R. (1980). *Work design.* Reading, MA: Addison-Wesley.

Harman, G. (1977). *The nature of morality: An introduction to ethics.* New York: Oxford University Press.

Hawkins, B. (1998). The dominant images of black men in America: The representation of O. J. Simpson. In G. Sailes (Ed.), *African Americans in sport* (pp. 39-52). New Brunswick, NJ: Transaction.

Hemphill, D. (1983). Social responsibility of a professional sport franchise to a community. Unpublished manuscript, University of Tennessee, Knoxville, TN.

Hertz, J. H. (Ed.). (1980). *The Pentateuch and haftorahs* (2nd ed.). London: Soncino Press.

Hobbes, T. (1962). *Leviathan: Or the matter, forme and power of a commonwealth ecclesiasticall and civil* (M. Oakeshott, Ed. & R. S. Peters, Intro.). New York: Collier Books. (Original work published in 1651)

Hoberman, J. (2000). Offering the illusion of reform on drugs. In P. Donnelly (Ed.), *Taking sport seriously: Social issues in Canadian sport* (2nd ed., pp. 28-30). Toronto: Thompson Educational.

Hudson, W. D. (1970). *Modern moral philosophy.* London: Macmillan.

Hughes, R., & Coakley, J. (1984). Mass society and the commercialization of sport. *Sociology of Sport Journal, 1,* 57-63.

Hums, M. (1990). *Model for moral development: A life issues approach for a sport management curriculum*. Unpublished manuscript.

Hunt, S. D., & Vitell, S. (1986, Spring). A general theory of marketing ethics. *Marketing Journal of Macromarketing, 6*, 5-16.

Hunt, S. D., Chonko, L. B., & Wilcox, J. B. (1984, August). Ethical problems of marketing researchers. *Journal of Marketing Research, 21*, 309-324.

Jennings, B., Callahan, D., & Wolf, S. M. (1987). Public interest and private good. *Hastings Center Report, 17*, 3-10.

Jones, R., Murrell, A. J., & Jackson, J. (1999). Pretty versus powerful in the sports pages: Print media coverage of U.S. women's Olympic gold medal winning teams. *Journal of Sport and Social Issues, 23*, 183-192.

Josepheson, M. (1992). *Making ethical decisions*. Marina del Rey, CA: The Josepheson Institute of Ethics.

Kant, I. (1959). *Foundations of the metaphysics of morals* (L. W. Beck, Ed. and Trans.). Indianapolis, IN: Bobbs-Merrill. (Original work published 1785)

Kekes, J. (1993). *The morality of pluralism*. Princeton, NJ: Princeton University Press.

Kinder, T. M. (1993). *Organizational management administration for athletic programs* (3rd ed.). Dubuque: IA: Eddie Bowers.

Kjeldsen. E. (1992). The manager's role in the development and maintenance of ethical behavior in the sport organization. *Journal of Sport Management, 6*(2), 99-13.

Knight Foundation Commission on Intercollegiate Athletics. (1991, March). *Keeping faith with the student-athlete: A new model for intercollegiate athletics*. Charlotte, NC: Knight Foundation.

Kohlberg, L. (1963). The development of children's orientations toward a moral order. I. Sequence in the development of human thought. *Vita Humana, 6*, 11-33.

Kohlberg, L. (1969). Stage and sequence: The cognitive-developmental approach to socialization. In D. A. Goslin (Ed.), *Handbook of socialization theory and research* (pp. 347-480). Chicago, IL: Rand McNally.

Kohlberg, L. (1987). *Child psychology and childhood education: A cognitive-developmental view*. New York: Longman.

Korner, S. (1955). *Kant*. London: Penguin Books.

Kretchmar, R. S. (1993). Philosophy of ethics. *Quest, 45*, 3-12.

Kretchmar, R. S. (1994). *Practical philosophy of sport.* Champaign, IL: Human Kinetics.

Kultgen, J. (1988). *Ethics and professionalism*. Philadelphia: University of Pennsylvania Press.

Laczinak, G., & Murphy, P. (1993). *Ethical marketing decisions: The higher road.* Englewood Cliffs, NJ: Prentice-Hall.

Laczinak, G., Burton, R., & Murphy, P. (1999). Sports marketing ethics in today's marketplace. *Sport Marketing Quarterly, 4*, 43- 53.

Lawson, H. A. (1999). Education for social responsibility: Preconditions in retrospect and in prospect. *Quest, 51*, 116-149.

Lee, T. (1992). Sports and the ethical tug-of-war. *Ethics: Easier Said Than Done*, 16, 30-39.

Leith, L. M. (1983). The underlying processes of athletic administration. *The Physical Educator, 40*, 211-217.

Leonard, W. M., II. (1993). *A sociological perspective of sport* (4th ed.). New York: Macmillan.

Lessig, W. J., & Alsop, W. L. (1990). Intercollegiate athletics and professional sport. In J. B. Parks & B. R. K. Zanger (Eds.), *Sport & fitness management: Career strategies and professional content* (pp. 17-33). Champaign, IL: Human Kinetics.

Lickona, T. (Ed.). (1969). Moral development and behavior: Theory, research, and social issues. pp. 34-35. New York: Holt, Rinehart, and Winston.

Lickona, T. (Ed.). (1969). *Moral development and behavior: Theory, research, and social issues*. New York: Holt, Rinehart, and Winston.

Lumpkin, A., Stoll, S. K., & Beller, J. M. (1999). *Sport ethics applications for fair play*, 2nd ed., Boston: McGraw-Hill.

Mackie, J. L. (1977). *Ethics: Inventing right and wrong*. London: Penguin Books.

Malloy, D. C. (1996). A perspective on ethics in sport administration curricula. *Avante, 2*(1), 79-82.

Malloy, D. C., & Zakus, D. W. (1995). Ethical decision making in sport administration: A theoretical inquiry into substance and form. *Journal of Sport Management, 9*, 36-58.

Marias, J. (1967). *History of philosophy* (S. Appelbaum & C. C. Strowbridge, Trans.). New York: Dover. (Original work published 1941)

Marx, K., & Engels, F. (1948). *The communist manifesto*. New York: International. (Original work published in 1848)

Matson, W. I. (1987). *A new history of philosophy: Modern* (Vol. 2). New York: Harcourt Brace Jovanovich.

McCracken, J., Martin, W., & Shaw, B. (1998). Virtue ethics and the parable of the Sadhu. *Journal of Business Ethics, 17,* 25-38.

McPherson, B. D., Curtis, J. E., & Loy, J. W. (1989). *The social significance of sport: An introduction to the sociology of sport.* Champaign, IL: Human Kinetics.

Meenaghan, T. (1994, September/October). Point of view: Ambush marketing: Immoral or imaginative practice? *Journal of Advertising Research, 34,* 77-88.

Melchert, N. (1991). *The great conversation: A historical introduction to philosophy.* Mountain View, CA: Mayfield.

Mill, J. S. (1956). *On liberty.* (C. V. Skield, Ed.). Indianapolis, IN: Bobbs-Merrill Library of Liberal Arts. (Original work published 1859)

Mill, J. S. (1969). Utilitarianism. In E. M. Albert, T. C. Denise, & S. P. Peterfreund (Eds.), *Great traditions in ethics: An introduction* (2nd ed., pp. 227-252). New York: D. Van Nostrand. (Original work published in 1861)

Miller, L., & DeSensi, J. T. (in press). Legal and ethical considerations in sport management. In J. B. Parks, B. R. K. Zanger, & J. Quarterman (Eds.), *Contemporary sport management* (2nd ed). Champaign, IL: Human Kinetics.

Minton, A. J., & Shipka, T. A. (1990). *Philosophy: Paradox and discovery* (3rd ed.). New York: McGraw-Hill.

Mintz, S. M. (1996). Aristotelian virtue and business ethics education. *Journal of Business Ethics, 15,* 827-838.

Mishkin, B. (1988). Responding to scientific misconduct: Due process and prevention. *Journal of the American Medical Association, 260,* 1932-1936.

Molander, E. A. (1987). A paradigm for design, promulgation and enforcement of ethical codes. *Journal of Business Ethics, 6,* 619-631.

Morgan, W. J., & Meier, K. V. (Eds.). (1996). *Philosophic inquiry in sport* (2nd ed.). Champaign, IL: Human Kinetics.

Mothershead, J. L., Jr. (1955). *Ethics: Modern conceptions of the principles of right.* New York: Holt, Rinehart and Winston.

Mullin, B. J. (1980). Sport management: The nature and utility of the concept. *Arena Review, 4,* 1-11.

NASPE-NASSM Joint Task Force. (1993). Standards for curriculum and voluntary accreditation of sport management education programs. *Journal of Sport Management, 7,* 159-170.

National Alliance for Youth Sports (June 25, 2002). www.nays.org.

National Athletic Trainers' Association (Winter, 1990). NATA Code of Professional Practice. *Athletic Training Journal of the National Athletic Trainer's Association, 25,* p. 341

National Christian College Athletic Association. (n.d.). Accessed 2002. www.thenccaa.org/

National Small College Athletic Association. (n.d.). Accessed www.thenscaa.com

NCAA Committee on Athletics Certification. (1993). *1993-94 Division I athletics certification handbook.* (Available from The National Collegiate Athletic Association, 6201 College Blvd., Overland Park, KS 66211-2422)

Nielsen, W. V. (1994, Winter). Ethics in coaching: It's time to do the right thing. *Olympic Coach, 4,* 2-5.

Nixon, H. L., II, & Frey, J. H. (1996). *A sociology of sport.* Belmont, CA: Wadsworth.

Nowell-Smith, P. H. (1967). Religion and morality. In P. Edwards (Ed.), *The encyclopedia of philosophy* (Vol. 7, pp.150-158). New York: Macmillan and The Free Press.

Nozick, R. (1974). *Anarchy, state, and utopia.* New York: Basic Books.

O'Sullivan, P., & Murphy, P. E. (1998). Ambush marketing: The ethical issues. *Psychology and Marketing, 15,* 367-383.

Olson, R. G. (1967). Teleological ethics. In P. Edwards (Ed.), *The encyclopedia of philosophy* (Vol. 8, p. 88). New York: Macmillan and The Free Press.

Ostrow, R. (1985, March 21). Tailoring the ballparks to fit needs. *USA Today,* pp. 1C, 2C.

Palmer, D. (1991). *Does the center hold?: An introduction to Western philosophy.* Mountain View, CA: Mayfield.

Parks, J. B, Zanger, B. R. K., & Quarterman, J. (Eds.). (1998). Contemporary sport management. Champaign, IL: Human Kinetics.

Pepper, S. C. (1960). *Ethics.* New York: Appleton-Century-Crofts.

Perry, M., Chase, M., Jacob, J. R., Jacob, M. C., & Von Laue, T. H. (1989). *Western civilization: Ideas, politics & society* (3rd ed.). Boston: Houghton Mifflin.

Pitts, B. G., & Stotlar, D. K. (1996). *Fundamentals of sport marketing.* Morgantown, WV: Fitness Information Technology.

Porter, B. F. (1980). *The good life: Alternatives in ethics.* New York: Macmillan.

Pride, W. M., & Ferrell, O. C. (2000). *Marketing.* Boston: Houghton Mifflin.

Quarterman, J. & Li, M. (1998). Managing sport organizations. In J. Parks, B. R. K. Zanger, & J. Quarterman (Eds.). *Contemporary sport management,* (pp. 103-118). Champaign, IL: Human Kinetics.

Rachels, J. (1986). *The elements of moral philosophy.* Philadelphia: Temple University Press.

Rachels, J. (Ed.). (1989). *The right thing to do: Basic readings in moral philosophy.* New York: Random House.

Raphael, D. D. (1981). *Moral philosophy.* Oxford: Oxford University Press.

Rawls, J. (1971). *A theory of justice.* Cambridge, MA: Harvard University Press.

Robin, D. P., & Reidenbach, R. E. (1987, January). Social responsibility, ethics and marketing strategy: Closing the gap between concept and application. *Journal of Marketing, 51,* 44-58.

Rosenstein, J. (1996). *In whose honor? American Indian mascots in sports.* Rosenstein Productions, Champaign, IL.

Ross, S. (1989). Locus of responsibility: Ethical behavior in sport. *International Journal of Physical Education, 26,* 19-22.

Ross, W. D. (1930). *The right and the good.* Oxford: Clarendon Press.

Russell, B. (1959). My philosophical development. London: George Allen and Unwin, Ltd.

Russell, P. S. (February, 1991). *Setting sanctions for misconduct.* Paper presented at Scientific Integrity Symposium, Harvard Medical School, Boston, MA.

Sage, G. H. (1990). *Power and ideology in American sport: A critical perspective.* Champaign, IL: Human Kinetics.

Salmon, M. H. (1989). *Introduction to logic and critical thinking* (2nd ed.). Englewood Cliffs, NJ: Prentice-Hall.

Sandler, D., & Shani, D. (1989). Olympic sponsorship vs. ambush marketing. *Journal of Advertising Research, 29,* 9-14.

Schneewind, J. B. (1967). John Stuart Mill. In P. Edwards (Ed.), *The encyclopedia of philosophy* (Vol. 5, pp. 314-323). New York: Macmillan and The Free Press.

Seefeldt, V. (1979). Young athletes have a bill of rights: Do we need a code of ethics for coaches? *Spotlight on Youth Sports, 2,* 1-6

Shirk, E. (1965). *The ethical dimension: An approach to the philosophy of values and valuing.* New York: Appleton-Century-Crofts.

Simon, R. L. (1991). *Fair play: Sports, values, and society.* Boulder, CO: Westview Press.

Slack, T. (1997). *Understanding sport organizations: The application of organization theory.* Champaign, IL: Human Kinetics.

Slote, M. (1992). *From morality to virtue.* New York: Oxford University Press.

Smith, M. (1983). *Violence and sport.* Toronto: Butterworths.

Solomon, D. (1997). Internal objections to virtue ethics. In D. Statman (Ed.), *Virtue ethics: A critical reader* (pp. 165-179). Edinburgh: Edinburgh University Press.

Solomon, R. C. (1997). Corporate roles, personal virtues: An Aristotelian approach to business ethics. In D. Statman (Ed.), *Virtue ethics: A critical reader* (pp.205-226). Edinburgh: Edinburgh University Press.

Statman, D. (1997). Introduction to virtue ethics. In D. Statman (Ed.), *Virtue ethics: A critical reader* (pp. 1-40). Edinburgh: Edinburgh University Press.

Stead, W. E., Worrell, D. L., & Stead, J. G. (1990). An integrative model for understanding and managing ethical behavior in business. *Journal of Business Ethics, 9,* 233-242.

Steiner, G. A. (1972, Winter). Social policies for business. *California Management Review, 15,* 17-24.

Stieber, J. (1992). The behavior of the NCAA: A question of ethics. *Ethics: Easier Said Than Done, 16,* 50-53.

Strong, K. C., & Meyer, G. D. (1992). An integrative descriptive model of ethical decision making. *Journal of Business Ethics, 11,* 89-94.

Sutton, W. A., & Gladden, J. (1998). Professional sport. In J. B. Parks, B. R. K. Zanger, & J. Quarterman (Eds.), *Contemporary sport management* (pp. 243-261). Champaign, IL: Human Kinetics.

The University of Notre Dame Mendelson Center for Sport, Character, & Culture. (2001). Accessed www.nd.edu/~cscc/aboutcscc/aboutcsccindex.html.

Title IX of the Education Amendments of 1972, 86 Stat. 235 (codified at 20 U.S.C.§ 1681-1688 [1900]).

Trevino, L. K. (1986). Ethical decision making in organizations: A person-situation interactionist model. *Academy of Management Review, 11,* 601-617.

Ulrich, D. (1997). *Human resource champions: The next agenda for adding value and delivering results.* Boston: Harvard Business School Press.

Urban, W. M. (1930). *Fundamentals of ethics: An introduction to moral philosophy.* New York: Henry Holt.

Velasquez, M. G. (1992). *Business ethics: Concepts and cases* (3rd ed.). Englewood Cliffs, NJ: Prentice-Hall.

Vroom V. H., & Yetton, R. N. (1973). *Leadership and decision-making.* Pittsburgh: University of Pittsburgh Press.

Webster's new collegiate dictionary. (1977). Springfield, MA: G. & C. Merriam.

Weiler, K. H., & Higgs, C. T. (1999). Television coverage of professional golf: A focus on gender. *Women in Sport and Physical Activity Journal, 8,* 83-100.

Weiss, M. R., & Bredemeier, B. J. (1990). Moral development in sport. In K. Pandolf (Ed.), *Exercise and sport sciences reviews* (Vol. 18, pp. 331-378). Baltimore: Williams & Wilkins.

Weiss, P. (1969). *Sport: A philosophic inquiry.* Carbondale, IL: Southern Illinois University Press.

Wellman, C. (1975). *Morals & ethics.* Glenview, IL: Scott, Foresman.

Werther, W. B., David, K., Schwind, H. F., Das, H., & Miner, F. C. (1985). *Canadian personnel management and human resources* (2nd ed.). Toronto, ON: McGraw-Hill Ryerson.

Wheelwright, P. (1959). *A critical introduction to ethics* (3rd ed.). New York: The Odyssey Press.

White, P. G. (2000). Employee fitness. In P. Donnelly (Ed.), *Taking sport seriously: Social issues in Canadian sport* (2nd ed., pp. 59-60). Toronto: Thompson Educational.

White, T. I. (1988). *Right and wrong: A brief guide to understanding ethics.* Englewood Cliffs, NJ: Prentice-Hall.

Williams, B. (1972). *Morality: An introduction to ethics.* Cambridge, UK: Cambridge University Press.

Wright, D. L. (1988). *The relationship between women athletes' ways of knowing and moral reasoning about authority/power in daily life and sport.* Unpublished doctoral dissertation. The University of Tennessee, Knoxville.

Young, T. R. (1984, November). The sociology of sport: A critical overview. *Arena Review, 8,* 1-14.

Young, T. R., & Massey, G. (1980). The dramaturgical society: A macro-analytic approach to dramaturgical analysis. *Qualitative Sociology, 1,* 78-98.

Zeigler, E. F. (1984). *Ethics and morality in sport and physical education: An experiential approach.* Champaign, IL: Stipes.

Zeigler, E. F. (1989). Proposed creed and code of professional ethics for the North American Society for Sport Management. *Journal of Sport Management, 3*(1), 2-4.

Zeigler, E. F. (1992). *Professional ethics for sport managers* [Monograph]. Champaign, IL: Stipes.

Zeigler. E. F. (1990). *Sport and physical education: Past, present, future.* Champaign, IL: Stipes.

About the Authors

Joy T. DeSensi, Ed.D., earned her doctoral degree at the University of North Carolina at Greensboro. She is currently a professor and department head in the sport and leisure studies department at The University of Tennessee. Her research interests include the areas of gender, race, and ethnicity in sport, women in sport, multiculturalism, and ethics in sport management. She has made numerous state, district, national and international presentations and is the author and coauthor of book chapters and articles that appear in *Quest, Journal of Sport Management* and the *Journal of Physical Education, Recreation and Dance.* She has served on the editorial boards of scholarly journals, as the editor of the *Journal of Sport Management,* and is the current associate editor of *Quest.* She is a founding member of the North American Society for Sport Management and has served as the President of the Southern Academy of Women in Physical Activity, Sport and Health, The Philosophic Society for the Study of Sport, and the National Association for Physical Education in Higher Education. Her professional recognitions include distinguished alumna awards from the University of Memphis and the University of North Carolina at Greensboro, service awards, and recognitions for teaching and research. She also received scholar lecture awards including the Delphine Hanna Lecture Award from the National Association for Physical Education in Higher Education and the Earle F. Zeigler Lecture Award from the North American Society for Sport Management.

Danny Rosenberg, Ph.D., is an associate professor in the Department of Physical Education and Kinesiology at Brock University, St. Catharines, Ontario, Canada. His primary research interests include sport and physical education philosophy, sport ethics, sport history, sport and ethnicity, and sport management. He was the founding Program Director and then Chair of the Department of Sport Management at Brock University. He was also a visiting scholar at the Zinman College of Physical Education and Sport, The Wingate Institute, Israel, during a sabbatical leave in 1998-1999. He has authored or coauthored articles and essays in journals such as the *International Journal of Physical Education, Canadian Journal of Sport History, Avante, Journal of the Philosophy of Sport,* and the *Journal of Sport History.* His works have also been published as book chapters and in conference proceedings. Dr. Rosenberg serves on several professional committees in both Canada and the U.S. and is a reviewer for a number of journals. He is currently working on a book that investigates Jews and sport in Toronto during the interwar period. He holds degrees from the University of Western Ontario and the University of Tennessee, Knoxville.

Index

moral pluralism. *See* pluralism

moral questions, features of, 26–27

moral reasoning, 39–42

    elements of, 40

    and impartiality, 41–42

moral responsibility, 11

morality, 2, 30–35, 108

    basic features of, 31–32

    distinguishing rights of, 31–32

    in sport, 9–11

    terms, 33

    and types of moral questions, 26–27

Mothershead, J. L., 61

Mullin, B. J., 153

Murphy, P. E., 194, 197, 206

N

NASPE/NASSM Guidelines for Curriculum in Sport Management, 135

National Association of Intercollegiate Athletics (NAIA), 113, 230

National Association for Sport and Physical Education (NASPE), 137, 146

    code of conduct, 147–148

National Athletic Trainer's Code of Professional Practice, 148–149

National Basketball Association (NBA), 232

National Christian College Athletic Association (NCCAA), 231

National Collegiate Athletic Association (NCAA), 113, 115, 127, 228–230

    and the Committee on Athletics Certification, 131

    divisions of, 228

National Football League (NFL), 232

National Hockey League (NHL), 232

National Intramural and Recreational Sport Association, 151

National Junior College Athletic Association (NJCAA), 230

National Small College Athletic Association (NSCAA), 231

Neilsen W. V., 138

North American Society for the

Sociology of Sport (NASSS), 145

North American Society for Sport Management (NASSM), 142–143, 145, 151

    Ethical Creed of, 142–143

Nowell-Smith, P. H., 34

Nozick, R., 95, 96

O

Older Workers Benefit Protection Act (1990), 212

Oldham, G. R., 157

ostensive definitions, 23

O'Sullivan, P., 197

other-regarding motives, 35

P

Pepper, S. C., 45

personal ethics, 13–15, 16, 111–112

    and the athlete, 117–118

    and the athletic director, 116–117

    and the coach, 119–120

        unethical behavior of, 119

    and the media, 120–123

        and gender bias, 121

    and the spectator/fan, 123–125

    and the sport manager, 115–116

philosophical relativism, 42–45

    cultural, 42, 43

    descriptive, 42, 43

    moral, 11

    normative (ethical), 42

Pitts, B. G., 189

Plato, 80

play, rules surrounding, 114

pluralism, 106–108

Porter, B. F., 43

Pregnancy Discrimination Act (1978), 212

Pride, W. M., 188

prima facie duties, 78–80

Principles of Medical Ethics of the American Medical Association, 143

professional ethics, 13–15, 16. *See also* professional ethics, and social responsibility

professional ethics, and social responsi-

bility, 127
meaning and relevance, 128–130
Professional Golf Association (PGA), 232
prostitution, 29

Q

Quarterman, J., 154, 155

R

race logic, 122
"Race Logic and 'Being Like Mike'" (Dufur), 122
Rachels, J., 43, 58, 59, 107–108
Raphael, D. D., 92
Rawls, J., 91–94, 115
criticisms of, 93–94
Rehabilitation Act (1973), 212
Reidenbach, R. E., 130
relative terms, 22
relativism. *See* philosophical relativism
responsibility, 111
terms of, 111
Reynolds, Butch, 233
rights, concepts of, 102–103, 109, 168
as entitlements, 103
and obligations, 103–104
imperfect, 104
perfect, 104
protection of, 130
types of rights, 104–106
civil, 105
legal, 104
moral, 104
political, 105
positive, 105–106
prima facie, 105
Robin, D. P., 130
Rose, Pete, 13
Rosen, B., 67, 79
Ross, W. D., 78–80
list of *prima facie* duties, 79
rules in sport competition, 113–114
Russell, P. S., 151–152

S

Sage, G. H., 5

Sandler, D., 197
sexual harassment, 119, 137, 217
Shani, D., 197
Shields, David Light, 249, 250
Shirk, E., 73
Simon, R. L., 41, 53, 93
on basic benefits of sport, 96–97
situation ethics, 65–66
and *agapism*, 65–66
Slack, T., 214, 216
slavery, 29
Smith, M., 124
social responsibility, 132. *See also* professional ethics, and social responsibility
corporate, 128
and education, 129
in intercollegiate athletic programs, 130–131
in professional sport, 132–133
and sport and fitness clubs, 133
social utility, 82
Solomon, D., 82
Solomon, R. C., 83
sport, future of, 247–249
sport, and society, 4–6
economic role in, 5–6, 8
and social responsibility, 6–9
social role of, 6
and violence, 123–125
sport business as amoral, 129
Sport Canada, 227
sport leagues, 5–6
Sport Management: Macro Perspectives (Chelladurai), 153
sport managers, 11–13, 74, 115–116, 158. *See also* ethical responsibilities, and the functions of sport managers; ethics in sport management; personal ethics, and the sport manager; social responsibility
and organization, 155–156
and potential problems with fans, 125
sport marketing, 189. *See also* ethics, and sport marketing
ambush, 197, 198–199
and ethnic stereotypes, 194–195